NATIONAL GEOGRAPHIC

TRAVELER
Egypt

NATIONAL GEOGRAPHIC
TRAVELER
Egypt

Andrew Humphreys

Contents

Page 1: Decoration on papyrus
Pages 2–3: Giza's great pyramids
of Khufu and Khafre
Left: An herb and tea vendor in
Luxor relaxes with a sheesha.

How to use this guide

See back flap for keys to text and map symbols.

The National Geographic Traveler brings you the best of Egypt in text, pictures, and maps. Divided into three main sections, the guide begins with an overview of history and culture. Following are eight regional chapters with featured sites selected by the author for their particular interest and treated in depth. Each chapter opens with its own contents list for easy reference.

The regions, and sites within them, are arranged geographically, each one introduced with a map highlighting the featured sites. Walks and a cycle ride, plotted on their own maps, suggest routes for discov-

ering an area. Features and sidebars offer intriguing detail on history, culture, or contemporary life. A More Places to Visit page generally rounds off the regional chapters.

The final section, Travelwise, lists essential information for the traveler—pre-trip planning, special events, getting around, and what to do in emergencies—plus a selection of hotels and restaurants arranged by region, shops and entertainment.

To the best of our knowledge, site information is accurate as of the press date. However, it is always advisable to call ahead when possible.

Color coding

206

Each region is color coded for easy reference. Find the region you want on the map on the front flap, and look for the color flash at the top of the pages of the relevant chapter. Information in **Travelwise** is also color coded to each region.

Catacombs of Kom al-Shuqafa

- 178 C1
- Al-Nasseriyya St.
- 03/486 5800
- Closed after 4 p.m.
- $$. Camera $, video camera $$$
- Karmouz

Visitor information

Practical information for most sites is given in the side column (see key to symbols on back flap). The map reference gives the page number of the map and grid reference. Other details are address, telephone number, days closed, entrance charge in a range from $ (under $4) to $$$$$ (over $25), and nearest public transport in Cairo. Some sites charge visitors for the use of videos and cameras, and these charges are indicated as above. Other sites have information in italics and parentheses in the text.

TRAVELWISE

Hotel & restaurant prices

An explanation of the price bands used in entries is given in the Hotels & restaurants section (beginning on p. 359).

REGIONAL MAPS

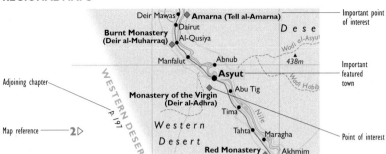

Important point of interest

Adjoining chapter

Map reference

Important featured town

Point of interest

- A locator map accompanies each regional map and shows the location of that region in the country.
- Adjacent regions are shown, each with a page reference.

WALKING TOURS

Red numbered bullets link sites on map to descriptions in the text.

Featured site (in bold) on walk route

Start point

Building outline

Direction of walk route

Walk route

Point of interest

- An information box gives the starting and ending points, time and length of walk, and places not to be missed along the route.

CYCLING TOUR

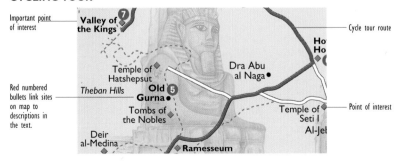

Important point of interest

Red numbered bullets link sites on map to descriptions in the text.

Cycle tour route

Point of interest

- An information box gives the starting and ending points, time and length of tour, and places not to be missed along the route.

NATIONAL GEOGRAPHIC

TRAVELER

Egypt

About the author

Brought up in northern England, Andrew Humphreys first traveled to Egypt in 1988 on a brief vacation, but he liked it so much he decided not to go home. Since then his life has been divided between the color and chaos of Cairo and the rather more leaden skies and ordered deadlines of the London publishing world. On assignment for a variety of periodicals, including NATIONAL GEOGRAPHIC TRAVELER and *The Wall Street Journal*, over the years he has explored every part of Egypt, cruising Lake Nasser, watching the sun rise from Mount Sinai, and sleeping beneath the stars in the Grand Sand Sea. His greatest fascination, however, remains with Cairo, its people, and their culture. In 1997 he cofounded an English-language newspaper, *The Cairo Times*, all the better to immerse himself in the goings-on of Um al-Dunya, "the Mother of the World." He is also the author or co-author of several guides to Cairo and Egypt, as well as to Syria and the Middle East.

Contributions to this guide were also made by Dr. Joann Fletcher (Pharaonic Culture), Siona Jenkins (The White Desert, Dakhla and Kharga Oases, St. Catherine's, and Mount Sinai), and Richard Hoath (Bird Life of Egypt).

History & culture

An "Upper Egyptian" from the south of the country

Egypt today

EGYPT IS THE WORLD'S ORIGINAL TOURIST DESTINATION. ANCIENT GRAFFITI in stone at the archaeological site of Saqqara, just outside Cairo, indicates that visitors have been marveling at the country's wonders for more than three millennia. And in one of the earliest examples of travel writing, penned about 450 years before the birth of Christ, the Greek geographer Herodotus (484–424 B.C.) pronounced: "Nowhere are there so many marvelous things, nor in the whole world beside are there to be seen so many things of unspeakable greatness." It's a statement that still holds true today.

Modern-day architects may build towers more than a hundred stories high; man may have walked on the moon and landed probes on Mars; we may have instantaneous communication between any two parts of the globe. But ancient Egyptian achievements such as the Pyramids and the Great Hypostyle Hall at Karnak leave us speechless with awe in a way that skyscrapers, rockets, and computers somehow never can. What is even more startling is that when that ancient publicist Herodotus stood before the Pyramids, they were almost as remote from his time as he himself is from ours. Small wonder that many people believe they must have been built by aliens: Egypt simply confounds.

Yet before the 19th century, Egypt was scarcely visited by Western travelers. The first recorded American to reach Cairo was John Ledyard, who died there in 1788 before he could set off on his planned exploration of interior Africa. It took a failed military expedition, led ten years later by the French general Napoleon, to awaken wider interest. Once the door was opened, Egyptomania swept Europe and America. As the first steps were being taken in France to decoding hieroglyphics, the government of the newly independent United States of America was busy incorporating the symbolism of Egypt into its civic identity, most prominently in the unfinished pyramid on the Great Seal (now to be seen on the back of every dollar bill). Cairo, Illinois? Memphis, Tennessee? They were founded in 1818 and 1819 respectively, in the first flush of excitement at the rediscovery of the antique land. American consulates were set up in Cairo and the port city of Alexandria in 1832, and at least 65 Americans are known to have visited in the decade following. Elizabeth Kirkland, wife of a former president of Harvard College,

carved her name at the top of the Great Pyramid in 1830, while the Reverend Stephen Olin of Connecticut sailed up the Nile and produced two volumes on his travels in 1843. More famously, Mark Twain came and poked fun at everything except the donkeys, which he termed "indescribably gorgeous." And like a virus, transmitted by the sketches, journals, and artifacts that these first intrepid voyagers carried back home, the symbols, forms, and mysteries of Egypt spread. Scarabs and sphinxes enlivened buildings in Paris, London, and New York. Pharaonic motifs decorated porcelain and furniture. Verdi wrote his bombastic ancient Egyptian opera *Aida*. The curse of the pharaohs began to claim its first victims in short stories by Edgar Allan Poe and Arthur Conan Doyle.

Judging by the conquest of the best-seller lists by Christian Jacq's "Ramses II" novels, and Wilbur Smith's take on ancient Egyptian adventure, Hollywood's belief that there is cinematic life yet in the mummy, and the fact that Las Vegas deemed Luxor worthy of rebuilding in the Nevada desert—albeit as a casino and hotel complex—the West's appetite for Egypt has yet to wane.

REAL LIFE EGYPT

Egyptians tend to leave the pharaohs, their monuments, and their mysteries to the tourist. They have little choice—they are too busy with real life.

Egypt is a country that Western strategists describe as "developing," which means it's considered to be lagging behind a little in the progress stakes. If it is, that's hardly surprising.

Despite millennia of history, Egypt is a young country, with 36 percent of the population below the age of 14.

From the moment Cleopatra succumbed to the bite of the asp and Egypt fell to Rome, the country suffered continuous foreign dominion and was sucked dry of revenue and resources. That situation only ended with revolution in 1952. Subsequently, under the leadership of the charismatic President Gamal Abdel Nasser, Egypt became the diplomatic hub of the Arab world, a role it maintains today. At peace with its neighbors, Egypt is the voice of moderation in a troubled region, and has good relations with most other world nations, particularly the United States from whom it receives some $2.3 billion annually, explicitly as a reward for being the first Arab state to make peace with Israel. However, in charge of their own destiny for barely half a century, the Egyptians are faced with some major domestic problems. Less than 10 percent of this desert country is cultivable and into that is crammed 90 percent of a population that increases by about a million

every nine months (in 2000 the figure was 65.2 million).

About a quarter of all Egyptians live in Cairo. It is, according to the United Nations, the most densely populated urban area in the world, with a population thought to be somewhere between 12 million and 16 million. In some central districts there are reckoned to be up to 700,000 people per square mile. The city's infrastructure gave up the ghost long ago. Housing shortages mean married chil-

Almost a quarter of Egypt's population lives in the capital, Cairo, one of the world's most densely populated cities.

dren share their parents' home, probably with the grandparents living there, too. Schools operate in up to three shifts. Major roads are jammed from morning until midnight.

What keeps the city from imploding is the resilience of the Cairenes. They are past masters in the art of making do and getting

by. Just look at some of the cars on the streets: Three models welded into one, with the gaps between them covered with tinplate, run as much on sheer willpower as on fuel. It is not unusual for a wage earner to be juggling two or even three jobs, working as a poorly paid, underemployed civil servant during the day, or running a small family business, while moonlighting as a taxi driver. Strike up a conversation with your cab driver and odds are he trained as an engineer, pharmacist, or doctor.

Aiding every Cairene in his or her daily struggle is the whole of the rest of the city. There is a palpable air of "we're all in this together." Strangers fall into conversation at the first chance, and jokes and wisecracks are traded with anyone in hearing. Privacy is unheard of, but then so is loneliness.

The most popular TV programs tend to be homegrown soaps, peering into the loves, lives, and tribulations of working-class families. Box-office favorites at the movies are

locally produced comedies in which the little guy manages, through wit and a sharp tongue, to bring some pompous and pampered types crashing down to earth. Singing and dancing play a big part, and it takes only the slightest of cues for someone to sling a scarf around their hips and break into a belly dance.

FAMILIES & FAITH

Families are still the keystone of Egyptian society. Getting married and raising children

Islam permeates day-to-day life for the more than 90 percent of Egyptians who are Muslims.

are probably the main priorities of almost every boy or girl over 16. However, progress toward this end is invariably slowed by the convention that requires the potential groom to provide an apartment and furnishings (even if it's only a furnished room in his parents' home). On a typical salary of about

$60 a month, accumulating the cash to secure a bride can take the average worker ten years or more. With sex before marriage taboo, little wonder that young Egyptian males are riveted by the casual heavy petting and bed hopping seen in the Hollywood movies that make it to the local theaters—even if the censor's scissors have snipped out all exposed flesh.

Pregnancy usually follows fast after marriage, almost invariably within the first year. Problems can arise if it doesn't. Witness the case in Alexandria in 1999, when a court of law ordered a nuclear scientist to put aside her research for a year and have a baby after her husband filed suit claiming he had a legal right to reproduce. Boys are favored, reflecting the preeminent status of men in Egyptian society. Egypt does have its high-profile feminists, such as internationally published writer Nawal al-Sadawi; but her most famous work, *The Hidden Face of Eve*, detailing the situation of Arab women, is banned in Egypt. Meanwhile

women collude in their second-rank status. In a national survey of adolescents carried out in 1999, some 60 percent of girls believed that a wife must accept her husband's opinion, even if she disagrees with it, while 89 percent held that a wife should never act without his permission. While the proportion of women who enter the workforce has risen steadily in recent years, only a fifth of Cairene women work outside the home, a figure that falls dramatically once outside the capital.

Every year, millions of visitors flock to see Egypt's ancient wonders, making tourism an important source of national revenue.

Inarguably, this patriarchal attitude stems from Islam, which clearly favors the male. Religion permeates Egyptian life, although not in an uncompromisingly authoritarian manner as in Iran or Saudi Arabia—no music? no dancing? black clothes? Egyptians would never stand for that—but at a low-key, almost

unconscious level. Ask after someone's health and they will reply *Alhamdilallah*, "Fine. Praise to God." Say to a tour guide, "See you tomorrow," and the answer will be *Insha'allah*, "God willing." Few pray the specified five times a day, but almost all men heed the amplified call of the *muezzin* each Friday at noon, when the crowds spill out of the mosques to block streets and sidewalks.

Likewise, the whole of the country's Muslim population is united in its celebration of Ramadan, the holy month of the Islamic calendar, when all who are capable of it have to refrain from eating, drinking, and smoking, from sunup to sundown. After the endurance test of the day come the celebrations of the evening, beginning with *iftar*, the breaking of the fast. Typically a communal event, each night this takes on the appearance of a nation-wide street party. Those with money to spare court blessings by sponsoring "mercy tables," where food is served free of charge to all. This

Alexandria is Egypt's second city. Its population is swollen each summer by Cairenes fleeing the heat.

being Egypt, as many turn up for the company as for the chicken and rice.

Other Islamic festivals and holidays are dotted throughout the year. A major occasion is Eid al-Kebir, the "big feast." As welcome to sheep as Thanksgiving must be to turkeys, this is a time when those who are squeamish or vegetarian should stay indoors, as backstreets become makeshift slaughterhouses.

Alongside Muslims, some five million Coptic Christians call Egypt home. Reputedly first brought by St. Mark the Evangelist (martyred in Alexandria in A.D. 63), the teachings of Christ gained a foothold in Egypt during Roman rule. The Copts of today wear their heritage proudly with crosses tattooed on their wrists. Occasional stories in the media screaming persecution of Christians by Egypt's

Muslims are off the mark. But when the Egyptian government says there is no problem at all, that's more than a little disingenuous, too. The truth is somewhere in between, but it would be fair to say that interfaith relations are relatively harmonious.

BEING EGYPTIAN

Muslim or Copt, being Egyptian comes first. And this is perhaps a defining characteristic: the Egyptians' love of their home country.

Harsh economics drive many abroad, particularly to the Arab Gulf countries, where work is plentiful and well paid. It is estimated that at any one time this overseas workforce numbers about 3.5 million. In some Delta villages practically every family has at least one son working in Kuwait or Bahrain or Saudi Arabia, and the money they send home constitutes one of Egypt's three top economic earners. Living and working overseas suits some, like Egyptian scientist Ahmed Zewail, who won the

1999 Nobel Chemistry Prize for his ground-breaking work at the California Institute of Technology in Pasadena, or Sir Magdy Yacoub, London-based pioneer of open-heart surgery. But most can't wait to get home.

As you clear immigration at Cairo International Airport, look around at the other arrivals. Among the overseas visitors, edgy with anticipation of the promised sights, there will always be a handful of young Egyptian men looking like out-of-uniform

Belly dancing—known to its practitioners as raqs al-sharqi, or Oriental dance—has been performed since pharaonic times.

Santas as they steer their trolleys piled high with boxes and bags. They are bringing home the spoils of years spent working abroad. Their excitement is broadcast on their faces. Incoming visitors might have yellow sands, camels, palms, and pyramids to look forward to, but these homecomers have Egypt. ∎

The land

SEEN FROM THE HEIGHT OF A SATELLITE, EGYPT IS A BLANK YELLOW expanse bisected by a single, dark blue vein that, toward the very top, spreads in a fan to meet the sea. In this one view is the truth of the often repeated statement, "The Nile is Egypt." The country may have a total area in the region of 400,000 square miles (1,000,000 sq km), but its millennia of civilization, history, and monuments are all crammed into that one life-giving thread, the Nile Valley.

Rising in twin sources in east Africa, which converge in Sudan, the Nile flows for 4,132 miles (6,650 km) before emptying into the Mediterranean. North of Khartoum, the Sudanese capital, it describes a broad S-curve; once in Egypt it flows almost straight, from the south (Upper Egypt) down to the sea in the north (Lower Egypt). From Aswan northward to Cairo the river lies in a trench-like valley filled by a rich belt of agricultural land that gradually increases to a width of about 12 miles (19 km). This is the gift of the Nile. Each year, as a result of the heavy seasonal rainfall on the Ethiopian Plateau, the river rises, beginning in May and reaching its maximum level in August. Before the completion of the first dam at Aswan in 1902, by September every year the whole of Egypt's Nile Valley used to be covered by water. Its retreat a few weeks later left a thick, silty residue of the richest soil in which farmers could scatter their seeds. "These people," wrote the Greek geographer Herodotus in the fifth century B.C., "get their harvests with less labor than anyone else in the world." Far from taking their good fortune for granted, on occasion the priests of ancient Egypt would throw virgins off the cliffs at Aswan to ensure a bountiful flood. These days, the young women of Upper Egypt can sleep secure, as water management is no longer left to the gods. The completion of the High Dam in the 1970s, with its massive reservoir Lake Nasser, for the first time in history allowed the annual flood to be controlled by man. Unfortunately, there are also several negative side effects, chief of which is a decrease in fertility, and hence agricultural productivity, caused by the loss of alluvial silt.

Nowhere are these problems more keenly felt than in the Delta, the rich, flat, bright green fan that spreads north of Cairo. It was formed by the Nile splitting into as many as seven branches, although its waters are now concentrated in two, the Damietta Branch to the east, and the Rosetta Branch to the west. Burdened with the task of feeding the whole of the country, the land is among the world's most intensively cultivated. Farmers here grow three crops a year, with the premier produce being cotton, maize, rice, and wheat. The climate is also conducive to a vast range of fruit and vegetables, from green beans to grapes to palms laden with dates. Taking a train ride through the Delta can seem like passing through some vast and bounteous Garden of Eden. However, it is countries overseas that are the beneficiaries of the harvest because the best of the produce is exported for vitally needed hard currency. Strawberries, for example, a major local crop, are sold in vast quantity to Europe, to the extent that they are practically impossible to find in the markets of Egypt. The lack of the annual replenishing of fresh black soil means overuse of fertilizers and high levels of salinity. Also, inch by inch, the northern Delta, which lies only just above sea level, is being eaten away by the Mediterranean. In an effort to reverse this trend, patches of cultivable land are now being reclaimed from coastal salt marshes.

Taking to the air again, it is startling to see the division between the cultivated land and desert all along the Nile Valley. There is no gradual fade or bleed; it is a harsh precise line, green on one side, yellow on the other. The crops stop dead, there is a small bump of earth, and then the sand takes over. Egypt is in fact one great desert plateau divided unequally by the Nile into the vast Western Desert and the Eastern Desert.

The Western Desert comprises two-thirds

A hot-air balloon drifts over the Theban Hills that are lit by the early morning sun.

of the land surface of Egypt, an area of about 262,800 square miles (680,600 sq km). If you ignore the political boundaries on the map, it stretches right across the top of North Africa under its better known name of the Sahara. Suffering extremes of temperature, barren and forbidding, the desert is not completely devoid of life. A series of wind-sculpted depressions allows water to come to the surface, creating a string of cultivable oases. Inhabited for thousands of years, these islands of greenery

prospered in ancient times as important staging posts on trade routes between Egypt and neighboring Libya. More recently, the Egyptian government has been attempting to develop the oases as part of a "New Valley" project, intended as an alternative settlement area to the Nile Valley. Since the 1950s landless farmers and city families have been encour- aged to move out to the desert, and in the 1990s grand plans were announced to attract industry by linking the oases to Lake Nasser

by means of a canal. Work on this pharaonic-scale scheme, known as the Toshka Canal, has yet to begin—and indeed may never happen because of cost concerns. Meanwhile the population of the Western Desert remains minimal.

Much smaller than its western counterpart, the Eastern Desert stretches between the Nile Valley and the Red Sea coast. It is devoid of sand and dunes, and instead is characterized by stony, mountainous terrain, extensively dissected by wadis (dry riverbeds). It is almost

The owner of a rice farm near Tanis in the Delta surveys laborers from the shade of a parasol.

completely unpopulated, save for a series of small ports strung along the Red Sea coast, such as Quseir and Berenice, which served ancient trade routes between the Nile Valley and Yemen, the Horn of Africa, and beyond. Through here the pharaohs imported exotic spices, live elephants, and slaves. In return,

they could offer the mineral wealth of the Eastern Desert mountains—in particular, gold. Later, the Romans quarried the same areas for porphyry, a dense roseate stone that they hacked into blocks, dragged overland to the Nile, and shipped to Rome where it was highly prized by masons and sculptors as a raw material most suitable for imperial busts. It remains today a wilderness, and what most visitors and Egyptians alike see of the Eastern Desert is the view out of the window of an air-conditioned bus as it follows age-old caravan routes between the Nile and the coast.

The Sinai Peninsula separates Africa from Asia. It is essentially a continuation of the Eastern Desert that was ripped away about 40 million years ago, when the African and Arabian continental plates began to move apart. This tectonic shift created the shallow Gulf of Suez and the much deeper Gulf of Aqaba. The latter is part of the Great Rift Valley, which, filled with a series of rivers,

gulfs, and lakes, extends from the Dead Sea for some 4,000 miles (6,400 km) all the way down the east coast of Africa to Mozambique in the south. Southern Sinai is covered by a gaunt mountain mass that includes Egypt's highest peak, Mount St. Catherine (Gebel Katerina), 8,668 feet (2,642 m) high. In the steep valleys between peaks there is enough hardy vegetation to sustain a variety of wildlife, including the rare Sinai leopard. North of this is a plateau sloping down to the Mediterranean,

The romance of epics such as *Lawrence of Arabia* persists in the vast sand seas of the Western Desert.

traditionally sparsely populated, save for roaming Bedouin tribes. However, the government has built a new pipeline, the Al-Salam Canal to bring fresh water from the Suez Canal region. Since the 1980s, tourism has also created new population centers all along the south and eastern coasts of the peninsula. ■

History of Egypt

CAST YOUR MIND BACK TO THE OPENING SCENES OF 1996's OSCAR-SWEEPING film, *The English Patient*. Kirsten Scott Thomas is copying into her notebook swimmers painted on a cave wall deep in the desert. It is a fictional episode but based on truth. In the 1930s such crudely daubed figures were indeed found at Gebel Uweinat, a remote massif near the Libyan border in the Western Desert, today more than 400 miles (640 km) from the nearest water. Historians take this as evidence that Egypt must have been inhabited as far back as the Paleolithic period, before 25,000 B.C., when the whole of North Africa was a vast habitable grassy savanna with abundant wildlife and lakes.

A dramatic change in climate turned the grasslands to desert, forcing early man to migrate toward sources of water, either oases or the valley of the Nile. Settlements dating from the Neolithic period, about 5000 B.C., have been found in the western oases of Siwa and Kharga, and in the Fayoum. The people lived by agriculture and fishing and were sufficiently advanced to produce pottery and woven materials. Little is known about them except that by the fourth millennium B.C., they had formed two geographically defined groups: Upper Egypt along the Nile Valley, and Lower Egypt, based in the fertile Nile Delta.

THE PYRAMID BUILDERS

Lost among the overload of exhibits at Cairo's Egyptian Museum is a shield-shaped piece of

slate carved with battle scenes. One side shows a king wearing the white crown of Upper Egypt about to deal a fatal blow to a kneeling figure. On the reverse is the same king wearing the red crown of Lower Egypt. Known as the Palette of Narmer and dating from about 3100 B.C., it is the museum's earliest artifact and one of its most significant. With its single king wearing two crowns, it depicts the first unification of Egypt under one ruler. This is ground zero—the event usually taken as marking the beginning of Egyptian civilization. From here begins a line of royalty that stretches for more than 3,000 years, encompassing 170 or more kings and pharaohs. The term "pharaonic Egypt" is used for the whole of this period, even though the king took the

The shadow of more than four and a half millennia of history is cast over modern Egypt.

title "pharaoh" (see p. 44) only in the New Kingdom, starting about 1550 B.C.

The basic skeleton of ancient Egyptian history comes from a list compiled in the third century B.C. by a high priest of Heliopolis named Manetho. He divides Egypt's rulers into 30 dynasties, or ruling houses. Modern Egyptologists then group these into three major periods (Old Kingdom, Middle Kingdom, and New Kingdom), each separated by periods of decline known as Intermediate Periods. Historians naturally could not rely on one uncorroborated source, and Manetho is backed up by several other ancient chronologies, including extensive "royal lists" such as that inscribed on the walls of the temple of Seti I at Abydos (see p. 227), and a fragmentary papyrus known as the Royal Canon of Turin, after the museum in which it is to be found (the Egyptian Museum in Turin, Italy). Of course, many discrepancies exist between the various sources, with the result that the whole time frame of pharaonic Egypt is still open to passionate debate.

Nowhere is this more the case than in the Early Dynastic period, the run-up to the Old Kingdom. Next to nothing is known of Narmer, the unifier of ancient Egypt, or of those who followed, including a king called Menes, who may actually be Narmer under a different name. Menes is important because it is to him that historians have traditionally ascribed the founding of Memphis, capital of Egypt for most of the pharaonic period. Appropriately, the new city was sited at the point where Upper and Lower Egypt met, making it well suited for controlling both the Nile Valley and the Delta.

Herodotus described Memphis as a "prosperous city and cosmopolitan center," and we have to take his word for it, because next to nothing of the city has survived. We can only get an idea of its glories through its vast necropolis, which developed in tandem with the living city during the period of the Old Kingdom (2686–2181 B.C.), a period otherwise known as the "pyramid age." These fantastic funerary monuments appeared in the 3rd dynasty, heralded by the Step Pyramid at Saqqara built during the reign of Djoser (R.2667–2648 B.C.). During the next three dynasties some 21 other major pyramids were

built, but the truly gigantic pyramids were all completed by father, son, and grandson in less than 80 years. Sneferu (R.2613–2589 B.C.) achieved true pyramid perfection first, at Dahshur, replacing steps with an even (on the second attempt) slope. He was outdone by his son Khufu, or Cheops (R.2589–2566 B.C.), who built his Great Pyramid at Giza even bigger. For reasons unknown, Khafre, or Chephren (R.2558–2532 B.C.) chose not to challenge his father Khufu, and built his neighboring pyramid marginally smaller.

This spectacular program of pyramid building speaks volumes about the power of the Old Kingdom rulers, who were able to marshal the vast workforce needed. Pyramid specialist Mark Lehner estimates that a constantly rotating workforce of 20,000 men must have labored for 20 years on Khufu's pyramid. This workforce had to be organized, fed, housed, and paid, which must have required an extraordinarily well-developed system of administration.

Khafre's was the last of the giant pyramids. Many followed during the 5th and 6th dynasties, but all on a much smaller scale. This was a symptom of the erosion of the king's power. Unified rule gave way to rival princi-palities and, inevitably, civil war. When the dust settled, following more than a century of chaos, control of the country had shifted from the north to Upper Egypt, and to a family of princes based at Thebes, site of modern-day Luxor.

THEBES & KARNAK

The rise of Thebes marks the beginning of the Middle Kingdom, which stands as something of an intermission between the glories of the Old and New Kingdoms. Continued disrup-tion and strife held progress in check, and few of its 11 dynasties of kings are well known outside the world of Egyptology. Mentuhotep II (R.2055–2004 B.C.) is credited with reunify-ing Egypt, and Senusret III (R.1874–1855 B.C.) has a high profile through his granite portraits at the Cairo and Luxor museums. However, these are very minor figures compared with the great pharaoh-gods to come.

The Middle Kingdom ended with Egypt partially occupied by invaders from the north, a Palestinian people called the Hyksos. Their introduction of the horse and chariot into warfare and their skill in archery enabled them to conquer the whole of the Delta region. It was only when the Theban Egyptians adopted this new military technology that they finally defeated the Hyksos and established Ahmose I (R.1550–1525 B.C.) as the first king of the 18th dynasty, and founder of the New Kingdom (1550–1069 B.C.).

So begins the golden age of the pharaohs. Over the next 500 years, Egypt would rise to unequaled greatness, and its rulers would create a legacy of awe-inspiring temples, tombs, and treasures that continue to captivate our imaginations today. Their names echo still: Tuthmose, Ramses, Akhenaten, and, most famously, Tutankhamun.

The first two New Kingdom rulers were concerned with consolidating Egypt's borders, but by the time of Tuthmose I (R.1504–1492 B.C.) domestic affairs were stable enough for the pharaoh to embark on a series of brilliant military campaigns; he raised a stela at Abydos that reads: "I made the boundaries of Egypt as far as that which the sun encircles…I made Egypt the superior of every land."

Tuthmose III (R.1479–1425 B.C.) surpassed his grandfather Tuthmose I in military prowess. He made no less than 17 successful campaigns into western Asia. He was nick-named "the Napoleon of ancient Egypt" by 19th-century American archaeologist James Henry Breasted.

All this empire building laid the founda-tions for the most prosperous and stable period of ancient Egyptian history. Wealth accumulated from foreign expeditions went to embellish Egypt's temples and palaces, not least that of Karnak, the vast complex at Thebes dedicated to Amun-Re, chief of the gods. During the almost 40-year-long reign of Amenhotep III (R.1390–1352 B.C.) in particu-lar, hardly any military activity was called for and instead manpower was lavished on great building works such as Luxor Temple, and there was a flowering in all aspects of the arts. Some of the most magnificent statuary dates from the reign of this pharaoh, including

Opposite: The Great Hypostyle Hall at Karnak, constructed in the New Kingdom and rediscovered in the mid-19th century

several pieces in the Luxor Museum (see pp. 244–45), and a colossal statue of the pharaoh and his queen that stands in the main atrium at Cairo's Egyptian Museum (see p. 74).

Was he spoiled by riches and indolence, or divinely inspired? The jury is still out on Amenhotep IV (*R*.1352–1336 B.C.), better known as Akhenaten, who ushered in a revolutionary period in ancient Egyptian history (see pp. 218-221). His short-lived removal of the capital to Amarna in Middle Egypt, and promotion of the cult of the sun disk, Aten, over Egypt's traditional gods, caused Akhenaten to be vilified by his successors when orthodoxy was restored on his death. Subsequently his name was left off the royal lists, such as the one at Abydos. Akhenaten's immediate successors suffered similarly and were also written out of history by revisionist scribes. It is ironic then that one of them, a very minor pharaoh called Tutankhamun, who took the throne at the age of nine and was dead at 18, should wind up as the best known of all ancient Egypt's rulers, thanks to the world-famous 1922 discovery of his intact and treasure-filled tomb by Howard Carter (see pp. 278–79).

Tutankhamun's early death briefly left the succession in question. Aye, a royal official, seized the opportunity and hastily married the young widowed queen, this despite the fact that she was actually his granddaughter. On the death of Aye, the throne passed not to a blood heir but to an army commander, Horemheb, and on his death to another general, Ramses I, founder of a dynasty of warrior pharaohs. Mightiest of these was Ramses II (*R*.1279–1213 B.C.), or simply Ramses the Great. Immortalized by the 19th-century English poet Shelley as the "king of kings," Ramses II is the epitome of the all-powerful pharaoh-god. His Herculean temple at Abu Simbel, the Hypostyle Hall at Karnak, and the great mortuary temple called the Ramesseum at Thebes practically define ancient Egypt in the popular imagination. No other pharaoh built so prolifically (and on such a scale), or raised so many colossi (or usurped those of others), or fathered so many children (over a hundred). He also gathered together the largest force of Egyptian troops ever seen, some 20,000 men, and led them against the

Hittites at the Battle of Kadesh (1275 B.C.), fought in what is now Syria.

Ramses II may have lived to be as old as 92 years of age. Although his tomb was discovered empty, the actual body of this extraordinary ruler was found as part of the cache of royal mummies at Gurna in 1881 (see p. 270). In 1976 he was flown to Paris for a Ramses II exhibition where, despite being dead for 3,200 years, he was met at the airport with a full presidential guard of honor. He now lies in the Royal Mummy Room at the Egyptian Museum in Cairo.

By the time Ramses III came to power, some 30 years after his illustrious namesake, Egypt was already in decline. Disunity had once more set in, and the country was under siege from outsiders. Before long, the kings of

Libya had captured the Delta, Nubians from the south had taken Thebes, and other civilizations, such as those of the Assyrians and Persians, were invading the Nile Valley. Egypt was bankrupt and powerless, and it fell to an outsider to rescue the country and resurrect former pharaonic glories.

ALEXANDRIA & THE PTOLEMIES

When Alexander the Great entered Egypt in 332 B.C., he was hailed as a savior. The Persians, who occupied the country, had already fallen before him the year previously at Issus in what is now southeastern Turkey. He marched straight to Memphis, where he was welcomed as a pharaoh, before crossing the desert to consult the famed oracle of Amun at the oasis of Siwa.

Tutankhamun's gold coffin exemplifies the pinnacle of ancient Egyptian prosperity and artistic magnificence in the New Kingdom.

On the Mediterranean coast Alexander founded the city of Alexandria. And then he was gone, campaigning across Asia and into India. When he died in 323 B.C. in Babylon, his enormous empire was divided between his generals. Alexander's boyhood friend Ptolemy claimed Egypt.

The newly crowned Ptolemy I (305–285 B.C.) had to defend his interest against rival claimants but did so successfully, and founded a dynasty of 15 Hellenistic rulers that lasted 335 years. Although Egypt now inevitably became part of the Mediterranean world, with Alexandria supplanting Memphis and

Cleopatra has long captured the imagination of writers and artists. In 1883 British painter Alma-Tadema depicted the queen on her barge on the Nile after the battle of Actium.

Thebes in national importance, the Ptolemies strove to maintain continuity with the age of the pharaohs. They kept the existing political and religious structures, adopted pharaonic dress and artistic styles, repaired and restored temples, and built some anew. Almost all the most complete temples in Egypt today— Dendara, Edfu, Kom Ombo, and Philae—are Ptolemaic, not ancient Egyptian. This means that well over a thousand years separate Luxor Temple and that at Esna, 50 miles (80 km) to the south. However, the Ptolemies used the earlier temples as their blueprints, and in doing so preserved for us building forms and styles that otherwise might have been lost.

As the Ptolemaic dynasty progressed, it took on all the qualities of a murderous soap opera, full of domestic intrigue and backstabbing (literally). The result was serious internal weaknesses in the country. Rome, the rising power of the region, was quick to exploit the situation and began to involve itself in the affairs of the exceedingly wealthy Egypt. In the end, it was the actions of Cleopatra VII, *the* Cleopatra of play and movie, that provided a pretext for the Romans to invade Egypt.

Daughter of Ptolemy XII, Cleopatra became queen on his death in 51 B.C., sharing a co-regency with her brother, Ptolemy XIII (*R.*51–47 B.C.), before he ousted her from power. The two siblings were set to battle it out when they were interrupted by the arrival of a Roman fleet led by Julius Caesar. He was in pursuit of Pompey, his rival for control of Rome, recently defeated and now seeking asylum in Egypt. Ptolemy had Pompey executed and presented his head to Caesar.

Far wilier, Cleopatra had herself smuggled into the palace of Alexandria in the dead of night and delivered to Caesar hidden in a rolled carpet. The next morning, Ptolemy was astonished and furious to find his sister with Caesar. Cleopatra was restored to power and kept secure there by her new lover, to whom she bore a son, Caesarion, or "little Caesar."

Contrary to the popular image of a voluptuous, ravishing vamp—as portrayed on the big screen by Vivien Leigh (1945) and Elizabeth Taylor (1963)—Cleopatra's charms were apparently not based on her looks. "Her actual beauty…was not in itself

The Bible was first translated into the Coptic language in the 2nd century A.D. The term Coptic refers to the last stage of ancient Egyptian language script as well as to Egyptian Christians.

remarkable," wrote Greek biographer Plutarch (A.D. 46–119). Her seductiveness, he reports, was in her "bold wit" and "the charm of her society."

Following the assassination of Caesar in Rome, Cleopatra sailed to Tarsus in Asia Minor at the behest of the new rising star of the Roman Empire, Mark Antony. The two entered into political alliance: Antony sought money, Cleopatra wanted power and territories. They became lovers, produced two children, and later married. But Antony already had a wife, whose brother was Octavian, legal heir to Caesar. Rome was turned against Antony and his queen in Alexandria, and in 32 B.C. the senate declared war. At the naval Battle of Actium the following year, Octavian defeated Antony, whom he pursued to Egypt. Antony committed suicide. Cleopatra tried her charms on Octavian to little avail. She herself then committed suicide, possibly by means of an asp (a venomous snake), preferring death to the humiliations she foresaw.

Octavian ordered the death of Cleopatra's eldest son and heir, Caesarion, appointing himself pharaoh and bringing to an end Ptolemaic rule in Egypt.

AL-QAHIRA, THE CITY VICTORIOUS

The Romans cared little for Egypt. For six centuries they used it as a granary, taking what they required and leaving nothing in return. Almost no monuments stand to their rule in Egypt.

The most significant legacy of the Romans' time is the emergence of the Christian faith in Egypt. Tradition has it that the teachings of Christ were spread in Alexandria by no less a personage than the gospel writer St. Mark from about A.D. 45—making the church in Egypt one of the oldest in Christendom. When Christianity was adopted as the official religion of the Roman Empire, under Constantine, Christians were allowed to worship and evangelize freely. Coptic (meaning "Egyptian") Christians, over time, had adopted an understanding of Christ's nature that was at variance with that of the main church. The Copts consequently found themselves cast as heretics and persecuted. So when

Cairo was shaped by successive Islamic dynasties, each of which left its mark on the city with imposing architecture.

an invading Arab army appeared in A.D. 641 under the flag of Islam, it was welcomed by the predominantly Christian Egyptians. The Copts survived the rise of Islam and remain a strong religious entity today.

Ignoring Alexandria, the Arab army camped beside a Roman fortress on the Nile across from the old pharaonic capital of Memphis. This encampment, called Fustat, gradually took on a more permanent aspect and became a city in its own right. In these early years of Islam (founded by the Prophet Muhammad around 610 A.D.), Egypt passed through the hands of several warring dynasties as the line of succession from Muhammad was disputed. With each dynasty the new Arab city was extended a little farther north. In A.D. 969, it was the turn of the Fatimids, a North

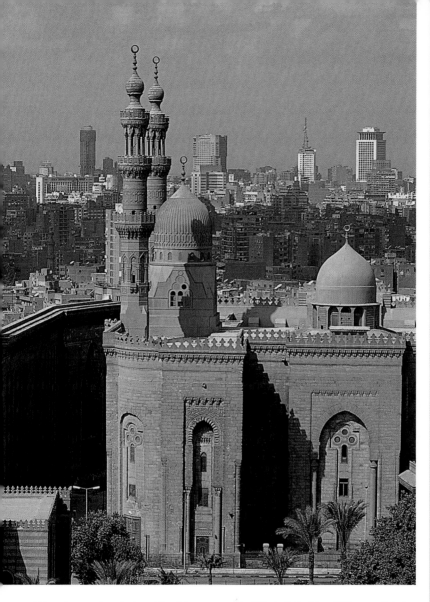

African dynasty whose leaders claimed descent from the Prophet's daughter. Their extension to the city included palaces and mosques, plazas and thoroughfares, all wrapped around by high fortified walls. They gave this new city the name Al-Qahira, "the Victorious," later corrupted by European tongues to "Cairo."

Its walls were strengthened by the famous military leader Salah al-Din (better known in the West as Saladin), successor to the Fatimids, who ruled as sultan (1171–1193) from the

Citadel he built for himself. However, Cairo's greatest glories came during the 267-year rule of a strange warrior caste, the Mamluks. The word *mamluk* means "one who is owned," and by origin they were slaves—mainly from the Caucasus region bridging Europe and Asia— purchased at a young age and brought to Egypt as palace guards. Their military service was rewarded by land and eventual freedom.

By the middle of the 13th century the Mamluks were the most powerful force in the

Napoleon told his troops before defeating the Mamluks: "40 centuries of history look down upon you from these Pyramids."

land, and were able to dispossess the heirs of Saladin and claim Egypt for themselves. Raised as warriors, they were a fearsome caste and swept through Palestine and Syria, carving out an empire that extended northward as far as eastern Turkey.

This put the Mamluks in control of all East-West trade, and the profits from this made Cairo one of the largest and richest cities in the world. It became a conduit for spices and silks from China, India, and Arabia, traded on to Florence, Genoa, and Venice and through them to the rest of Europe. Incidentally, along with the precious goods,

the Western world also imported vocabulary: so from the Arabic *ruzz* we have "rice"; from *kammun* we have "cumin"; from *zafaran*, "saffron"; from *qahwa*, "coffee"; from *sharbat*, "sherbet"; from *sukkar*, "sugar"; and from *makhzan*, the Arabic word for a place of storage, "magazine."

Leonardo Frescobaldi, an Italian merchant, writing in 1384, claimed that more people dwelled on a single street in Cairo than in all of Florence. Precise figures are uncertain, but Cairo's population may have been as large as half a million, making it twice the size of Paris, then Europe's biggest city, and five times the size of Constantinople. As historian Max Rodenbeck writes in his splendid *Cairo: The City Victorious* (1998), for sheer scale and density, enterprise and

unimaginable cruelty. With no system of hereditary lineage, succession went to the strongest. To become sultan meant first eliminating all potential rivals. Once a ruler was in power, assassination lurked around every darkened corner. Rare was the Mamluk sultan who died of old age.

One who died at least *in* old age, if not of it, was Qansuh al-Ghouri. When he assumed power in 1501 he was the 46th Mamluk sultan. He had begun as a slave and page boy to former sultans and had clawed his way up the ladder carefully and slowly, so that by the time he reached the summit he was already 60 years old. He is known to have been fond of the perfume of flowers, but would not have balked at having miscreants sawn in half alive—a favorite Mamluk punishment. In 1516, when he had already held power three times longer than the average reign, he was obliged to ride out to meet the threat of the Ottoman Turkish Empire. His Mamluk army, for two and a half centuries the scourge of the Near East, was defeated in battle. In January of the following year the Turks entered Cairo.

In the late 15th century, two other events had taken place that would critically affect the future of Cairo and Egypt in general. In 1498 the Portuguese explorer Vasco da Gama successfully rounded the Cape of Good Hope and reached the coast of southwest India. Six years earlier, Genoese mariner Christopher Columbus had reached the Americas, opening up a whole new world of riches. Europe no longer had any need of the Mamluk middlemen. From being the center of the world, Cairo was downgraded to a provincial capital, subject to Istanbul. Egypt shrank in on itself, and became ever more isolated.

EGYPT & EUROPE: NAPOLEON

Just as with Alexander the Great some 2,000 years previously, it took another exceptional and hugely ambitious young general to bring Egypt back to the world's attention at the end of the 18th century. Napoleon Bonaparte was looking for a way to hurt the English, with whom France was at war, and he concluded that the shrewdest answer was to capture Egypt. From there he could threaten British interests in India. His dreams went further, as he was later to write: "I saw myself founding

economic success, medieval Cairo was the New York of its day.

The bounty of the Mamluk era is reflected today in the buildings they left behind, which represent a pinnacle of Islamic architecture in Egypt. Characterized by slender, multitiered minarets, exquisitely carved stone domes, and delicate inlays of marbles and other colored stone, Cairo retains some 200 Mamluk structures, ranging from mosques and palaces to fountains and even a hospital, founded 700 years ago and still in use today. It is a legacy that is largely unknown and unseen by most visitors to Egypt, but one that is arguably every bit as impressive as the heritage of the pharaohs.

Yet, in addition to fostering wealth and beauty, this was an age of bloody violence and

The Suez Canal was opened on November 17, 1869, in the presence of German crown prince Frederick William and other European royalty, with no expense spared.

a religion, marching into Asia, riding an elephant, a turban on my head, and in my hand the new Koran that I would have composed to suit my needs."

In the event, his campaign ended disastrously. Napoleon and his army landed in 1798 near Alexandria only to be stranded when the French fleet was blasted out of the water by the English admiral Horatio Nelson in an engagement remembered as the Battle of the Nile. However, in a famous confrontation fought in the shadow of the Pyramids, the French did defeat Egypt's Mamluks, back in power in the absence of any real control from Istanbul, but the country remained hostile.

Unable to exert control, battered and humiliated, by the end of 1801 the expedition was over. But the military failure was counterbalanced by the achievements of Napoleon's other army, the 154 scientists, painters, physicists, anthropologists, and more, who spent three years investigating everything in and about Egypt. The results were gathered in 24 volumes as *Description de l'Egypte* (*Description of Egypt)*, and through its publication Europe rediscovered its interest in this ancient land.

EGYPT & EUROPE: MUHAMMAD ALI

Napoleon's defeat of the Mamluks also cleared the way for new blood. Into the power vacuum in Egypt stepped an Albanian mercenary named Muhammad Ali who, within five years of the French army's departure, had successfully maneuvered to become Ottoman viceroy of Egypt.

Muhammad Ali (*R*.1805–1848) was keen to continue the affair begun between Egypt and Europe. He encouraged foreigners with talent to come to Cairo. One to take up the invitation was a French veteran of the Napoleonic Wars named Joseph Sèves, who trained the viceroy's armies. He later converted to Islam, becoming Suleyman Pasha, and his statue used to stand in downtown Cairo until the 1952 revolution relegated him to the Citadel.

Muhammad Ali also hired Western teachers and experts in all fields to help resurrect his adopted country. At the same time, Egyptian students and scholars were dispatched to Europe to learn Western ways. Politically Muhammad Ali supported the Ottoman sultan at first, but his own military victories in Greece, Arabia, and the Sudan gave

Opened up to the West by Muhammad Ali and his successors, Egypt became an attraction for tourists from the mid-19th century onward.

him the confidence to challenge his masters. When Sèves's troops decisively defeated an Ottoman army in 1839, Muhammad Ali was poised to attack Istanbul. In return for the hereditary right to rule Egypt, he backed down and gave up his gains in Syria.

EGYPT & EUROPE: THE CANAL

Though not without its warts, Muhammad Ali's rule is generally viewed favorably for nurturing the seeds of the modern Egyptian state. However, the dynasty he founded (which ruled with the title of "khedive") came to be increasingly reviled by the Egyptian people, who labored under heavy taxes to support new projects that seemed primarily to benefit European powers.

Egypt was seen as the fast overland route to the East. Under Abbas (R.1848–1854) a railroad line was constructed by the British from Alexandria to Cairo, then under Said (R.1854–1863) a concession was given to the ruler's friend, the French engineer Ferdinand de Lesseps, for the cutting of a canal across the Isthmus of Suez. The work was completed in 1869. The French-educated and devoutly

Francophile Ismail, (R.1863–1879), grandson of Muhammad Ali, orchestrated the lavish inaugural celebrations. The royalty of Europe and their retinues came in great numbers, all at Egypt's expense. Hotels and palaces were specially built: The result was bankruptcy.

Ismail was forced into exile, and financial advisers were appointed by Britain and France, Egypt's two main creditors. An Egyptian did not have to be a passionate nationalist to conclude that the country was being run for, and by, foreigners. But when the people objected too loudly, with rioting in Alexandria in 1882, the British stepped in and assumed control of the country. The heirs of Muhammad Ali remained on the throne, but all real power was concentrated in the hands of the British consul general. Promises of Egyptian self-rule made in 1914 in return for help in World War I were not honored, and in 1919 Egyptians vented their anger in rioting. Within three years Britain was forced to proclaim the end of its protectorate and recognize Egypt as an independent state with a hereditary constitutional monarch, although British influence and soldiers remained.

A 1936 treaty formally ended British occupation, but that was all but negated by the outbreak of war in 1939, when Egypt became vital to British strategy. Battalions were barracked beside the Pyramids and on the banks of the Nile. While the fighting went on in the desert, Cairo and Alexandria became fleshpots for troops on leave. Militant weekend in 1952, remembered as "Black Saturday." Clouds of acrid smoke swallowed the whole of central Cairo as some 700 stores, hotels, and premises in the European quarter were torched by rampaging mobs. Six months later, on July 23, a group calling itself the Free Officers, led by Gamal Abdel Nasser, occupied the ministries, palaces, and parliament in a

Egypt's first president, the charismatic Gamal Abdel Nasser (1918–1970), was a hero to his own people and those of all developing nations.

Egyptian nationalists conspired with German spies. It was a time of turmoil and some danger, but also plenty of romance, the inspiration for a whole slew of literature.

THE ARAB REPUBLIC OF EGYPT

By the end of the war, new forces were emerging in Egypt, impatient with both the king and existing political representations for having failed to secure independence, and for having collaborated with the British. Then came the disaster of the 1948 Arab-Israeli conflict, in which the Egyptian army was defeated by the newly formed state of Israel. Egyptian anger at the humiliation found an outlet on a January

bloodless coup. The last king of Egypt, Farouk, was forced to abdicate and dispatched into exile, and in June 1953 the Republic of Egypt was proclaimed.

Confirmed as president the following year, Nasser became the first native Egyptian to wield power in his own country since the last of the pharaohs. British and French nationals were sent packing, along with other colonials. Rich pashas had their land confiscated and parceled out among the *felaheen*, the peasant classes. Nasser was a socialist hero, especially after the defiant stance adopted during the Suez Crisis in 1956 when he faced down the combined forces of Britain, France, and Israel after he nationalized the canal. Nasser came to symbolize anti-imperialism and social justice, as well as pan-Arabism. He was the John F. Kennedy of Egypt, until his magic was ended not by a single bullet, but by the Israeli air force's precision bombing on June 5, 1967. The scale and suddenness of Egypt's military defeat in the Six Day War, as its air forces were

Islamic extremist. He was succeeded by his vice-president, Hosni Mubarak. A pragmatic leader, lacking the charisma or flamboyance of his predecessors, Mubarak has proved solid. Egypt may no longer be the center of the Arab world, but regional relations are good, and international standing has been enhanced by Cairo's good-neighborly role in negotiating

President Anwar Sadat (1918–1981) achieved peace with Israel, but at a price: He was assassinated by extremists.

Incumbent president Hosni Mubarak exerts a moderating influence on the Middle Eastern political scene.

caught napping on the ground and Israeli troops advanced across Sinai, totally destroyed the aura of Nasser's new Egypt. He died three somber years later.

His successor, Anwar Sadat, took Israel by surprise in October 1973, when he initiated a new military campaign (see p. 142). The Egyptian army's initial successes, regardless of later reversals, were a boost for the country's morale. They opened the way for peace talks that culminated in the signing of the American-brokered Camp David peace treaty on March 26, 1979.

Sadat was assassinated in 1981 by an

between the Palestinians and Israel.

The threat of violence from religious extremists seems to have been met at the start of the 21st century, and the focus is on self-development. Schemes are afoot to reclaim more living space from the desert, privatization has given a shot in the arm to the moribund state economy, literacy is up, population growth is down, and ever more areas are being opened up to tourism. After 4,500 years of often tumultuous recorded history, if Egypt can't quite yet rest on its laurels, it is at least in a position to make a decent tourist buck off past achievements. ■

Pharaonic culture

FOR MOST PEOPLE, THE PHARAONIC CULTURE OF ANCIENT EGYPT CONSISTS of little more than temples and gods, tombs and mummies, and the archaeologists who discovered them. Although these things tend to give the impression that the ancient Egyptians were obsessed by death, theirs was a culture firmly rooted in the belief in eternal life, which they went to enormous lengths to ensure with help from their many gods.

PHARAONIC RELIGION

Ancient Egyptian religion was a highly complex system of ritual and belief at the core of which lay the need to maintain cosmic order in a perfect balance of opposites. This was only possible with the help of the gods, who were honored with endless rituals designed to keep the universe in harmony.

Initially worshiped as representatives of the natural world, the Egyptians' many deities developed more complex personalities as the myths surrounding them became more numerous. Each myth also had its local variant, with even the story of creation preserved in at least three different forms. Although all creation myths were based on the belief that life first appeared from the waters of chaos on a mound of earth, a number of places claimed to be the original site of this mound. The life it supported was believed to have been created by the deities associated with that particular place, be they the nine gods of Heliopolis, the eight gods of Hermopolis, or the one god of Memphis.

In the "solo" version of creation, the god Ptah simply thought the world into being before naming everything in it and creating life quite literally by "the word of god." Elsewhere, credit was given to Atum, the creator god of Heliopolis, who had produced his own children Shu and Tefnut by "sneezing out one and spitting out the other"—or simply by ejaculating them. These two gods then produced the earth god and sky goddess, whose own children in turn were Isis, Osiris, Seth, and Nephthys.

Others believed in more cataclysmic events, during which life was created by eight mysterious gods. Their combined energies sparked life into being and formed the primeval mound from which the sun burst forth in the earliest version of the big bang theory. Always at the center of Egyptian life,

the sun was regarded as all powerful and as capable of taking life as of creating it. The god most often associated with this power was the falcon-headed god Re, although at dawn the sun was also identified with the scarab beetle Khepri, with Horus as it rose in the east, and Atum as it sank in the west. Then as it entered the underworld, the sun once again became Re, traveling through the hours of the night to conquer the forces of darkness before returning victorious each dawn to begin the eternal cycle all over again.

As the sun god's representative on earth, the king ("pharaoh" from the Egyptian *per-wer* meaning "great house") was always acknowledged as the "Son of Re," and even when local god Amun became the national deity for political reasons, his status was assured by using Re's name to create Amun-Re, king of the Gods.

It was essential that male deities had female counterparts since Egyptian belief required complete balance between dualities, an idea embodied by the goddess Maat, who held the universe together. It was she who set the rules by which each king must govern, protected by an array of largely female deities.

Honored by massive cult temples to which only their priesthood had access, Egypt's numerous gods were also worshiped by the majority of the population in small domestic shrines, together with a whole range of protective household deities such as Bes, Taweret, and the spirits of each family's ancestors. Gods great and small were an essential part of daily life, and as protective funerary deities they accompanied the dead into the eternity of the afterlife.

The gilded wooden figure of Selket is one of the four protector goddesses of the dead who stand around the canopic shrine of Tutankhamun in Cairo's Egyptian Museum.

GODS & GODESSES

The ancient Egyptians represented their deities in both human and animal form, and as a combination of both. Many of them shared characteristics, titles, and attributes creating an incredibly complicated pattern of religious belief. Here is a cast list of key players in the divine dramas.

name means "the house of Horus" as protector of the god, the king, and all dead souls, and her cult center was Dendera.

Horus Usually represented as a falcon, the son of Isis and Osiris was conceived after his father's resurrection to avenge and succeed him (see box p. 309) and was the god with whom all living kings were identified.

Nut stretches her body protectively over the dead as shown on the underside of the stone sarcophagus lid of King Merneptah.

Isis kneels at the foot end of the stone sarcophagus of King Amenhotep II, whose mummy, discovered in 1898, she protected.

Ammut This composite figure of a lion, hippopotamus, and crocodile ate the hearts of sinners after death.

Amun Local deity of Thebes whose name means "the hidden one," he became king of the gods when combined with Re as Amun-Re. His cult center was Karnak.

Anubis Jackal-headed god of embalmers and guardian of cemeteries.

Atum The great creator god known as "the one who came into being of himself"; like Re he was worshiped mainly at Heliopolis.

Bes Grotesque dwarflike god of the household and protector of women in childbirth.

Geb The son of Shu and Tefnut, Geb represents the earth and is shown as a green man.

Hathor Goddess of love, pleasure, and beauty, she is often represented as a cow. Her

Isis The great goddess of magic who reassembled Osiris's dismembered body to create the first mummy and conceive Horus. Her name was written with a throne sign, and her cult center at Philae was the last outpost of the ancient religion.

Khepri The sun god at dawn in the form of a scarab beetle.

Maat Goddess of universal order and symbol of truth, identified by her feathered plume against which the hearts of the dead were weighed for sin.

Nekhbet Vulture goddess of Upper Egypt whose outstretched wings protect the king. Together Nekhbet and Wadjet were known as the "Mighty Ones."

Nephthys Sister of Isis. Together they were the protectors of the dead.

PHARAONIC CULTURE

47

Nut The sky goddess is portrayed as a woman whose body forms heaven, arcing over that of her brother Geb, with the pair held apart by their father Shu, god of air.

Osiris Initially an earthly ruler and bringer of fertility, his name is also written with the throne sign; after his murder and resurrection as the first mummy he became savior of the

figure wearing a feather on his head. He was created when Atum sneezed him into being.

Taweret Hippopotamus goddess of childbirth.

Tefnut Goddess of moisture and twin sister of Shu, she was created when her father Atum spat her out—her name is sometimes written with the hieroglyph sign of lips spitting.

Amun-Re in his tall double-plumed crown acknowledges the kneeling Hatshepsut as pharaoh in this relief carving at Karnak.

The jackal-headed Anubis prepares the mummy of the tomb-builder Sennedjem (ca 1200 B.C.) in his tomb at Deir al-Medina.

dead and lord of the underworld. His cult center at Abydos was a place of pilgrimage.

Ptah Creator god and patron of craftsmen whose cult center was Memphis.

Re Preeminent form of the sun god whose name means "the sun," generally portrayed as a falcon-headed figure with the sun's disk on his head. His cult center, Heliopolis, is the area now partly beneath Cairo airport.

Sekhmet Fearsome lioness goddess of destruction whose name means "the powerful one," she directed the forces of aggression against all enemies of the state. The center of her cult was Memphis.

Seth God of chaos and storms, murderer of his brother Osiris, he was represented as a mythical animal.

Shu God of the air represented as a human

Thoth Ibis-headed god of wisdom and patron of scribes, he was worshiped at Hermopolis.

Wadjet Cobra goddess of Lower Egypt, represented by the protective serpent, or uraeus on the brow of the king's headdress.

Pharaonic deities have many different aspects and there are lots of overlaps, as you can see in the above list. Also, certain gods are particular to specific regions, fulfilling roles filled by another god elsewhere.

THE TEMPLE

The temple lay at the heart of Egyptian life and formed the focus of each settlement. It combined the roles of town hall, college, and medical center as well as performing a religious function. But whereas the modern

Great entrance gateway ("pylons") flanked by huge temple flagpoles

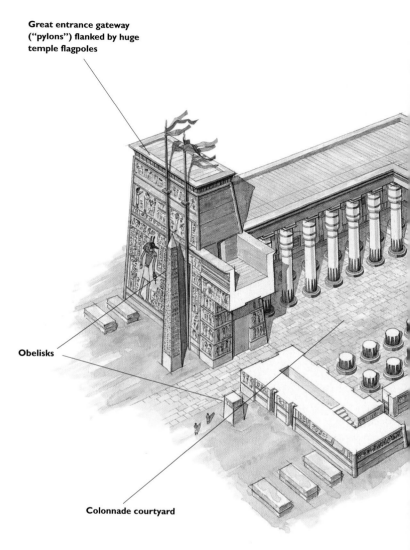

Obelisks

Colonnade courtyard

church or mosque has a congregation, only the priesthood were allowed inside the ancient temples, where their role was simply to serve the gods whose divine powers could then be harnessed for the benefit of all.

Each day in temples all over Egypt, the high priest, standing in for the king, acted as intermediary between the mortal and divine worlds. He used traditional rituals in which the gods were honored with a constant flow of offerings intended to encourage them down

to inhabit their statues, housed inside small shrines to which only the king and high priest had access.

The clergy themselves ranged from the most highly educated priest to the man who tended the sacred cattle. They lived in their own small communities attached to the temple, often close to its sacred lake in which they were required to bathe twice each day and twice each night, since ritual proceedings required total purity.

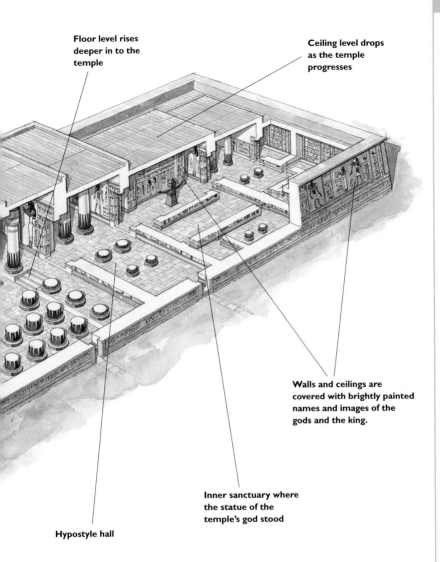

Floor level rises deeper in to the temple

Ceiling level drops as the temple progresses

Walls and ceilings are covered with brightly painted names and images of the gods and the king.

Inner sanctuary where the statue of the temple's god stood

Hypostyle hall

Although the priests' houses, storerooms, and subsidiary buildings were made of standard mud brick, the temples themselves were constructed of stone, their every surface covered in brightly painted images and texts. Scenes of warfare and destruction on the outside walls contrasted sharply with the calm scenes of devout worship inside, graphically illustrating the idea that the source of universal order could only be found within the temple walls.

A generic example of a classic New Kingdom temple

TOMB ART

The distinctive style of ancient Egyptian art was established at the very beginning of the pharaonic period, about 3100 B.C., and remained largely unchanged for more than three millennia. Despite its instantly recognizable appearance to the modern viewer, the reasons why it was created are still

very much misunderstood. Unlike art produced to be appreciated for its own sake,
Egyptian sculpture and painting were meant
to be functional rather than simply decorative.

The breathtaking beauty of the art is therefore all the more remarkable given that the
paintings, reliefs, and sculpture were made
mainly for religious and funerary purposes.
Hidden away from public gaze, they were
either in the darkness of temple interiors or
buried with the dead in their tombs to protect

them in the afterlife. This explains the nature
of painted and relief scenes in particular.
Their deceptively simplistic appearance and
lack of perspective have a functional purpose
since it was vital that the subject be portrayed
with every relevant feature shown as clearly as
possible. Human figures were given a clear
profile of nose and mouth, whereas the eye
was shown as whole: It was thought that the
correct rituals would reanimate the subjects
and that only the clearest of representations

would enable the senses to work efficiently on that reanimation.

Inanimate objects were also represented as clearly as possible, with the vast quantities of food and drink offered in temples and tombs duplicated on the walls to ensure a constant supply for eternity. The offerings are shown piled up in distinct layers, often to the extent of "floating" in suspension, and the contents of boxes were similarly portrayed. Although working within strict stylistic conventions, the

Repeated figures of Horemheb, in a striped headcloth presenting offerings to the gods, decorate a tomb in the Valley of the Kings.

ancient artists still managed to capture the vitality of images inspired by the world around them. These images repeatedly emphasize the concept of life and rebirth and were thought capable of transmitting the very vitality they depicted. They include scarab beetles and tilapia fish, believed capable of self-generation, the animals and plants offered as food for the deceased and the gods, and the life-giving lotus flower (the heraldic symbol of Upper Egypt, as the papyrus reed was of Lower Egypt).

Art's functional nature was also enhanced by a careful use of bright primary colors. The land of Egypt, represented politically by the White Crown of Upper Egypt and the Red Crown of Lower Egypt, was also divided into the fertile black land and the red desert wastes. This distinction explains the choice of black and green in representations of Osiris, god of fertility and eternal life, in contrast to the red-ness associated with his murderous brother Seth, god of chaos. The ethereal blue of the sky also had divine associations and was used in representations of the gods in general, with the golden yellow of the sun employed for its protective qualities. Even humans were repre-sented with different-colored skin tones, the red-brown of men contrasting with the paler, more yellowed tones of female figures.

HIEROGLYPHS & CARTOUCHES

The beginnings of ancient Egyptian writing were thought to have emerged about 3100 B.C., until recent discoveries indicated that it was actually in use almost two centuries earlier, making it the world's oldest script, predating that of Mesopotamia. The Egyptians first developed writing as a means of organizing resources, using a pictorial script that came to be known as hieroglyphs from Greek words meaning "sacred carved letters." In continuous use for more than 3,500 years, hieroglyphs evolved from a simple script made up of a handful of signs to a highly complex com-pendium of more than 6,000, each sign repre-senting either one, two, or three consonants, or simply acting as a determinative. The lack of vowels, punctuation, and spacing, together with the practice of writing hieroglyphs hori-zontally right to left and left to right as well as vertically only added to their cryptic nature.

Although a "shorthand" form (known as hieratic) soon developed for day-to-day transactions, hieroglyphs were retained for religious purposes. They were regarded as "the words of Thoth" after the ibis-headed god of writing, and their magical nature was enhanced by the fact that only one percent of

the ancient population was literate, with those who had direct access to this "divine wisdom" forming an elite scribal class.

Their aesthetic appearance made hieroglyphs a perfect medium for both tomb and temple inscriptions in which they form an integral part of scenes, both words and pictures infused with divine power. The symbols of strength, prosperity, and above all life were regarded as especially potent, as were the names of the king and the gods, written again and again to preserve them for eternity.

The Egyptians sincerely believed that "to speak the name of the dead is to make them live," the name being as essential to an individ-ual's identity as his or her soul. The loss of either would result in permanent oblivion, the fate of those unfortunate enough to incur

The royal cartouche punctuates funerary liturgy carved into the wall of a tomb.

official censure, whether commoners, kings, or even the gods themselves. To counteract this, the names of the most powerful individuals were not only repeated, but protected with epithets such as *ankh, wedja, seneb* ("life, prosperity, health"). Parts of the royal name were also written inside a protective fortress wall *(serekh)*, which later developed into an oval-shaped cartouche (from the French for "cartridge"). The cartouche enclosed two of the five names given to each king, first the "King of Upper and Lower Egypt" name, which was written with a sedge plant and a bee and assumed at the coronation, followed by his "Son of Re" name, written with a sun disk and a goose; this name was given at birth.

As a good luck charm, names frequently incorporated those of the gods, such as Amenhotep meaning "Amun is content" or Ramses, "born of Re." An individual could also be given a simple name such as Nefer meaning "beautiful" or "happy," or Seneb meaning "healthy," while some chose to name their children after aspects of the natural world, including Miwt ("Cat") or Seshen ("Lotus").

The last hieroglyphic inscription is dated to A.D. 394, after which time the acceptance of Christianity led to the closure of the temples and all the knowledge they contained. Ancient Egypt had been lost and remained so until revealed once again with the decipherment of hieroglyphs in 1824 (see p. 171). ∎

Timeline of the pharaohs

THE PRECISE DATES OF THE EGYPTIAN DYNASTIES AND OF INDIVIDUAL reigns are still the subject of much heated scholarly debate. The following table, based on the chronology presented by the *British Museum Dictionary of Ancient Egypt* by Ian Shaw and Paul Nicholson, is also selective, including only the major kings and pharaohs, usually those who have left enduring monuments to their reign.

EARLY DYNASTIC PERIOD
ca 3100–2686 B.C.
Formative period in which many major aspects of pharaonic culture and society emerge.

1st dynasty	*3100–2890*
Narmer/Menes	ca 3100
2nd dynasty	*2890–2686*

OLD KINGDOM
2686–2181 B.C.
Rise of Memphis as Egypt's capital and growth of absolute power of pharaohs who erect pyramids as monuments.

3rd dynasty	*2686–2613*
Djoser	2667–2648
Sekhemkhet	2648–2640
4th dynasty	*2613–2494*
Sneferu	2613–2589
Khufu (Cheops)	2589–2566
Djedefra	2566–2558
Khafre (Chephren)	2558–2532
Menkaura (Mycerinus)	2532–2503
5th dynasty	*2494–2345*
Userkaf	2494–2487
Sahure	2487–2475
Neferirkare	2475–2455
Nyuserra	2445–2421
Unas	2375–2345
6th dynasty	*2345–2181*
Teti	2345–2323
Pepi	2321–2287
Pepi II	2278–2184

FIRST INTERMEDIATE PERIOD
2181–2055 B.C.
Unified rule gives way to rival principalities and civil war. Power of the pharaohs declines.
7th–11th dynasties

MIDDLE KINGDOM
2055–1650 B.C.
Continued turmoil until Egypt is reunified under the rulers of Thebes, which now becomes increasingly important. Power shifts to Upper Egypt.

11th dynasty	*2055–1985*
Mentuhotep II	2055–2004
12th dynasty	*1985–1795*
Amenemhat I	1985–1955
Senusret I	1965–1920
Amenemhat II	1922–1878
Senusret II	1880–1874
Senusret III	1874–1855
Amenemhat III	1855–1808
Amenemhat IV	1808–1799
13th–14th dynasties	*1795–1650*

SECOND INTERMEDIATE PERIOD
1650–1550 B.C.
Egypt is occupied by the Hyskos, foreign settlers from the north.
15th–17th dynasties

NEW KINGDOM
1550–1069 B.C.
Golden age of the pharaohs as Egypt rises to unequaled greatness under a succession of powerful kings; Thebes now the southern capital and Egypt's religious and funerary center.

18th dynasty	*1550–1295*
Ahmose I	1550–1525
Amenhotep I	1525–1504
Tuthmose I	1504–1492
Tuthmose II	1492–1479
Tuthmose III	1479–1425

A statue in Cairo's Egyptian Museum depicts King Menkaura of Upper Egypt, flanked by Hathor and the local deity of Hardai; it comes from the king's temple at Giza.

Hatshepsut	1473–1458
Amenhotep II	1427–1400
Tuthmose IV	1400–1390
Amenhotep III	1390–1352
Akhenaten	1352–1336
Tutankhamun	1336–1327
Aye	1327–1323
Horemheb	1323–1295
19th dynasty	*1295–1186*
Ramses I	1295–1294
Seti I	1294–1279
Ramses II	1279–1213
Merenptah	1213–1203
Seti II	1200–1194
20th dynasty	*1186–1069*
Ramses III	1184–1153
Ramses IV	1153–1147
Ramses V–XI	1147–1069

THIRD INTERMEDIATE PERIOD

1069–747 B.C.

Pharaonic rule breaks down. Tanis in the Delta supercedes Thebes. Libyans invade and rule. *21st–24th dynasties*

LATE PERIOD 747–332 B.C.

Simultaneous dynasties of rival rulers in Thebes and the Delta. Egypt comes under both Kushite (a dynasty from the south) and Persian rule. However, the 26th dynasty (664–525 B.C.) saw native rule based at Sais. *25th–30th dynasties*

GRECO–ROMAN PERIOD

332 B.C.–A.D.395

Ptolemaic Period	332–30
Alexander the Great	332–323
Ptolemy I	305–285
Ptolemy II	285–247
Ptolemy III	246–221
Cleopatra	51–30

The arts

FOR ALL THAT WE IN THE WEST KNOW OF IT, EGYPTIAN CULTURE MIGHT have died with the pharaohs. But to the Arab-speaking world, Cairo is their Hollywood and New York rolled into one, a powerhouse of film, TV, music, theater, and literature.

LITERATURE

Ancient Egyptian stories and legends have long made their mark on the psyche of Americans and Europeans via movies such as *Cleopatra*, *The Prince of Egypt*, and the countless undead risings of the *Mummy*, but probably the last time modern Egypt and international culture crossed paths in any

Nobel Prize-winning writer Naguib Mahfouz contemplates the streets of Cairo, raw material for many of his novels.

major way was when Omar Sharif wowed female audiences in David Lean's *Lawrence of Arabia* and *Doctor Zhivago*.

However, keen readers and news followers may have noted another Egyptian entry onto the international scene in 1988, when Cairo-born novelist Naguib Mahfouz was awarded that year's Nobel Prize for Literature, thus joining the ranks of the likes of Gabriel García Márquez, John Steinbeck, and Ernest Hemingway. Born in 1911, Mahfouz is the grand old man of Arabic letters. He started writing at age 17 and has since produced around 50 novels and collections of short

stories. He can claim to have almost single-handedly shaped the nature of Egyptian literature this century, shepherding its transition from European imitation to a form with a distinct national voice of its own. The best of his work—which includes the novels *The Harafish* and *Children of the Alley*—harks back to the indigenous narrative arts of Arabic literature, drawing inspiration from medieval story cycles like *The Thousand and One Nights*, and those found in the Koran, the Muslim holy book. Many of his works have been translated into English, and they are, in the words of *The Washington Post*, "a marvelous read."

How much better it would be, however, if the stories were delivered by a master storyteller. This is how it once was. Tales such as those that make up *The Thousand and One Nights*, a bawdy collection of parables and entertainments, many of which have a setting in the Cairo of the Mamluks, were never meant to be read. Instead they were perpetuated by itinerant showmen, who carried the stories in their heads and related them in backstreet coffeehouses. Skillful manipulators of an audience, they would end each tale on a note of high suspense, commanding a tribute of coins to reveal what happened next. Sadly, public storytelling is an art that has largely failed to survive the 20th century, supplanted in the coffeehouses first by radios, then by television. Only during the holy month of Ramadan does the storytelling recommence, revived by a young actress called Sherine al-Ansari, who gathers an audience each night in one of the old houses of Islamic Cairo to entrance them with the tales of Sheherazade.

Part of the appeal of Mahfouz is that he transports his readers to a time before the advent of television. Ironic then that, despite his fame, Mahfouz is actually little read in his

Musicians play traditional instruments including the oud, Arabic lute, and tabla—the expressive drum tucked under the arm.

الهام شاهير نور الشريف محمد زهدى احمد الطاهر صلاح الدمرداش

عريس النها

السلبين مجدى نور محمد المعتصم

عادل الأخضر

CINEMA Miami ميامى

Giant movie billboards represent a vibrant form of street art, at odds with the rather moribund mainstream art scene.

home country. Egyptians are not great readers and the books that do sell tend to be lurid accounts of scandals or gaudily packaged bits of journalistic sensationalism. Instead, Mahfouz's fame at home comes from film and TV adaptations—even his own daughters confess to knowing their father's work through the screen rather than the printed word.

THE LADY

Virtually unknown in the West, one figure stands even taller than Naguib Mahfouz in the Egyptian cultural pantheon—a large woman with dark glasses and a handkerchief, often referred to with great reverence simply as Al-Sitt, "the Lady." She is Umm Kolthum, the 20th century's greatest Arabic singer. Born into poverty in a small Delta village, she gained early fame as a reciter of the Koran at weddings. She gave her debut radio broadcast in 1935 and rapidly became the voice of a nation. For almost 40 years until she retired in 1973, the first Thursday of every month became a celebrated occasion, eagerly anticipated by millions of Egyptians, as Umm Kolthum gave her monthly concert. Kings, presidents, and princes would fly in from all over the Arab world to attend, while the streets of Egypt's towns and cities would become deserted as families stayed home to listen to the performance broadcast live on the radio. Her songs were great epics, with lyrics by famous poets

than thousands of railways or telephone lines. Get in your car on the night of her concert and roam around the Arab countries, and you'll easily identify its borders," wrote critic Mustafa Mahmoud.

She had her male counterparts in Abdel Halim Hafez and Farid al-Atrash, Egypt's answers to Bing Crosby and Frank Sinatra.

A portrait of Umm Kolthum is carried aloft by mourners who thronged the streets at her funeral in 1975.

They were crooners with enormous popular appeal, but they never came close to attracting the adulation of the Lady. When she died in 1975 her funeral was attended by a bevy of Arab leaders, and the streets of Cairo filled with over two million mourners.

Since her death classical Arabic music has become much less popular. Egypt has experienced a population boom and the mean age has decreased. A new generation of singers has emerged. Egypt has its own take on pop, and rap, and other modern musical trends, and has its own homegrown hit parade of stars and starlets. For people of a certain age, however, the songs of Umm Kolthum remain as pinnacles, reminders of a great golden age of Arabic culture. They are constantly played on radio and TV, and a cheap cassette of *Inta Omri* (*You Are My Life*) or *Al-Atlal* (*The Ruins*), two of the Lady's seminal works, is an essential part of any Cairo taxi-driver's kit.

set to tunes by contemporary composers. A single song could last up to an hour or more. Toward the end her voice would rise to an almost sobbing intensity, which would have her audiences shouting out of sheer ecstasy. It has been said that the whole country was enslaved to her voice.

The Lady's popularity was at its peak, in the heady days of the 1950s, when newly independent Egypt was a torch to the whole Arab world and the developing nations of Africa, still struggling to free themselves from colonial rule. Charismatic firebrand Gamal Abdel Nasser may have been the president, but Umm Kolthum was the real embodiment of the Arabs' cultural renaissance. "Umm Kolthum is more effective in connecting the Arab world than thousands of airlines, more powerful

HOLLYWOOD ON THE NILE

During her lifetime Umm Kolthum appeared in six movies, including 1936's *Wedad,* the first long feature to be made by Studio Misr, Egypt's equivalent to MGM. In the halcyon years of the 1940s and '50s, Cairo's film studios rolled out 50 to 100 movies annually, with many reaching technical standards that matched the best European and American productions. Egypt produced its own home-grown stable of square-jawed leading men and swooning starlets. Musicals, romances, and melodramas spread the Cairene dialect throughout the Arab-speaking world. Just as every kid in America at one time grew up familiar with the sights of New York via the big screen, so too children from Casablanca to Baghdad had their fantasies fueled with the glamorous settings of celluloid Cairo.

This is less the case today. Production has dropped and critics complain of a decline in quality. Egypt no longer has the cinematic cachet that it once did. However, within Egypt itself local product still has the edge over Hollywood imports and fills more of the country's screens. Walk around any town or city and large, lurid, hand-painted billboards advertise the latest movies, with their stars, standing many times larger than life-size, bearing down on the passersby below.

Unfortunately, the Egyptian product has never translated beyond its Arabic-speaking audience. In that sense, it is a little like the output of India's Bollywood—too firmly tailored to its home audience to appeal to non-natives. Typical fare is slapstick comedy, full of raised voices, exaggerated gestures, and high-pitched hysterics. There are exceptions: Shadi Abdelsalam's *The Night of Counting the Years* (1969) is a beautiful and truly original film based on the story of the tomb-robbing Abdel Rassoul brothers (see p. 270). Among film critics it ranks as the finest Egyptian movie ever made.

Also highly regarded is the output of director Yousef Chahine, who has been called Egypt's Fellini and was honored with a lifetime's achievement award at Cannes in 1997. Born in 1926, he has directed around 40 films to date in a career that defies classification. Chahine's films are also some of the very few Egyptian productions that are ever subtitled into English or French, and they regularly do the rounds of international film festivals. It was Chahine who discovered the young Omar Sharif, casting him in three films in the early 1950s. Sharif acted only in Egyptian films until his role as Sharif Ali in *Lawrence of Arabia.* For anyone who was wondering what happened to Sharif, he is now back in Egypt making undistinguished made-for-television films and TV commercials.

BELLY DANCING

One of the staples of the majority of Egyptian films is a wiggle of the belly. A truly indigenous art form, there is strong evidence from sources such as tomb paintings that the belly dance dates back to the time of the pharaohs. During medieval times dancing became institutionalized in the form of the *ghawazee,* a caste of dancers who traveled in groups and performed publicly or for hire. The female ghawazee, who according to 18th- and 19th-century descriptions danced in baggy pants and loose shirts sometimes open to the navel, were also often prostitutes.

Belly dancing began to gain credibility and popularity in Egypt with the advent of movies, when the dancers were lifted out of nightclubs and given roles on the big screen. Movies imbued belly dancing with glamour and made household names of a handful of dancers. Slinkiest of all was Tahiyya Carioca, who named herself after a Latin American dance, the carioca, popularized by Ginger Rogers and Fred Astaire. From the 1930s to the 1990s she appeared in over 200 films and was married no less than 12 times. Artists such as Carioca started the modern phenomenon of the belly dancer as superstar, someone who can command Hollywood-style fees for an appearance. Current dancers at the top of the league, including names such as Fifi Abdou, Lucy, and Dina, can expect as much as $10,000 for a single performance.

Despite the celebrity and wealth of some of its practitioners, belly dancing is still not considered to be completely respectable,

A superstar in the world of belly dancing, Fifi Abdou draws admirers to a performance at a hotel in Cairo.

especially not by Egypt's Islamic fundamentalists. For a time in the early 1990s, pressure was successfully exerted on the dancers to cover up their midriffs, but today they are once again exposed.

Away from the glitz of the professional scene, dance in Egypt thrives at a grassroots level. At the humblest of weddings the

This is at odds with the rather moribund mainstream art scene. Although in the past Egypt has produced fine artists of merit and originality, notably Abd al-Hady al-Gazzar (see p. 125) and Mahmoud Said, who has a museum devoted to his work in Alexandria (see p. 194), and the sculptor Mahmoud Mokhtar (1891–1934), the contemporary

Wonderfully decorated walls at Gurna, near Luxor, are a popular art form. Designs often celebrate a pilgrimage to Mecca.

unmarried girls sway to the beat of the *tabla,* the Egyptian hand-held drum, hands clasped above their heads and pelvises gyrating in a blatant bid to attract male attention and a possible future groom of their own.

Belly dancing is an exclusively female pursuit, but there is also a male dance performed with wooden staves. It involves lots of stick-twirling and mock fighting and comes across as rather contrived, although the hotel nightclubs that present it in performances billed as "folkloric dancing" insist that it is an authentic rural tradition.

ART
The billboards advertising local films represent a wonderfully vibrant form of street art.

scene is straitjacketed by a state teaching system that continues to penalize originality and stifle experimentation.

ARCHITECTURE FOR THE POOR
Folk tradition unquestionably lies at the heart of the architecture of Hassan Fathy (1900–1989), one of the few Middle Eastern names in the field that is also known in the West, and reputedly the favorite architect of Britain's Prince Charles. He is, however, known as more than just an architect. Fathy was also a philosopher, artist, humanitarian, and even a visionary. From his base in Cairo (which, in his latter years, was a house in the city's Islamic quarter, beside the Citadel), Fathy devoted himself to housing the poor in developing nations.

Utilizing ancient design methods and materials, he integrated a knowledge of peasant economics with a mastery of age-old, common-sense, design techniques; for example, dense mud-brick walls to minimize heat transfer, so rooms stay cool in the day and hold their warmth when the sun goes down at night, and natural air-conditioning achieved

GOING GLOBAL

Fathy has gained international recognition, as has Naguib Mahfouz, and the belly dance has been exported world wide, where it competes with Jane Fonda videos and Pilates programs as a fun way to keep fit. Now there are signs that other aspects of Egypt's rich modern culture might finally be breaking through. In summer

Ahdaf Soueif's *The Map of Love,* a historical novel about 20th-century Egypt rich with detail and debate, was shortlisted in 2000 for the Booker Prize.

by carefully situated apertures.

Fathy's efforts, ahead of his time, did not always meet with success. His showpiece village of New Gurna (see p. 256) on the West Bank at Luxor remains empty to this day. However, his ideas on sustainability, an architectural way to deal with our dependence on dwindling natural resources, are coming of age, and posthumously Fathy is gaining in influence.

New hotels, such as the Adrere Amellal in Siwa (see p. 369), are being designed along his principles. Not only are the results environmentally sound, but with their domed roofs, and myriad internal courtyards open to the stars, they are beautiful buildings to look at and inhabit.

2000, lawyers claimed that American rap artist Jay-Z had stolen the riff to one of his hit singles from an old Abdel Halim Hafez song. In November 2000 an article in *Vanity Fair* magazine included the works of Umm Kolthum in a list of the 500 best recordings ever made. Cairo-born Ahdaf Soueif was shortlisted in 2000 for the Booker Prize, for her historical novel of Egypt, *The Map of Love.* In 2001 the works of Cairo-born contemporary artist Chant Avedissian were exhibited at the Smithsonian Institution in Washington, D.C.

Meanwhile, Cairo is still the center of Arabness, and worn as it is, the city still draws the best in Arab arts. As Abdel Halim might have sung had he lived longer, "If I can make it there, I'll make it anywhere...." ■

Food & drink

MUCH OF THE FOOD EATEN IN EGYPT IS NOT UNIQUE TO THE COUNTRY, BUT is shared with other Middle Eastern neighbors and near neighbors. Most of the dishes Egyptians claim as their own are arguably Turkish, Lebanese, or Persian, but there are a few specialties that can truly be claimed as national dishes.

Chief of these national dishes is *fuul*, also known as *fuul medames*, which are small brown beans, soaked overnight, then boiled for eating. Considered something of a poor man's dish in a country where the greater part of the population lives on the breadline, it has become a national staple. In fact, fuul is claimed to have been eaten in Egypt as far back as the time of the pharaohs. In its most refined form the beans are sprinkled with olive oil, have a little lemon juice squeezed over them, and are seasoned with salt, pepper, and cumin, and maybe garnished with a chopped boiled egg. Much more common, though, is for them to be mashed to a paste and ladled into small pockets of flat pita bread as a sandwich. For many Egyptians a fuul sandwich serves for both breakfast and lunch.

Egyptians are also big consumers of *felafel* (called *taamiyya* in Cairo), patties made from dried white broad beans (*fuul nabeid*), spiced and flavored and deep-fried in oil. Although felafel is ubiquitous throughout the Middle East (especially in Israel and Lebanon, where it is made with chickpeas), again it is claimed that the dish dates back to ancient Egypt. As part of a meal the felafel are served whole on a small plate, but they, too, are often eaten as a street snack, broken up and stuffed into a pita sandwich along with salad and small pieces of pickles known as *torshi*.

Stuffed vegetables are popular, particularly eggplant (*bedingan*) and peppers (*filfil*). These are eaten hot and cold. Eggplant is also grilled and mashed and seasoned with tahina (a sesame seed paste), olive oil, and garlic to make a purée known as *baba ghanoug*. Also common are stuffed grape leaves, a dish called *warak enab*. In addition to ground meat, a spicy mix of rice, chopped tomatoes, onion, mint, and cinnamon—or some similar variation—is also often used to stuff these leaves.

Wheat is the staple cereal of the country-side, but rice is more often used as a base or side dish to most meals. It is given an unusual twist by the addition of small, very thin strands of noodles. Beans of all types, split peas, lentils, and chickpeas also form an important part of the diet. They are used in the many different soups and stews that Egyptian women are so fond of cooking—which, unfortunately, rarely find their way into restaurants—and, in the case of chick peas, are ground into a paste known as hummus, also often served as a side dish, to be eaten with bread.

A meal without bread is absolutely unthinkable, and in fact the Arabic word for it, *aish*, also means "life." Bread types are wide and varied, but the most common form is a round flat disk the size of a dinner plate, made from a coarsely ground flour.

When it comes to meat, lamb is the favorite and predominates. Beef is much less common, and, because of the dietary laws of Islam, no pork is ever eaten. Traditionally the cost of meat has been prohibitive and so it tends to be served in small chunks, flame grilled, known as kabobs, or stretched to go far in a stew, or ground and used as part of a filling in vegetables. Chicken is common, as are pigeons, which are something of an Egyptian delicacy, especially when stuffed. In Alexandria it is also possible to find quail on the menu.

One dish to seek out is the infamous *molokhiyya*, made from the molokhiyya leaf, which looks a little like spinach. It is boiled up into a soup with an extraordinary glutinous texture that makes eating it a little like swallowing warm, savory Jell-O. It is a sensation that many find unpleasant. Nevertheless, the dish has acquired a symbolic, almost patriotic importance in Egypt and you ought to try it at least once.

The influences of Turkey, Lebanon, and Iran reflect Egypt's long history, but Egyptian cuisine does have its own character.

SWEET TREATS & DESSERTS

Given the Egyptian addiction to very sweet, sticky pastries, it is no wonder that dentistry is such a popular profession. The generic term for these sugar-loaded confections is baklava: layers of wafer-thin filo pastry filled with crushed nuts and pistachios and drenched in syrup. It is baked in great trays and then typically sliced into small diamond-shaped pieces sold by the kilogram. *Konafa* is another generic type; this is made by straining liquid batter onto a hot metal sheet so it sets in strands, which are quickly swept off so they remain soft. These are then piled on top of a soft cheese or cream base. Konafa is often associated with feasts and is always eaten during Ramadan.

Around the markets and bazaars, you sometimes see vendors pushing small, wheeled glass cabinets filled with dishes of what looks like blancmange; this is *muhalabiyya*, a milk cream thickened by cornstarch or ground rice,

Sharing meze (appetizers) at a streetside café

often flavored with rose water, and with chopped almonds or coconut sprinkled on top. For the sake of your stomach, though, it is better to try it in a restaurant. There you might also have the option of *om ali*, a pastry layered with nuts and raisins, soaked in cream and milk, and baked in the oven.

DRINKS

Tea *(shai)* and coffee *(ahwa)* are served at every opportunity and are an integral part of culture and hospitality. Business meetings never begin and bargaining in the souq never finishes before all parties involved have sat and drunk at least one cup. Both drinks are taken strong and sugary.

Tea comes in a glass with the leaves swirling around in the bottom (although asking for "shai lipton" will get you a brew from a tea bag), while coffee Egyptian-style (also known as Turkish coffee) comes in tiny cups half full with grounds. It is often flavored with cardamom, but is still very bitter. "Of all the unchristian beverages that ever passed my lips," wrote grouchy American humorist and traveler Mark Twain, "Turkish coffee is the worst. The bottom of the cup has a muddy sediment in it half an inch deep. This goes down your throat, and portions of it lodge by the way, and produce a tickling aggravation that keeps you barking and coughing for an hour." If you would prefer Western-style instant coffee, ask for "neskaf."

A far healthier option is to take advantage of Egypt's abundance of fresh fruit. A platter of fruit is usually served at the end of a meal, but on practically every street throughout Egypt there is also a juice stand at which you can get a drink squeezed out of just about any fruit in season. Most common are guava *(guafa)*, mango *(manga)*, orange *(bortuaan)*, sugarcane *(asab)*, and lemon *(limoon)*; the latter drink is also offered in most cafés and restaurants.

In coffee shops, during the colder winter months, many patrons like to drink *sahlab*, a milky drink thickened with the powdered bulb of a type of orchid and flavored with chopped nuts and cinnamon. In summer, try *karkade*, made from boiled hibiscus leaves, which is a beautiful deep crimson color and drunk from a tall beaker filled with ice.

In this Islamic country, the consumption of alcoholic drinks is not part of the culture. However, hotels and restaurants catering for tourists will serve beer or wine if asked. Locally brewed Stella beer is very acceptable, and Egypt produces a number of wines, both red (Omar Khayyam is the one most usually offered) and white. ∎

Look beyond the Pyramids and Tutankhamun's treasures and you'll find the capital of Egypt—and the Arab world—is a nonstop whirl of culture, arts, good humor, and hospitality.

Cairo

A theater poster in downtown Cairo

Cairo

IF NEW YORK CITY IS CHARACTERIZED BY ITS SKYSCRAPERS, AND LONDON BY its parks, the leitmotif of Cairo is its traffic. You hit it the moment you leave the airport, and it provides the finest possible introduction to the city. Cairo's traffic is composed of oddities and spectacles: Cars are dented and patched; passengers cling to the outside of buses like barnacles; a single small motorbike carries a family of five as it moves at high speed—weaving, darting, braking—accompanied by a frenetic chorus of beeping horns.

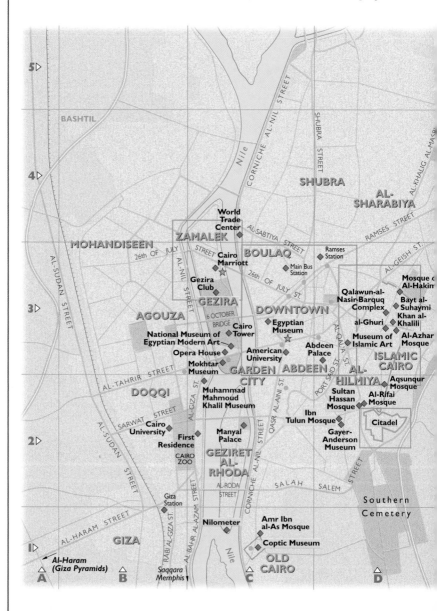

Cairo

Area of map detail

STREET

Quba Palace

Merryland

HELIOPOLIS

Airport

Nasser's Tomb

Cairo Stadium

Sadat's Tomb

SALAH SALEM STREET

Northern Cemetery

Muqattam Hills

MADINET AL-MUQATTAM

0   2 kilometers
0   1 mile

E   F

When it comes to driving, highway rules appear nonexistent, and seemingly anything goes. Yet there is a system, one that relies on unwritten understandings backed by nods, winks, and waves. Against all the odds it works, a bit like Cairo itself really. Half the cars in Egypt are in the capital because, in a sense, all roads lead here. Rarely is a country so completely dominated by a single city. Politics, finance, media, and popular culture scarcely exist beyond its boundaries. Only when it comes to tourism does any other city rate seriously. Tellingly, in the Egyptian language the word for Cairo and for Egypt is one and the same: *Masr*.

Cairo now sprawls over something like 175 square miles (450 sq km), which is a little over half the size of New York City, but with twice as many residents. That number swells almost daily as ever more *fellaheen*, or rural peasants, pour into the city looking to improve their lot. Incomes are, of course, better in the city, but it is also a fact that Cairenes live longer and have a far lower child mortality rate than their country cousins.

Cairo has always absorbed more than its fair share of outsiders in its role as Umm al-Dunya, or Mother of the World. In the 19th and early 20th centuries, it was Europeans and Americans for whom the city was a temperate winter playground. Now it is the Gulf Arabs, who arrive each summer, fleeing the seasonal heat back in Saudi or Kuwait. To them, Cairo is the Arabic Hollywood and Big Apple rolled into one. Its streets and squares are familiar from countless movies, and its street talk and slang are emulated from Baghdad to Riyadh. Something like a million Gulf Arabs annually reserve suites and entire floors of hotels to indulge in a season of slapstick theater, movies, nightclubs, and casinos. Similarly for Eritreans, Ethiopians, and Sudanese, here as students, economic migrants, or refugees from Africa's internecine wars, the Egyptian capital is the ultimate uptown experience.

Unfortunately, when it comes to present-day tourism, the tour-company trend is to reduce the city to a two-day stopover en route to the pharaonic monuments of Upper Egypt or the beaches of Sinai. Wonderful as the Pyramids and Egyptian Museum are, there really is a lot more to Cairo. ■

Egyptian Museum

THOUGH MANY WESTERN MUSEUMS CONTAIN IMPRESSIVE collections of ancient Egyptian antiquities (see box p. 73), none begins to rival the riches on display at Cairo's Egyptian Museum. Devoted entirely to the legacy of the pharaohs, the museum has more than 120,000 items of antiquity on display, ranging from delicately crafted jewelry to towering granite colossi of kings.

A scarab jewel from the treasures of Tutankhamun

The museum is not especially big, and the floor plan of both upper and lower floors is simple: rectangular, with a series of rooms around a central court linked by a perimeter corridor. The collection on the ground floor is organized chronologically. As you enter, bear left for the Old Kingdom and continue clockwise through the Middle and New Kingdoms, ending up in the Greco-Roman period. You can then take the southeast staircase to the upper floor, where the exhibits are arranged thematically.

Ideally, try to arrive as close to the 9 a.m. opening time as possible, as the museum gets very crowded toward the middle of the day.

PLANNING YOUR VISIT

Egyptian Museum

⬛ 68 C3

✉ Tahrir Square

☎ 02/575 4319

💲 $$, extra fee ($$$) for Royal Mummy Room. Camera $, video camera $$$

Opposite: The famous gold mask of Tutankhamun— the exhibit that everyone wants to see

You may not get lost, but you may become bewildered and possibly overwhelmed. There is simply too much to take in. Added to which, the century-old museum is something of an antique piece itself, a product of the age when it was considered enough simply to catalog an artifact and pop it in a glass case. Labeling (in Arabic, English, and French) remains not just poor but frequently nonexistent. One good strategy to deal with this is to read a description of the museum before you go and identify pieces of interest, perhaps even noting their location on a map. If you have the time, plan for two visits, tackling one

floor only on each occasion. If your itinerary is too tight for this, then you could at least take time out in the museum garden. There is also a café of sorts on the ground floor, entered from the garden via the gift shop.

When considering what to see, most visitors would agree that the highlight has to be the treasures of Tutankhamun. His golden funerary mask and coffins are possibly the most stunning objects on display in any museum anywhere in the world. Save them until last because the dazzle eclipses everything that comes afterward. The museum's other big draw is the Royal Mummy Room, which brings you face to face with several of the greatest of the pharaohs, including Seti I and Ramses II. The mummies and Tutankhamun are on the upper floor. On the ground floor, many of the best pieces are in the Old Kingdom rooms and include the statue of Khafre (see p. 74), the wooden statue of Ka-Aper (see p. 74), and the double statue of Rahotep and Nofret (see p. 75). Also impressive is the Amarna collection of objects from the reign of Akhenaten, the "heretic king" (see p. 76).

The perpetually crowded bookshop at the entrance has plenty of further reading about the museum and ancient Egypt in general. The official guide is not particularly good as it does not locate any of the objects that it catalogs. Far better is *Cairo: The Egyptian Museum & Pharaonic Sites* by Muhammad

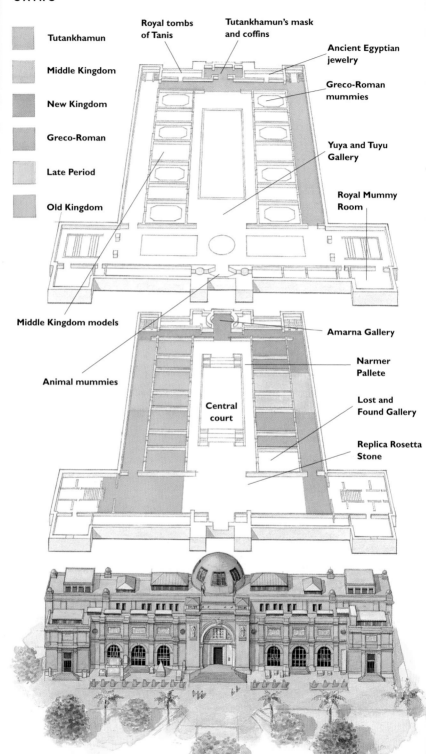

Tutankhamun

Middle Kingdom

New Kingdom

Greco-Roman

Late Period

Old Kingdom

Royal tombs of Tanis

Tutankhamun's mask and coffins

Ancient Egyptian jewelry

Greco-Roman mummies

Yuya and Tuyu Gallery

Royal Mummy Room

Middle Kingdom models

Animal mummies

Amarna Gallery

Narmer Pallete

Central court

Lost and Found Gallery

Replica Rosetta Stone

Salah, which describes 50 of the most important pieces accompanied by good color photographs.

GROUND FLOOR

Passing through security you emerge beneath the museum's rotunda; the chronological sequence starts off to the left, but directly ahead is the **Central Court**, containing monumental sculpture from all ages. Look for the crude limestone statue of King Djoser (or Zoser), which dates back to the 27th century B.C., making it one of the oldest pieces in the museum. It was discovered in 1924 within its *serdab* beside the Step Pyramid at Saqqara (see pp. 149–150). Opposite, set into the wall, is a replica of the Rosetta Stone, which provided the key to

Like some vast warehouse, the central court of the museum is filled with monumental antiquity.

Egyptian treasures overseas

After Cairo, the world's largest collection of pharaonic antiquities belongs to the Egyptian Museum in Turin, Italy. It includes some magnificent colossal statues removed from the Temple of Amun at Karnak, as well as the complete funeral paraphernalia from an intact 18th-dynasty tomb. Berlin's Egyptian Museum, founded 13 years before the one in Cairo, houses some of the most valued treasures of Egyptology, including a striking 3,350-year-old painted head of Nefertiti. Smuggled out of Egypt by an archaeological expedition in 1912, this is a piece that the Egyptian authorities would dearly love to see returned. Another disputed item is the Rosetta Stone in London's British Museum, which also has a fine granite bust of Ramses II, as well as a series of important papyri and a great many mummies and coffins. Best of all, the Metropolitan Museum of Art in New York has a complete temple, a gift from Egypt in recognition of American efforts to save the monuments of Nubia from the rising waters of Aswan's High Dam during the 1970s. ∎

Visitors to Room 32 are confronted with the gaze of the royal couple, Rahotep and Nofret, who lived 4,600 years ago.

Opposite: Small figurines called ushabti were put into the tomb with the deceased to carry out any labor in the afterlife.

unlocking the mystery of hiero-glyphics (see pp. 52–53). The original is still in the British Museum in London, despite frequent requests from the Egyptian antiquities authorities for its return.

Moving into the court, you pass between two funerary barks (see pp. 251–52), recovered from the pyramid site of Dahshur (south of Cairo), and descend to a collection of sarcophagi. The sarcophagus of Psusennes I (circa 1000 B.C.) has a relief figure of the sky goddess Nut on the underside of its lid covering the pharaoh in a protective embrace (a star-spangled Nut is often depicted across the ceilings of tombs).

The centerpiece of the court is a painted floor from the Amarna period (see pp. 218–221); unusually for this museum, it has a good caption. Sitting in stately fashion at the end of the hall is an imposing group of colossi representing Amenhotep III, his wife Queen Tiye, and their daughters. These statues were discovered in fragments on the West Bank at Luxor and painstakingly reassembled here.

The **Old Kingdom Galleries** begin with **Rooms 47** and **46.** The most striking things here are three slate triads—sets of three standing figures about 3 feet (1 m) high—depicting the pharaoh Menkaura (Mycerinus) flanked by the horned goddess Hathor on his right and the female personification of one of the territories under his jurisdiction on his left. Four of these triads were discovered at the pharaoh's temple beside his pyramid at Giza.

In **Room 42** another of the pyramid builders, Khafre (Chephren), is represented by a superb, larger-than-life-size black diorite statue that was also discovered on the Giza plateau, in the pharaoh's valley temple. The wings of the falcon god Horus protectively embrace his head. In the same room is the wooden statue of Ka-Aper, an amazingly lifelike figure with a potbelly, fleshy face, and lively eyes. Workers present at the discovery at Saqqara nicknamed him Sheikh al-Balad (the head of the village) because of the statue's resemblance to their own chief.

Equally lifelike are the statues of Prince Rahotep and Princess Nofret, which take center stage in **Room 32.** It is hard to imagine as you look at Rahotep, with his neat mustache, well-groomed hair, and simple heart-shaped pendant hung around his neck, that you are gazing on the face of someone who died more than 4,600 years ago. The royal couple were discovered in a tomb at Meidum in the Fayoum region, as were the friezes on the wall to the left depicting with great skill a gaggle of feeding geese. To this day the lakes at Fayoum remain a popular spot with bird-watchers (see p. 158).

The beginning of the **Middle Kingdom Galleries** is marked by the red-crowned seated figure of Mentuhotep II, the first pharaoh of this particular era. He came to light at Deir al-Bahri (see p. 274) when a horse ridden by Howard Carter (finder of Tutankhamun's tomb) put its foot into a hole in the ground. This chance led to the discovery of an unsuspected burial chamber.

The central exhibit in **Room 22** is a complete example of a Middle Kingdom burial chamber, also from Deir al-Bahri, with its limestone sarcophagus. The ten surrounding statues of Senusret I have nothing to do with the burial chamber; they are from a slightly later period and were discovered in the Fayoum region.

A parade of shaggy, gray granite sphinxes from the Delta city of Tanis (see p. 169) introduces the transition to the **New Kingdom Galleries. Room 12** is devoted to some of the early New Kingdom pharaohs of the 18th dynasty. They include the great conqueror Tuthmose III, seated in a traditional pose with his enemies symbolically represented as nine bows under his feet, and Hatshepsut, ancient

The remains of Ramses II lie in state in the Royal Mummy Room.

Egypt's only female pharaoh (see p. 274). Hers is the pink granite statue with arms at its side; she wears a king's costume and false beard and has been given a masculine physique, but her face is noticeably feminine.

Midway along the northern wing is the **Amarna Gallery,** a room displaying finds from the era of the rebel pharaoh Akhenaten (see pp. 218–21). Artistic style took a strange new turn under his rule, evident in the four fragmented colossi of the pharaoh, showing him with bulbous belly, almost feminine hips and thighs, elongated skull, and sensuous facial features, notably heavy-lidded eyes and bee-stung lips.

Several stelae depicting Akhenaten and his family at rest and worshiping the sun disk, Aten, make the pharaoh look even more alien. However, a sculpted quartzite head of Akhenaten's wife Nefertiti shows her to have been anything but freakish, with high cheekbones and an exotic beauty that would not look out of place on the cover of *Vogue* magazine.

Two monumental heads of Ramses II, long-lived builder of the Ramesseum on the West Bank at Luxor and the great temple at Abu Simbel, mark the start of the east wing, which continues with the **Late Period Galleries.** The rulers of this era were mostly foreign, and under their imported influence the archetypal sleek, hardened forms of pharaonic sculpture begin to loosen up. This culminates in a full-blown metamorphosis into classicism following the invasion of Alexander the Great and the subsequent era of Greco-Roman rule.

Room 44 is an unusual attraction called **Lost and Found,** which contains priceless objects recovered from would-be smugglers of antiquities.

From here take the staircase on the left to the upper floor.

UPPER FLOOR

From the top of the southeast staircase the Tutankhamun Galleries begin off to your right, starting with Room 45. Leaving those for later, buy a ticket (sold at

the top of the stairs) for the **Royal Mummy Room.** There are 11 desiccated royals entombed in glass cases in this darkened room, including Seti I and his son Ramses II, Tuthmose II, and Queen Meret Amun (wife of Amenhotep I). Once you have seen the human mummies, you might want to head for **Room 54** to see the **Animal Mummies,** a bizarre collection that includes cats, monkeys, a falcon, and even a fish. (For information on the hows and whys of embalming see "Making Mummies" on pp. 242–43.)

From the mummies, walk straight ahead to **Room 43,** the **Yuya and Tuyu Gallery.** Before Carter discovered Tutankhamun's tomb, this cache of funerary furniture, found in 1905 intact in the tomb of these two nobles (parents of Queen Tiye, wife of Amenhotep III), had constituted the biggest find in Egyptian archaeology. Displayed in this gallery are a number of items for use in the afterlife, including beds, biers, a chariot, and several coffins. The two former occupants of the coffins are now

among the inhabitants of the Royal Mummy Room.

Moving clockwise around the central atrium, **Rooms 37, 32,** and **27** contain **Middle Kingdom models,** providing a fascinating glimpse of daily life circa 2000 B.C. The lovingly detailed scenes include a weaver's workshop, fishing boats, and a herd of cattle being counted by a master and his scribes. They may look like children's toys, but these models were funerary offerings, and 25 of them were found sealed within the tomb of an official on the West Bank at Luxor. Part of the find is displayed at the Metropolitan Museum of Art in New York.

Room 14 contains **Greco-Roman mummies,** many adorned with what have come to be known as "Fayoum portraits" (see p. 157). Unfortunately, the mummies are not so much displayed as stashed—in stacks of grimy glass cabinets; this effectively makes it impossible to view the painted faces. Many of the other rooms along this upper east wing are particularly badly presented, and

In a Middle Kingdom model, herdsmen drive cattle past officials sitting in the shade of a pavilion.

tomb survived intact to be discovered by Howard Carter in 1922 (see pp. 278–79). Of the unimaginable treasures found chaotically heaped inside—which took four years to catalog and remove—some 1,700 objects are displayed here.

Entering **Room 45** you pass between two life-size, bitumen-coated wooden statues of the boy-king, which stood as guardians outside the antechamber where his body lay. Many of the objects in this first area are connected with hunting, such as leopard-skin shields and a wooden casket depicting the king hunting—a reminder that Egypt was once home to rich and varied wildlife. **Room 35** is filled with small figurines, which include a series of gods placed in the tomb to protect Tutankhamun, and some of the 400-plus *ushabti:* miniature effigies of the king that would carry out any tasks or labors on his behalf in the afterlife. Also here is the royal "lion" throne, covered with sheet gold and inlaid with glass and semiprecious stones; on the back is a colorful tableau of Tutankhamun being anointed by his queen.

Rooms 25 and **20** contain delicately made alabaster jars, lamps, and a chalice. **Room 15** has several intricately rigged model ships for the journey in the afterlife, but the real crowd-pleasers begin in **Room 10** where the king's three animal-headed funerary couches stand. Beside the couches is an alabaster chest; during the embalming process the internal organs were removed from the body and placed in canopic jars or urns, four of which you see here with their stoppers fashioned in the likeness of Tutankhamun. The chest containing the canopic jars was then enclosed within the neighboring golden canopic shrine, protected at its corners by the four

A quartet of Tuts carved from alabaster serve as stoppers on jars containing the king's internal organs.

although they contain objects of great interest, few visitors have the patience to investigate. You could be excused for hurrying on, back to the top of the southeast staircase and to the first of the rooms devoted to Tutankhamun.

TUTANKHAMUN GALLERIES

Tutankhamun was a relatively minor pharaoh who reigned for less than ten years (1336–1327 B.C.) before dying of unknown causes at the age of 18. He may well have been murdered. The name of this son-in-law and heir to the heretic king Akhenaten was erased from all monuments, and he would have merited no more than a footnote in ancient Egyptian history if it were not for the fact that his

goddesses, Isis, Neith, Nephthys, and Serket.

The gilded wooden boxes in **Rooms 7** and **8** fitted into each other like Russian dolls, and at their center were the sarcophagus and a series of inner coffins encasing the king. The outer, quartzite sarcophagus remains in the tomb at Thebes, but in **Room 3** are the inner coffins, one of gilded wood set with semiprecious gems and the innermost of solid gold weighing over 440 pounds (200 kg).

The body of Tutankhamun lay within this, the smallest and most precious of the coffins, wearing the fabulous death mask that takes center place in this room. Made of solid gold, it is an idealized portrait of the young king, with the eyes fashioned from obsidian and quartz, and the outlines of the eyes and the eyebrows delineated with lapis lazuli. If this was the treasure of only a minor pharaoh, one has to wonder what the looted tomb of a great pharaoh such as Ramses II might have held.

On either side of the main Tut room are two well-organized galleries; **Room 2** contains finds from the Royal Tombs of Tanis (see p. 169), five intact New Kingdom tombs found in the Delta region in 1939. The objects include a dazzling silver anthropoid coffin of the pharaoh Psusennes I (1039–991 B.C.) with the head of a falcon. **Room 4** on the other side displays some of the museum's finest pieces of ancient Egyptian jewelry, as well as items from the Greco-Roman era, found in the Western Oases. ■

A silver-robed queen anoints her king on Tutankhamun's golden "lion" throne.

Collecting ancient Egypt

Egyptology is a very young science, with almost everything known about ancient Egypt's 5,000-year history discovered in the last two centuries. Enlightenment first came from the scholars who accompanied Napoleon Bonaparte's military expedition to Egypt in 1798; their resulting 24-volume work, *Description de l'Egypte (Description of Egypt)*, has formed the cornerstone of all future research.

Following Napoleon, in the first decades of the 19th century, Egypt was rediscovered by a flood of intrepid travelers. One unfortunate consequence of this Egyptomania was the wholesale looting of the country. With no law against removing antiquities, the *Description de l'Egypte* was used as a catalog by European agents in Egypt who systematically plundered the land of anything that could be carried off.

Among the roll call of treasure-hunting adventurers, one name in particular stands out, that of the Italian Giovanni Belzoni. Born in Padua in 1778, he at one time earned a living in London on the music-hall stage with a strongman act that involved him carrying 12 people at once. Traveling to Egypt, Belzoni found employment with the British consul

general and supplied the British Museum with some of its key items, including a massive head of Ramses II transported from the Ramesseum at Thebes. In such a way, from around 1810 to 1850, was the core of the Egyptian antiquity collections of the great European museums created.

It was a Frenchman, Auguste Mariette (1821–1881), who put a stop to the pillaging. A former teacher from Boulogne, Mariette developed a passion for Egyptology, leaving his job for a menial position at the Louvre, then securing a small stipend to head out for the deserts to dig. In 1851, acting on a passage from Greek geographer Strabo (64 B.C.–A.D. 23), Mariette achieved success with the discovery of the Serapeum at Saqqara. The Egyptian viceroy Said Pasha invited Mariette to become the head of the newly founded Egyptian Antiquities Service with a remit to "collect stelae, statues, amulets, and any easily transportable objects…in order to secure them against the greed of the local peasants or the covetousness of Europeans."

To house the fruits of the service's excavations, in October 1863 Mariette inaugurated the first Egyptian Museum in the Cairo suburb of Boulaq. But the collection rapidly

The head of Ramses is depicted being transported from the Ramesseum in this watercolor by Belzoni.

expanded to fill its initial warehouse premises and outgrew a second home, too, before moving in March 1902 into its present specially built, dusky pink premises on Tahrir Square. Mariette did not live to see the Tahrir Square museum, but he was reburied in its garden with an impressive monument erected to mark the resting place of the institute's founder and first director.

A century later, the number of finds made in the last hundred years and shut away in storage in the Egyptian Museum's basement has come to outnumber the artifacts on display. Consequently, a new antiquities museum is currently being planned for a site out beside the Pyramids at Giza. ■

Members of the grandly titled "Commission des Sciences et des Arts de l'Armée d'Orient" survey antiquities for Napoleon.

Tahrir Square (Liberation Square) is the perpetually crowded center of modern Cairo.

Central Cairo

NO ONE WOULD CLAIM THAT THE MODERN CENTER OF Cairo is beautiful. Certain streets do have a worn charm and there is the odd architectural gem. But for the most part the city center is under siege from neglect, unregulated planning, and the destructive demands of the automobile. Yet anyone who spends more than a little time here quickly realizes that what central Cairo lacks in initial appeal, it more than makes up for on further acquaintance.

Tahrir Square is to Cairo what Times Square is to New York: not a grand plaza with statues and fountains, but a clamorous crossroads, filled night and day with people and a great deal of traffic. For tens of thousands of Cairenes, Tahrir is a commuting hub; it is where they arrive each morning from the suburbs by busy bus, overcrowded subway, or cab. Many are filing into the square's monolithic state office building, the Mogamma, workplace for 20,000 paper-swamped civil servants. The formerly elegant sweep of buildings on the east side of the square is home to travel agents, importers and exporters, and myriad other miscellaneous small businesses. On the sidewalk

out front, traders sell anything from watches to a shoeshine. At dusk the square is lent some glamour by a curve of neon signs along the building tops.

Every visitor spends time around Tahrir, if for no other reason than this is where you will find the famous **Egyptian Museum** (see pp. 70–79). Conveniently sited beside the museum is the **Nile Hilton,** the first modern five-star hotel to be built in Cairo (in 1959) and a distinctive city landmark. The glory days when the hotel welcomed the likes of Frank Sinatra are long past, but the courtyard coffee shop remains a popular meeting place for Cairo's moneyed classes.

Across the square, in a block of shabby travel agencies and snack bars, the Ali Baba Cafeteria is patronized by a more modest clientele, largely made up of middle-aged civil servants from nearby government offices. Internationally acclaimed author Naguib Mahfouz (see p. 56) used to have coffee here each morning until the tragic knife attack that almost ended his life. His favored seat was upstairs by the window, and it is a fine place to watch the theater of Cairo street life, so vividly captured in the Nobel laureate's writing.

One block to the south, housed in a former cigarette factory, is the **American University in Cairo,** where the wealthy pay big bucks to confer on their sons and daughters the prestige of a Western-style education. The university bookstore has an excellent stock of

The main residence of the Manyal Palace sits among beautiful gardens.

Abdeen Palace
- 🅰 68 D3
- ✉ Al-Gamaa St., Abdeen
- ☎ 02/391 0042
- 🕐 Closed Fri.
- 💲 $. Camera $, video camera $$$

Egypt-related titles, and the **Sony Gallery** hosts some good exhibitions of art and photography. You need to present your passport to get onto the campus.

Following either Muhammad Mahmoud or Sheikh Rihan Streets east past the university leads to another large square, on the far side of which is **Abdeen Palace.** Designed by a French architect in a graceless neoclassic style, the palace was completed in 1874 as a residence for Egypt's khedival rulers. Since the 1952 revolution and the exile of the last king, Farouk, Abdeen has served as government offices, with the grander rooms reserved for receiving visiting heads of state. In 1998 part of the rear of the building was opened to the public as a museum. Unfortunately, the rooms that everyone really wants to see, like the Byzantine Hall with its art deco "pharaonic" frescoes, remain behind closed doors. Those halls that can be visited are plainly decorated and house an endless array of daggers, swords, pistols, and other firearms, plus medals and decorations, royal silverware, and ceramics. There is a certain raised-eyebrow factor in items like a set of gold-plated machine guns presented by a Gulf Arab dignitary to President Hosni Mubarak. Another oddity is the small domed mausoleum of a 19th-century Muslim saint, which lies off one of the fountain courtyards. The mausoleum predates the palace and, rather than see it demolished, the architect incorporated it into the overall design.

In contrast to the austerity presented by the rooms at Abdeen is central Cairo's other remaining former royal residence, the wildly eccentric **Manyal Palace.** This is located on the island of Rhoda, about a mile (1.5 km) south of Tahrir Square. Inside a walled compound are five separate buildings, executed in pastiches of Islamic styles and set amid luxuriant banyans, palms, and rubber trees—all that remains of an extensive royal botanical garden that once covered the whole island. The palace was commissioned by Prince Muhammad Ali Tewfik (1875–1955), a monarch-in-waiting who never made it to the throne. This did not prevent him from building his own private Throne Hall, complete with red carpet, gilt furniture, and the ranked portraits of his illustrious forebears.

Another of the buildings is the prince's actual residence, or *haramlek.* Its overblown interiors include a Turkish room covered in Iznik tiles and a Syrian room with an exquisitely painted wood ceiling. Oriental paintings, ceramics, and carpets further decorate the salons. French composer Camille Saint-Saëns (1835–1921) was a sometime house guest here and entertained the prince's circle with private recitals. He is said to have composed his Piano Concerto No. 5, "The Egyptian," while in residence. Also within the grounds are a mosque with a Turkish-tiled interior and an adjacent, crudely fashioned Moorish tower.

Near by is the **Hunting Museum.** In addition to a menagerie of shot and stuffed animals—including a hermaphroditic goat—this long hall contains an astounding testament to excess in the form of the mounted heads of more than 300 gazelle, all bagged by Farouk and his cronies.

The most convenient way to get to Manyal is to take a taxi, but a more pleasant alternative is to walk from Tahrir Square down the **Corniche,** Cairo's extensive Nile-side boulevard. This is one of the city's main north-south traffic arteries, but with the cars and trucks partially screened from the sidewalk by trees, and cool breezes coming off the river, it is a popular place for strolling.

Located on the Corniche are the **Semiramis** (see p. 361) and **Shepheard's,** modern incarnations of hotels that, in their time, were as famous as the London Ritz and Singapore's Raffles Hotel, and attracted a similar class of international high society. The original Shepheard's, a vast Victorian edifice with Moorish halls, stood just north of Opera Square and it was here, according to the hotel's historian Nina Nelson, that "practically every world-renowned person has sat at one time or another on the famous terrace." Theodore Roosevelt was there in 1910, and T.E. Lawrence (of Arabia) stayed; Noel Coward, staying there in 1942, gave impromptu performances on the hotel piano. Sadly, the original hotel was burned down in the Black Saturday riots of 1952. Its concrete replacement has nothing to recommend it and the only continuity is a dedication plaque in the entrance hall, rescued from the ashes.

From a landing opposite the hotels it is possible to rent a *felucca,* the graceful lateen-sailed boats that have been plying the Nile since antiquity. For a charge of around five dollars an hour a captain will take a party out, tacking back and forth across the river. Watching the sun set over the city skyline while languidly drifting on the Nile makes for a stress-relieving end to a busy day's sight-seeing. ■

Manyal Palace
- 68 C2
- Al-Saray St., Manyal
- 02/368 7495
- $. Camera $, video camera $$$

Downtown Cairo walk

Determined to modernize Egypt along European lines, Khedive Ismail (R.1863–1879) planned a new Paris-on-the-Nile on the swampy floodplain between the old medieval city and the river. His dream was realized in the creation of a quarter with wide, tree-lined boulevards, grand squares, and public gardens, capped by an Italianate opera house. This walk revisits the past of Ismail's belle epoque Cairo.

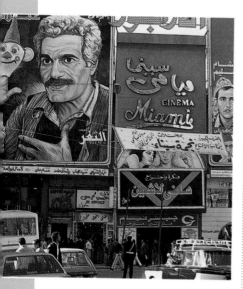

Egyptian screen idol Omar Sharif looms over Talaat Harb, advertising his latest movie.

Start at Tahrir Square and head north up Talaat Harb, the main street of *al-balad*, or downtown. If you have not yet eaten breakfast, you could drop in at the **Café Riche** ❶ *(17 Talaat Harb St., tel 02/392 9793)*, a haunt of artists and intellectuals since it opened in 1908. Allegedly Gamal Abdel Nasser and his coplotters used to meet and talk revolution here. A little farther on, a portly statue presides over one of Ismail's Parisian-style *places;* the figure is Talaat Harb, a financier who gave money to the nationalist cause and his name to this square. Fittingly, the statue has its back to **Groppi** *(Talaat Harb Sq., tel 02/574 3244),* a Continental-style tearoom established in 1925 that was once a byword for glamour and excess. All that was extinguished by the nationalization that came as a

consequence of Nasser's long afternoons in the Riche, but the beautiful floral mosaics around the entrance still have their sparkle.

Follow Talaat Harb's gaze and head down Qasr al-Nil Street, lined with boutiques and shoe shops with more bright, shiny color than a package of M&Ms. Take the second small street on the right to face the **Cosmopolitan Hotel** (see p. 362), opened in 1902 as the Metropolitan, and a gorgeous example of some of the fine architecture hidden in the downtown backstreets. Next door to the hotel is the **Bourse** ❷, or stock exchange. At the time it was built, in the early 20th century, Egypt's economy was booming and its stock exchange was rated among the world's top ten. Since the government initiated a program of privatization in the mid-1990s, share trading has become big business once again, meriting a face-lift for the Bourse, and for the surrounding streets.

From the Bourse rejoin Qasr al-Nil Street beside the **Trieste Insurance Building** ❸ *(11 Sharifeen St.),* designed by one of the many European architects Ismail commissioned to help him create his new capital, a prolific Italian named Antoine Lasciac. Across from Lasciac's elegant building, modern Cairo reasserts itself on pedestrian-only Shawarby Street, full of shops selling jeans and jackets and loud with pop soundtracks emanating from half a dozen music cassette stores. Halfway along on the left, a little alley leads back to Talaat Harb, emerging beside a popular bakery called **Al-Abd** *(19 Talaat Harb St.).* Perpetually packed right up until closing at midnight, it serves Cairo's best baklava and other syrupy, nut pastries, costing just a couple of dollars for a half pound to take out.

This upper end of Talaat Harb marks the beginning of Cairo's entertainment district, with theaters and low-rent belly-dancing

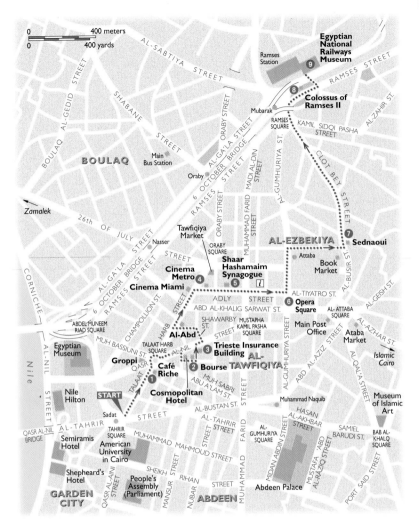

Map of Downtown Cairo Walk

NOT TO BE MISSED

- Pastries at Al-Abd
- Painted hoardings at the Miami and Metro cinemas
- Facade of the Shaar Hashamaim Synagogue

joints. Most of these advertise with huge, garish, often hand-painted billboards, as seen at the **Cinema Miami,** which screens Egyptian movies. Across the road, the jaggedly art deco **Cinema Metro** ❹ first opened house in 1939 with *Gone With the Wind* and still shows mostly Hollywood fare.

Adly Street runs east off Talaat Harb beside the Metro building, and along here is what looks like a movie-set construction for a Babylonian epic but is in fact one of the few remaining monuments to Cairo's once sub- stantial and influential Jewish community, the **Shaar Hashamaim Synagogue** ❺.

Founded by a Swiss confectioner, Groppi once supplied chocolates to the British royalty.

Downtown Cairo is at its busiest once the sun goes down and the heat of the day is over.

Jews were founders of the national bank and were heavily involved in the development of the city during the early decades of the 20th century, but most left following the creation of the state of Israel in 1948. Numbers are now so low that although the synagogue still opens for Shabbat there are not enough people for a minyan (the minimum ten required for a service). Beyond the synagogue is the visitor information office (*5 Adly St., tel 02/391 3454*), where the staff are friendly but poorly resourced.

Continuing on, Adly links with **Opera Square** ❻. It's hard to imagine now, but this large, open plaza was originally the centerpiece of Ismail's Cairo. As the name suggests, it was once graced by an opera house, hastily built just in time for the celebrations accompanying

the opening of the Suez Canal in 1869. It was to have been inaugurated with a performance of *Aida,* a new opera with an Egyptian theme specially commissioned for the occasion from Italian composer Giuseppe Verdi. In any case, *Aida* was not ready in time, so the first-night guests were entertained with Verdi's *Rigoletto* instead. Fire destroyed the Opera House in 1972 and it was replaced with a building far more suited to modern Cairo life: a multistory parking garage. The equestrian statue is of Ibrahim, father of Ismail, who ruled Egypt for just 40 days before his death in 1848.

Greenery is a rarity in central Cairo, an almost extinct phenomenon. The flat green patch on the north side of Opera Square is all that remains of what until not too long ago was a wooded park, the Ezbekiyya, with paths

around a lake and pavilion cafés where bands played. It has the appearance of a site waiting for a building to happen. One paved corner is taken up by the cabins of a secondhand book market, beyond which is Khazinder Square, site of the **Sednaoui department store ❼**. Modeled on Galeries Lafayette in Paris and opened in 1913, it merits a look inside for the grandiose central atrium.

From Sednaoui head north along **Clot Bey Street,** named for a French physician to the 19th-century Egyptian court. You are now leaving European Cairo behind and entering an old residential quarter, little changed in character since the time of the good doctor. Streets become narrower and the architecture more ramshackle. During World War II, Clot Bey was more commonly known as the "Birka," and was a seamy red-light district. It would be wrong to suggest that Clot Bey has since become gentrified. Instead, it is prostitution that has gone upscale. At its northern

end, Clot Bey joins numerous other streets in spilling into Ramses Square, the most chaotic spot in Cairo. All routes from the north of the city converge here, spewing cars, buses, and taxis into one great screeching, horn-honking melee. At the center of it all stands a **colossus of Ramses II ❽**, the great warrior pharaoh. It was unearthed at Memphis and erected on this site in 1955. Conservation fears led to the recent removal of the original statue (now in storage) and its replacement with the replica you see today. Beyond the statue, reached by a pedestrian bridge, is Ramses Station. Part of the station building houses the **Egyptian National Railways Museum ❾** (Tel 02/575 3555, closed Mon.), which has a tiny royal locomotive with plush seating for four only, presented to Egypt by Empress Eugénie of France at the opening of the Suez Canal.

From Ramses Square it is a brief three-stop ride on the subway back to Tahrir Square (metro: Sadat), where this walk began. ■

Islamic Cairo

UNESCO, THE CULTURAL WING OF THE UNITED NATIONS, includes Islamic Cairo on its select World Heritage list, which puts it on a par with the Pyramids, the Great Wall of China, and Venice. It is a historic area that contains the greatest concentration of medieval Islamic monuments to be found anywhere. The skyline is a spiky signature of minarets and domes, reflecting a time when Cairo was the wealthiest capital in the world.

Islamic Cairo is the term for the part of the city that dates back to before the development of the new European quarters—modern-day central Cairo. Because the word "Islamic" is unfortunately at times associated with terrorism, the Egyptian authorities are now promoting the less emotive term "Fatimid" Cairo. This is valid, given that the core of the area is the fortified city founded by the Fatimids in A.D. 969 (see pp. 98–100). The walls that once ran around the city are long gone, but hundreds of monuments still line the traditional historic thoroughfares. These range from modest streetside marble fountains to splendid stadium-size mosques, the equal of Europe's great cathedrals in scale and beauty. In age, they cover the spread of Islamic history from the 10th century to the 19th.

Unlike historic districts elsewhere in the world that have been preserved, sterilized, and pickled, Islamic Cairo makes few concessions to the visitor. It has not been able to afford to. Lying at the heart of the metropolitan area, it is home to a dense 21st-century population still living in what are essentially medieval quarters. Plumbing and sewer systems gave up long ago, and those who could afford it moved out. This is now one of the poorer areas of the city. When you encounter a printing shop cranking out flyers on hand-operated presses, this is not part of a heritage industry—the antique machinery survives because there is no money to replace it. The decay and neglect may be sad, but as a consequence, Islamic Cairo retains a vital human presence, making it something more than a mere open-air museum.

PLANNING YOUR VISIT

Islamic Cairo covers an area of several square miles, and exploring it could occupy days, if not weeks. Fortunately, there are several key clusters of buildings, all conveniently located along one linear route. This stretches perhaps a mile and a half (2.5 km) in length and can be walked end to end in an hour, but there is so much to see that it is better to pace yourself and, if time allows, make several visits.

Begin at Khan al-Khalili, the extensive bazaar at the heart of the area. With its miles of lanes, alleys, and cul-de-sacs, cruising the Khan requires a day in itself, though you could combine it with a visit to the neighboring Al-Azhar Mosque. Your next trip could take in the Northern Walls and include visits to Al-Hakim's Mosque, Bayt al-Suhaymi, and the three great Mamluk complexes on Bayn al-Qasreen. A third expedition might begin at the Al-Ghouriyya and involve a walk down to Bab Zuwayla and the Tentmakers' Market. Non-Muslims are welcome to visit any Islamic monument

Opposite: Merchants and shopkeepers have been trading in the narrow alleys of Khan al-Khalili since the 14th century.

Islamic Cairo's profusion of domes and minarets creates an impression of piety.

other than the Al-Hussein Mosque beside Khan al-Khalili. The only stipulation is that footwear must be removed. In some cases tie-on cloth covers are provided to slip over your shoes. To avoid giving offense, dress modestly. A headscarf is not necessary, but women must not be dressed in shorts, short skirts, or sleeveless tops or dresses. Men should wear long pants.

KHAN AL-KHALILI

To reach Islamic Cairo from down-town, you can walk the half mile (1 km) from Ataba Square along crowded Muski Street, or just take a taxi and be whisked along the Al-Azhar overpasss. Either way you end up around Al-Hussein Square, on the fringes of one of the world's oldest shopping districts, the bazaar of Khan al-Khalili. This is Cairo at its most frenetic and seductive: the Cairo of Ali Baba and Aladdin, loud with the sound of bargaining. Salesmen hiss and beckon. Boys glide about with trays of tea. Everything sparkles and glitters— at least until you get it home, where the luster quickly wears off.

Merchants have been trading on this site since at least the 14th century. In 1384 an emir named Al-Khalili built a great *khan* here, a three-story hostelry intended to accommodate traveling merchants and their wares. Buyers visited the khan for the goods brought in on the merchant caravans, and the selling and bartering spread to the streets around. Al-Khalili's khan was demolished in the 16th century, but by then the area had become

firmly established as the city's commercial center. The earliest surviving parts of the bazaar today are several great stone gateways that date back to the 1500s.

To an extent, the type of goods on offer have changed surprisingly little over the centuries. The slave market closed in 1870, and no longer do you find silk, jewels, or diamonds, but cloth remains important. The aroma of spices is very much present on Al-Muizz li-Din Allah Street, where stalls are heaped with variously colored powders and sacks of seeds and pods. Farther east on the same street, coppersmiths hammer out platters and tureens, and create coffeepots and enormous crescent-shaped tops for minarets. However, it is unlikely that medieval citizens of Cairo would recognize the stuffed leather camels, alabaster pyramid paperweights, and their ilk that pile the stalls in the central section of the bazaar.

Whatever you are buying, expect to bargain. It is a ritual of the bazaar, equally applicable to local Egyptian customers and foreign visitors. There are no hard-and-fast rules except one, which is that if you do not bargain, then you will certainly end up paying seriously over the odds. One tip: If you see something you like, check the price of similar items at other stalls. Armed with an idea of relative values, you can go back and bargain more effectively. Keep your maximum price fixed in mind, and if the shop owner will not meet it, you can always walk away.

A tourist inspects the goods in the Carpet Bazaar, which is part of Khan al-Khalili.

For a respite from the sales patter, retreat to **Fishawi's,** Cairo's oldest and most celebrated coffeehouse. Its rickety wooden chairs and tall, copper-topped tables line a narrow alley one block north of Al-Hussein Square. Huge, heavy-framed antique mirrors adorn the walls. It is open 24 hours and really comes to life late in the evening when most visitors have left and the place returns to the locals. (For more on coffeehouses see pp. 110–11). One famous regular here was Egypt's Nobel Prize-winning author Naguib Mahfouz (see p. 56). He grew up in the neighborhood and later held weekly literary gatherings in a back room heavy with the sweet smoke from the *sheeshas*, or water pipes, that many Egyptians smoke.

Around the corner is an upscale tourist café named after Mahfouz; its air-conditioned interior is a world away from all that he wrote about, but it is a good place for a lunchtime snack when sightseeing, and for freshening up. The Khan al-Khalili Restaurant in the same

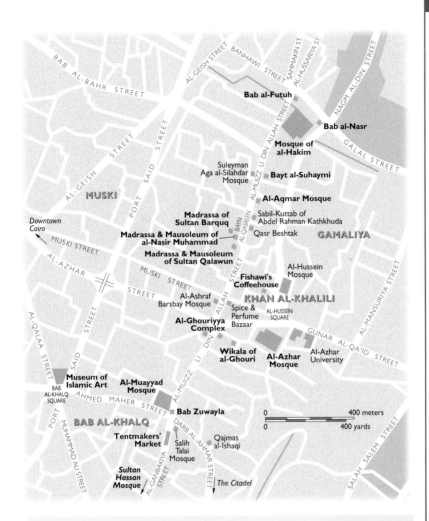

Bab al-Futuh
Bab al-Nasr
Mosque of al-Hakim
Suleyman Aga al-Silahdar Mosque
Bayt al-Suhaymi
Al-Aqmar Mosque
Sabil-Kuttab of Abdel Rahman Kathkhuda
Madrassa of Sultan Barquq
Qasr Beshtak
GAMALIYA
Madrassa & Mausoleum of al-Nasir Muhammad
Madrassa & Mausoleum of Sultan Qalawun
Al-Hussein Mosque
Fishawi's Coffeehouse
Al-Ashraf Barsbay Mosque
KHAN AL-KHALILI
Al-Ghouriyya Complex
Spice & Perfume Bazaar
AL-HUSSEIN SQUARE
Wikala of al-Ghouri
Al-Azhar Mosque
Al-Azhar University
Museum of Islamic Art
Al-Muayyad Mosque
BAB AL-KHALQ SQUARE
BAB AL-KHALQ
Bab Zuwayla
Tentmakers' Market
Salih Talai Mosque
Qajmas al-Ishaqi
Sultan Hassan Mosque
The Citadel

MUSKI
Downtown Cairo
MUSKI STREET
AL-AZHAR

BAB AL-BAHR STREET
AL-GEISH STREET
PORT SAID STREET
AL-GEISH STREET
BANHAWI STREET
AL-GEISH STREET
SANMAKIN ST.
AL-HUSSARIYA ST.
NAGM AL-DIN STREET
GALAL STREET
AL-MUIZZ LI DIN ALLAH STREET
BAYN AL-QASREN
MUSKI STREET
STREET
ALLAH STREET
AL-MANSURIYA STREET
GUNAR
AL-QA'ID STREET
AL-QALAA STREET
PORT SAID STREET
MUHAMMAD ALI STREET
AHMED MAHER STREET
AL-MUIZZ LI DIN
DARB AL-AHMAR STREET
AL-GANBAKIYA STREET
SALAH SALEM STREET

0   400 meters
0   400 yards

What to buy

Spices are extremely cheap, as are perfume essences. You can get local blends as well as imitations of Western name brands, sold in small, delicately decorated bottles. Despite the profusion of sellers, gold and silver work is not impressive unless you can find old pieces. In general, beware of claims of antiquity—most things come straight from the factory. Buy an item because you like it, not because it is "old." Wood jewelry boxes and small chests inlaid with mother-of-pearl are both attractive and cheap. For something more original, simple backgammon boxes resembling those used in coffeehouses are sold for a few dollars on Al-Muizz li-Din Allah Street, and there is a riotously glitzy belly-dancing costumer at the eastern end of Muski Street. Remember to bargain hard. ∎

Local women pick through beads at a jewelry stall in Khan al-Khalili.

building is an atmospheric choice for dinner (see p. 364).

To see what Al-Khalili's khan might have looked like in its original state, cross Al-Azhar Street via the pedestrian underpass at Al-Hussein Square and pay a visit to the **Wikala of al-Ghouri.** A *wikala* is essentially a larger version of a khan. At one time Cairo possessed more than 350 such structures, but of the handful left today this is in the best condition by far. Enter through a high, decorated gateway into the central courtyard where the caravans would have unloaded. Goods were stored and animals stabled on the ground floor, while the merchants took rooms above. Those rooms now serve as ateliers and workshops for local artists, some of them open to the public. Local handicrafts also are sold here.

As you leave the wikala, turn right and follow the road past a small open-air fruit and vegetable market, and then to the left. You are now walking in the shadow of the towering walls of one of Islamic Cairo's most important buildings.

Wikala of al-Ghouri

🗺 Map p. 95

✉ Tablita St., off Al-Azhar St.

☎ 02/511 0472

💲 $

AL-AZHAR MOSQUE

Cairo has several hundred old mosques; if you visit only one, it probably should be the Al-Azhar Mosque. Founded in A.D. 970 as a place of worship and learning, the mosque remains one of the most important centers of Islamic theology more than a thousand years later, annually receiving a new intake of Muslim students from all over the world. Throughout Cairo's history, the holy men in their precincts have been a channel of communication between the country's rulers and the ruled; sometimes a force for moderation, other times a focus for discontent. When Napoleon invaded Egypt in 1798 one of his first actions was to try to win over Cairo's clerics. He failed, and resorted to ordering a

cavalry charge into the mosque as the only way to subdue the rebellious city. The sheikh of Al-Azhar remains the highest religious authority in the land, and pronouncements from his office carry more weight than governmental decrees. Al-Azhar is also a showpiece of Islamic-era Cairene architecture, as over the centuries a roll call of sultans and emirs added their imprint to the building.

You enter through the double-arched **Gate of the Barbers,** where freshmen students had their heads shaved. To the left and right, courts lead to two *madrassas,* or teaching schools; the one on the left, complete with its own dome and minaret, was added in 1340 and is worth entering for the glass-mosaic decoration in the prayer

niche. Straight ahead is the central court, surrounded by an arcade of keel arches—so-called because the shape of the arches resembles a ship's keel turned upside down. This is the oldest part of the building and dates back to Fatimid times. Across the court is the carpeted prayer hall, which used to extend only to where the prayer niche stands but was enlarged by a further four arcades in the mid-18th century. The courtyard also provides a good view of the three main minarets, which, from right to left, date from 1340, 1469, and 1510. The 1510 minaret with its twin finials, was added by the last of the Mamluk sultans, Al-Ghouri, who was also responsible for the nearby wikala (see p. 96) and the Al-Ghouriyya complex (see p. 104).

Remodeled over the centuries, the prayer hall of Al-Azhar Mosque has been the spiritual heart of Egypt for over a thousand years.

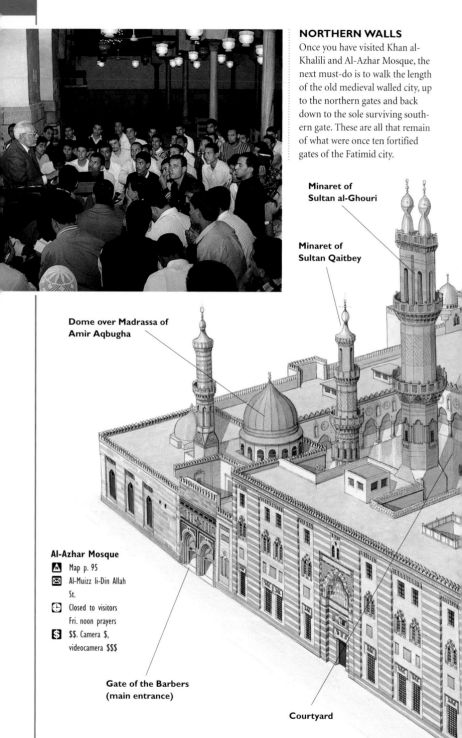

NORTHERN WALLS

Once you have visited Khan al-Khalili and Al-Azhar Mosque, the next must-do is to walk the length of the old medieval walled city, up to the northern gates and back down to the sole surviving southern gate. These are all that remain of what were once ten fortified gates of the Fatimid city.

Minaret of Sultan al-Ghouri

Minaret of Sultan Qaitbey

Dome over Madrassa of Amir Aqbugha

Al-Azhar Mosque
🅐 Map p. 95
✉ Al-Muizz li-Din Allah St.
🕐 Closed to visitors Fri. noon prayers
💲 $$. Camera $, videocamera $$$

Gate of the Barbers (main entrance)

Courtyard

Left: A lecturer addresses students at Al-Azhar.

Below: The venerable mosque of Al-Azhar

Square-towered **Bab al-Nasr** and semicircular **Bab al-Futuh** are the two northern gates. First constructed in 969, then rebuilt in 1087, they are massively solid pieces of masonry. Their impact today is less than it formerly was, as the ground level has risen considerably over the centuries—originally ramps ran up from the street to the gates. You can visit the interiors and walk from one gate to the other along a corridor within the walls. As you do, look for fragments of hieroglyphic inscriptions and even a relief carving of a large hippopotamus, evidence that Cairo's early fortifications were built with stones quarried from the ruins of the ancient capital of Memphis.

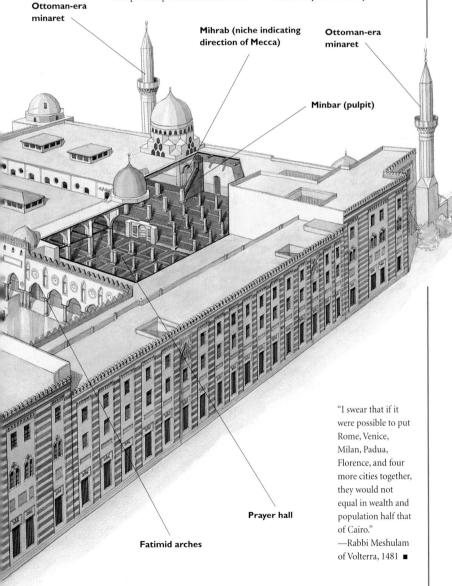

Ottoman-era minaret

Mihrab (niche indicating direction of Mecca)

Ottoman-era minaret

Minbar (pulpit)

Prayer hall

Fatimid arches

"I swear that if it were possible to put Rome, Venice, Milan, Padua, Florence, and four more cities together, they would not equal in wealth and population half that of Cairo."
—Rabbi Meshulam of Volterra, 1481 ■

The northern gate of Bab al-Futuh was the main entrance to medieval Cairo.

Mosque of al-Hakim & Northern Walls & Gates

🅰 Map p. 95

✉ Al-Muizz li-Din Allah St.

🕐 Closed to visitors Fri. noon prayers

💲 $$

collection of the Museum of Islamic Art, and a school. For much of its recent history it stood in ruins, but it was almost completely rebuilt in the 1980s. Only the strange minarets, looking like pepperpots on boxes, are original.

In front of the mosque, a widening of the street serves as a pungent open-air market for onions, garlic, and lemons, brought in from the surrounding country-side. The street in question is the former main thoroughfare of medieval Cairo, **Al-Muizz li-Din Allah Street,** named for the Fatimid caliph in whose name the city was founded. It runs all the way down to the southern gate of Bab Zuwayla and beyond to the Citadel, former seat of the city's rulers. Too narrow for present purposes, it is almost permanently congested with a low-tech jam of handcarts and donkeys almost invisible under their mountainous loads.

After 200 yards or so of slow progress down Al-Muizz li-Din Allah, you come to a small alley off to the left, conspicuous for its blindingly whitewashed appearance, the result of a makeover by the Egyptian antiquities department. This is stage one of an ambitious project for the eventual restoration of the main spine of Islamic Cairo. The pilot work here has focused on the showpiece **Bayt al-Suhaymi,** Cairo's finest example of the traditional family mansion built throughout the city from Mamluk times to the 19th century. The *bayt* (meaning "house") presents a typically blank facade to the street, but once through the tunnel-like entryway the visitor emerges into a beautiful inner courtyard, overlooked by all the rooms. Guests were received in an impressive *qa'a,* or reception room, off the court-yard, graced with a polychrome marble fountain inset in the floor

Further evocative detail comes in the form of French names carved above the tower doorways—echoes of Napoleon Bonaparte's brief occupation of Egypt (1798–1801), when some of his troops were garrisoned in these towers.

The gates are entered via the roof terrace of the neighboring **Mosque of al-Hakim,** another survivor of Fatimid times. Al-Hakim (*R.*996–1021) was the third caliph, or ruler, of the Fatimids and was noted for his eccentricities. A lover of night, he banned business activity during the day; and a hater of women, he forbade the manufacture of women's shoes in order to keep them off the streets. Over the centuries his mosque has served as stables, a prison, a storehouse for the objects that later made up the and a high, painted wood ceiling. Upstairs are the family quarters, with the wood-lattice windows known as *mashrabiyya* that allowed the women to observe the goings on below without being seen themselves. The rooms are kept cool by devices called *malqaf,* angled wind-catchers on the roof that direct the prevailing northerly breezes down into the building. It is an amazingly effective system and, as far as both aesthetics and running costs go, it certainly beats mechanical air-conditioning.

Returning to Al-Muizz li-Din Allah, on the next left-hand corner is the neat little **Al-Aqmar Mosque.** Its name means "moonlit" and it is supposedly inspired by the luminous quality of the stone. Perhaps in the 12th century, when the mosque was built, it did shine, but centuries of dust and grime have left it down at the heels and dulled. It is nevertheless notable for the exquisite carving on the facade.

BETWEEN THE PALACES

At the center of the Fatimid city, two great palaces faced each other across a large public square. The palaces were long ago replaced by the monuments of later dynasties, but they are remembered in the name **Bayn al-Qasreen,** or Between the Palaces, still used for the stretch of Al-Muizz li-Din Allah south of the little Al-Aqmar Mosque. Of the royal residences themselves, only some finely carved wood friezes survive; these are displayed in the Museum of Islamic Art (see pp. 106–107).

Although credited with the founding of Islamic Cairo, it is not the Fatimids whose stamp is most dominant on the old city today. That distinction falls to the Mamluks (see pp. 37–39). Of the scores of domes and minarets that grace the skyline, the most magnifi-

cent and ornate were erected over the prayer halls and mausoleums of the soldier-slave dynasty that ruled from 1250 to 1517. The wealth of their conquests in Palestine, Syria, and Arabia went into these buildings. Since life was often short, and power was not hereditary, the Mamluk rulers were inclined to spend while they could. There was perhaps also an element of public relations involved: If the Mamluk warlords appealed enough to the glory of God, the people of Cairo might eventually forget their savage rule and sinful deeds.

Bayn al-Qasreen represents Mamluk Egypt at the zenith of its vigor and prosperity. Here three massive complexes stand shoulder to shoulder in a sequence of spectacular facades spanning 150

Al-Hakim's unusual pepperpot minarets are some of the earliest structures in Islamic Cairo.

years. The northernmost is the **Madrassa of Sultan Barquq,** founded in 1386 as an Islamic teaching center. Most madrassas typically also functioned as mosques, and the terms are somewhat interchangeable, but if you enter the main courtyard you will find a door at each corner leading to four sets of classrooms, one for each of the four schools of Islamic law. Under the dome, reached via the prayer hall, is a highly decorated mausoleum, which contains not the sultan (he is buried elsewhere in Cairo) but his daughter Fatima.

Next door to the Barquq's complex is the **Madrassa and Mausoleum of al-Nasir Muhammad,** erected by one of the most prolific builders in the history of Cairo. During his long reign from 1293 to 1340, Al-Nasir endowed the city with some 30 mosques, of which the best known is up at the Citadel (see p. 113). His madrassa-and-mausoleum complex on Bayn al-Qasreen is squeezed between two giant neighbors, but still manages to make an impact with its almost symmetrical facade. The white marble Gothic doorway came from a Crusader church in Acre (now in Israel), while the minaret, directly above, is covered in lacelike stucco patterning of North African influence. The interior is unfortunately in very poor condition and it is not usually open to visitors.

The last, earliest, and most outstanding in the sequence is the **Madrassa and Mausoleum of Sultan Qalawun.** It is said to have been built in a single year in 1285, and that to achieve this feat the sultan's soldiers forced hapless passersby to join the labor gangs. The city's sheikhs were so outraged that they at first declared prayer there unlawful. However, such is the magnificence of Qalawun's legacy

that his misdeeds are forgotten and he is praised as one of the greatest Mamluks—no doubt his intention.

Entrance to the complex is through an imposing bronze door. Immediately within, off to the left, is the madrassa, and to the right is the mausoleum, modeled on the Dome of the Rock in Jerusalem, which the Mamluks had recently recaptured from the Crusaders. The mausoleum's walls are faced from floor to ceiling with colored stone and decorative marble panels spelling out the name of Muhammad. Under a dome raised high on four massive pink-granite pharaonic columns is the cenotaph containing Qalawun.

As part of his complex, Sultan Qalawun also endowed a *maristan,* or hospital, which according to the Moroccan traveler and historian Ibn Battuta, visiting Cairo in 1325, contained "an innumerable quantity of appliances and medicaments." If such historical accounts are to be believed, the hospital treated up to 4,000 patients a day in its prime. Incredibly, an eye clinic still occupies a part of Qalawun's complex, maintaining an unbroken tradition of more than 700 years of medical care.

SOUTHERN CITY GATE
In the early 20th century, the creation of Al-Azhar Street broke the traditional spine of the old city. Previously all traffic had flowed north-south; now the main stream is east-west as cars thunder off the overpass, weave between the medieval mosques, and race on to link up with the road that encircles the city and runs out by the historic cemeteries. One solitary, shabby footbridge now links the two broken halves of Al-Muizz li-Din Allah Street to allow visitors to continue uninterruptedly along a route that has been in use for over a thousand years.

Complexes of Barquq & Qalawun
- Map p. 95
- Bayn al-Qasreen
- Closed to visitors Fri. noon prayers
- Both $

Opposite: **Mashrabiyya windows at Bayt al-Suhaymi allowed women to view the street scene below without themselves being seen.**

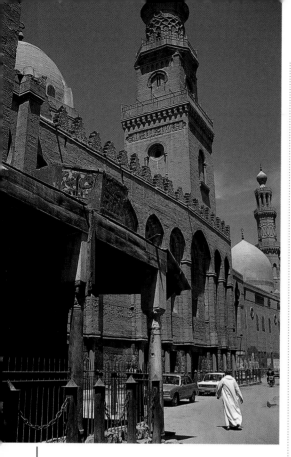

instead lies the body of Tumanbey, who ruled for the time it took the Turks to march down and claim possession of Egypt.

The madrassa's square minaret with the strange five-bulbed top is one of the tallest in the city; the dome that once covered the mausoleum was also once one of the biggest, but it collapsed three times and has been replaced with a flat wood roof. A wood canopy once stretched across the street between the two buildings, and in the covered space below was the silk market. Canopy and silk merchants are now gone, but the surrounding alleys are filled with narrow storefronts packing a colorful abundance of textiles and rugs.

Cloth gives way to clothes as you move south, but before then, on the right-hand side, are the city's two sole remaining makers of the *tarboosh,* the little burgundy-colored flowerpot hat known elsewhere as a fez. Prerevolution, no *effendi*-about-town would be seen without one, but now the only buyers are hotels and tourist restaurants for staff uniforms. Also somewhat out of fashion these days is the *attar,* or herbalist, across the street, who sells the likes of dried lizards for use in concocting home medicines.

The hard sell and clamor continue for perhaps half a mile until they are brought up short by the towering **Bab Zuwayla,** built in 1092 and the third of the Fatimid gates that remain standing. The two minarets were added much later, in the 15th century, and belong to the neighboring **Al-Muayyad Mosque.** If you enter the mosque and tip the guardian, he will unlock the door in the prayer hall that gives access to the gate tower, from where you can reach the minarets and ascend for some of the best views in all Cairo.

Massively imposing, the Madrassa and Mausoleum of Sultan Qalawun is one of three adjoining complexes on Bayn al-Qasreen.

Al-Muayyad Mosque

- Map p. 95
- Al-Muizz li-Din Allah St..
- Closed to visitors Fri. noon prayers
- $$

To the south of the bridge are the matching pink-striped blocks of the **Al-Ghouriyya,** another fine piece of Mamluk civic building. There is a mausoleum on one side and a madrassa on the other, but more than anything the complex stands as an architectural epitaph to the princely era when Cairo was more dazzling than Rome, Florence, and Venice put together. Little more than ten years after the Al-Ghouriyya was finished in 1504, the resplendent, 5,000-strong Mamluk army paraded past, accompanied by drums and trumpets and led by three caparisoned elephants, only to be slaughtered in battle by the Ottoman Turks. The sultan Al-Ghouri had fallen from his horse; his body was never recovered. In his mausoleum

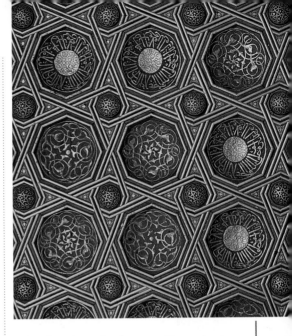

Outside the gate, which was closed each night until as recently as the 19th century, is an untidy and chaotic intersection of three streets. West leads to the **Museum of Islamic Art** (see pp. 106–107), which is no more than a five-minute walk away. To the east, the uneven road rambles by yet more mosques and madrassas before climbing up toward the **Citadel** (see pp. 112–15); a walk of maybe 15 minutes.

Straight ahead from the Zuwayla Gate is the **Street of the Tent-makers,** Cairo's only remaining medieval covered market. It takes its name from the bright, block-printed fabric traditionally sold here and still used today for the large street tents erected for funerals, weddings, shop openings, and feasts. This is also a center for appliqué panels and covers, sewn in nearby workshops and sold in the cell-like spaces that line the passage. Prices are reasonable and some of the calligraphic work is very beautiful, making for an interesting alternative to the usual souvenirs.

From the market, you can either return the way you came or continue south, in which case a walk of 15 minutes will bring you to the great **Sultan Hassan Mosque** (see pp. 108–109). ■

The wood-and-ivory-inlay ceiling at Qalawun's madrassa shows the Mamluk's mastery of geometric decoration.

Whirling Dervishes

Every Wednesday and Saturday evening a group of Whirling Dervishes puts on a 90-minute display of Sufi dancing at the Al-Ghouriyya (adm. free). Sufism is a semi-mystical branch of Islam with a somewhat unorthodox approach to prayer. Urged on by the hypnotic pulse of drums and pipes, the dancers spin in a blur of multicolored skirts. Originally, the dance had the ideal of attaining a trancelike union with God. It may not now be wholly authentic, but it is a great spectacle. ■

A colorful Sufi dancer in action

The Islamic art museum contains some fine pieces from Egypt's medieval past.

Museum of Islamic Art

THE CORE OF THIS COLLECTION COMES FROM THE LOOSE bits and pieces of Cairo's mosques and monuments, gathered together in the late 19th century to prevent them from being carried off by European treasure hunters. Objects were stored in the Mosque of al-Hakim until, in 1902, a permanent museum was created on the ground floor of what was then the National Library.

Museum of Islamic Art

- Map p. 95
- Port Said St.
- 02/390 1520 or 02/390 9930
- Closed to visitors Fri. noon prayers
- $$. Camera $, video camera $$$

The museum is an imposing chocolate-and-buff striped neo-Islamic block, easily spotted, though located off the tourist trail. It is only a 20-minute walk due east of Tahrir Square, but few visitors ever make it—which is a shame, because it really is worth the effort. Historically, the interpretation of a Koranic injunction against the representation of Allah (God) led Muslims to reject figurative forms;

instead they developed exceptional skills in floral geometric, and epigraphic forms, applying fantastic patterning to wood, glass, metal, stone, textiles, ceramics, bone, and paper, all of which are represented here. There are carved wood pulpits, panels, and doors, finely worked mosque lamps, and marble fountains from houses and palaces in the old Islamic city. Many items in the museum originated elsewhere, having found their way to medieval Cairo simply because it was one of the richest cities in the world. So the collection includes Armenian and Anatolian tiling, Persian manuscripts and carpets, and Moorish luster-painted dishes.

Labeling in the museum is typically poor. To understand what some of these objects are, where they fitted, and how they were used, visit *after* a walk through Islamic Cairo, where you will see in situ many of the architectural objects represented in this museum.

Entrance is through a small garden off Port Said Street and then directly into the central hall. The collection is arranged by type with only the loosest attempts at imposing any chronology, so it doesn't matter in which sequence the rooms are visited. One highlight is straight ahead: an exquisite, large *mashrabiyya* screen. Made from thousands of small pieces of individually turned wood, screens like this were a highly practical medieval alternative to glass. They filtered the harsh rays of the sun, while allowing ventilating breezes. And in a society in which women were obliged to remain out of sight, the mashrabiyya made it possible to see without being seen. Until the 19th century, all the houses of Cairo's wealthier citizens had bay windows fashioned in this style, but few good examples remain today.

Pass under a coffered wood ceiling with stalactite carvings dating from the Ottoman Turkish period to see two beautiful marble fountains that would have taken center place in the reception hall of a noble's house. You can see similar in several of the preserved houses of Islamic Cairo such as Bayt al-Suhaymi (see p. 100) and the Gayer-Anderson Museum (see p. 117).

Bearing left takes you into a series of rooms with large pieces from the Mamluk era, including a set of stained-glass windows and another fountain, which the caretaker will sometimes switch on. Fixed to the wall at the far end is a series of friezes that are unusual in that they are figurative. Carved into the wood are musicians, hunting scenes, and even men pouring wine. These are believed to be the work of the Fatimids, the North African dynasty that ruled Egypt from the mid-10th to the 12th century. Later, when the Fatimids were overthrown and their buildings torn down, these friezes were

reused in the decoration of the Madrassa and Mausoleum of Sultan Qalawun (see p. 103), but they were laid facing inward so as not to offend the pious. The Fatimids belonged to the minority Shiite branch of Islam, which had its greatest following in Iran, where a figurative tradition also existed— for instance, in the painting of miniatures, a few examples of which are exhibited in the book room at the far end of the museum.

Continuing counterclockwise, there are more rooms of woodwork and metalwork and then an array of tiling, mostly of Armenian, Iranian, or Turkish origin. The Egyptians rarely decorated their buildings with ceramics, preferring inlaid stone and marble, available from quarries south of Cairo. ■

The museum building belongs to a 19th-century revival of Mamluk architectural styles.

Mamluk artisans excelled in marble inlay decoration, seen to great effect in Sultan Hassan's prayer hall.

Sultan Hassan Mosque

SULTAN HASSAN'S CREATION IS REGARDED AS ONE OF THE major monuments of the Islamic world. Its hulking size and brutal grandeur belie an inner simplicity and lightness, although given the mosque's turbulent history the real wonder is that it still stands at all.

Sultan Hassan Mosque

- 68 D2
- Al-Qalaa Sq.
- Closed to visitors Fri. noon prayers
- $$

Al-Rifai Mosque

- 68 D2
- Al-Qalaa Sq.
- Closed to visitors Fri. noon prayers
- $$

Hassan became sultan in 1347, at the age of 13. He was deposed four years later in favor of an even younger brother, but was restored as sultan in 1354. Work on his mosque began two years later. The site was a prestigious one, overlooking the hippodrome at the foot of the royal Citadel (now predictably a traffic circle). Such a colossal project was expensive, but the population of Cairo had recently been decimated by the Black Death, and the properties of those who died intestate were used to bolster the royal treasury. Even so, the construction of the mosque nearly bankrupted the state. It continued for seven years, which proved to be too long for Hassan, who was assassinated in 1362.

Tragedy clung to the mosque. While under construction, a minaret collapsed, killing 300 onlookers. Once it was finished, the mosque's monumental scale and location opposite the Citadel proved a liability. During the frequent Mamluk skirmishes in

pursuit of power it was used as a fortress, with soldiers on its roof firing catapults at the sultan in his palaces. One canny ruler ripped out the staircase to prevent a repeat occurrence, while another began dismantling the mosque until public outrage forced him to stop.

Battle damage may have been responsible for the toppling of another minaret in 1659 (replaced by the smaller, less ambitious structure that survives today) and for the collapse of the dome just two years later (also rebuilt since, in a more modest form). The battering continued right up until the 19th century, when Napoleon turned his cannon on the mosque while quelling one of the frequent popular uprisings that were taking place against his occupation of the city. The facades still bear the scars.

Possibly the single most impressive element of the mosque is the towering, recessed entrance portal. Architectural historians identify strong similarities with portals in Anatolia in present-day Turkey, while some of the decoration is clearly inspired by Chinese flower motifs, evidence set in stone of the trading links between 14th-century Egypt and the world at large.

Right: A domed central fountain was used for ritual ablutions before prayer.

Inside, a dark, bent passageway leads to the sudden brightness and humbling dimensions of the main courtyard. It has a central fountain for washing before prayers and four large, arched recesses known as *iwans*, where the Koran would have been taught—the mosque also served as a madrassa, or Islamic school. Each of the four doors off the courtyard leads to six stories of student cells. In all, this building provided free lodging for about 500 students, as well as a large staff that included professors, calligraphers, prayer-callers, and Koran readers. The many long, hanging chains in the iwans once held decorated glass lamps, now displayed at the nearby Museum of Islamic Art (see pp. 106–107).

Beyond the prayer hall, with its fine marble *minbar,* or pulpit, is the domed mausoleum meant for Sultan Hassan. He never occupied it, as his murdered body mysteriously

disappeared. Two of his sons are buried here instead.

Next to Sultan Hassan's mosque is a similarly monumental building that looks as though it could be a close relative. In fact, 600 years separate the two: The **Al-Rifai Mosque** was completed as recently as 1912. It was commissioned, in an imitation Mamluk style, by the mother of Khedive Ismail, to serve as a grandiose tomb for herself and her descendants. Royals buried here include Ismail, Farouk (Egypt's last king), and the last Shah of Iran. Chased out by Ayatollah Khomeini, the shah sought asylum in Egypt in 1979. When he died the next year, his casket was paraded through Cairo, with Egypt's President Sadat and former President Richard Nixon leading the cortege. ■

The coffeehouse

"Cairo, city of a thousand minarets." So says the old cliché, but if there is one institution found in more abundance than the mosque, it is the *ahwa*, or coffeehouse. A Turkish traveler to Cairo in the late 16th century wrote, "Also [remarkable] is the multitude of coffeehouses in the city of Cairo, the concentration of coffeehouses at every step." And that is still very much the case today. Not only is there virtually one on every corner, you will pass at least two in between.

Large water heaters at the rear of the coffeehouse ensure a constant supply of hot *shai* (tea) and *ahwa* (coffee).

exclusively male (women are welcome but may feel a little self-conscious). In Egypt, the house is the woman's domain; everything else belongs to the man. While wives visit with each other at home, husband and friends sit around in the coffeehouse.

It can be anything from a rag-covered bench served from a hole in the wall to a terrace with rattan chairs and menus, but typically a coffeehouse is just a collection of cheap tin plate-topped tables and wood chairs in a sawdust-strewn room open to the street. Waiters shuffle around shouting orders back to the boys at the water boilers and gas rings, while the *muwaalim*, the boss, sits at his desk, watching over proceedings and trading welcomes and backslaps with customers.

Coffee reached Cairo some time in the mid-15th century, some three centuries before it took hold in the West, and more than half a millennium before the first Starbucks. Initially the beans were viewed with distrust as an intoxicant, all forms of which were—and, of course, still are—forbidden by the Koran. Coffeehouses were associated with drug use, prostitution, and idleness—none of which prevented them from quickly becoming a keystone of Egyptian society. Today, most Egyptian men will drop into a coffeehouse on an almost daily basis. It is not that anyone is particularly addicted to coffee. There are no debates over the merits of mocha versus espresso. Coffee is coffee—Arabic coffee, that is, black and gritty, served in tiny cups holding no more than a half dozen sips. Occasionally it might be flavored with cardamom, nutmeg, or cloves. However, no one chooses to frequent a particular coffeehouse because of the quality of its brew.

Coffeehouses are not cafés. Rather they combine the functions of a bar, a social club, a street corner. They are a place to meet and talk, trade gossip, catch up on the news, read the paper, even watch TV. They are also almost

In Cairo especially, each coffeehouse fills its own niche. There are those frequented by intellectuals and writers, others by chess players, and a few known to keep particularly good tobacco that are visited by connoisseurs of the *sheesha*, the burbling water pipe. In one part of town, several competing establishments screen videos nonstop. Elsewhere, in an alley off downtown's Tewfiqiyya market, is where theater musicians go after the show, sometimes putting on impromptu performances. In the same neighborhood casting agents looking for movie extras patronize the Al-Shams Coffeehouse; it has become known through the backpacker bibles, and many young travelers manage to extend their stay in the city by picking up occasional film work here. ■

Most men spend a part of every day at a coffeehouse, dropping in for morning tea, finishing the day with a *sheesha*, or both.

The Citadel

FROM ITS RAISED ROCKY PLATFORM ON THE EDGE OF THE city, the Citadel dominates Cairo's eastern skyline. It was begun in 1176 by the famed Muslim general Saladin, who had its muscular walls and towers constructed with stones stripped from the Pyramids at Giza. The fortress served as Egypt's seat of power for the next 700 years, remodeled in the image of each successive dynasty.

Egypt's rulers moved out of their medieval quarters in the 1870s to the newly built Abdeen Palace (see p. 84), but the Citadel retained its military role until the 1970s. Soldiers still have a foothold and some areas are out of bounds, but today most of the complex is open to visitors and it is quite possible to spend half a day visiting the various mosques, museums, and other monuments enclosed within its walls. There are a couple of cafés for pit-stop refreshments.

By far the best reason to visit the Citadel is for the views from its **Western Terraces.** On a clear day it is possible to pick out such vertical landmarks as the Ramses Hilton on the edge of the Nile, the

Cairo Tower on Gezira, and—right on the horizon, marking the westernmost edge of the city—the distinctive zigzag of the Pyramids. It's a panorama that alone almost justifies the admission fee.

The Citadel's next biggest draw is the **Muhammad Ali Mosque,** a relatively late addition to the fortress, but one that by virtue of its prominent site and bulk—it is the most visible monument in Cairo—serves to symbolize the Citadel in the minds of most visitors. Ironically, the mosque is designed wholly along Turkish lines and owes nothing to the architectural traditions of Egypt.

Muhammad Ali was the Albanian mercenary who, after a bloody

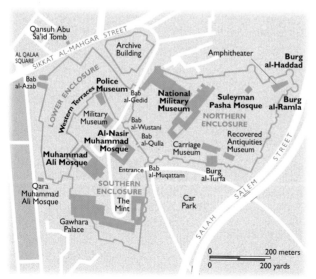

Qansuh Abu Sa'id Tomb

SIKKAT AL-MAHGAR STREET

AL QALAA SQUARE

Archive Building

Amphitheater

Burg al-Haddad

Bab al-Azab

LOWER ENCLOSURE

Police Museum

Bab al-Gedid

National Military Museum

Suleyman Pasha Mosque

Burg al-Ramla

Western Terraces

Military Museum

Bab al-Wustani

NORTHERN ENCLOSURE

Al-Nasir Muhammad Mosque

Bab al-Qulla

Carriage Museum

Recovered Antiquities Museum

Muhammad Ali Mosque

Entrance

Bab al-Muqattam

Burg al-Turfa

Qara Muhammad Ali Mosque

SOUTHERN ENCLOSURE

The Mint

Car Park

SALAH SALEM STREET

Gawhara Palace

| 0 | 200 meters |
| 0 | 200 yards |

The Citadel

🅜 68 D2

✉ Salah Salem St.

☎ 02/512 1735

💲 $$$. Camera $, video camera $$$

contest with rival claimants, seized power in 1806 and went on to rule for 43 years, founding a dynasty that would last until it was removed by revolution in 1952. His mosque was begun in 1839 and took 18 years to complete. Modeled on the great mosques of Istanbul, it sadly lacks their elegance and grace, and the best thing about the interior is that it is at least cool. Muhammad Ali lies in the marble tomb to the right as you enter. Out in the court-yard, the iron clock was a gift from King Louis-Philippe of France in exchange for the obelisk that stands on the Place de la Concorde in Paris. The clock was damaged dur-ing transit and has never worked.

To make room for his own monuments and palaces, Muhammad Ali tore down a great many earlier buildings in the Citadel, but one structure that escaped the demolition was the **Al-Nasir Muhammad Mosque,** completed in 1335. Considering it was only spared for use as stables, it is still in a good state of repair. The courtyard is attractive, with an arcade supported on a variety of pharaonic and Roman-era columns, and the minarets are unusual in that they are decorated with blue and green mosaics in a style more usually associated with Persia.

When you leave the mosque, across the plaza you'll see a pastiche Gothic gate that leads to another terrace with fine views and to the **Police Museum.** There is little of interest inside, but at the base of the staircase is a frieze of carved stone

Napoleon bombarded the city into submission from the Citadel's terraces, which today provide fine views.

lions, evidence of the 13th-century Lions Tower on top of which the museum is built. If you step across to the terrace wall from here, you look directly down upon the lower enclosure of the Citadel and a narrow defile of a roadway, which on March 1, 1811, was the site of one of the bloodiest episodes in the history of Cairo.

The greatest challenge to Muhammad Ali's rule came from the Mamluks, former overlords of Egypt and still figures of power and influence. On the occasion of a celebration for his son, Muhammad Ali invited 500 of the leading Mamluk lords to the Citadel. They arrived with great pomp, feasted, and enjoyed the pasha's hospitality. As they departed, bellies full, in a mounted procession down toward the lower gate, the doors were slammed shut and Muhammad Ali's soldiers opened fire from the surrounding rooftops. Penned in and panicked, with no room for maneuver and no way to retreat, all 500 were slaughtered. Their heads were exhibited on stakes outside the city gates. According to an often recounted tale, a Mamluk by the name of Amin Bey survived by jumping his horse over the Citadel walls (a famous painting of the equestrian leap hangs in Manyal Palace). In fact, Amin Bey did survive the infamous massacre, but only because he failed to turn up for the feast that day.

The alabaster-lined arcades of Muhammad Ali Mosque provide some shelter from the sun.

The buildings adjacent to the Police Museum are part of the former **Military Prison,** established in the late 19th century by the British, whose forces were garrisoned here until as recently as the 1940s. The twin rows of small cells were in use until 1983. An imposing gate opposite the north side of the Al-Nasir Muhammad Mosque leads through into a large open area with well-tended lawns.

Directly ahead is the former Harem Palace, built in 1827 as the residence of Muhammad Ali and his family, and since 1949 home to the **National Military Museum.** Uniforms and ceremonial weaponry account for the bulk of the exhibits, but some of the rooms themselves are notable for their decorative excesses.

Two more small museums in this part of the Citadel are devoted to ceremonial carriages and to recovered stolen antiquities. More worthwhile than either is the beautiful little **Suleyman Pasha Mosque,** which, constructed in 1528, was the first mosque to be built in Cairo following the imposition of rule from Istanbul in 1517. Like Muhammad Ali's great mosque, this one is built along

wholly Turkish lines, but with its graceful tumble of domes and half-domes it is far more successful. It's a very introverted structure half-hidden behind a wall, with fine delicate decoration in the prayer hall and a particularly attractive, leafy central courtyard. The elderly guardian of the mosque often encourages visitors to sit and take tea, which makes for a very relaxing break from sight-seeing.

The solid walls that wrap around this part of the Citadel are the oldest elements in the whole complex. They were constructed under the command of Saladin himself around 1183 and strengthened 25 years later by his nephew Al-Kamil, using captured European Crusaders as labor. Walk across the concrete amphitheater to enter the twin half-round towers, known as the **Burg al-Haddad** (Blacksmith's Tower) and **Burg al-Ramla** (Sand Tower), which controlled the pass between the Citadel and the rocky hills behind. Al-Kamil felt they were too small in their original form, so he had them totally encased in new towers; Saladin's original window slits were broken open to serve as doorways into the new rooms.

Look for the "No. 7" above one doorway, which was painted by Napoleon's troops in 1798; they numbered all the towers to avoid using the unfamiliar Arabic names. It is possible to ascend the stairs to the upper levels but at the present time you cannot walk around the ramparts and have to return the way you came. ∎

The soaring central prayer hall was created for 19th-century ruler Muhammad Ali.

Underused today, the whole royal quarter of 9th-century Cairo would assemble at the mosque for Friday prayers.

Ibn Tulun Mosque

IBN TULUN'S IS THE OLDEST MOSQUE IN EGYPT. THIS FACT will excite an architectural historian, but for the casual visitor the main interest lies in its curious "open-air minaret"—which is an easy and rewarding climb—and in the adjacent Gayer-Anderson house, preserved as Cairo's most fascinating and quirkily individual museum. The mosque is a little awkward to get to from the city center and a taxi is the only option, but it is a mere half mile from the Citadel and the two can be combined in one half-day trip.

Ibn Tulun Mosque

🗺 68 D2

✉ Saliba St.

🕐 Closed to visitors Fri. noon prayers

💲 $$

Ahmed ibn Tulun (Ahmed son of Tulun) was sent to rule Cairo in the ninth century by the caliph of Baghdad. Ibn Tulun took advantage of his distance from court to turn his fief into an independent state and founded a mini-dynasty that ruled Egypt for three generations. With the tribute withheld from the caliph, the family built palaces and pleasure gardens and, according to legend, a pool filled with quicksilver where the ruler floated on an air bed. The Tulunid legacy largely perished after reconquest of Egypt by Baghdad, but, as a building dedicated to God, this mosque survived.

A commemorative plaque tells that it was opened for prayers in May 879. Its design is like nothing else found in Egypt and reflects Ibn Tulun's Iraqi origins. Architectural historians point out the similarities to the Great Mosque at Samarra, built around 30 years previously, especially the spiral minaret. The use of an outer enclosure is another Iraqi feature and is unique in Egypt. This is where today you buy your entry ticket, at a small wooden hut—although with so few visitors, the attendant has often wandered away and may have to be tracked down. The enclosure was meant to act as a buffer, keeping the

surroundings at a respectful distance from the place of worship, but what worked in Iraq was not necessarily going to work in crowded, commercial medieval Cairo; for much of its history Ibn Tulun's outer enclosure was filled with a bazaar. The shops and stalls were cleared in the 19th century.

A flight of steps leads up into the mosque proper. Cloth coverings are provided for shoes (for which you will be expected to tip). This is to prevent soiling of the carpets on which the worshipers kneel to pray. In plan the mosque is almost square, with a vast central courtyard surrounded on four sides by shady arcades, two aisles deep on three sides but stretching back for five aisles on the side facing Mecca, which acts as the prayer hall. The decorative designs of the small windows that punctuate the back walls of the aisles are said to be all different with no repetition.

The minaret is reached from the outer enclosure, and from the tiny cockpit at the top a fine view of the mosque is laid out below. The panorama also takes in the minarets of Sultan Hassan's mosque and the distinctive silhouette of the mosque of Muhammad Ali at the Citadel to the east.

Equally if not more impressive than Ibn Tulun's mosque is the neighboring **Gayer-Anderson Museum,** which is off to the left, through a small entrance way, as you first enter the outer enclosure. The museum is a complete Orientalist fantasy: Two 16th-century houses joined by a covered bridge, with jasmine-scented courtyards, floor cushions and fountains, twisting passageways, and secret viewing galleries. All it lacks are its dark-eyed *houris*, although even they were briefly provided when Hollywood came here to film the James Bond adventure *The Spy*

Right: The qa'a, or reception hall, of the Gayer-Anderson Museum

Gayer-Anderson Museum

🅜 68 D2

✉ Saliba St.

☎ 02/364 7822

🕐 Closed to visitors Fri. noon prayers

💲 $$. Camera $, video camera $$$

Who Loved Me (1977).

The Gayer-Anderson for whom the place is named was a British officer in Egypt, a keen collector of antiquities. Around 1930, he was allowed to occupy these houses — until that time family residences — in return for financing their restoration and upkeep. During the decade or more that he lived here he repaired and rebuilt, and added a vast miscellany of paintings, statuettes, small pharaonic antiquities, and tribal artifacts to fill the maze of rooms. On his return to England he bequeathed his work and collections to the Egyptian government. There are some wonderful local legends attached to the houses, including one concerning the courtyard well—said to be a passageway down to the domain of Sultan Watawit, Lord of the Bats.

Straight across the road from the museum and mosque as you leave is Khan Misr Touloun, an emporium stocked with pottery, glass, carvings, handwoven textiles, and all sots of beautiful objects made by artisans and craftspeople throughout Egypt. ■

Coptic Cairo

ARCHAEOLOGICAL EVIDENCE SUGGESTS THAT COPTIC
Cairo is where the modern city began. But successive later conquerors
shifted the urban center ever northward, to the point that Coptic
Cairo now lies out on the southern fringes, well away from all the
clamor and noise. Its high stone walls enclose a compound of silent
narrow lanes, ancient holy places, and an important small museum.

**Opposite and
below: Newly
restored, the
Church of the
Virgin Mary is the
spiritual home of
Egypt's Coptic
Christians.**

For a few hundred years following
the decline of the old pharaonic
religions and before the arrival
of Islam, Egypt was Christian.
Alexandria was the seat of power
and the country's only city of
importance. Cairo-to-be existed as
a modest port and river crossing in
use since pharaonic times, and as a

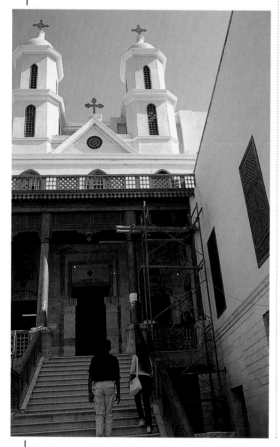

Roman fortress that went by the
name Babylon-in-Egypt.

As you arrive today by subway at
Mar Girgis station, you have been
traveling along the line of the banks
of the Nile before the river changed
its course 700 or more years ago.
Steps down from the platform face
the remains of two round Roman
towers that formed the western
gateway to the fortress, built in
A.D. 98 by Emperor Trajan. As you
pass between them, you are really
standing on top of the walls
because centuries of mud and
debris have raised the ground level
by some 30 feet (10 m). Excavations
down to the base of the right-hand
tower have revealed traces of an
ancient dock. Its twin on the left
has been pressed into service as
the foundations for the circular
Greek Orthodox **Church of St.
George.** George (in Arabic
"Girgis") was an early Palestinian
Christian martyr, executed by the
Romans about A.D. 300. Returning
Crusaders popularized his cult in
Europe, and some time around the
13th century he was adopted by the
English as their patron saint. His
veneration in Cairo dates back earlier, and there has been a church
dedicated to him in Coptic Cairo
since the tenth century, although
the present round basilica dates
from the early 20th century.

Across a small garden with
shady gazebos is the **Coptic
Museum.** Founded in 1908, the
museum houses a fascinating
collection representing a period

of great change in world cultural history, when all around the eastern Mediterranean the old pagan gods—Greek, Roman, and Egyptian—were being usurped by the beliefs and icons of Christianity. Here you can see how Greek goddess motifs have become crosses, as have pharaonic ankhs, and the hawk-headed pharaonic deity Horus nestles at the corners of Coptic basket-weave capitals.

All these objects are on the lower floor of the museum's **New Wing,** which is to the left on entering. On the upper floor are textiles, early Bibles, manuscripts, and an array of 17th- and 18th-century icons. The exhibits are almost upstaged by the museum's beautifully painted wooden ceilings and *mashrabiyya* windows. The **Old Wing** is even finer, but since the violent earthquake of 1992, it has been closed while structural defects are attended to. If the wing has reopened, take the chance to descend the staircase off the south side of the courtyard, which leads down into an area enclosed by the **Water Gate,** another twin-towered portal from the Roman fortress.

Built right on top of the Water Gate is the **Church of the Virgin Mary,** also known as the Hanging Church (Al-Muallaqa, "the suspended" in Arabic) because it rests on top of, and literally hangs over, the Roman towers. It was probably founded in the ninth century, so it is not the oldest of Coptic Cairo's half dozen ancient churches, but it is arguably the most beautiful. You enter the church from the museum garden up a steep staircase to a twin-towered 19th-century portico. In an inner court, stalls do a good business in reproduction icons, taped liturgies, and videos of papal sermons. Inside, much of

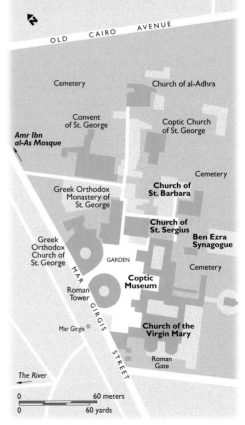

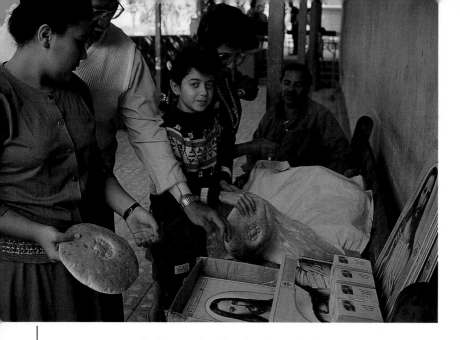

Egyptian
Christians buy
communion
bread outside a
Coptic Cairo
church.

Coptic Museum
- Map p. 119
- Mar Girgis St.
- 02/363 9742
- $$. Camera $, video camera $$$

the decoration dates from the 13th century, including the bone-and-ivory screens shielding the altars. Mass is still held celebrated here each Friday and Sunday morning.

On leaving the church, return to the main road and walk north beside the subway line to a flight of stairs that leads down, through a short tunnel, and back into the Coptic compound. Through a gate on the left in the high-walled alley is the **Convent of St. George,** closed to the public except for the main hall and chapel.

Farther on down, past several large "antiques" emporiums and around the corner, is the **Church of St. Sergius,** also called Abu Serga. You have to descend another flight of stairs, which is an indication of the building's age—around here, the lower you go the older things are. Historians dispute the age of this church but the likely consensus is fifth century. According to tradition, it is built over a crypt in which the Holy Family took shelter during their stay in Egypt (see p. 222). In more recent times the crypt has been

flooded by rising groundwater and cannot be visited.

At the end of the same lane, a left turn leads to the 11th-century **Church of St. Barbara,** while a right brings you to a small gate through which you'll find the **Ben Ezra Synagogue.** Venerated as the oldest synagogue in Cairo (it was founded in the 9th century and remodeled in the 12th by Abraham Ben Ezra, Rabbi of Jerusalem), it is associated by tradition with the prophet Jeremiah, whose temple is said to have stood on this spot.

Another tradition has this as the place where the pharaoh's daughter found Moses in the bulrushes. The real find, however, happened in the 19th century with the discovery of the synagogue's intact *geniza*, or treasury. Since the 11th century, Cairo's Jewish community had been depositing documents in this chimney-like space in the synagogue because any paper bearing the name of God had to be preserved. The thousands of letters, promissory notes, deeds, accounts, contracts, and petitions recovered amounted to an account of

medieval life comparable in completeness to the Domesday Book, William the Conqueror's 1086 survey of England. This priceless collection was rapidly spirited away to academic institutions abroad—most of it to Cambridge, England—and not one single bundle or sheaf remains in Cairo.

A short walk north of the walls of the Coptic compound is the **Amr ibn al-As Mosque,** established by the Arab general who captured Cairo in A.D. 640 and claimed Egypt for Islam. As it exists today,

the mosque is a patchwork of countless rebuildings and restorations, but it holds a special place in the story of Cairo as the site where Islam was first introduced into Egypt. To get to the mosque, follow Mar Girgis Street which runs beside the metro line north for 200 yards (180 m).

From Coptic Cairo it is just a brief walk to the **Nilometer** (see pp. 122–23): Cross the bridge over the subway tracks and keep going west until you reach the river where a footbridge takes you across to the island of Rhoda. ∎

The Ben Ezra Synagogue was restored to a pristine state in the 1980s, even though Jews no longer pray here.

The riverboat

You can ride the metro down to Coptic Cairo; Mar Girgis station is just four stops south of Tahrir Square (where the station is called Sadat), and a ticket costs the equivalent of just a few cents. But how much better to go by boat! Blue-and-white river buses depart from the Maspero Quay across from the Television and Radio Building, which is just a few minutes' walk north of the Egyptian Museum. Broad and flat like water beetles, the boats take the greater part of an hour zigzagging leisurely up the Nile to finish the trip at Masr al-Qadima, or Old Cairo. From the landing stage, it is another walk of a few minutes directly inland to the subway tracks. Cross over the footbridge and you are in Coptic Cairo. ∎

Nilometer

FROM PHARAONIC TIMES UNTIL AS RECENTLY AS THE beginning of the 20th century, the cycle of Egyptian life was governed by the annual flooding of the Nile. Prosperity depended on inundation by the river's waters—but only by the right amount, as too much could also be disastrous. So it was necessary to be able to read the rising flood in order to know what to expect. For this reason a whole series of Nilometers was constructed along the Nile Valley, the most elaborate being this one on the island of Rhoda in Cairo.

Nilometer

⬛ 68 CI

✉ Al-Malek al-Salah
St., Rhoda

💲 $. Camera $, video
camera $$$

Rhoda, which lies in the river off Old Cairo, has been inhabited since the era of the Pyramids. It was at various times a port and a ship-building center, and the Romans built a fortress here, the twin of that at Babylon (see p. 118). In the tales of *The Thousand and One Nights* the island is described as a garden paradise. It is no longer that, but the ranks of modern apartment blocks do at least stop short of the southern tip, which is an attractive vantage point. Over half a mile (1 km) wide at this point, the river looks splendid and mighty, with reed beds lining the far banks. It was wider still in ancient times,

Water was let in by three tunnels at different heights, all now sealed. A good year was when the waters rose to the 16th of the column's graduated divisions, known as ells. This was greeted by city-wide festivities and celebrations. Much more than 16 ells meant disastrous flooding; much less meant drought and famine. In the event of a shortfall, celebrations were canceled, their place taken by emergency prayers and fasting.

To improve the chances of just the right amount of flooding, Koranic verses carved on the walls of the Nilometer praise Allah and water as his blessing. In earlier times, the ancient Egyptians would occasionally sacrifice young virgins to the river gods. Other decorations include four recesses with pointed arches resembling the Gothic arches seen in medieval European architecture. However, these prefigure the Gothic style by several hundred years; it has been suggested that they may be the first pointed arches anywhere in the world. Although not particularly old, the elaborate carved and painted arabesques on the wooden ceiling are very impressive.

On leaving the Nilometer, turn left and follow the terrace path around the **Munasterli Palace,** built in 1851 on the site of the Nilometer Mosque, which had existed since the 11th century. For a time the headquarters of the Arab League (the organization is now in a grim building just off Tahrir Square), the palace is now used intermittently as an arts center.

An annex is currently being fitted out as the **Umm Kulthum Museum,** devoted to the greatest singer that the Arab world has ever known (see pp. 58-59). It is to hold a collection of memorabilia and an archive of her recordings, and is expected to open in 2002. ■

when a pontoon bridge of boats connected Rhoda to the mainland. These days, only a narrow channel separates the island and the Corniche, spanned by a wooden footbridge that gives access to the Nilometer from Coptic Cairo (see pp. 118–121).

There has been a Nilometer here since pharaonic times, although the existing one dates only from A.D. 861, and the unusual little conical-capped kiosk over it is a modern re-creation of a Turkish building. The Nilometer takes the form of a great stone-lined pit that descends well below the level of the Nile. At the bottom is an octagonal column, measured off and marked. (Vertigo sufferers beware: The narrow stair that winds down to the bottom of the pit has no handrail.)

The Gezira Club,
an oasis of green

Gezira

GEZIRA IS THE ARABIC WORD FOR "ISLAND," BUT IF YOU
hear it said in Cairo, chances are the speaker is referring to one
particular island that lies midstream in the Nile between the city
center and the west bank. Uninhabited until the 19th century, when
it became a royal garden, Gezira these days is home to an arts complex, an exclusive sporting club, and Cairo's premier soccer team.
But it also remains the greenest and leafiest part of the city.

Mokhtar Museum

⬛ 68 C3

✉ Tahrir St.

☎ 02/735 2519

🕐 Currently closed for
renovation

💲 $

Cairo Opera House

⬛ 68 C3

✉ Tahrir St.

☎ 02/739 8144 or
02/739 8132

🕐 Only open for
performances

From central Cairo's Tahrir Square,
the elegant **Qasr al-Nil Bridge**
forms a link to the southern end of
Gezira. Originally built in 1871, it
was completely overhauled in
1931 by Dorman Long & Co., the
British firm responsible for
Australia's famous Sydney Harbour
Bridge. The splendid lions that
stand guard, a pair at each end,

belong to the original crossing.
  At the Gezira end, the bridge
empties into Saad Zaghloul Square,
named for an Egyptian nationalist
leader of the early 20th century;
that's him, on top of the plinth at
the center of the traffic island. The
statue is the work of Mahmoud
Mokhtar (1891–1934), the preeminent Egyptian sculptor of modern

times. The **Mokhtar Museum,** dedicated to his output, is due west along Tahrir Street, but is currently closed for renovation. Meanwhile, the collection is housed in the National Museum of Egyptian Modern Art (see below).

Southern Gezira is dominated by the **Cairo Opera House** complex. After fire destroyed the old downtown Opera House (see p. 88), the city was left without a major concert venue until the Japanese stepped in during the late 1980s. They made a gift of the present building, which is a beautiful, cool white modernist update on Islamic architectural themes. It maintains a busy program of opera, ballet, theater, and music, and has a strict jacket-and-tie policy.

Adjacent to the opera is the **National Museum of Egyptian Modern Art.** Although they remain largely unknown on an international level, there are several outstanding Egyptian artists whose work deserves to reach a much wider audience. Chief of these are Mahmoud Said, who now has a museum devoted to him in Alexandria (see p. 194), and the surrealist Abd al-Hady al-Gazzar; both are represented here. Unfortunately, with its poor lighting and sparse collection, the museum does none of its artists justice. Two other major galleries within the Opera House grounds are used to host temporary exhibitions. Look for the larger-than-life statue of a woman on the lawn beside the main path; this is Umm Kolthum, the legendary Egyptian singer (see pp. 58–59).

Just a short distance north of the Opera House is another local icon, the **Cairo Tower.** It owes its conception to the Cold War of the 1950s, when Egypt was a part of the Middle Eastern chessboard

pondered over by U.S. and Soviet policymakers. The story goes that after Nixon declined to bankroll Egypt's High Dam project, the U.S. State Department offered President Nasser a sweetener of one million dollars toward arms purchases. Furious

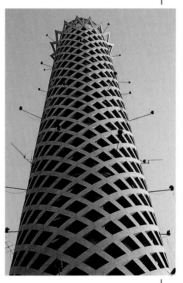

at the assumption he could be bought, Nasser took the money and used it to send a message back to Washington in the form of a great big raised finger. On a clear day from the top of the 614-foot (187 m) tower you can pick out the minarets of the Citadel to the east and the Pyramids to the west. Last admission is not until 11 p.m., and it is worth going late to view Cairo by night.

You also can look down over the swath of green in the island's center. This is the **Gezira Club,** founded by the British in the 1880s as an officers' club. It retains its exclusivity today with a membership restricted to the elite who can afford the large annual subscription fee. ■

Right: The Cairo Tower, symbol of defiance pointed at America

National Museum of Egyptian Modern Art
- 68 C3
- Opera House grounds, Tahrir St.
- 02/341 6667
- Closed 1–5 p.m. & Mon.
- $

Cairo Tower
- 68 C3
- Hadayek al-Zuhreya St.
- 02/735 7187
- Last adm. 11 p.m.
- $$$. Video camera $

Zamalek walk: Fine living & fine art

An island neighborhood on the north end of Gezira, Zamalek is Cairo's Manhattan, the city's most desirable address. Its well-to-do residents love it for its leafy streets and its vaguely European air, a legacy of the early 20th century when the neighborhood was the preserve of diplomats, colonial officials, and aristocracy.

Kitkat Mosque, named for a notorious World War II nightclub, is a vertical counterpoint to the picturesque sweep of houseboats on the island of Zamalek.

One of the first to grace the district with her presence was Empress Eugénie, wife of Napoleon III of France, who was accommodated on Gezira while visiting Egypt for the opening of the Suez Canal in 1869. A lavish palace was specially constructed for the occasion, with a striking facade of Islamic-style arches in cast iron. The Gezira Palace survives as the core of the **Cairo Marriott Hotel** ❶ (*Saray al-Gezira St., tel 02/735 8888;* see p. 360). Modern wings have been added, but the central building is original and remains regally opulent. If you are not a guest, then it is well worth visiting for lunch or an evening drink in the garden.

Royal overspending on extravagances such as the Gezira Palace led, predictably, to bankruptcy. By 1879 creditors were laying claim to the land and possessions of the khedive,

including Gezira. They carved up the island and sold it off, triggering a real-estate boom, out of which was born Zamalek.

Leave the Marriott by the main drive. The apartments here on Saray al-Gezira Street

⬛ See area map pages 68–69
▶ Cairo Marriott Hotel
⬌ 2 miles (3 km)
⏱ 2 hours
▶ Cairo Marriott Hotel

NOT TO BE MISSED
- The garden of the Cairo Marriott Hotel
- Pizza at Maison Thomas
- The view of houseboats from Zamalek Bridge

overlooking the river are some of the most sought-after in town. They are a favorite with international correspondents, who no doubt appreciate being able to observe the goings-on at the towering white Foreign Ministry directly across the water. At No. 14, up on the second floor, is **Nomad Gallery** 2 *(tel 02/736 1917),* a beautiful little shop specializing in Bedouin and traditional Egyptian jewelry and dress.

From Nomad, backtrack slightly and walk alongside the Marriott to come out opposite the Gezira Club (see p. 125), and then follow the road around. Opposite the club entrance is a smart little 19th-century villa, once a private residence, now the **Museum of Islamic**

Ceramics 3 *(1 Sheikh al-Marsafi St., tel 02/736 8672, closed Fri.).* It contains a lovely collection of tiles, bowls, pitchers, and vases, spanning ten centuries, and drawn not just from Egypt, but also from Persia, Morocco, Turkey, and Andalusia (southern Spain).

From here, head north across the small square and then take a left (passing Cairo's prestigious British International School) and a right to come to **26th of July Street** 4, the hub of the neighborhood. If you are hungry, then across the road and to the right you'll find **Maison Thomas** 5 (see p. 365), Cairo's only Continental-style deli, trading since 1930 and source of the best pizza in town. And a few steps beyond that is the

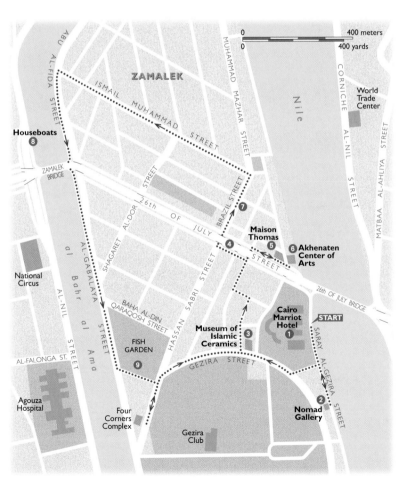

Cast-iron arcades originally part of a royal palace now provide an ornate frontage to the Marriott hotel.

Akhenaten Center of Arts ⑥ (*1 Aziz Abaza St., tel 02/735 8211, closed Fri.*), a government-run gallery complex with regularly changing exhibitions. Otherwise, head left down toward the crossroads with the traffic lights and a newsstand on three out of four corners—this is the best place to find yesterday's *Wall Street Journal* or this week's *Time.*

Cross the street and head north up **Brazil Street** ⑦. Among the butchers, the bakers, and the guy who mends carpets are a great many small boutiques selling good-quality cotton Egyptian clothing, as well as a fair scattering of antique stores and fine art galleries. Do not expect any bargains though; these people have copies of Sotheby's and Christie's auction catalogs on their bedtime reading tables. Continue to the top of Brazil Street, and turn left along Ismail Muhammad Street. Follow it to the end and you will arrive at the far side of the island.

Unfortunately, untidy riverside buildings obscure the views, but go south and walk up onto Zamalek Bridge at the end of 26th of July Street. From here, a beautiful panorama to the north takes in a curving sweep of river fringed by a chain of old wooden double-decker **houseboats** ⑧. Continuing south beside the river will bring you to the **Fish Garden** ⑨, a small landscaped park with grottoes and aquariums that was once part of the Gezira Palace gardens.

From here turn inland along the road past the Gezira Club and bear left to return to the Marriott. Alternatively, you could turn right and try one of the restaurants that make up the Four Corners complex: La Piazza is excellent for lunch; Justine is superb for dinner. ■

Western Cairo

AS FAR AS THE VISITOR IS CONCERNED, CAIRO IS CONFINED to one bank of the river. West of the Nile does not even appear on most tourist maps. That's because it is where a sizable proportion of Cairo lives, in an area dense with mid-rise apartment blocks and six-lane highways that fly past strips of Arbies, Baskin Robbinses, and KFCs. While this is not somewhere to go strolling, there are several places worth flagging down a taxi for.

Visitors associate Giza with pyramids, but to Egyptians it is most famously home to Cairo University.

It's hard to imagine now, but until well into the 20th century palm-decked farmland lay just over the river from central Cairo, bisected by a single, long, tree-lined road aimed straight at the Pyramids. A wealthy elite maintained "country homes" beside the Nile with gardens running to the water's edge. Population pressure has seen the majority of the villas give way to the more egalitarian high-rises, but there are some survivors. One such is a splendid, late 19th-century, Parisian-styled mansion, preserved as the **Muhammad Mahmoud Khalil Museum.** Khalil was a cabinet minister during the 1930s and a wealthy, compulsive collector of international, and particularly

Muhammad Mahmoud Khalil Museum
- 🅰 68 C2
- ✉ 1 Kafour St., off Giza St.
- ☎ 02/336 2379
- 🕐 Closed Mon.
- 💲 $$. Camera $, video camera $$$

French, art. He bequeathed his house and acquisitions to the state, endowing Cairo with one of its best-kept secrets—a world-class collection of Impressionist paintings and other works by well-known European artists.

On display in well-lit, temperature-controlled surroundings are sculptures by Rodin, several paintings by Corot, Pissarro, Sisley, Millet, and Renoir, works by Degas and Monet, two gorgeous Gauguins, a luminous Toulouse-Lautrec, and one of van Gogh's iris series. The house itself, which was well restored in the 1980s, is quite charming. As you gaze out of the back windows toward the Nile, note the nicely kept grassy lawn; 20 years ago that was a tarmac helicopter landing pad used by President Sadat, who commandeered the house as part of his residence.

Half a mile (1 km) south of the museum, along Giza Street, is **University Square,** a traffic circle with a striking monument at its center; this is "The Awakening of Egypt" (1928), the most lauded work of Egyptian sculptor Mahmoud Mokhtar (see p. 62). Originally, the statue stood in Ramses Square until the present Ramses II colossus took its place. It is a little lost here, almost permanently cordoned off by fast-flowing traffic, but presumably its siting is intended to stimulate the students at nearby **Cairo University,** whose domed main building squats at the end of the avenue.

Across from the statue is the entrance to **Cairo Zoo,** established in 1894 on the grounds of the former royal Harem Gardens. The first animals came from the personal menagerie of Khedive Ismail, and the collection rapidly grew to make this one of the finest zoos in the world. Sadly, under-funding and neglect mean that

today the place is a shadow of its former self, with little in the pens beyond lots of big birds, such as ostriches, emus, flamingos, and the like. This makes it fantastically popular with Cairo's roaming cat population. Nevertheless, as one of the largest green spaces in the city, it continues to attract big crowds, especially on weekends and public holidays.

Although the zoo is no Central Park, it is overlooked by Cairo's most talked-about piece of real estate, the twin-towered **First Residence.** Apartments here start at 1.3 million dollars, while the penthouse is rumored to have gone for 14 million dollars. Back at ground level, the First Mall is a chichi air-conditioned shopping experience, with an atrium café

that provides expensive respite from the heat outside.

Children will enjoy **Dr. Ragab's Pharaonic Village** (*3 Al-Bahr al-Azam St., Giza, tel 02/568 8601, $$$*), an ancient Egypt theme park on Jacob's Island, situated in the middle of the Nile, south of Giza. Visitors sail in small boats through the reed beds viewing scenes of pharaonic daily life re-created by costumed actors. At the end of the boat journey you reach several small, lively museums. One is devoted to early Egyptian history, including an absorbing mock-up of Tutankhamun's tomb as it was discovered by archaeologist Howard Carter, and another displays a new collection devoted to Alexander the Great and Hellenistic Egypt. ∎

Above: Young men paint wall panels for a replica of a waterside Ptolemaic temple, an attraction at Dr. Ragab's Pharaonic Village.

Cairo Zoo
- 68 B2
- Giza St.
- 02/570 8895
- $

Opposite: Bactrian camels are not native to Egypt, but they can be seen at Cairo Zoo.

The Pyramids

TRIVIA BUFFS, BUT PERHAPS NO ONE ELSE, KNOW THAT
the Seven Wonders of the Ancient World were the Pyramids of Egypt,
the statue of Zeus at Olympia, the Colossus of Rhodes, the Temple of
Artemis at Ephesus, the Mausoleum of Halicarnassus, the Pharos of
Alexandria, and the Hanging Gardens of Babylon. But only the
Pyramids are still with us. And modern visitors continue to find
the Pyramids no less wondrous and mysterious than the ancients did.

The Pyramids
🗺 68 AI & 145 C4
💲 $$, plus additional
fee ($$ each) to
enter Great
Pyramid, Khafre's
Pyramid, Menkaure's
Pyramid, Solar Boat
Museum. Sound-and-
light show $$
☎ 02/383 8823

There are two fundamental charac-
teristics of the Pyramids: They are
big and they are old. But despite
these being fairly straightforward
concepts, exactly how big, and how
old, is something that is still quite
hard to grasp. Until as recently as
the 19th century, the Great Pyramid
of Khufu, built 4,400 years earlier,
was the tallest building in the
world. Napoleon, having conquered
Egypt in 1798, calculated that it
contained enough stone to build
a wall 3 feet (1 m) high around the
whole of France. The dashing
young general also spent a night
alone inside the Great Pyramid
from which he reputedly emerged
shaken, never to discuss the
experience. As for their age, the
Pyramids were already ancient at
the time of the birth of Jesus
Christ, year zero for much of the
Western world. In fact, Christ's
birth is closer in time to us than it
is to the building of the Pyramids.
As the world celebrated the arrival
of the new millennium in 2000,
the Pyramids were entering their
fifth set of one thousand years. An
ancient Arabic saying sums it up
best: "Man fears time, but time
fears the Pyramids."

VISITING THE PYRAMIDS

*Opposite: Time
has not lessened
the mystique of
the world's oldest
tourist attraction.*

In spite of the awesome spectacle
("Like a thing of nature, a moun-
tain…with something terrible
about it, as though it were going to
crush you," wrote French novelist

Gustave Flaubert of the Great
Pyramid in 1849), a first visit can
be disappointing. All the countless
pictures and images—and the
Pyramids must be the most pho-
tographed monuments in the world
—show the Pyramids in the middle
of the desert, but suburban Cairo
actually creeps right up almost
to the paws of the Sphinx. Were
hunger to strike the great beast
now, it only need stretch out one of
those paws to flag some service at
the neighboring branch of an inter-
national pizza chain.

Of course, it wasn't always so.
Giza Plateau, the rocky foundation
on which the Pyramids and Sphinx
rest, is 10 miles (16 km) southwest
of central Cairo. It once took a
horse ride through the fields to
reach the monuments, where they
stand on the edge of the desert.
Then in the 19th century, a road
was built and along it ran a tram.
Now that road, Al-Haram, or
Pyramids Road, is four lanes of
horn-honking traffic, blocked solid
night and day. The tram is gone,
but in its place are buses, and there
is a good air-conditioned service
that runs between Tahrir Square in
central Cairo and the Giza Plateau.
Alternatively, a taxi costs about five
dollars one way.

There are two approaches to the
site: one through the village of
Nazlet al-Samaan, the other up a
curving slip road, an extension of
Pyramids Road, passing the Mena

House Hotel to the right. Either way, entry tickets are purchased at a kiosk on the edge of the plateau. Separate tickets are necessary to go inside the Pyramids. Just 300 people per day are allowed to enter each one, with tickets sold on a first-come first-served basis. An ongoing program of restoration means that usually only two out of the three Pyramids are open at any one time. Get there early. An early morning visit also means that you avoid the worst of the heat.

It is only when you get up close to the Great Pyramid that you truly appreciate the scale.

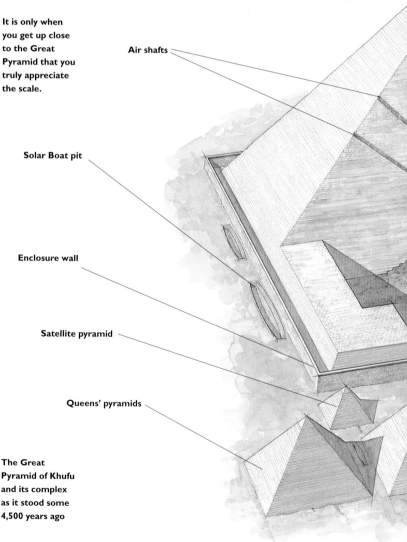

Air shafts

Solar Boat pit

Enclosure wall

Satellite pyramid

Queens' pyramids

The Great Pyramid of Khufu and its complex as it stood some 4,500 years ago

The **Great Pyramid of Khufu** is the first one to appear if you approach from Pyramids Road, as most visitors do. Khufu (who is also known by his Greek name of Cheops) is thought to have ruled about 2589 to 2566 B.C., although these dates are far from undisputed. His pyramid is the oldest and the largest of the trio. It is estimated to contain about 2.3 million limestone blocks, each thought to weigh on average 2.5 tons (2.3 tonnes), although some of the stones at the

A guide leads the way through a tomb deep inside a pyramid.

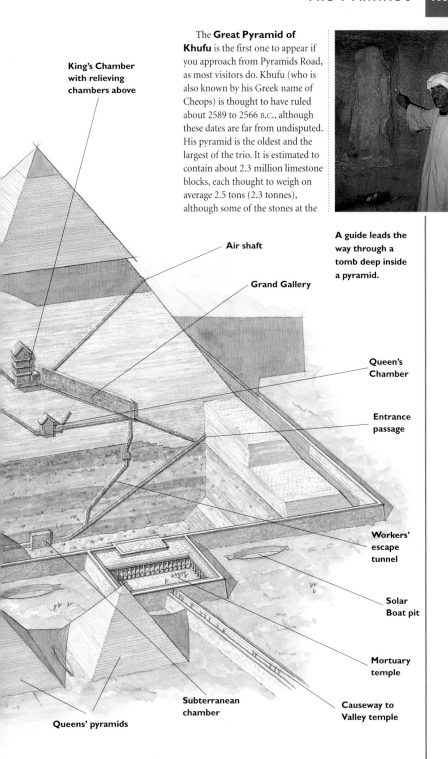

King's Chamber with relieving chambers above

Air shaft

Grand Gallery

Queen's Chamber

Entrance passage

Workers' escape tunnel

Solar Boat pit

Mortuary temple

Causeway to Valley temple

Subterranean chamber

Queens' pyramids

The descent into the Great Pyramid is steep and constricted, and can have visitors' leg muscles aching for days afterward.

base may weigh as much as 16.5 tons (15 tonnes). Originally 482 feet (147 m) high, it is now a little lower because of the removal of its outer limestone casing and capstone.

Visitors can climb a few feet of staircase purposely cut into the exterior face of the Great Pyramid and make their way inside through an opening, which was forced by the Egyptian ruler Caliph al-Mamun in A.D. 820. From the entrance a low, narrow corridor descends into an unfinished room, from which a second corridor ascends to another unfinished room, known as the **Queen's Chamber.** Visitors then go through the magnificent high **Grand Gallery** to the **main burial chamber,** right at the very center of the pyramid. In this chamber is an empty pink granite

sarcophagus, all that was ever found. As the sarcophagus is too big to get through the door, Egyptologists deduce that the room and pyramid must have been built around the sarcophagus. Whether it ever actually contained the body of Khufu, nobody can say for sure. Negotiating the steep slopes and confined spaces is arduous and not recommended for serious claustrophobes or for those with heart problems, but everything is clean and well lit, and there are handrails and wooden ramps.

In its original form, the pyramid was the focal point of a small complex. It was surrounded by a high wall enclosing a limestone court. Entrance to the court was via a mortuary temple, itself reached by a long, sloping causeway. When the Greek historian Herodotus visited, somewhere between 449 and 430 B.C., Khufu's causeway was still intact with "polished stone blocks decorated with carvings of animals," and he described it as a work "of hardly less magnitude than the pyramid itself." At the bottom of the causeway was a second small "valley" temple below. This lay beside a lake, which was fed by the Nile once a year during the annual flood. Both temples are gone, but the stone flagging of the causeway survives.

Either side of the causeway are large rectangular pits. In 1954, when covering slabs were lifted off one of these for the first time since antiquity, the dismantled planking of a boat was revealed. Its 1,224 separate cedarwood parts were painstakingly reassembled like a giant 3D jigsaw, and the reconstructed boat is now displayed in its own specially built **Solar Boat Museum** on the south side of Khufu's pyramid. A second pit was explored in 1985 by a combined team from the National Geographic

Society and the Egyptian Antiquities Authority, and that too was found to contain a disassembled boat. It has been left untouched beneath the sand.

The **Pyramid of Khafre** (or Chephren, as he is also known) is slightly smaller than that of Khufu, his father. It appears taller because it is built on higher ground. It is distinguished by a cap of smooth white stone—this is all that remains of a hard, polished outer limestone casing that once sheathed all three pyramids. It would have given them the appearance of pure, gleaming geometric prisms, but it was stripped away to build the palaces and mosques of Cairo.

Inside, the burial chamber lies just below ground level, incised into the bedrock. It is reached by a single descending passage, and the effort involved in a visit is much less than that required in the Great Pyramid.

The **Pyramid of Menkaura** (Mycerinus) is the smallest of the group. It has a base area of less than a quarter of that of the pyramids built by Khufu and Khafre. Archaeologists speculate that perhaps the Egyptians were running out of room. It may also be that the power of the pharaoh was waning, and it was no longer possible to raise the large workforce necessary for another truly gigantic monument. The great vertical gash in the north face is from a 12th-century attempt made to dismantle the pyramid by Othman ibn Yousef, son of Saladin (see p. 37). But in eight months all his laborers had achieved was merely the creation of this large slot, and so the sultan gave up the attempt.

From the entrance, also on the north side, a passage descends to an unfinished chamber with a series of panels carved with a stylized false door motif. A further passage leads

down to the burial chamber, in which was found a beautiful basalt sarcophagus, subsequently lost when the ship carrying it to England sank at sea. The pyramid is flanked by three small queens' pyramids, two of which are unfinished, left stepped like Zoser's pyramid at Saqqara (see pp. 149–150).

THE SPHINX—THE FATHER OF TERROR

From the foot of Khafre's pyramid, another causeway descends to the east to the king's partially reconstructed valley temple. A striking diorite statue of Khafre that was found here is now exhibited in Room 42 of the Egyptian Museum (see pp. 70–79). The temple now serves as a viewing platform for audiences entranced by the Sphinx,

One theory is that the Solar Boat was a funerary bark that carried Khufu's body from Memphis to his pyramid tomb.

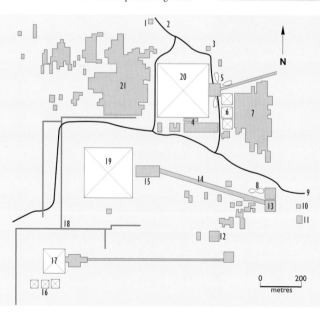

the mysterious creature with a lion's body and a human face, known to the early Arabs as Abu al-Hol, or the Father of Terror. Although subject to much dispute—with one claim that it predates ancient Egypt and is an artifact of some older, vanished civilization—most archaeologists now agree that the Sphinx was carved during Khafre's reign (2558–2532 B.C.). It is thought that it is a representation of the King, the lion being an archtype of royalty, and the King's head, framed by a flared *nemes* (the headdress worn by pharaohs), symbolizing power.

It was carved from a single outcrop of bedrock, with blocks used to build up the legs and paws, and it represents the earliest truly colossal piece of ancient Egyptian sculpture. Parts of the creature are gleaming white as a result of renovations undertaken in the 1990s, but repairs have been ongoing since at least as far back as the 18th dynasty, when a small temple was added between the forepaws along with a

KEY TO SITE PLAN

The Pyramids

1 Ticket office
2 Site entrance
3 Office for tickets to enter inside the Pyramids
4 Solar Boat Museum
5 Solar Boat pits
6 Queens' pyramids
7 East cemetery
8 Sphinx
9 Site entrance
10 Ticket office
11 Sound-and-light pavilion

The mighty Sphinx surveys Giza, with the Great Pyramid of Khufu rising beyond.

stela describing how the pharaoh Tuthmose IV (*R.*1400–1390 B.C.) rescued the Sphinx from the sands that covered it. More recently, it was an Italian, Caviglia, who reexcavated the Sphinx in the 19th century, discovering as he did so the ashes of the last sacrificial fire burned there, probably in late Roman times. He also found Tuthmose's stela and fragments of the Sphinx's royal beard, part of which went to the British Museum in London in the 19th century. ■

The mystery of the Pyramids

The breathtaking accuracy and alignment of the Pyramids at Giza have given rise to much theorizing. Khufu's pyramid is laid out with its sides oriented to within just three degrees of true north. The pyramid's base, which has sides over 756 feet (230 m) long, is level to within 1 inch (2.6 cm), and the greatest difference in the length of the four sides is just 2 inches (5.2 cm)—a margin of error of less than 0.2 percent.

Another striking statistic: The southeast corners of the three main pyramids line up on an exact diagonal. Such phenomenal precision in such ancient structures inspires many pyramid enthusiasts to look for more alignments, always with the suspicion of hidden greater meanings and possible treasures. ■

Heliopolis

NOT TO BE CONFUSED WITH ANCIENT HELIOPOLIS, THE pharaonic City of the Sun (of which nothing remains but a lone obelisk), the Heliopolis of today is an eccentric Cairo suburb with fantastical architecture and a relaxed, almost Mediterranean air.

Moorish colonnades bring a stage-set Orientalism to the northern suburb of Heliopolis.

Heliopolis
69 F4

Heliopolis is the creation of a wealthy Belgian industrialist, Baron Edouard Empain (1852–1929). In the early 20th century, he acquired a large tract of desert north of Cairo, where he constructed a small satellite city of theatrically Moorish terraces and Oriental villas separated by green avenues.

Close to a hundred years later, the ever expanding metropolis has swallowed up Empain's oasis, but it still has a unique charm and quirky character that set it apart from the rest of the city. It also still has plenty of social cachet. President Hosni Mubarak resides here, close to his administration's headquarters, the **Uruba Palace** on the corner of Al-Ahram and Al-Mirghani Streets. Formerly the Heliopolis Palace Hotel, this was

once Africa's most luxurious accommodations. The only guests now are visiting foreign dignitaries.

A wide avenue (Al-Ahram Street) with central streetcar lines runs north from beside the palace to a squat neo-Byzantine **basilica,** where Baron Empain lies in a black granite crypt *(not open to the public)*. His residence while he lived was even odder, exactly resembling a Hindu temple, with an exterior covered in carved temple dancers and gods. Known as the **Baron's Palace,** it stands neglected half a mile (1 km) east of the basilica on the road to the airport.

It is worth walking around some of the streets crossing Al-Ahram for their wonderful whitewashed architecture of arcades, sculpted windows, and teardrop turrets. ■

An Egyptian Air Force fighter plane points its nose skyward outside the rotunda of the October War Museum.

More museums in Cairo

AGRICULTURAL MUSEUM

A badly neglected group of pavilions contains exhibits on early farming methods and ancient life in the Nile Valley. The highlight is a mummified bull from the Serapeum at Saqqara (see p. 151); low points are the mounted animals which wear a somewhat moth-eaten appearance and the large jars full of stuffed birds. One of the pavilions houses the **Cotton Museum,** tracing the history of Egypt's main cash crop from its introduction to the country in the 19th century.

✉ Off Wizaret al-Ziraa St., Doqqi

☎ 02/760 8682

🕐 Closed after 2:30 p.m. & Mon.

💲 $

Ⓜ Metro: Doqqi

THE CHILD MUSEUM

Located in a small wooded park just north of central Heliopolis (which makes it somewhat difficult to get to), this is nevertheless an excellent place for keeping the children quiet for an hour or two. As a relative newcomer on the scene, the museum makes full use of multimedia technologies, and there are plenty of buttons to push that open up cross sections of pyramids, activate film clips of animals, and play music. There is also an **Arts Hall,** where children can paint and draw.

✉ 34 Abou Bakr al-Siddik St., Heliopolis

☎ 02/639 9915

🕐 Closed after 2:30 p.m.

💲 $

Ⓜ Metro: Darrasa

DR. RAGAB'S PAPYRUS INSTITUTE

If you are considering buying some decorated papyrus to take home, then a visit here is not a bad idea. Housed on a boat moored a little south of the Cairo Sheraton, it is really a salesroom rather than an "institute." But the people here at least really do know about papyrus, and demonstrate the treatment necessary to turn the original reeds into sheet papyrus. They will be selling you the real thing, not banana leaves, which is what you may well be sold at Khan al-Khalili and from other disreputable sources.

✉ Corniche al-Nil, Doqqi ☎ 02/748 8177
🕐 Open daily 9 a.m.–9 p.m. 💲 $
🚇 Metro: Doqqi

ENTOMOLOGICAL SOCIETY MUSEUM

Dusty wood-and-glass cabinets, combined with the general appearance of a Victorian-era schoolroom, make this the museum that time forgot. Its collection of pinned insects and mounted birds dates from the British occupation of Egypt at the turn of the 20th century, a time when the colonial powers were busy collecting and cataloging the world. A real period piece, the museum itself deserves to be encased in clear plastic and preserved whole for posterity.

✉ Wizaret al-Ziraa St., Doqqi ☎ 02/761 4999 🕐 Closed after 2:30 p.m. & Mon.
💲 $ 🚇 Metro: Doqqi

NATIONAL POSTAL MUSEUM

Housed in an annex of Ataba Square's main post office (itself a nice old building with an attractive courtyard), this small but busy museum serves as a reminder that Egypt was one of the first countries to issue stamps (in 1866). Philatelists might also be interested in visiting the stamp shop, which is on Sherif Street at the corner of Abdel Khalek Sarwat in downtown Cairo.

✉ 55 Abdel Khalek Sarwat St., Ataba Sq.
☎ 02/391 0011 🕐 Closed p.m. & Fri.
💲 $ 🚇 Metro: Ataba

OCTOBER WAR MUSEUM

The series of 20th-century wars with Israel still looms large in the Egyptian national consciousness. Pride was wounded by the defeats in 1948 and 1967, but in 1973 some succor was provided by the success of an attack launched across the Suez Canal that took the Israeli army completely by surprise. It is this breaching of the so-called Bar Lev Line, which took place on October 6, 1973, that is celebrated in this museum. Assorted military hardware fills the forecourt of the museum, while inside the purpose-built, circular exhibition hall a large model depicts the famous canal crossing. The museum is just off the airport road and is most easily reached by taxi.

✉ Al-Uruba St., Heliopolis
🕐 Closed Tues. 💲 $

PRINCESS FATMA MUSEUM

Cairo's newest museum is named in honor of a daughter of Khedive Ismail famed for her benevolence and charity. The grand villa in which she lived from 1853 to 1920 contains some 500 pieces of art and other so-called rare possessions confiscated from the royal family in the wake of the 1952 socialist revolution. Twenty-one rooms contain an eclectic assortment ranging from carpets and fine art to a collection of early 20th-century cameras. The most pleasant feature is the rooftop "Roman-style" garden, complete with mosaics and statuary.

✉ Wizaret al-Ziraa St., Doqqi
☎ 02/761 4999, 02/761 6785, 02/337 2933
🕐 Closed after 2:30 p.m. & Mon.
💲 $$ 🚇 Metro: Doqqi

TAHA HUSSEIN MUSEUM

Taha Hussein (1889–1973), blind from the age of three, is one of the most celebrated figures of Arabic literature—as scholar, novelist, and political writer. Trained at Al-Azhar University and the Sorbonne in Paris, he was a revolutionary thinker whose groundbreaking ideas occasionally brought him into conflict with the authorities. His novels display sympathy with the poor and oppressed and a desire for social justice. The museum occupies the chic white villa in which he spent the last 15 years of his life in the shadow of the Pyramids. Airy and elegant, it contains the writer's personal effects, including his 7,000-volume library.

✉ 11 Dr. Taha Hussein St., Haram ☎ 02/585 2818 🕐 Closed Mon. 💲 $ ■

Taking in stunning desert scenery, a lush oasis, and plenty more pyramids, the region around the capital offers a host of antidotes to the bustling urban experience.

Around Cairo

A man stops by the roadside at Saqqara to read the Koran.

Around Cairo

THE PRESENCE OF THE PYRAMIDS OFTEN FOOLS VISITORS INTO BELIEVING that Cairo must be a very ancient city. It is not. At heart, it is tenth century, founded by the Fatimids, and by Egyptian standards that is modern. However, as the great and mysterious monuments at Giza attest, civilization in the immediate vicinity dates back far, far earlier, and within just a short drive of Cairo's city limits are some of the oldest and most important ancient Egyptian sites in the country.

Long before the founding of Cairo proper, the mighty capital of the Old Kingdom of Egypt was Memphis, located not far southwest of the modern capital. This was where the legendary King Menes, who first united the southern valley and northern delta (circa 3100 B.C.), laid the foundations for the civilization of the pharaohs. Only a museum marks the site today, the rest is buried or vanished, but the

ancient imperial city's glories are reflected in its vast necropolis at Saqqara, one of the finest archaeological sites in Egypt, if not the world. Dominated by its Step Pyramid—the prototype for all the pyramids to follow—Saqqara was in use as a burial ground for over 2,500 years. It covers a vast area and comprises so many separate tombs and tomb complexes that it is impossible to take it all in on a single visit. Much of the site still has to be excavated, and fresh archaeological discoveries are made here on a regular basis.

North and south of Saqqara are the associated pyramid fields of Abu Sir and Dahshur. All of these monuments predate the better known temples of Luxor and Upper Egypt by several hundred years, and represent the formative steps of an architecture and art that would reach fruition at Karnak and in the Valley of the Kings.

A visit to these sites should arguably take third place on the itinerary of any visitor to Cairo, after the Pyramids of Giza and the Egyptian Museum. All four locations—Memphis, Saqqara, Abu Sir, and Dahshur—are connected by one highway, which runs south from Giza along the edge of the fields, where they suddenly stop and the desert begins.

The sites could be visited in a day, but that is inviting acute ancient Egypt overload. A far better plan is to visit Saqqara and Memphis on one day, and Abu Sir and/or Dahshur on another. Most Cairo hotels organize excursions, as do many of the city's independent tour agencies, including companies like American Express and Thomas Cook. Failing that, there is also the option of renting your

Originating in Sudan, a herd of camels is trucked through the desert south of Cairo to market at Birqash.

own taxi and driver, which costs around $25 to $30 for a full day. There is no public transportation that will take you to these sites.

What is highly noticeable on trips like these is how little time it takes to be free of the apartment blocks and overpasses and out into the countryside. Despite being home to any-

where between 12 million and 16 million people (nobody is quite sure of the number), Cairo does not sprawl. It ends abruptly, in luscious green fields to the north and south, lunarlike rocky landscapes to the east, and endless sand to the west.

One of the best ways to enjoy the contrast in scenery is to make a trip to Fayoum Oasis, Egypt's biggest oasis, just a 90-minute drive from central Cairo. It offers lakes and palm groves, tranquility and wildlife all surrounded by spectacular sand hills. An easy excursion from the city, it is at the same time a whole other world. ■

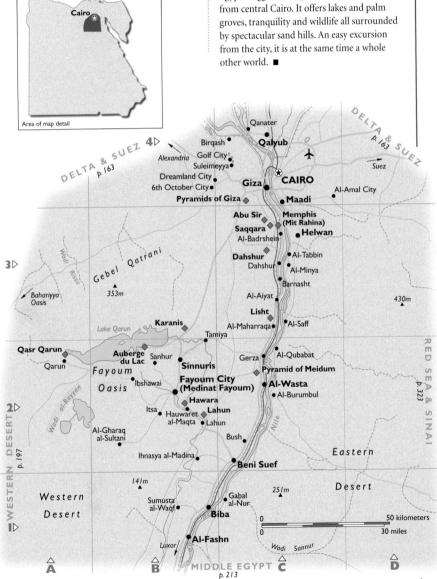

Abu Sir

DESPITE BEING OPEN TO THE PUBLIC ONLY SINCE THE MID-1990s, Abu Sir has long been known to the most casual of Egyptologists as the place of discovery of a cache of important papyri unearthed in the last years of the 19th century. More recently, in February 1998, a team of archaeologists chanced upon the rare find of an undisturbed ancient Egyptian burial, putting Abu Sir back in the limelight once again.

Abu Sir
145 C3
02/383 8823

Located several miles south of Giza, Abu Sir is marked by a cluster of three pyramids belonging to little-known kings and queens from the 5th dynasty (2494–2345 B.C.). All are considerably smaller than even the smallest of the three Pyramids of Giza. They are also quite dilapidated, giving them a slumped appearance. What makes the site charming is its isolated setting on a sandy ridge, where the desert rises away from the palm groves of the Nile plain. Few visitors come here.

Abu Sir marks the continuation of a trend begun with the Pyramid of Menkaura at Giza; as the pyramids decrease in size, their accompanying temple complexes become proportionately larger, with a greater emphasis on decoration. At Abu Sir, the remains of the various mortuary and valley temples are by far the most interesting elements of the site.

Northernmost of the group, the **Pyramid of Sahure** (*R.* 2487–2475) is the only one it is possible to enter—via a descending passage that is terrifyingly constricted and leads only to a single, small burial chamber. On the east side of the pyramid are the remains of Sahure's mortuary temple. Some of the walls have been reconstructed up to a height of about 18 inches (0.5 m), which is enough to give some indication of the floor plan. Reliefs decorated much of the wall surfaces and included scenes depicting the

trio. Unfinished at the time of the pharaoh's death, its outer sheathing was hastily completed with perishable mud brick that has eroded, revealing a six-stepped stone inner core similar to Djoser's pyramid at Saqqara (see pp. 148–150). It is in Neferirkare's mortuary temple, on the east side of the pyramid, that a celebrated set of papyri was discovered. When deciphered, the expressive pictograms (written in hieratic, a shorthand form of hieroglyphics) revealed themselves to include priestly schedules, inventories of furniture and equipment, and accounts. Taken together, these offer a fascinating insight into the day-to-day administration of the Abu Sir temples of 4,000 years ago. Much is still to be learned from the papyri, which are being studied at the British Museum in London.

The third, and most dilapidated, of the pyramid trio was built for **Nyuserra** (*R.*2445–2421), son of Neferirkare. His desire to nestle his funerary monument between those of his father and his uncle has limited the size of the pyramid. ■

The slumped pyramids of Abu Sir are near neighbors of the Pyramids of Giza.

pharaoh's victories over a Libyan army. Most of these reliefs are now in the Egyptian Museum in Cairo, but a few fragments remain in situ, making the area worth exploring.

Sahure was succeeded by his brother **Neferirkare** (*R.*2475–2455 B.C.), whose pyramid is the southernmost and largest of the

Uncovering history

Abu Sir is also the site of a sixth-century B.C. cemetery of shaft tombs. In 1995 a team of Czech archaeologists began excavating one of these shafts. At 70 feet (21 m) below the surface, workers reached the burial chamber, located a small doorway, and removed the stones that sealed it. Inside, well-preserved inscriptions and reliefs covered the walls, identifying the occupant as Iufaa, a priestly palace administrator who lived about 500 B.C. Hundreds of artifacts lay intact just as they had been left, but most of the chamber was taken up by a large, white limestone sarcophagus. Further exami-

nation was delayed by an earthquake that collapsed part of the shaft, and it was not until February 1998 that, using beams and jacks, the 24-ton lid was inched off to reveal a mummy-shaped sarcophagus of gray basalt covered with hieroglyphs. When the sarcophagus lid was hoisted off, it revealed a mummy covered with a magnificent shroud of ceramic beads. A once-in-a-lifetime find for the archaeologists involved, Iufaa's grave represents a wealth of new knowledge about ancient Egypt. ■

The face of Iufaa is revealed again after 2,500 years.

Saqqara

ONLY 15 MILES (24 KM) SOUTHEAST OF CENTRAL CAIRO,
Saqqara is one of the richest archaeological sites in Egypt. In fact,
few sites in the world can compare. It is a vast desert necropolis built
for the kings and nobles of the Old Kingdom, and among its highlights are the very first pyramid, some splendid tomb paintings, and
one of the great oddities of Egyptology, the Serapeum, a haunting
burial place of mummified sacred bulls.

Saqqara

 145 C3

☎ 02/383 8823

Saqqara was founded as the
necropolis, or burial city, for the
Old Kingdom capital, Memphis
(see p. 154). Its earliest tombs date
from the 1st dynasty (3100–2890
B.C.), its latest from the Persian era
(circa 500 B.C.). However, all this
was unknown until a French former schoolteacher named Auguste
Mariette (see pp. 80–81) began
excavating at Saqqara in 1850. He

discovered a half-buried sphinx in
the sand and remembered a passage
from the first-century Greek
geographer Strabo that mentioned
a Serapeum at Memphis and
sphinxes in the sand. Following this
lead, Mariette began digging and
succeeded in uncovering the avenue
of sphinxes and, from that, the
Serapeum. His discovery sparked
the extensive and continuing

Imhotep, who was both high priest and the world's first big name in architecture. Though less than half the height of the two largest pyramids at Giza, and much less well known, Imhotep's monument represents a far greater achievement. Before Saqqara, the building material of choice had been mud brick, and the common building form was the *mastaba* (from the Arabic word for "bench"), a simple, rectangular, slablike structure covering a burial pit. Imhotep took the mastaba, constructed it in stone, and added to it five times, one on top of the other, each successive layer being smaller than those below to create a pyramidlike effect. The high priest surrounded his king's pyramid with a host of secondary structures and enclosed them all within a bastioned perimeter wall 32 feet (10 m) high.

Entrance was, as it is today, via a gate in the southeastern corner and along a corridor of 40 pillars, their design inspired by bundles of tied reeds. This leads into the **Great**

excavation of the site. Much more has been found since then, but archaeologists believe that the monuments seen at Saqqara today represent only a fraction of what might still be buried. Even so, there is more than enough uncovered and open to the public to make a visit to Saqqara a bewildering experience. Three main groupings of monuments should head any visitor's list, centered on the Step Pyramid, the Pyramid of Teti I, and the Serapeum. You should allow at least half a day to explore them.

THE FIRST PYRAMID

Centerpiece of Saqqara is the **Step Pyramid** and surrounding enclosure of Djoser (also spelled Zoser), king of Egypt from 2667 to 2648 B.C. It was built for the king by

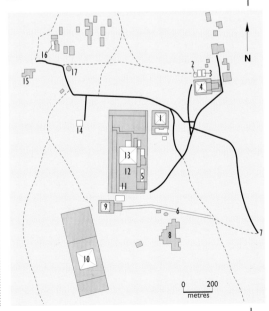

South Court, an open area the size of a soccer field in front of the pyramid. Decoration is sparse, but in the southwest corner is a building projecting into the court that has a frieze of rearing cobras. This venomous reptile was a symbol of royalty, and it is here to protect the **Southern Tomb,** sunk deep below, where the king's *ka,* or life force, was put to rest in the form of a statue. If you ascend the stairs to the top of the wall you can look down the shaft, but the tomb is closed to visitors.

On the east side of the court is what's known as the **Heb-sed Court,** linked to a ritual in which the king renewed his rule by re-enacting his coronation. To the north are the remains of two pavilions, one dedicated to Upper Egypt, the other to Lower, the two kingdoms united under Djoser. In the first of these, protected under clear plastic, is the world's oldest known example of tourist graffiti (12th century B.C.), in which visitors from Thebes express their admiration for the king and his monuments.

A little farther north, the most intriguing aspect of the complex is usually indicated by a milling crowd of visitors; they are in line to see Djoser himself. Here at the foot of the pyramid's north face is a stone kiosk, known as a *serdab,* with a slot through which you look to meet the level stare of the king, enshrined within a life-size, painted statue. This arrangement enabled the king's ka to communicate with the outside world. The statue is a copy; the original is displayed in the atrium of the Egyptian Museum in Cairo.

South of Djoser's enclosure, a misshapen mound represents the slumped remains of the **Pyramid of Unas,** resting place of the last king of the 5th dynasty (*R.* 2375–2345) When the pyramid was entered in 1881, the walls were found to be covered in hieroglyphs, the earliest example of texts found in any ancient Egyptian burial. Unfortunately, because of the damage caused by visitors, the pyramid is now closed to the public. Its causeway is flanked by a number of well-preserved tombs, and several of these are usually open.

A worker in the Step Pyramid kneels beside a statue of a sacred bull that rests on the symbol for stability.

TOMB PAINTINGS

Although the writings on the walls of the Pyramid of Unas are off-limits to visitors, similar early "pyramid texts" can be seen in the **Pyramid of Teti** (first king of the 6th dynasty, *R.* 2345–2323). These vertical columns of script, which include hymns, litanies, and spells of protection, are the first flowerings of a tradition that would later blossom into the full-blown, full-color, floor-to-ceiling wall paintings seen in the tombs of the Valleys of the Kings and Queens in Luxor. Long before that time, however, tomb art had already become quite sophisticated, as can be seen in two later 6th-dynasty tombs adjacent to Teti's pyramid. Closest is the **Tomb of Ankh-ma-Hor,** also known as the Physician's Tomb because of its scenes depicting ancient surgical operations, including surgery on a man's toe and a circumcision. (Bodies of Egyptians from burials as early as 4000 B.C. have been found to be circumcised.) Adjacent is the **Tomb of Mereruka,** a son-in-law of Teti, which is a large complex of 33 chambers, many bearing magnificent reliefs. In the very first chamber, Mereruka hunts from a boat among birds, fish, and hippo, scenes that have taught Egyptologists a great deal about the wildlife of ancient Egypt.

THE SERAPEUM

Mariette's Serapeum remains one of the great discoveries of Egyptology. It is a series of eerie catacombs created for the burial of sacred bulls, known as Apis bulls. Animals in ancient Egypt were often associated with gods, and bulls with particular markings—black with a white spot on the forehead and another near the tail—were regarded as the physical manifestations of the Memphite god Ptah, and later of the Greco-Roman deity Serapis. These creatures roamed the grounds of Ptah's Temple in Memphis, and when they died they were buried in the subterranean galleries of the Serapeum at Saqqara.

The catacombs date back to at

least as early as the 18th dynasty (1550–1295 B.C.) and continued in use until the Ptolemaic period (332–30 B.C.). When Mariette entered in 1851, he discovered a series of passageways with side chambers containing 25 massive granite coffins, each weighing up to 80 tons (72 tonnes). All had been robbed in antiquity, save for one, in which was a solid gold statue of a bull (now in the Louvre in Paris) and an inner sarcophagus containing a mummified bull (Agricultural Museum, Cairo, see p.141).

Near the Serapeum is the **Philosophers' Circle,** a collection of statues of Greek philosophers and poets, set in place by the Ptolemies. A short distance away is another of Mariette's discoveries, the **Mastaba of Ti,** the burial complex of a court official who served under three kings. Its wall paintings are unrivaled for the wealth of information they present on life in Old Kingdom Egypt. The best reliefs are in the farthest chamber, which also has three slits in the far wall through which Ti's statue can be viewed in its serdab. ■

Mereruka strides forward from a niche in his tomb.

The pyramid builders

In the space of about 500 years, Egypt's kings raised more than 80 pyramids in a strip between Giza and the oasis of Fayoum. But despite being perhaps the most famous monuments in the world, Egypt's pyramids still keep many secrets, even down to the very basics such as how they were built and why.

Archaeologists, Egyptologists, and pyramidologists (for the study of the pyramids has become a science in its own right) have a great many theories between them, but there are a good deal fewer certainties. By the time of the Romans, the art of deciphering hieroglyphs was lost and real knowledge of the pyramid builders was drowned in a sea of myths and legends. The Greek historian Herodotus began the swell of misinformation with the story that Khufu forced his daughter into prostitution to pay for his pyramid. Three centuries later, Roman Jewish historian Josephus Flavius included pyramid building among the hardships that the Jews had to endure during their years of labor in Egypt. In the 20th century, Hollywood director Cecil B. DeMille presented a panoramic vision of legions of whiplashed slaves toiling away to complete their king's work.

It is DeMille's vision that is the latest to be debunked. In 1993 archaeologists discovered fields of ancient graves at the Giza Plateau, which are most likely the burials of the actual builders of the pyramids. Bodies found in the graves showed evidence of the strains and stresses of physical labor, as well as of emergency medical treatment. They also discovered dwellings, which, while modest, are definitely not the abodes of slaves.

The prevailing belief now is that the pyramids were built by a willing labor force

King Khufu immortalized himself by building a huge pyramid at Giza, but why?

of peasants, employed perhaps in rotation, paid in foodstuffs, and led by a few thousand skilled craftsmen. Only during periods of great wealth and stability could the realm provide the authority and administration necessary for such an undertaking. Given this need, the age of the pyramids begins soon after Egypt was first unified and ends when centralized power broke down at the end of the 6th dynasty.

As to how the pyramids were built, we are still some way from a universally agreed theory. The most common suggestion is that huge ascending ramps, either straight like causeways or spiraling around the structure, were laid and the massive stone blocks were hauled up these, but there is no hard evidence to either prove or disprove this idea.

Similarly, the mathematical precision of the pyramids' construction begs another question yet to be answered conclusively: What purpose do they serve? While most archaeologists agree that they were tombs, they disagree about what other functions these massively proportioned monuments might have had. For example, the purpose of some of the internal chambers is not yet known, and the significance of the pyramids' alignment is hotly debated.

Our knowledge of the pyramids is still expanding. Everything we know could so easily be entirely rewritten by a single find. Investigating the pyramids now requires a team of scientists, including specialists in bone and plant remains and in radiocarbon dating, in addition to those who probe the structure of the pyramids themselves with remote-controlled robots. There is always the suspicion that the pyramids must hold more secrets. ■

New theories dispel the popular perception of vast teams of slaves hauling up blocks under a foreman's whip. Excavations are revealing housing that possibly accommodated a well-kept workforce.

Memphis

ALMOST 4,000 YEARS BEFORE THE FOUNDING OF CAIRO, Memphis was the capital of Egypt. One of the greatest cities of the ancient world, today it is marked solely by an open-air museum of meager finds, partially redeemed by its one outstanding exhibit, the remains of a mighty statue of Ramses II.

Larger than life as pharaoh, Ramses II spread his likeness across Egypt, including colossi at Memphis.

Memphis
- 145 C3
- 02/383 8823

The city itself lies buried beneath the modern-day village of Mit Rahina. It was already in decay when the Arab al-As armies conquered Egypt in A.D. 641. They, and their successors, used ancient Memphis as a quarry to provide building materials for their new capital—later to be known as Cairo. Silt deposits from the annual flood of the Nile gradually covered the pharaonic city, until Memphis became no more than a lumpy alluvial plain on which palms rooted and peasants founded their villages.

The presence of these villages, combined with a high water table (a result of the damming of the Nile at Aswan), means that archaeologists have never been able to excavate the site. However, over the decades, as a new drainage ditch or

the foundations of a house were dug, a chink of spade against stone would signal the discovery of some ancient building block or a fragment of statue. Some of these finds are displayed at a small museum. Most striking is a **colossus of Ramses II,** discovered in 1820. Missing his lower legs, the king lies on his back in a specially constructed viewing pavilion, but in its original state the statue would have stood as tall as a five-story building.

The garden contains more statues of Ramses II, indicating that the great pharaoh built as prolifically here as he did in Upper Egypt. You have to wonder what has been lost. Similarly with the sphinx here—at 80 tons the largest alabaster statue ever found. Was this just one in an avenue of sphinxes, as at Karnak? ■

Dahshur

DAHSHUR IS A SMALL PYRAMID FIELD IN AN ISOLATED desert setting to the south of Saqqara. Only accessible to the public since the mid-1990s, it has yet to be added to the tour-bus trail. Anyone making the journey down here is likely to have the site completely to themselves.

In pyramid chronology, Dahshur comes after Saqqara but before Giza and Abu Sir. The two main pyramids here were both built for the pharaoh Sneferu (R.2613–2589 B.C.), father of Khufu, builder of the Great Pyramid at Giza.

The **Bent Pyramid** was begun first. It can lay claim to being the first pyramid proper—all those that had come before were stepped. So it is perhaps understandable that the builders erred in their calculations: The pyramid started to rise at an angle of 55 degrees, but halfway up it must have become clear that the structure was becoming unstable, and it was completed with a less steep slope of around 44 degrees. The result is the distinctive "bent" look.

Uniquely, the Bent Pyramid retains much of its original white limestone casing. From nearby, you can appreciate how smooth the surfaces of not just this, but all pyramids would originally have been.

For reasons that remain unknown, in the 30th year of his reign, Sneferu abandoned his first pyramid and began a new one. Known as the **North Pyramid** (also called the Red Pyramid), this was constructed with a gentler slope of 43 degrees. A stair on the north face allows visitors access to the interior. From the entrance 100 feet (30 m) up, an excellent view to the south takes in the pyramids of Saqqara, Abu Sir, and Giza. A 70-yard (65 m) passage leads down to three chambers, the first two of which have high corbeled ceilings, foreshadowing the Grand Gallery of the Great Pyramid at Giza. ■

Clouds mass over the Bent Pyramid, misshapen prototype of the Pyramids of Giza.

Dahshur
145 C3
02/383 8823

Fayoum Oasis

FAYOUM, 60 MILES (100 KM) SOUTHWEST OF CAIRO, IS Egypt's largest oasis and a popular getaway for smog-choked inhabitants of the city. While it has temples and archaeological sites and a history of settlement that goes back to pharaonic times, what attracts most people to Fayoum is greenery and serenity.

For this reason, most visitors avoid **Fayoum City** itself (Medinat al-Fayoum), which is an ugly, modern town with little to recommend it, and instead head for the real heart of the area, **Lake Qarun.** Formed 70,000 years ago when the Nile flowed over into the Fayoum depression, the lake is kept supplied with water by a series of canals connecting it to the river. These channels were first dug during the reign of the 12th-dynasty pharaoh Amenemhat III (*R.* 1855–1808 B.C.). The ancients cultivated Fayoum and made it into a "garden of Egypt"—a role that it still plays today, producing an abundance of fruit and vegetables. Unfortunately, the lake is becoming increasingly saline, and the surrounding beaches have become encrusted with salt.

Unsuitable for swimming, the lake is nonetheless beautiful from the vantage point of a rented rowboat. The views can also be enjoyed from the promenade café of the **Auberge du Lac** (see p. 365), a luxury hotel that was once King Farouk's hunting lodge, and where Allied leaders met after World War II to carve up the Middle East.

Lake Qarun supports a huge number of birds (see pp. 158–59), most of which are migrants and winter visitors. We know that this was also the case in antiquity, as the ancient Egyptians recorded the wildlife of Fayoum in frescoes and friezes in local tombs and temples, most famously in the panels known as the Meidum Geese, displayed in the Egyptian Museum in Cairo.

Best preserved and most accessible of Fayoum's pharaonic remains is the small Ptolemaic temple of **Qasr Qarun,** at the very western end of the lake. It was dedicated to the crocodile god, Sobek, whose "offspring" flourished in the marshes and waters of the oasis in ancient times. The temple was heavily restored in 1956, and it is possible to descend into underground chambers (beware of snakes) and climb up to the roof for a view of the surrounding desert. Fayoum's other main ancient site is **Karanis** (known locally as Kom Oshim), a ruined third-century B.C. city, at the eastern end of the lake. There are two minor temples, plus a museum with pottery, glassware, and terracotta figures found on the site.

Left: Young village girls collect water from a well.

Fayoum Oasis
⬛ 145 B2

PYRAMIDS

Fayoum also has four pyramid sites, all lying slightly to the east of the oasis, in a desert strip between it and the Nile. Those at Hawara, Lahun, and Lisht are in bad shape and of little interest to all but keen pyramidologists—although Hawara is notable as the site of a great find of 146 Fayoum Portraits (see box below), discovered in the early 19th century.

The **Pyramid of Meidum,** however, is impressive, if nothing like a conventional pyramid. It exists as a three-stepped tower rising above a mound of debris. This tower is the inner structural core, exposed after the outer casing and packing that filled in the steps collapsed and slid away. The failed pyramid is traditionally attributed to Sneferu, who went on to more successful endeavors at Dahshur (see p. 155). The famous painted wildfowl were found in one of the subsidiary buildings close to the pyramid. ■

The sun sets over Lake Qarun, a haven for migratory bird life.

The Fayoum Portraits

Although the Fayoum Oasis receives few foreign visitors, its name is familiar to many people thanks to several recent high-profile international exhibitions of the so-called Fayoum Portraits.

Painted in the first to third centuries A.D. while their subjects were still alive, these hauntingly lifelike portraits were cut to life size, and then at death they were laid over the face of the corpse after it had been mummified.

Since their discovery (in several caches), most of the portraits have been detached from their mummies, and they are now displayed at Cairo's Egyptian Museum and at other institutions throughout the world, including the Metropolitan Museum of Art in New York. They provide a wealth of information about the clothing, hairstyles, adornment, and physical characteristics of Egypt's wealthier inhabitants during Roman times. ■

Bird life of Egypt

It is not just humans that take advantage of the incongruous fertility of the Fayoum. To other creatures, too, it is an oasis, and none are more obvious than the birds.

Year-round, the Fayoum is home to a variety of species reflecting not only the diversity of habitat from reed bed to desert, but also Egypt's position at the junction of the African and Asian continents. Some, like the Senegal coucal, Senegal thick-knee, common bulbul, and little green bee-eater, are African at or near the northernmost limits of their range. Cattle egrets, kestrels, and palm doves are more widespread, while the little owl is a European species for which Egypt is a southerly outpost.

The god Horus is represented as a falcon on the tomb of Inkerhau at Deir al-Medina.

Olive groves play host to the incessant *zitzit* of the graceful warbler. The reed beds are full of clamorous reed warblers living up to their name, and you may be lucky enough to glimpse the elusive purple gallinule or crepuscular painted snipe. On the desert margins look for wheatears, especially the dapper white-crowned black wheatear. In winter these residents are joined by vast numbers of wildfowl and waders from more northerly breeding grounds.

The water regime of the Fayoum may be man made and recent, but this gathering of the avian clans was well documented by the ancients. Some birds were worshiped. Thoth, the god of wisdom, for instance, is often portrayed as an ibis; sadly no longer found in Egypt, the species is still called the sacred ibis. Birds are depicted in tomb friezes throughout Egypt. The immaculately painted Meidum Geese, now in Cairo's Egyptian Museum, come from the site of Meidum, southeast of the Fayoum. At Saqqara, friezes of papyrus swamps, alive with many of the birds still found in the Nile Valley and Delta, cover the tombs of Ti and Mereruka.

But it is farther south, at Beni Hassan (see pp. 216–17), that the greatest of all pharaonic wildlife panoramas lies. Vividly colored and accurate paintings of birds still familiar, such as the resident hoopoe, with its head shaped like a hammer, and migrants like masked and red-backed shrikes and redstarts, enliven the walls of the Tomb of Khnumhotep III.

Many of Egypt's more than 400 recorded species are migrants, using Egypt as a staging post every spring and fall as they journey to and from their European breeding grounds. The smaller birds—the warblers, chats, flycatchers, buntings, and so on—pass through in millions. In autumn, Egypt's north coast is a bird-watcher's paradise, first landfall for birds from Europe crossing the Mediterranean, where anything from a willow warbler to a nightjar can be seen flying in off the sea at places such as the Zaranik Protectorate near Al-Arish in northern Sinai (see p. 336).

However, it is for the large birds—the white and black storks, the raptors, cranes, and pelicans—that Egypt is of most importance. These birds channel down specific migration corridors since, because of their large size, they are dependent on thermals of rising warm air for prolonged flight. Since thermals are weak over open water, these species bottleneck at each end of the Mediterranean to avoid the sea. Many have to come through Egypt, converging at key points such as Suez, Ain Suhkna, and Gebel Zeit, and providing one of the world's great wildlife spectacles. ■

Above: A spoonbill seeks out food among the reed beds.
Below: White and black storks stop for a rest near the Red Sea during migration, creating an impressive sight for bird-watchers.

Wadi al-Rayyan

Little more than an hour and a half's drive from Cairo awaits stunning desert scenery.

OUT IN THE DESERT EAST OF FAYOUM, WADI AL-RAYYAN IS a large depression among the dunes into which excess water from the oasis has been channeled to create three freshwater lakes and a shallow waterfall. Stocked with fish, the lakes are a major nesting ground for birds and a big draw for picnicking visitors.

Wadi al-Rayyan
🅰 145 A2

Absolutely unspoiled by any form of development—and with protected status to ensure that it stays that way—the scenery is intensely dramatic. Although the lakes are attractive, it is the desert surroundings that really impress. Aside from the single thread of black tarmac road, all else is just oceans of yellow sand, sculpted into great wavelike hills by the wind.

Today, wildlife is among the wadi's chief attractions. The desert environment is home to some 15 species of animals, including gazelle, sand foxes, wildcats, and wolves. An estimated 134 species of birds inhabit or visit the wetlands surrounding the lakes. Among them are rare species of hawks, as well as kestrels, kites, egrets, and herons. There are plans to establish an information and bird-watching center, funded by the tolls cars pay to enter the reserve. At the moment, however, most visitors head straight for the water and the much vaunted "waterfalls." These falls, in reality, have been created by piping water into rock-based reed beds just a few feet above the level of the lake. Nevertheless, it is an idyllic spot for swimming and sunbathing; avoid weekends and public holidays, when families crowd the place.

Access is by car only, via Fayoum Oasis. A trip combining these two places makes for a great excursion from Cairo, and is highly recommended for anyone who does not have the time to make the trip out to the Western Oases or Sinai and might otherwise miss the country's spectacular desert scenery. ■

Birqash camel market

NOT FOR THE FAINT-HEARTED, CAIRO'S FRIDAY CAMEL market is dusty, smelly, and unbelievably loud. It is held 22 miles (35 km) to the northwest of the city at Birqash. Proceedings start at first light and most of the business is done by nine, so it is advisable to get an early start. Public transportation is tricky, with no direct buses, and the best option is to arrange a taxi for the whole morning.

Camels are not indigenous to Egypt. Their absence from pharaonic art (which frequently depicts animals) strongly suggests that they were unknown in ancient Egypt. Historians believe that the Persians introduced the animals around the sixth century B.C. Since that time they have become indispensable as hard-working, low-maintenance beasts of burden.

Although camels are now bred in Egypt, hundreds are brought into the country each week from northern Sudan. First stop is Daraw, just north of Aswan, the largest camel market in Egypt, from where a great many of the beasts are sent on in trucks to Birqash.

There is a market here every day, but Friday attracts the largest number of traders and animals. Grand men in *galabiyyas* (gowns) and turbans huddle on straw mats around trays of tea and discuss prices, while herders keep the bawling animals in line. Each camel is sold with a booklet issued by Ministry of Agriculture officials at Daraw, which includes its state of health, age, and place of origin. The latter can also be identified through tribal brand marks. According to herders, a good camel is characterized by a big hump and sturdy bones. Tests on teeth, gums, and eyesight usually only apply to the bigger animals, which are sold for farming; the smaller beasts usually go to the slaughterhouse. According to one herder, "They can be cooked like chickens." ∎

Not long after dawn, traders mill around the market on the outskirts of Cairo in search of a good camel.

Birqash
⚠ 145 C4

Oranges are gathered and crated in orchards around the Nile-side town of Qanater.

More places to visit around Cairo

DREAMLAND CITY
On the edge of the Western Desert, a ten-minute drive north of the Giza Plateau, is the mirage-like vision of Dreamland City, one of Cairo's new, and ever so slightly surreal, suburban communities. It could be California—or at least, that is the hope. Designed to offer wealthy Cairenes an alternative lifestyle to the cramped, congested, and creaky old city, projects such as this combine condominiums and villas with malls, hotels, luxury amenities, and mosques. Dreamland comes complete with a theme park of Disney-type rides and an 18-hole, par 72 golf course with fairway views of the Pyramids.
A 145 C4

GOLF CITY
Strange as it may seem, given the arid climate and scarcity of useable land, Egypt is seeking to market itself as an international golfing destination. Thirty minutes' drive north of Cairo on the Desert Road to Alexandria is Golf City, opened in 2000 with 90 holes available to play, and more to come. What was once scrub and sand has been transformed by imported

turf—rumored to require 1.2 million gallons of water each day. This is just one of—at last count—eight world-class courses scattered through the country (see p. 381). Each comes with pro shops, caddies, power carts, club houses, health spas, and restaurants. The Mena House Hotel beside the Pyramids has had a course since the 19th century, on which players once rode donkeys between the tees.
A 145 B4

QANATER
Roughly 15 miles (24 km) downriver from Cairo, Qanater is a small town on the Nile at the point at which the river forks into eastern (Damietta) and western (Rosetta) branches. Its main attractions are the Nile barrages, a series of early 19th-century locks, decoratively arched and turreted, spanning both branches of the river, with an area of wooded parkland between. The trip to Qanater is a joy in itself, along the Nile on a ferry, caught from a landing just north of the Ramses Hilton in central Cairo. The journey takes around two hours. Avoid Fridays and public holidays when the boats become uncomfortably overcrowded.
A 145 C4 ∎

Fanning north from Cairo, the Delta is Egypt's bread basket, dotted with historical sights. To the east, the Suez Canal offers the spectacle of ships in the desert, and two interesting canalside towns.

The Delta & Suez

A Coptic monk in distinctive embroidered hood

The Delta & Suez

A GREEN FAN AND A BLUE LINE: TOGETHER THE NILE DELTA AND THE SUEZ Canal represent two of Egypt's greatest riches. The Delta is the triangular swath of fertile land between Cairo and the Mediterranean coast, and a vital source of agricultural wealth; Suez is the preeminent engineering feat of the 19th century, an international waterway whose revenues provide a significant portion of the country's national income.

Most visitors only see the Delta through the windows of a train, speeding through on the way to Alexandria. Scenes of brightly dressed *felaheen* working the lush green fields flash by, and there are quickly snapped images of lumpish, gray water buffalo driving wooden waterwheels, and of feathery date palms bowed under the weight of their fruit. The Delta population centers barely

register; small, provincial places such as Damanhur, Mansura, and Zagazig are hard-working farmers' towns, with little to offer visitors beyond hospitality. But in antiquity the Delta was a battleground and a strategic

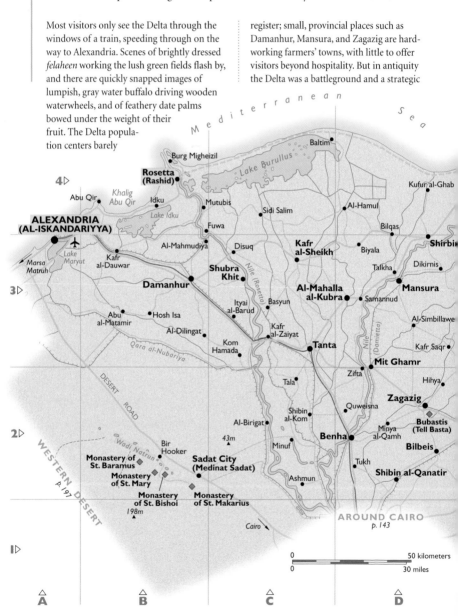

prize for victorious invaders. The Semitic Hyksos, the Libyans, and the Persians engaged the ancient Egyptians here, winning the right to settle, found cities, and reap the harvests. They have left their own riches in the form of the ruins of their civilizations. Archaeologists view the Delta as one of Egypt's richest remaining sites for excavation.

As the Delta approaches the sea, there is a marshy transition zone between land and water, with a chain of salty lakes running parallel to the coast. The need for fresh land has pushed the Egyptians to attempt to reclaim these seacoasts, in much the same way as they are attempting to green the deserts. Historically, habitation in this region of Egypt has been confined to the fertile zones where the two main branches of the Nile empty into the sea. Rosetta (see pp. 170–71) and Damietta, the two

Produce from the Delta includes dates, as well as cotton, corn, rice, and wheat.

estuary towns, flourished while the Nile was a navigable route, but the 19th-century resurgence of Alexandria, along with the arrival of railroads, sentenced the two towns to a gentle decline.

At about the same time, Egypt gained two new ports in Port Said (see pp. 174–75) and Suez, north and south gateways respectively to the Suez Canal. Both suffered badly in the wars with Israel in the second half of the 20th century, in which the canal was a vital strategic goal. From an aesthetic point of view, the town of Suez has never recovered, but Port Said is worth a visit for its harborside architecture. For visitors interested in the canal and ships, a better spot is Ismailia (see p. 176). ■

Area of map detail

Wadi Natrun

EGYPT IS REGARDED AS THE PLACE WHERE CHRISTIAN monasticism began. St. Anthony from Upper Egypt is credited with being the first Christian monk, retreating into the desert some time in the latter part of the third century A.D. Wadi Natrun is not quite that old, but there has been a monastic presence here since the fourth century. A visit today remains an expedition back in time to the roots of the Christian faith.

Wadi Natrun

 164 B2

Bus from Cairo to Bir Hooker, then taxi to monasteries

Wadi Natrun was known to the ancient Egyptians as a source of natron (from which it takes its name), a form of sodium carbonate deposit used in the mummification process (see p. 242). After the advent of Christianity, the wadi (a dried-up river) attracted large numbers of Coptic followers of St. Anthony, who sought not only an ascetic existence but also an escape from Roman persecution. Numbers grew quickly, and in the fifth century the area was said to contain as many as 60 monasteries. Although only four survive, monastic life is enjoying something of a resurgence, attracting plenty of recruits. In all, some 500 monks live in the wadi at the present time.

Despite having chosen a life of seclusion, the monastic communities are exceptionally welcoming to visitors. The wadi is only a one-hour drive from Cairo, just off the Alexandria Desert Road. Buses from Turgoman bus terminal in central Cairo run to a small village called Bir Hooker, where it is possible to rent a taxi for a few hours to make the rounds of the monasteries, along roads that are more potholes than surface.

Most frequently visited of the four is the **Monastery of St. Bishoi** (Deir Anba Bishoi), the official residence of the Coptic Patriarch, Pope Shenouda.

St. Bishoi was a fifth-century hermit who performed the act of kindness of washing the feet of a stranger, who subsequently revealed himself to be Jesus Christ. At the heart of the walled compound is a church built around Bishoi's cell, where he used to tie his hair with a rope hooked to the ceiling, a device to wake him if he should fall asleep during his prayers. A sealed tube, kept at the church, is said to contain the saint's miraculously preserved body. Each year on July 17 the tube is carried in procession around the church, and the bearers are said to clearly feel the weight of a whole body within.

In addition to seclusion, these monasteries had to provide protection from Bedouin bandits. At the Monastery of St. Bishoi, the massive fortified keep, entered by a drawbridge, contained a well, kitchens, church, and storerooms to hold enough provisions for a year. Up on the roof, trapdoors open to small cells that acted as makeshift cemeteries for those who died while the tower was under siege, as it often was during the Middle Ages.

Equally popular with visitors is the **Monastery of St. Mary,** also known as Deir al-Suriani, the Monastery of the Syrians, because it was for centuries occupied by monks from that country. The central church here, dedicated to St. Mary, is famous for its wall paintings and icons, some of which date back to the seventh century. One of the monks takes visitors around the rest of the compound, including a look at a series of ninth-century cells. Apparently some of the monks use these cells to prepare for the life of a hermit; when they are ready, they move to desert cells where they pray in seclusion for six days of the week, joining the rest of the community over the Sabbath.

A little to the north, the **Monastery of St. Baramus** (Deir al-Baramus) contains no fewer than five churches. The **Monastery of St. Makarius** (Deir Abu Makar) is more secluded, lying 12 miles (20 km) to the southeast. Both are less visited than the other two because they do not accept tour groups. Individuals, however, are welcome. ■

The mud-brick building style of the desert monasteries has not changed in six centuries.

Bubastis

Bubastis
 164 D2
Train from Ramses
Station in Cairo to
Zagazig, then walk

BUBASTIS WAS THE LOWER EGYPTIAN CAPITAL DURING A brief period of Libyan rule around the tenth century B.C. Today it is a small archaeological site on the outskirts of the charmingly named town of Zagazig, with a famous temple to Bastet, the elegant cat goddess.

Bastet was originally depicted as a lioness, but later more commonly as a cat.

Known locally as Tell Basta (Hill of Basta), the former city is now no more than a modest, weed-covered mound strewn with huge blocks of smooth, carved granite, and packed with gaping archaeological pits. It enjoyed a long life span, flourishing from the 4th dynasty to the end of Roman rule (circa 2613 B.C. to A.D. 395). The city was renowned for its

temple to Bastet, who was honored with licentious festivals.

The Greek historian Herodotus visited Bubastis in the fifth century B.C. and wrote of hundreds of thousands of pilgrims gathering there for the goddess's annual celebration, described by him as was one of the greatest festivals in Egypt. He described how revelers consumed more wine than during the whole of the rest of the year. Although a few papyrus-bud columns have been reerected, it is impossible to get a sense of any structure today. Instead, most visitors' interest is taken by what is known as the "cat cemetery," which lies 200 yards away on the road to Zagazig town center. This series of underground earthen tombs is extensive enough to wander around. When they were excavated in the mid-20th century, some 400 human mummies, as well as many neatly packaged mummified cats, were found.

Another Bubastis curiosity is a thousand-year-old holy well. Local Coptic Christians claim the Holy Family stopped here when they passed through on the journey to Egypt (see p. 222). Possibly this is why still today the well is considered to have special fertility properties. Women hoping to conceive use clay pots to scoop up the water, pouring it over their heads before smashing the pots against a nearby weathered statue of Bastet.

Zagazig is 50 miles (80 km) from Cairo and easily accessible by bus. From here, you can hire a taxi to visit the nearby site of Tanis. ∎

Tanis

FEW VISITORS EVER MAKE IT TO TANIS, A CAPITAL OF THE Delta region during the Late Period (747–332 B.C.), when the pharaonic age was drawing to a close. Yet it was a major burial site, and yielded one of the most spectacular finds of Egyptology.

The lack of visitors is not so surprising, as Tanis lies far up in the northeast corner of the Delta, 42 miles (70 km) beyond the town of Zagazig. You need a car to reach it; from Cairo allow a day for the trip.

In its heyday, Tanis—known to the ancient Egyptians as Djanet—was a busy commercial city under the rule of pharaohs of the 11th and 12th dynasties. At its center was a large temple dedicated to Amun, surrounded by a number of smaller shrines and temples, all enclosed within a mud-brick wall. All that remains today is a large field with areas of weed-covered paving and a wealth of scattered blocks, column stubs, rubble, and broken statuary. Excavations were carried out as far back as the 1860s by Auguste Mariette (see pp. 80–81), but the important find came in 1939, when

French archaeologist Pierre Montet discovered some intact royal tombs —the only untouched tombs yet found aside from Tutankhamun's. Gold death masks, solid silver coffins, and superb jewelry belonging to 11th dynasty pharaohs were brought to light after 3,000 years.

However, the find was overshadowed by the advent of World War II, and the Tanis treasures have remained largely ignored by visitors to the Egyptian Museum in Cairo (see pp. 70–79), who bypass them en route to the treasures of Tut. That may one day change, as Egypt's antiquities authorities have plans to invest heavily in Tanis. So in the future, the obscure names of its pharaohs—Psusennes, Osorkon, and Sheshonq—might become as well known as those of Tutankhamun and Ramses. ■

A lone guardian walks beside the fallen colossus of Ramses II, brought to Tanis from some other earlier site.

Tanis
🔺 165 E3

Rosetta

IF THE TOWN OF ROSETTA IS KNOWN AT ALL TODAY IT IS only because its name is attached to the famous black stela that provided the key to unlocking many of the mysteries of ancient Egypt. The stone is now held by the British Museum in London, and the small Nile-side town where it was found has become little more than a historical footnote. However, Rosetta (Arabic name Rashid) is actually a very attractive place, and it can't be too long before it is rediscovered and put back on the tourist map.

Fishing contributes heavily to the north Delta economy.

Rosetta
🅜 164 B4

**Rosetta Museum
(Bayt al-Kili)**
✉ Al-Geish St.
☎ 045/921 733
🕐 Closed after 4 p.m.
💲 $$

Rosetta is located where the western branch of the Nile flows into the sea. During the Middle Ages it was Egypt's busiest port and a major player in the trade between Egypt and the Italian city-states. But the town's fortunes have always been inversely linked to those of Alexandria, and when that city experienced a rebirth in the 19th century, it was at the expense of Rosetta.

As you travel from Alexandria today, the road is almost a causeway in parts, with the Mediterranean on one side and reedy lakes on the other, colored by great shoals of small, bright blue and green fishing boats. The lakes feed roadside canals, irrigating groves of palms bowed by the weight of massive clusters of dates. Between them, the boats and the palms constitute a

thumbnail sketch of the local economy.

That Rosetta was once a far wealthier town is evident in its fine old Turkish-era houses, built by wealthy burghers and merchants. There are about 20 of these, all within a few minutes' walk of each other. Dating from the 17th and 18th centuries, and built three or four stories high in a distinctive Delta style of flat bricks painted alternately red and black, the houses represent the finest legacy of domestic architecture in Egypt. Studded with *mashrabiyya*-screen windows (see p. 101), many incorporate an assortment of blocks and columns, scavenged from ancient Delta sites. In their eccentric fashion, the Rosetta houses are like an Eastern version of England's half-timbered buildings.

Restoration of some of the finest residences has been ongoing since the 1970s, and several are now open to the public. **Ramadan House,** just downhill from the square where the local minibuses congregate, has a typical and fascinating interior. Its first floor is given over to stabling and warehousing, the second floor was for the men, and the third floor for women. The uppermost floor, with its terrace areas open to breezes, was used in the hot summer months as sleeping quarters. Both the men's and women's areas have reception rooms adorned with intricate wooden paneling. Partway up the stair between the two is a turntable at foot level that allowed the women to serve the men's food while remaining out of view.

Other houses are scattered on and just off the winding market street running north. The street emerges into a small square, with a grassy park at its center, across which is Bayt al-Kili, former residence of the governor during the town's heyday, and now the **Rosetta Museum.**

Just east is the river, wide and still as it broadens to meet the Mediterranean. Follow it north for 4 miles (6 km) to reach the restored Mamluk **Fort of Qaitbey,** also known as Fort Julien, which is where Napoleon's soldiers found the Rosetta Stone (see box below). ■

Composed of alternate red and black bricks, Rosetta's legacy of fine town houses is unique in Egypt.

The key to ancient Egypt

Arguably the most significant find in Egyptology, the Rosetta Stone was unearthed in 1799 by Napoleon's soldiers while restoring an old fort. An irregularly shaped slab of black basalt, it is inscribed in three scripts: Egyptian hieroglyphics, Egyptian demotic (a cursive script derived from hieroglyphics), and Greek. Napoleon's savants were quick to see that by comparing the demotic and the hieroglyphics with the Greek text, they could crack the previously baffling code of the pharaohs.

Linguists and academics applied themselves to the task, but it was not until 1824 that a Frenchman, Jean-François Champollion, was able to fathom the scripts. His achievement opened up many of the mysteries of ancient Egypt. ■

The Rosetta Stone, now kept and displayed at the British Museum in London

Suez Canal

Almost as startling and magnificent a sight as the Pyramids or temples of Upper Egypt is the vision of a giant oil tanker gliding between the dunes. Mirage or miracle? A miracle is exactly how the Suez Canal was hailed internationally when it first opened, but this verdict failed to recognize that the Egyptians had been digging enormous canals since the time of the pharaohs.

As early as the seventh century B.C., the 26th dynasty pharaoh Nekau II connected the Nile and Red Sea with an east-west canal. It was later renewed by Egypt's early Arab conquerors to tighten the tie between their new Nile territories and the homeland of Arabia. Appropriately, it was the canal-loving Venetians who, in the Middle Ages, first considered slicing north-south through the Isthmus of Suez to connect the Mediterranean and the Red Sea. The project became a pre-occupation of colonialist Europe in the early 19th century, but progress was stalled because of a misguided belief, based on calculations by Napoleon's engineers, that the Mediterranean was 33 feet (10 m) higher than the Red Sea.

A later report set the seas on a level, and the idea of a canal was enthusiastically taken up by a young French vice-consul, Ferdinand de Lesseps (1805–1894). He doggedly pursued his dream for 20 years until, with the succession of Said Pasha, a personal friend, to the throne of Egypt, De Lesseps was finally granted permission to proceed. Ground was broken on April 25, 1859.

Rather than following the shortest route across the isthmus, which is only 75 miles (120 km) at its narrowest, the canal utilized several lakes: Lake Manzala at its northern end, Lake Timsah and the Bitter Lakes farther south. By this route it measures 101 miles (163 km). To begin with, the canal was largely dug by hand, but after five years the Egyptian government refused to continue providing the 20,000 necessary laborers, and work continued with mechanized diggers.

Finally, after almost ten years of excavating, in March 1869 Mediterranean waters flowed into the basins of the Bitter Lakes. On Novem-

Above: A procession of royal yachts makes the first voyage through the canal on November 17, 1869.

ber 17, 1869, the Suez Canal was inaugurated with magnificently flamboyant festivities in the presence of guest-of-honor Empress Eugénie of France, wife of Napoleon III.

Ownership remained largely in French and British hands for the next 86 years. That changed when revolutionary leader Gamal Abdel Nasser nationalized the canal in 1956. Britain and France, in conjunction with Israel, invaded in an ungallant attempt to take it back by force, but had to retreat in the face of international condemnation of their actions.

Deepened and widened three times since it was completed, the canal is one of the world's most heavily used shipping lanes. An average of 60 vessels a day pass through in three convoys, in alternate directions. Shipping tolls bring the Egyptian treasury more than a billion dollars a year, making the canal one of the top five contributors to the economy. ∎

Above: Excavation of the canal took almost ten years, first by hand, then with mechanical aid.

Port Said

PORT SAID WAS FOUNDED IN 1859 AS THE MEDITERRANEAN gateway to the Suez Canal. It was the site of the inaugural celebrations in 1869, dubbed by the press of the time the "party of the century." Before too long the tag was the "wickedest town in the East," as the place became known for smutty postcards and brothels, pandering to the baser tastes of long-distance sea voyagers. A combination of a sobering revolution, devastation during the wars with Israel, and cheap air travel changed all that. These days, Port Said (Bur Said in Arabic) is a little-visited backwater, although with enough pockets of charm to make it a worthwhile day trip from Cairo.

Port Said
🅜 165 F4
Visitor information
✉ Palestine St.
☎ 066/235 289
🕐 Closed Fri.

The town grew out of shallow Lake Manzala, on land reclaimed with sand excavated from the canal. Ground zero was a single outcrop of rock just below water level, on which a landing dock was anchored to receive supply ships. This artificial islet is well buried by 150 years of development, but its site is marked by an empty plinth at the northern end of Palestine Street, on which for a long time stood a larger-than-life statue of Ferdinand de Lesseps, architect of the canal. It was very nearly something much grander. At the time of the canal's construction, French sculptor Frederic Auguste Bartholdi approached Khedive Ismail with the idea of a colossal torch-bearing statue to stand at the mouth of the canal; rejected for Port Said as too expensive, the proposed "Light of Asia" was found a new home where it received a new name—the Statue of Liberty. De Lessep's statue was

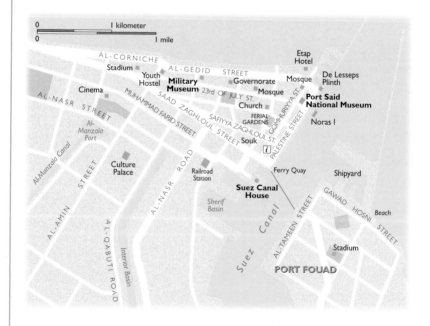

torn down in 1956 during the Suez Crisis, and the plinth has been vacant ever since.

Just south on Palestine Street find the **Port Said National Museum,** set in its own neat garden. Sadly, it has little about either the town or canal and instead concentrates on local prehistory and the pharaonic, Islamic, and Coptic eras. Modern history gets a look in at the **Military Museum,** with relics from the 1956 Suez Crisis, and the 1967 and 1973 wars with Israel; it is a mile west along 23rd of July Street. Close to the National Museum is the mooring place for the *Noras I,* a floating restaurant, which offers daily lunch and dinner canal cruises (see p. 366).

If there is no time for a trip on the *Noras I,* the next best thing is to take a ride on one of the cross-canal ferries shuttling over to the suburb of Port Fouad. From the deck you have a good view of the quayside **Suez Canal House,** the white colonnaded building with three green Byzantine domes. Built in 1869 as the Canal Company Offices, it still plays a part in

controlling the waterway and is off-limits to the public.

One block in from the ferry quay is Port Said's old commercial center, once a mix of Greek and Italian restaurants, French patisseries, Jewish stores, and Egyptian tailors, all of which would flicker into life, no matter what the hour, whenever a big liner docked. Echoes of this cosmopolitan past survive only in a legacy of raffishly elegant buildings with wooden balconies that are more New Orleans than Mediterranean. Look for faded signboards such as that of Simon Arzt, who arrived from New York in the late 19th century to found his fashionable department store, and Woolworth's, now a souvenir emporium.

In recent times Port Said has been blessed with a new lease on life as a free-trade zone. Its retailers are now kept busy by busloads of Egyptians on the hunt for cut-price clothing and electronics. Their main target is the souk, west of main Gomhuriyya Street, a clothes and household goods market occupying a grid of narrow lanes. ■

The white-painted frontage of Suez Canal House addresses the waterway it controls.

Port Said National Museum
- ✉ Palestine St.
- ☎ 066/237 419
- 🕐 Closed Fri.
- 💲 $

Military Museum
- ✉ 23rd of July St.
- ☎ 066/224 657
- 🕐 Closed after 3 p.m. & Fri.
- 💲 $

Incongruous amid the palm trees, the chalet-like house of De Lesseps is now used as a government guest house.

Ismailia

FOUNDED AS THE CENTER OF OPERATIONS DURING THE building of the Suez Canal, Ismailia is now better known as a popular day out for Cairenes, who each summer weekend flock to the beaches around Lake Timsah, just to the south of town.

Ismailia
📖 165 F2
Visitor information
✉ Governorate Building, Al-Togari St.
☎ 064/321 072
🕐 Closed after 3 p.m. & Fri.

Ismailia Museum
✉ Muhammad Ali Quay
☎ 064/322 749
🕐 Closed after 3 p.m. & Fri.
💲 $

The day-trippers tend not to visit the town of Ismailia itself, which offers little in the way of things to see. Nevertheless, if you are looking for a place to spend a few hours away from crowds and traffic, then the old center of Ismailia is an attractive option. Low-rise and leafy, it has an appealingly out-of-time colonial air. It covers a few blocks between the railroad tracks and the small **Sweetwater Canal,** which runs through green parkland beside the lakeshore. Ferdinand de Lesseps, the founder of the Suez Canal, had his chalet-style residence on Muhammad Ali Street across from the park, now used as a government guest house and closed to the public. North of the De Lesseps's house is Sultan Hussein Street, which probably qualifies as the town's main street.

Several blocks farther on, still heading along Muhammad Ali, is the **Ismailia Museum,** designed in pharaonic style. It houses objects from pharaonic and Greco-Roman times, the highlight of which is a beautiful fourth-century A.D. mosaic depicting characters from Greek mythology. A second museum is set to open in town within the next few years, devoted to the history of the Suez Canal. The cornerstone was laid in summer 2000.

To see the Suez Canal, head out of town. Most Egyptian visitors favor the beaches to the south, but these tend to be owned by clubs and hotels, and they charge for access. If you simply wish to see the ships sailing by, it is possible to do so from the main Cairo-Ismailia road, which runs parallel and close to the waterway to the south. ■

Alexandria is the European face of Egypt. Its setting on the Mediterranean provides cool breezes, plenty of good seafood, and a cosmopolitan café culture.

Alexandria

Catch of the day for sale at the fish market

Alexandria

WITH ITS KEY FIGURES OF ALEXANDER THE GREAT AND CLEOPATRA, ITS famed ancient library, and the towering Pharos lighthouse—counted by the ancients as one of the Seven Wonders of the World—the Alexandria of old is a city of legend bordering on myth. For some, the modern-day reality comes as a disappointment: all that history and so little to show. Yet the lack of visible monuments only adds to the mystique.

After staking his claim to the land of the pharaohs in 331 B.C., Alexander the Great decided that Egypt should have a new capital on the Mediterranean, tying his conquest to Europe by sea. Over the next 300 years this spot became the crossroads of trade from Britain to China, growing rich on commerce and in culture. Alexandria's library, part of the great research center of science, philosophy, and the arts known as the Mouseion, reputedly contained the sum total of knowledge available to the ancient world, earning the city the epithet the "most learned place on Earth." And just as New York celebrates its

glories with the Statue of Liberty and Paris with the Eiffel Tower, the ancient Alexandrians erected an enormous beacon, the Pharos, which trumpeted the successes of the city while guiding ships into their busy harbor.

But for all its learning and wealth, ancient Alexandria all but completely vanished. Its great temples and centers of learning were burned to the ground through the intolerance of Christians, while neglect and natural disasters took care of the rest. Earthquakes tipped the royal quarters into the sea and toppled the Pharos. When, after centuries of obscurity, the city experienced a revival in the 19th century, the ruins of antiquity were simply built over. Today, as you walk the streets of Alexandria, the past is quite literally under your feet. Some of the more portable remnants were carried off, like the two obelisks known as Cleopatra's Needles, which now grace Central Park in New York and the Thames Embankment in London.

Nevertheless, for a time Alexandria again

Area of map detail

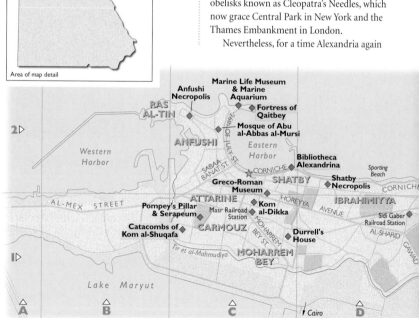

After a long night dragging their nets, fishermen take stock in Alexandria's Eastern Harbor.

burned bright. From the mid-19th to the mid-20th century it was a thriving, cosmopolitan Mediterranean port. "Five races, five languages, a dozen creeds," wrote English author Lawrence Durrell in the *Alexandria Quartet*, a study in decadence that in the four novels further embroidered the myth of the city (see p. 188). Then quite abruptly, this particular vital chapter was brought to a close when Egypt's socialist revolution of 1952 led to the mass exodus of Alexandria's foreign communities and the dismantling of its sophisticated and multicultural society.

Since that time the population has exploded, reaching the five million mark. The Alexandria of the 21st century is a wholly Egyptian and largely modern city of apartment blocks, traffic jams, fast food, and cell phones. However, scratch away the surface and antiquity pokes through. For instance, construction on a highway in 1997 had to halt when workers unearthed a Roman necropolis. More recently, the waters of the Eastern Harbor have begun to give up some of their treasures, too (see pp. 182–83). Alexandria's young population is busy coming to terms with its own history, and perhaps recognizing that their city's past may well be its future. ∎

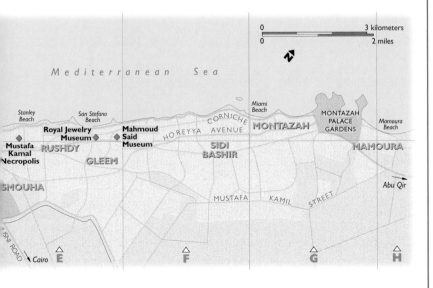

Greco-Roman Museum

Alexandria

⬛ 164 A3

Visitor information

✉ Saad Zaghloul Sq.

☎ 03/485 1556

Greco-Roman Museum

⬛ 178 C2

✉ 5 Al-Mathaf al-
Romani St.

☎ 03/486 5820

🕐 Closed Fri. noon–2 p.m.

💲 $$. Camera $, video
camera $$$

Kom al-Dikka

⬛ 178 C1

✉ Al-Muhafza St.

☎ 03/490 2904

💲 $. Camera $, video
camera $$$

ONE OF THE FEW PLACES IN ALEXANDRIA WHERE IT IS possible to get any sense of the city as it was 2,000 years ago is this small but densely packed museum. Its exhibits illustrate a fascinating period in Egyptian history, when pharaonic traditions and gods were being wedded to those of the occupying Ptolemaic Greeks and the Romans who followed them.

Appropriately enough, on entering and turning left into **Room 6,** the first exhibits you see are three heads of Alexander the Great, the city's founder. Two busts of a shaggy-haired man with a flowing beard of coils represent the god Serapis. In this wholly Alexandrian creation, Egyptian elements in the form of Osiris were combined with the Greek god Dionysus to create a deity that the city's two peoples could worship together. Most visitors' attention, though, is hijacked by the arresting wall-hung mosaics. They portray Queen Berenice II, wife of Ptolemy III, who ruled Egypt from 246 to 221 B.C. Several more mosaics are displayed in other halls, but these are just a fraction of the total (almost a hundred) that the museum possesses and is unable to show for lack of space.

You can meet more legendary figures from Alexandrian and world history elsewhere in the museum; there is a white marble head of an imperious Julius Caesar in **Room 14** and a supposed head of Mark Antony mounted on the wall of the museum's restful central garden. In **Room 24,** Cleopatra, lover of both men, is represented on a silver coin minted during her reign. Either the artist lacked skill, or Plutarch's remarks about the queen's looks (see p. 34–35) are indeed more truthful than the legend of her beguiling beauty.

Room 18 is devoted to terracotta pieces and has the only contemporary representations of the Pharos lighthouse (see p. 187) found in Alexandria. These are in the form of three-tiered lanterns, with the squared base, octagonal middle, and circular top that the Pharos is said to have had. Neighboring cabinets are filled with terra-cotta figurines of women of Alexandria dressed in richly pleated robes and sporting a third-century B.C. fashion spread of hairstyles and hats. According to contemporary accounts, the city's females were famous for the artfulness of their dress, coiffures, and cosmetics. But these dolls were no ornaments; they were made to be placed beside the deceased and were found in the city's necropolises, in the tombs of women who had died young.

Above: Another exhibit for the museum is unearthed at Kom al-Dikka.

Right: A statue of Emperor Septimius Severus

KOM AL-DIKKA

Further evidence of ancient Alexandria lies southwest of the museum. **Kom al-Dikka,** which translates as "mound of rubble," is a large city-center excavation of the ancient Panion, or Park of Pan, a Greco-Roman-era pleasure garden. Pride of the archaeologists is a small but beautifully preserved

Roman theater, the only one found in a city that once boasted 400 (according to the Arab general Amr ibn al-As in A.D. 642). Digging is ongoing, uncovering Roman baths and a villa where floor mosaics include a nine-panel masterpiece depicting a number of colorful birds. ■

The search for Alexander's tomb

When Alexander died in 323 B.C. in Babylon (in modern-day Iraq), his body was carried back to Alexandria, placed in a gold coffin, and buried near the crossroads of the city. In the first century A.D., Emperor Augustus paid his respects at the tomb, as did Emperor Caracalla in A.D. 215. But after that there are no further records of the tomb. Perhaps it was pillaged in the riots that took place in the third and fourth centuries A.D., or maybe Alexander's remains were moved to a secret, safer place. No matter what, the lost tomb constantly inspires new theories and renewed searches for its location. The idea that Alexander may still lie entombed beneath the streets of Alexandria is an enchanting one, and one day—who knows—someone might just sink a spade in the right place. ■

Rediscovering ancient Alexandria

Alexandria's classical glories were long thought lost, with Cleopatra's palace engulfed, the Pharos toppled into the sea, and the Mouseion and library burned down. In the 21st century, all three are reappearing, as two teams of archaeologists make fantastic discoveries on the seabed and a team of architects completes what has already been heralded as one of the seven wonders of the modern world.

Chief of the discoveries is what is being described as the palace of Cleopatra, venue of trysts with Mark Antony and setting for the dramatic finale of the queen's asp-assisted suicide (see p. 35)—that is, if such a thing ever happened. Practically everything we know about Cleopatra is based on literature and myth, and the truth about her remains hidden. Other than coins bearing her image and a few stone busts, all physical evidence of her reign disappeared during the fourth century A.D. when great cataclysms submerged a large part of the North African coast, including Alexandria's royal quarters.

However, a French-Egyptian team headed by explorer Franck Goddio has discovered ancient wooden piles, limestone paving, red granite columns, and a small temple to Isis on a sunken island in the Eastern Harbor. There is no conclusive proof that these are the remains of Cleopatra's palace, but Strabo (64 B.C.–A.D. 23), a Greek geographer visiting Alexandria about 27 B.C. (three years after the death of the queen), described the royal quarters as being on a small harbor island, known as Antirhodos. Anecdotal this evidence may be, but it has captured the world's imagination, particularly when in October 1998 a beautiful sphinx and statue of a priest of Osiris, unseen for one-and-a-half millennia, were raised out of the water before the assembled cameras of the world's media. Following the viewing and photo-op, the pieces were returned to the seabed until it is decided what to do with them.

Meanwhile, on the other side of the harbor, in the shadow of the Fortress of Qaitbey, another French-Egyptian team, led by archaeologist Jean Yves Empereur, has been diving an extensive field of over 2,000 large stone blocks lying 25 feet (8 m) below the water's surface. In all probability, these are the remains of the legendary Pharos lighthouse, shattered by its fall into the sea (see p. 187). The team has also found columns, fragments of obelisks, and a colossal statue in four parts which, reassembled, stands 41 feet (12.5 m) high. Empereur believes that the colossus, representing a Ptolemaic pharaoh, once stood at the foot of the lighthouse.

Feasibility studies are now being pursued for an underwater archaeological park

Above: The torso and upper legs of a
Ptolemaic pharaoh are raised from
Alexandria's Eastern Harbor.
Right: A diver carries out an underwater
survey of a capital that toppled into the sea
in ancient times.

incorporating the finds of both the Goddio
and the Empereur explorations, where visitors
would view objects in situ, either from
Plexiglas tunnels beneath the sea, by diving,
or from glass-bottom boats.

Complementing all the activity beneath
the waves, on a seafront site overlooking the
harbor, is a different sort of revival of the past:
a massively ambitious and architecturally
exciting new library and study complex, a
replacement for the lost Mouseion of old
(see p. 192). ■

Jackal-headed
figures of Anubis,
god of death,
guard the main
tomb.

Catacombs of
Kom al-Shuqafa

ALEXANDRIA IS RIDDLED WITH UNDERGROUND PASSAGES
and chambers belonging to catacombs, cisterns, and who knows
what else. In the early years of the 20th century, the disappearance
of a donkey into a hole that suddenly opened up in the ground
resulted in the chance discovery of an elaborate and unique Roman
burial complex.

**Catacombs of
Kom al-Shuqafa**

🅰 178 C1

✉ Al-Nasseriyya St.

☎ 03/486 5800

🕐 Closed after 4 p.m.

$ $$. Camera $, video
camera $$$

🚇 Karmouz

A rackety tram ride away from the
railroad station square, Kom al-
Shuqafa appears as a baked-earth
hillock surrounded by shabby con-
crete mid-rises in one of the poorer
quarters of the modern city. What
lies beneath, however, is a different
world altogether.

A descending stair spirals
around a central shaft down which
the bodies of the dead would have
been lowered (and down which the
unfortunate donkey plummeted).
It leads to three levels of tombs,
hollowed out of solid rock in the
second century A.D., probably as a
crypt for a wealthy family of nobles.
On the upper level is a rotunda
with a central well down to the

flooded and inaccessible chambers
of the lowermost level. Off to the
left is the *triclinium,* the banqueting
hall for funeral feasts. It is from the
discarded broken remains of plates
and dishes, perhaps from such
feasts, that the locale of the
catacombs gets its arabic name
"mound of potsherds."

Another stair descends to the
central burial chamber, the
showpiece of the complex, filled
with a bizarre confusion of the
iconography of death. On either
side of the doorway are bearded
Greco-Roman serpents, which also
wear the pharaonic double crown
of Egypt. Above the door is the
snake-haired Medusa of Greek

mythology, meant to turn would-be tomb robbers to stone. Inside the cramped tomb chamber is a figure of the usually fearsome jackal-headed god Anubis—with a pudgy body squeezed into the uniform of a Roman legionary. It's a clumsy mix and one found nowhere else in Egypt, but it does have the intended effect of looking fantastically funereal. If ever Hollywood finds itself short of a set for the next *Mummy* movie, this would be the place to come.

In keeping with the idea of all show and no sense, the lids of the chamber's three sarcophagi were never meant to open; instead the bodies were put in place from a passageway behind. Later, this passage was enlarged to create galleries lined with pigeonhole spaces, known as loculi, for several hundred more burials.

POMPEY'S PILLAR & SERAPEUM

Back in the realm of the living, there is another worthwhile site a short walk from the catacombs, helpfully indicated by the distinctive landmark of **Pompey's Pillar.** This 100-foot (30 m) red Aswan granite column was mistakenly thought by the Crusaders to mark the burial site of Julius Caesar's rival, the Roman general Pompey, murdered in Egypt in 48 B.C. (see p. 34). In fact, it was erected in honor of Emperor Diocletian about A.D. 300, and there is an inscription to that effect part way up the shaft. However, the pillar is something of a red herring, because the far more significant ruins are those to be found around it.

What is now an archaeological park, with neatly kept shrubbery surrounding a somewhat pock-marked rocky hill, is all that remains of Alexandria's acropolis, the **Serapeum.** Dedicated to the

city's homemade god, Serapis (see p. 180), this had as its centerpiece a vast temple that, according to contemporary accounts, was reached by one hundred steps and had an exterior made of marble and interior walls plated with precious metals. A colossal statue of Serapis, also made from precious metals, inspired awe in the worshipers within. But pagan worship was anathema to the growing Christian movement and, in A.D. 391, a mob led by the patriarch Theophilus reduced the Serapeum to ruins.

During the past century, archaeologists have rediscovered some of the Serapeum's treasures, such as an impressive life-size black basalt Apis bull (see p. 151) and a gold plaque commemorating the foundation of the Serapeum etched in both Greek and hieroglyphics; these are displayed at the Greco-Roman Museum (see pp. 180–81). Visitors to the site have to be content with broken column shafts, some Ptolemaic sphinxes, and several pharaonic oddments moved up here from ancient Heliopolis. And, of course, Pompey's Pillar. ∎

The top of Pompey's Pillar was a daring picnic spot for early travelers, who climbed up on rope ladders.

Pompey's Pillar & Serapeum
🄰 178 C1
✉ Amoud al-Sawari St.
☎ 03/486 5800 ext. 430
🕐 Closed after 4 p.m.
💲 $
🚏 Karmouz

Fortress of Qaitbey

THIS NEAT LITTLE FORTRESS LOOKS AS THOUGH IT WAS built for toy soldiers of days gone by. It has the most perfect location too, cast out on a spindly arm far into the Eastern Harbor. Long devoid of any military function, the place now serves as a small naval museum. But, this being Alexandria, it is what's *not* there that really excites, for the fortress occupies the site of the Pharos lighthouse, one of the ancient Seven Wonders of the World.

After enduring for more than 1,600 years, the lighthouse was rubble by the 14th century (see box opposite). In 1480 Mamluk sultan Qaitbey (*R.*1468–1498) made good use of the still solid foundations and fallen masonry to build a fortress as defense against the Turks, who were threatening Egypt. A prolific builder, Qaitbey has numerous monuments to his name in Cairo, including his mosque (depicted on the Egyptian one-pound note), but this is his only legacy to Alexandria. However, its current form is not as designed by the sultan; during a nationalist uprising in 1882, the fortress was targeted by a British naval bombardment, following which it was extensively rebuilt.

Today, the fortress is approached via a causeway with a sea wall that serves as a popular spot for anglers. A gatehouse provides access to the outer court, which has some passages and rooms to explore, but the main interest is the **keep.**

As you enter, you pass through a doorway whose lintel and door-posts are formed from large granite slabs, in all likelihood salvaged pieces of the Pharos. Inside, three floors contain a variety of maritime artifacts and displays, including bits and pieces recovered from Napoleon's fleet, sunk off Alexandria by Admiral Horatio Nelson in 1798 (see p. 40). Part of the keep was built as a mosque, and for four centuries a minaret towered high above the ramparts until it was blown away by the British navy. The oldest surviving mosque in Alexandria, it is no longer used for worship. Its structure includes five monolithic, red-granite columns that are probably more survivors from the Pharos.

Even if you are not interested in the fortress and its contents, it's still worth a walk down here for the views of central Alexandria seen across the Eastern Harbor.

On the peninsula leading to the fortress there is a **Marine Life Museum,** with kitschy dioramas and a few shabby, long-dead specimens of sea life. Across the street is the **Marine Aquarium,** where the fish, sea turtles, and Nile crocodiles, housed in small and dirty glass tanks, are barely more alive. ■

Left: Qaitbey's toytown castle was once flattened by Britain's Admiral Horatio Nelson.

Fortress of
Qaitbey
🗺 178 C2
✉ Eastern Harbor
☎ 03/480 9144
🕐 Closed after 4 p.m.
💲 $. Extra fee ($) for
    Naval Museum

Pharos lighthouse

Inaugurated in 279 B.C. during the reign of Ptolemy II (R.285-247 B.C.), the Pharos was a massive stone beacon built to aid ships navigating the featureless coastline of Mediterranean Egypt. More than that, it was the physical embodiment of the learning of Alexandria's Mouseion and a statement of the city's great wealth. Images of the Pharos appear in Roman mosaics in Libya, on a vase dug up in Afghanistan, and even in St. Mark's Basilica in Venice. From these, historians describe a structure about 500 feet (150 m) high, with a square lower section set with rows of small windows, an octagonal middle section, and a conical top.

It is thought that the tower became a functioning lighthouse in the first century A.D., but its workings remain a mystery. One idea that sounds plausible is that there was an oil-fed flame with sheets of polished bronze as reflectors, but a classical account describes a "transparent stone" through which ships invisible to the naked eye could be seen; did the ancient Alexandrians discover the lens? However the light beam was achieved, it was lost to the world about A.D. 700 when the lantern top fell. More natural disasters further reduced the tower until, in 1303, an earthquake shook the eastern Mediterranean and the Pharos was destroyed. ■

Now a spot for fishermen and courting couples, the tower that stood here was a wonder of the ancient world.

Marine Life Museum & Marine Aquarium
- 178 C2
- Eastern Harbor
- 03/480 1553
- Closed after 2:30 p.m.
- $

A walk through the Capital of Memory

It was the English novelist Lawrence Durrell (1912–1990), author of the *Alexandria Quartet*, who called the city "the capital of memory." He and his characters inhabited an Alexandria heavily shaded by memories of its classical past. Through the success of the *Quartet* a whole new layer of myth has been added. The ghosts of Alexander and the Ptolemies have been joined by the spirits of Durrell's Justine, Balthazar, Mountolive, and Cleo—ciphers for a cosmopolitan city now largely gone except for a handful of melancholic landmarks visited on this walk.

Durrell's book is almost an epitaph for the city of Alexandria. By the time the *Quartet* was published (the final volume came out in 1960), the city of which he wrote was gone. Cosmopolitan Alexandria was at its most boisterous in the 1920s and '30s. The city lived in a Babel of languages: It shopped in Greek, perused newspapers in French, skirted bureaucracy in English. Alexandrians, wrote historian Robert Ilbert, could have several nationalities,

If you cannot afford a room at the Cecil, at least visit for a drink at Monty's Bar, named for Britain's General Montgomery.

and they used them like credit cards. Foremost surviving symbol of this free-spirited age is the **Cecil Hotel** ❶ (*Saad Zaghloul Sq., see p. 366*), which is a good place to begin a walk. Built in 1929 in a Moorish style, it was at the center of the city's dinner-and-dance scene, when guests included the likes of writers Somerset Maugham and Noel Coward, and Durrell made it a haunt of the enigmatic Justine, heroine of the book of the same name.

At the center of grassy Saad Zaghloul Square in front of the hotel is a statue of Saad Zaghloul (1860–1927), a nationalist leader who did much to pave the way for eventual Egyptian self-rule. At the southeast corner of the square is the city's visitor information office (*Saad Zaghloul Sq., tel 03/485 1556*). At its northeast corner, Saad Zaghloul Square links with one of the hubs of the city, **Ramla Square** ❷. From here trams run west to the Fortress of Qaitbey (see pp. 186–87) and east toward—though not as far as—Montazah (see p. 195). Around the tram station are several grand old patisseries, of which a favorite is the Trianon. Its dining hall is decorated with

---

- ⓜ See area map pages 178–79
- ▶ Saad Zaghloul Square
- ⟷ 2 miles (3 km)
- ⏱ 4 hours
- ▶ Tahrir Square

NOT TO BE MISSED
- Cecil Hotel foyer
- Lemon tea and pastries at Pastroudi's
- The antique stores of Attarine

gorgeous Oriental murals, while the salon is a classy place for a Continental breakfast. Outside the Trianon's large picture windows, where the tram station is now, for almost two millennia stood two great obelisks. They were carved during the reign of Tuthmose III and originally adorned ancient Heliopolis. In the first century B.C. they were removed to Alexandria by Augustus Caesar. Nineteenth-century travelers dubbed them "Cleopatra's Needles." In the 1870s the British took one (it now stands beside the Thames in London), and then the Americans took the other; you can see it now in New York's Central Park.

On leaving the Trianon, bear right, then right again, so that you are now heading back west along Saad Zaghloul Street. Opposite the Brazilian Coffee Store, turn left on narrow An-Nabi Daniel Street, lined with small stores. Just

a few paces along is a large iron gate, almost rusted shut, which is a sad commentary on the fate of the city's **Great Synagogue ❸**. Jews have been living in Alexandria continuously since it was founded by Alexander the Great in the fourth century B.C. After their expulsion from Jerusalem in the second century A.D., Alexandria became for a time the world center of Judaism. At its peak the community numbered about 40,000, but tragically, today its numbers are dwindling due to anti-Jewish sentiment over the founding of Israel. There is a side entrance, guarded by soldiers, but the synagogue is rarely open.

Take the next left on Sultan Hussein Street and then cross to head south down little Sharm al-Sheikh Street, entering No. 4. A creaky, sparsely furnished apartment on the second floor is preserved as the **Constantine**

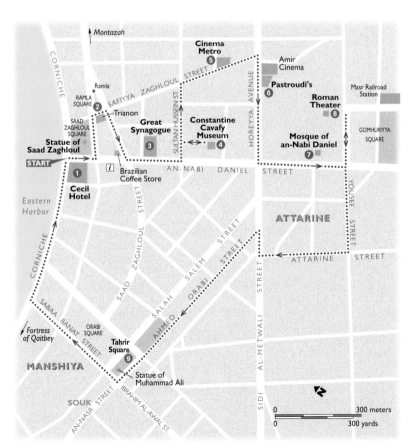

Cavafy Museum ❹ *(4 Sharm al-Sheikh St.).* Cavafy (1863–1933) was a Greek poet, whose work, despite being widely translated, is too little known outside the Mediterranean world, though his poem, *Ithaca,* was read at the funeral of Jacqueline Kennedy Onasis in 1994. Alexandria, the city in which he lived all but a few of his 70 years, was his muse. In turn, it was

Service is not what it was in Alexandria's heyday, but Pastroudi's still offers a fine slice of bohemian history.

Cavafy's verse that provided inspiration for Durrell, who immortalizes Cavafy throughout his *Quartet* stories as the "poet of the city."

Return to Sultan Hussein Street and walk to Safiyya Zaghloul Street, where you should turn right. Ahead is the **Cinema Metro** ❺ *(26 Safiyya Zaghloul St., tel 03/487 0432),* inaugurated in 1950 by MGM and still splendidly maintained, with colored marble floors, mahogany panels, and stylish geometric detailing. Beyond the Metro turn right on Horeyya Avenue, where past the Amir movie theater—with a great art deco foyer—is **Pastroudi's** ❻ *(39 Horeyya Ave., tel 03/392 9609),* another Greek patisserie. Founded in 1923, it is a haunt of Durrell's characters. Still one of the city's major thoroughfares, Horeyya Avenue is the modern incarnation of one of

the two main streets originally laid out by Alexander. At that time it was known as the Canopic Way and stretched between the eastern Gate of the Sun and the Gate of the Moon. A fifth-century bishop described how a row of columns went from one end of it to the other.

After a few minutes of walking you reach a busy intersection, where you turn left. This puts you on **An-Nabi Daniel Street,** named for a local saint, and host each day to booksellers who display their well-thumbed wares on sheets on the sidewalk. Partway along is the **Mosque of an-Nabi Daniel** ❼, which over the years has been a favorite site for hunters of Alexander's tomb (see box p. 181). Some people are convinced that it lies beneath the foundations, but the religious authorities will not allow any digging. Serious archaeologists dismiss this as a potential site, preferring a set of cemeteries to the east of the city center as a more likely location.

An-Nabi Daniel exits onto Gomuriyya Square, recently spruced up as part of a campaign to reverse the decline in the appearance of the city. After decades of neglect, wonders are now being achieved with cans of paint and brooms. If you haven't already visited the **Roman Theater** ❽ (see p. 181), it is to the left behind the high wall; otherwise bear right down Yousef Street for two blocks then right again on **Attarine Street,** the center of Alexandria's antiques trade. It is possible to spend hours rummaging through the stores in this warren of alleys, all filled with offcasts from the city's ornamented past.

At the far end of Attarine Street, turn right, then left to get on Ahmed Orabi Street, which you should follow to **Tahrir Square** ❾. Muhammad Ali (see pp. 40–41), whose equestrian statue rides high above the traffic, planned the square as the heart of his new Alexandria in 1830. It remains a grand space, although the vital institutions that once gave it life, such as the Bourse and law courts, are no longer present. Instead, it is better known now as the starting point for the city's main souq, or market, which stretches from here west. To find your way back to the Cecil, head for the sea and stroll back along the **Corniche.** ∎

Right: Skirting the Eastern Harbor, the Corniche makes for prime promenading.

Bibliotheca Alexandrina

Chief architect Christoph Kappeler poses outside his striking new Alexandrian library.

A STRIKING PIECE OF 21ST-CENTURY ARCHITECTURE THAT is pure high-tech while simultaneously evoking the glory of the ancient Ptolemaic capital, the new Bibliotheca Alexandrina is the largest and most advanced library in the Arab world, and has helped put the city back on the map.

Bibliotheca Alexandrina
- 178 C2
- Al-Silsila, Shatby
- Due to open in 2002

The library has an impressive precedent. The original Great Library, founded in the early third century B.C., shortly after the city itself, was perhaps Alexandria's finest achievement. It held as many as half a million texts, and legend has it that every vessel entering the city's harbor had to hand over any manuscripts for copying. The library was part of a larger institution known as the Mouseion, or House of the Muses, forerunner of universities everywhere. Here in Alexandria scholars first accurately measured the circumference of the Earth, mapped the stars and planets, and dissected bodies to discover the central nervous system. No one knows how the Great Library was destroyed, but when it disappeared much of this knowledge was lost.

This ancient wealth of learning is evoked on the new library's exterior walls, which are carved with giant letters, pictograms, hieroglyphs, and symbols from every known alphabet. The building itself, on the Corniche, close to the eastern promontory of Silsila, takes the form of a huge disk, tilted into the ground. Its near-circular roof is a mesh of interlocking glass panels that looks like an integrated circuit.

Set in the entrance foyer floor are mosaics uncovered on site while digging the library's foundations; the doleful-eyed dog sitting beside an overturned jug has an almost contemporary look, yet is more than two millennia old. A viewing gallery allows you to appreciate the reading hall, which has terraces cascading down ten levels. ∎

Royal Jewelry Museum

JEWELRY IS LESS THAN HALF THE STORY IN THIS SMALL BUT absorbing museum, which houses a glitzy collection of personal heirlooms and valuables formerly belonging to the family of Farouk, the last king of Egypt. Popular and well-liked when he took the throne, Farouk quickly became a byword for greed and excess.

Examples of the last king's lavish lifestyle provide glittering displays in the jewelry museum.

The king was a notorious womanizer and gambler. It was said that when he crashed parties, hostesses rushed to hide their daughters. In 1951, on one night of his 13-week honeymoon with his second wife, Farouk blew a record $150,000 in a baccarat game. A year later the hedonism ended: Egypt's rulers were unseated by the coup of 1952. Farouk was deposed, the royals were stripped of their properties, and most then departed for exile. Sequestered villas and palaces found alternative uses, serving as everything from presidential residences to primary schools.

Fortunately, the Fatma al-Zahraa Palace, built by French and Italian architects in 1923 for the family of Farida, Farouk's first queen, has survived largely unscathed. A modestly sized mansion set on beautifully kept grounds, the place has kept much of its wildly eclectic original decor, and this, rather than anything in the display cabinets, is the attraction.

One corridor is lined with a series of floor-to-ceiling painted-glass windows depicting a bright parade of waltzing courtesans. Ceilings are crowded with sickly pink cherubs frolicking on cottony clouds. A "Greek" room has stylized mock-classical friezes and stenciled frescoes. Best of all in this feast of gaudy taste is the trio of bathrooms, each with tiled scenes decorating the walls: in one a farmyard, in another fishing boats, and in the third a painted-glass beach scene.

Trinkets and follies make up most of the museum's collection. High points—or lows, depending on your humor—include a silver gardening trowel with ivory handle, a silver-plated shaving set, and—most impractical of all—an amber mouthpiece for a water pipe set with 204 diamonds. Considering this gratuitous squandering of Egypt's wealth (and at this time just 2 percent of the population owned more than 50 percent of the land), it is difficult to feel anything but empathy with the revolutionary leaders who kicked the royals out of their silk-sheeted beds.

To find the museum, alight from the tram at the Qasr al-Safa stop, beside the Faculty of Fine Arts, and look for the big white villa surrounded by a high wall. ∎

Royal Jewelry Museum

- 🅰 179 E2
- ✉ 27 Ahmed Yehiya Pasha St., Gleem
- ☎ 03/586 8348
- 🕐 Closed Fri. during noon prayers
- 💲 $$. Camera $, video camera $$$
- 🚃 Tram No. 2 from Ramla Sq.

Mahmoud Said Museum

**Mahmoud Said
Museum**

▣ 179 E2

✉ 6 Mohammed Said
Pasha St., Gianaclis

☏ 03/582 1688

⏱ Closed Mon.

🚊 Tram No. 2 from
Ramla Sq.

**A self-portrait of
Mahmoud Said.
His work is now
displayed in the
villa where he
once lived.**

A PIONEER OF EGYPTIAN MODERN ART, MAHMOUD SAID
was honored in 2000 by the opening of a museum of his works in
the eastern suburb of Gianaclis. The museum's setting, in a beautiful
Italianate villa in which Mahmoud once lived, is also worth seeing.

Said (1897–1964) was born into an
aristocratic family, the son of a former prime minister, and trained in
law. He painted only as a sideline
while pursuing a career in law that
culminated in appointment as a
judge. Nevertheless, he is arguably
the finest painter produced by
Egypt in modern times. In tune
with the renaissance of the 1920s
and '30s, he and other artists strove
to forge an Egyptian artistic identity by depicting scenes of rural life
and by drawing on motifs and
styles from the pharaonic and
Greco-Roman traditions. This is
seen most clearly in some of Said's
soulful self-portraits, which resemble nothing so much as the famed
Fayoum Portraits (see p. 157).

However, along with absorbing
his country's heritage, Said was also
taken with European and American
influences. There is a canvas called
"At the Ballroom" that is pure jazz
age. Best of all are the portraits in
the nudes room—which, in a sad
indictment of the current social climate, museum attendants usher
visitors past. Not lewd or lecherous,
these paintings are of honey-toned,
earthy women depicted against
richly colored landscapes. They are
wonderful pieces of work that
deserve to be far better known—as
it is, they are something of a
neglected national treasure.

Also of interest is a cartoonish
panorama of the opening of the
Suez Canal (see pp. 172–73), with
Khedive Ismail and his distinguished guest, Empress Eugénie.

The restored building has been
planned as an open university to
celebrate Egypt's contribution to
modern art. In addition to 54
paintings by Said, 115 works by the
Waneili brothers are displayed and
there are more than a hundred
exhibits in the accompanying
Modern Egyptian Art Museum.

To find the museum, take the No.
2 tram from Ramla Square to the
Gianclis stop, then walk on along the
tracks and take the first right. ■

Montazah Palace Gardens

TRADITIONALLY, ALEXANDRIA HAS ALWAYS BEEN THE place that Cairo escaped to during the punishingly hot summer months. Vacation apartments line the seafront, blooming into life each July and August. Egypt's rulers valued the cooling sea breezes too, and at the far eastern end of the Corniche, at the point where the city stops 11 miles (18 km) east of the center, Khedive Abbas Hilmy II (R.1892–1914) built Montazah as a royal summer residence.

Montazah is not so exclusive since the abolition of the monarchy, and for a small fee you can go into the grounds. Within the walls are the khedive's former residences and extensive, well-tended gardens, heavily planted with pines and palms and with even the odd flower bed. There's an attractive sandy cove (the beach is private) with a bridge running out to a small island. It is probably the most appealing spot in all Alexandria for walking, and on Fridays and public holidays the place is packed with picnicking locals.

Abbas Hilmy's palace, sited on a bluff overlooking the sea, is vaguely Moorish in style, with a definite Florentine twist—particularly in the tower, which is a direct steal from Florence's Palazzo Vecchio. During World War I the palace was loaned to the British for use as a Red Cross hospital, and for a time one of the orderlies was English novelist E.M. Forster. Returned to the royals, the palace was seized by the state after the revolution and now serves as a presidential retreat.

A few minutes' walk away is a second royal residence. Known as the **Salamlek,** it was built in an Austrian style as a hunting lodge and has recently opened as a luxury hotel (see p. 366). One of its two restaurants, Al-Farouk, once served as the study of the king of the same name, and it still has the original floors and ceilings. ∎

Montazah Palace, built for royalty, now serves as the Egyptian president's summer retreat.

Montazah Palace Gardens

- 179 G2
- Montazah St.
- 03/547 7152 or 03/547 7153
- Open daily 9 a.m.–sunset
- $

More places to visit in Alexandria

ABU QIR

East of Alexandria proper is Abu Qir, a small coastal settlement notable for the the naval battle fought just offshore in 1798. During what is known as the Battle of the Nile, Britain's Admiral Nelson surprised and destroyed Napoleon's French fleet at anchor in the bay. In 1994, Napoleon's sunken flagship *L'Orient* was discovered partially buried on the seafloor by divers. More recently, the bay at Abu Qir has proved a site for further spectacular finds, notably the three ancient cities of Canopus, Herakleion, and Menouthis, thriving cult centers in Greco-Roman times that subsequently vanished, perhaps drowned by an earthquake or tidal wave. Alexandrians flock here on weekends for seafood. The easiest way to get to Abu Qir is by minibus from the square in front of the main train station.

⚔ 179 H1

The turret room in which Lawrence Durrell wrote while living in Alexandria

ANFUSHI

The district of Anfushi, the narrow spit of land between the city's two harbors, is the one part of Alexandria that has a wholly Eastern feel. It developed during the Ottoman Turkish period, as the population gradually abandoned the ruins of the Greco-Roman city that lay to the south. It remains a warren of narrow alleys with listing buildings and plenty of time-worn, small neighborhood mosques. At the heart of the quarter is the modern but majestic **Mosque of Abu al-Abbas al-Mursi** (built in the 1930s), which occupies the site of a much earlier mosque founded by North African immigrants in honor of a venerated 13th-century Andalusian saint. The saint's body lies in a tomb beneath one of the soaring domes. On feast days and during Ramadan, the piazza beside the mosque is the focus of festivities, and the atmosphere is that of a fairground.

⚔ 178 C2   ✉ 26th of July St., Anfushi ☎ 03/480 1251   🕑 Closed Fri. during noon prayers

DURRELL'S HOUSE

Fans of Lawrence Durrell can seek out his Alexandrian residence at 19 Maamoun Street in the Moharrem Bay district, southeast of the train station. While occupying the turret rooms of this grand villa for two and a half years in the early 1940s, he wrote poetry and his short novel *Prospero's Cell*. Sadly, the house has been derelict for some years and is under threat of demolition to make way for yet another modern high-rise.

⚔ 178 C1

NECROPOLISES

A short walk northwest of the Mosque of Abu al-Abbas al-Mursi in Anfushi (see above) is the **Anfushi Necropolis** (*Map 178 C2, Ras al-Tin St., Ras al-Tin*), a complex of five tombs dating back to the third century B.C. A staircase cut into the limestone descends to a sunken open-air court, off which are the burial chambers. The walls are painted to resemble tiling, and there are faded scenes of Egyptian gods and the underworld. Similar tomb complexes have been excavated in the eastern suburbs, notably the **Shatby Necropolis** (*Map 178 D2, Port Said St., Shatby*). The terra-cotta "death dolls" displayed at the Greco-Roman Museum (see p. 181) were found here. At the **Mustafa Kamel Necropolis** (*Map 178 E2, Moaskar al-Romani St., Rushdy*), small sphinxes guard tombs that are otherwise wholly Greek in character. ■

V ast sand seas cover almost all of western Egypt, but travelers can follow a route that links four lush areas, or hug the north coast before striking south to discover the remote idyll of Siwa.

Western Desert

The preferred mode of transport in the oases

Egypt's pharaonic antiquities are overrun, but the vastness of the Western Desert remains well off the beaten track.

Western Desert

THE WESTERN DESERT COVERS MORE THAN TWO-THIRDS OF THE TERRITORY of Egypt. It starts at the banks of the Nile and stretches west into Libya; to the south it is bordered by Sudan, while to the north it is halted by the Mediterranean. It is a vast world of beauty, solitude, and utter silence, one that still has yet to be fully explored.

Although it appears desolate, the desert is not short of water. Rain is infrequent, but water is trapped in subterranean chambers, creating springs that support a scattering of oases dotted across the immense, empty expanse like a lonely constellation. Four—Bahariyya, Farafra, Dakhla, and Kharga—form a loop, connected by asphalt road to Cairo in the north and Luxor in the south. For the adventurous, a trip through the oases offers a chance of true discovery in a region still very little known even to the Egyptians themselves.

The oases have surprisingly long and rich histories. They were occupied in ancient times and were known to Herodotus, who called them the Islands of the Blest. During the Roman era they were thriving trade hubs on routes to the Libyan provinces. As a result, the Western Desert is now seen as Egypt's final archaeological frontier. Over just the last

couple of decades, hundreds of significant sites have been discovered, including the Valley of the Mummies (see p. 207), which brought camera crews from all over the world to a tiny village that, until recent years, had never even seen a television set.

High-profile finds like the mummies are attracting more and more travelers to the Western Desert, but there is one oasis that has long been a draw—Siwa. A place of legendary beauty, it also gains mystique through its relative inaccessibility. Lying way out of the oases loop, up in the northwest corner near the Libyan border, even today it requires tenacity to make the uncomfortable journey. The only way is via the northern coast, sticking to the Mediterranean as far as Marsa Matruh, then striking south into the desert. Alexander the Great took this very same route in 331 B.C., probably only too aware that some

200 years earlier, in 524 B.C., the Persian general Cambyses had set out for Siwa from the south at the head of an army of 50,000 men, none of whom was ever to be seen again: All were lost to the desert. ■

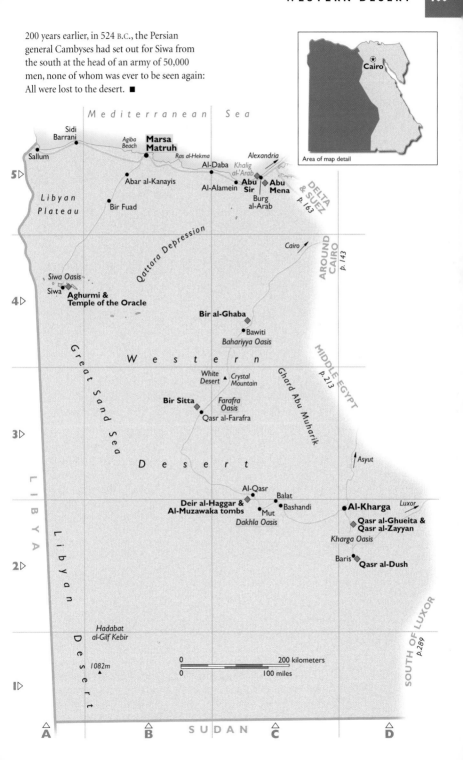

Area of map detail

Cairo

Mediterranean   Sea

Sidi Barrani
Sallum
Agiba Beach
Marsa Matruh
Ras al-Hekma
Alexandria
Al-Daba
Khalig al-'Arab
Abar al-Kanayis
Al-Alamein
Abu Sir
Abu Mena
Burg al-Arab
Bir Fuad

Libyan Plateau

DELTA & SUEZ p.163

AROUND CAIRO p.143

Cairo

Qattara Depression

Siwa Oasis
Siwa
Aghurmi & Temple of the Oracle

Bir al-Ghaba
• Bawiti
Bahariyya Oasis

Western

MIDDLE EGYPT p.213

White Desert   ▲ *Crystal Mountain*

Bir Sitta
Farafra Oasis
Qasr al-Farafra

Great Sand Sea

Desert

↑ *Asyut*

Al-Qasr
Balat
Deir al-Haggar & Al-Muzawaka tombs
•Bashandi
Mut
Dakhla Oasis

•**Al-Kharga**   *Luxor*
Qasr al-Ghueita & Qasr al-Zayyan
Kharga Oasis

Baris•
Qasr al-Dush

L I B Y A

Libyan

Desert

SOUTH OF LUXOR p.289

Hadabat al-Gilf Kebir

▲ *1082m*

0   200 kilometers
0   100 miles

5▷
4▷
3▷
2▷
I▷

△A   △B   S U D A N   △C   △D

Mediterranean Coast

Foreign visitors flock to the beaches of Sinai and the Red Sea coast, but the Mediterranean is where Egyptians holiday.

THROUGHOUT HISTORY THE EGYPTIANS HAVE LARGELY shunned their northern coast. Far removed from the life-sustaining Nile Valley, it involved too many days' travel across inhospitable desert. Instead, it has served as a lonely highway for traders and as a route for invading armies, from the Libyans in ancient times to Italians and Germans in World War II.

That has all changed. As Egypt's population has boomed in the last decades and acquired cars and surplus cash, developers have pounced on the long-uninhabited coastline. From the outskirts of Alexandria all the way west to Al-Alamein, the Mediterranean beaches have been barricaded off with an unbroken wall of vacation villages. Executed in a mishmash of architectural styles from neo-Moorish to neo-Disney, each village has a monumental roadside gateway, the modern-day equivalent of the pharaonic pylon.

There is a real pylon at **Abu Sir,** at Kilometer 47 on the coastal highway, part of the substantial remains of a Ptolemaic temple

dedicated to Osiris. Beside it is a small, white stone tower, with a square base, octagonal midsection, and circular (partially collapsed) top story—a miniature version of its big brother, the Pharos (see p. 187). It was part of an ancient chain of lighthouses strung along this coast.

The tower played a role in a curious episode in American history, involving the first U.S. foreign intervention by land. In 1805, Gen. William Eaton (1764–1811), a U.S. Army officer and adventurer, led an expedition across the Western Desert to oust the government of Tripoli (present-day Libya) and put a halt to piracy against American ships in the Mediterranean. Eaton hoped to

reinstate the exiled Pasha Hamet Karamanli, and a friendship treaty between the two men was signed in the Abu Sir tower.

Just past the tower, a road turns off south leading through the village of Burg al-Arab (Arab's Tower, the local name for the lighthouse) to the archaeological site of **Abu Mena.** One of Egypt's most revered Christian saints, Mena is believed to have been a conscript in the Roman army, martyred for his faith. Legend has it that the camel carrying his remains halted at this spot and refused to go any farther (hence, Mena is often depicted between two camels). Stories of miraculous events connected with the site turned it, from the fifth to seventh centuries, into a pilgrimage center supporting several churches, monasteries, bathhouses, shops, and inns. It lost its importance after the Arab conquest and eventually fell into ruin. Egypt's Coptic community is eager to resurrect the site's past glories, and monks from a new monastery, built in the 1970s, are usually happy to guide visitors through the ancient remains.

Back on the highway, the tourist villages peter out just short of the coastal village of **Al-Alamein,** famous as the site of one of the key battles of World War II. It pitted two master tacticians against each other: Field Marshal Erwin Rommel (1891–1944), the "Desert Fox," commanding German and Italian forces, and the British general Bernard Montgomery (1887–1976). In June 1942 the German army rolled across North Africa, threatening Alexandria and the Suez Canal. It was halted by a last-ditch line of defense at this remote desert spot. On October 23 of that same year, Montgomery's Eighth Army launched a devastating counteroffensive that drove the Germans all the way back into Libya. Casualties on both sides were high, and Al-Alamein today is a place of cemeteries and somber memorials. Those of the Italians and Germans are just off the main highway, while the British and Commonwealth cemetery is south, opposite the **Al-Alamein Museum** displaying artifacts from the battle and leftover pieces of hardware. ∎

Every October, Al-Alamein is the site of commemorative services, but as the years pass the number attending diminishes.

THE BATTLE OF AL-ALAMEIN

British war leader Winston Churchill wrote of the battle of Al-Alamein, "Before Alamein we never had a victory. After Alamein we never had a defeat."

Al-Alamein Museum

- 199 C5
- Medinat al-Alamein
- 046/410 0021
- Closed Fri. 1–2 p.m.
- $$

If the shops are
open it must be
summer: Matruh
is closed out of
season.

Marsa Matruh

MARSA MATRUH, 180 MILES (290 KM) WEST OF ALEXANDRIA,
is the only town of any size on the north coast. Even so, it has just
the one main street, and half of its businesses slumber for two-
thirds of the year. For the other third, Matruh rouses itself to be
transformed into Egypt's most popular summer retreat—albeit a
bargain-basement version of the resorts on the Red Sea.

Marsa Matruh
- 199 B5

Visitor information
- Omar Mukhtar St.
- 03/493 1841

Rommel Museum
- Rommel Beach, 2
  miles (3 km) E of
  town
- Closed after 3 p.m.
- $

The town is wrapped around an
attractive bay in use since classical
times, when it was a port called
Paraetonium. Shiploads of Greek
pilgrims regularly disembarked
here en route to consult the oracle
of Amun at the oasis of Siwa.
Unfounded legend has it that
Cleopatra and Mark Antony came
here shortly before doing battle
with Rome (see p. 35).

During the North African campaigns of World War II, first
Rommel, on the offensive, then
Montgomery, giving chase, set up
headquarters in town. Rommel's
headquarters was a cave, now
turned into a small, half-hearted
museum with a few photos and
maps, and what is claimed to be the
field marshal's overcoat. The more

urbane "Monty" took up residence
at the stylish Hotel Lido (where in
1950 Rita Hayworth checked in
during an African honeymoon).

Since then, Matruh has gone
decidedly downscale…and the Lido
has gone, period. (Although for
echoes of former grandeur there
is still the Beau Site Hotel; see
p. 369.) The resort is a summer
escape for Egypt's middle classes,
and in the hot months the beaches
that fringe the town completely disappear beneath bodies. However,
away from town some unspoiled
sandy sweeps border magnificent
turquoise waters, notably at **Agiba
Beach,** which is 15 miles (24 km)
west. Beyond that, there is next to
nothing on the coastal highway
until the border with Libya. ∎

Siwa Oasis

THE ULTIMATE REMOTE GETAWAY, SIWA IS A SMALL SPECK of life-sustaining greenery marooned far out in the Western Desert, almost nudging Libya on the map. Between it and Cairo is nothing but 340 miles (550 km) of sand. Famous in antiquity for its oracle—consulted by Alexander the Great—the oasis has been largely left alone ever since. It remains an appealing combination of tranquility, beauty, and inaccessibility.

Isolated throughout its long history from goings-on beside the Nile, the oasis has developed independently from the rest of Egypt. For instance, most Siwans speak Siwi, a Berber tongue, a reminder of their historic origins as wandering Bedouin. The community (pop. 15,000) also retains its traditional tribal structure, with the heads of the 11 tribes, the sheikhs, acting as the local council. Siwans are more conservative than other Egyptians: Alcohol is banned, and women are rarely seen unless swathed in a voluminous wrap known as a *milayah*.

Until as recently as the 1980s, Siwa had no television and no phones, and the donkey cart was the transportation of choice. But a new asphalt road linking the oasis to Marsa Matruh brought changes. The oasis is now firmly marked on the tourist map and is sprouting an ever increasing number of hotels and restaurants. It has logged on to the Internet with a free public-access cybercafé, and an airport is on the drawing board.

None of this has yet impacted significantly on the splendor of the oasis, with its dense, green groves of date-bearing palms and olive trees watered by more than 300 fresh-water springs and streams. At the heart is the modest market square, ringed by canvas-shaded stalls and dominated by the remains of the 13th-century, mud-brick enclave

Siwan villagers offer their handicrafts for sale to visitors.

Siwa Oasis

⚑ 199 A4

Visitor information

✉ Town center

☎ 046/460 2883

🕐 Closed after 2 p.m. & Fri.

Modern brick has replaced mud-brick; otherwise, isolation has prevented change in Siwa.

Siwan House Museum

 Town center

🕐 Open 10 a.m.–noon except Fri.

💲 $

of **Shali.** This was the original oasis settlement, surrounded by high walls as protection against attacks by marauding Bedouin. Finding it too dangerous to build outside the walls, the Siwans instead built upward, some of the houses rising four or five stories. Then, a freak three days of rain in 1926 was so damaging, dissolving the high salt content in the mud and causing the buildings to literally melt, that the inhabitants moved out. Looking like a canvas by Salvador Dalí, the abandoned Shali is a delight to explore, and from upper vantage points there are excellent views over the oasis to the desert and tabletop bluffs beyond.

Down below Shali, just to the left of the main Mosque of Sidi Suleiman, is the **Siwan House**

Museum, founded by a former Canadian ambassador to Egypt, who feared the complete demise of Siwa's mud-brick dwellings and associated way of life. It contains traditional dress, jewelry, and domestic implements.

OUTSIDE TOWN

Two miles (3 km) east of town is the ancient hilltop settlement of **Aghurmi** which, aside from a restored mosque, is even more ruined than Shali. Signs lead to the remains of the sixth-century B.C. **Temple of the Oracle,** once renowned throughout the Mediterranean world. In 331 B.C., Alexander the Great came, trekking eight days across the desert from the coast, seeking confirmation from the Oracle of Amun that he

was the son of Zeus, the Greek king of the gods. Nobody knows the oracle's reply (Alexander never told), but afterward he asked his generals to bury him at the oasis. It is unlikely that they carried out his request—historians believe he was laid to rest in Alexandria (see p. 181)—but of course, there are those who disagree. In 1995 two Greek amateur archaeologists announced that they had discovered the legendary lost tomb in Siwa; while they undoubtedly found a tomb, there is no evidence to suggest that it is Alexander's.

A short distance south lies the **Temple of Amun,** dedicated to the ram-headed Egyptian god of life. It is almost totally ruined, having been, unbelievably, dynamited for building materials in 1896.

Continuing south through the palms is a well-marked track leading to **Cleopatra's Bath,** a stone-lined pool filled by a natural spring. It is a popular swimming hole for local men, but the water's scummy surface discourages most visitors. A much better spot for a soak is **Fatnas Spring,** a large, palm-shaded pool on an island in salty Lake Siwa, accessible across a narrow causeway. This is about 4 miles (6 km) west of central Siwa.

Just a mile (1.6 km) north of town, off the Marsah Matruh road, is **Gebel al-Mawta** (Hill of the Dead), a wind-eroded bluff honeycombed with tombs dating back to Ptolemaic and Roman times. Four are locked, but it's worth finding the guardian with the keys to see some funerary paintings. In one tomb are colored reliefs of a Greek man and his family praying to Egyptian gods; another has a faded yellow crocodile, a representation of the god Sobek.

Desert trips are another popular Siwan activity. Lapping up against the oasis is the **Great Sand Sea,** the world's largest dune field, stretching west into Libya and for some 500 miles (800 km) to the south. Most hotels can organize a day's four-wheel-drive excursion into the dunes. ■

Siwan crafts

Siwan craftworks have become collectors' items to such an extent that, in the oasis itself, it is almost impossible to find the distinctive, finely embroidered dresses or heavy silver jewelry once produced here. All the best pieces have gone abroad, and with most of the original craftsmen dead, these reminders of oasis heritage are now lost to the Siwans themselves. However, in local craft shops you can still get wonderful silver rings, shaped differently for each finger and inscribed with geometric patterns. Siwa is also known for its baskets, woven from date palm fronds, and its pottery (water jugs, beakers, and incense burners), made from local clays and colored reddish brown with a pigment made from local earth. ■

Siwan girls display colorful locally made basketry.

Bahariyya Oasis

A Roman fort at Bahariyya embodies the centuries of foreign rule that recast Egyptian life.

AT 205 MILES (330 KM) SOUTHWEST OF CAIRO, BAHARIYYA is the closest of the four Western Desert oases to the capital. It was always regarded as the least interesting of the quartet until a series of significant archaeological discoveries in just the last few years put it on the map.

Bahariyya Oasis
199 C4
Visitor information
Town council building, Bawiti
011/802 167
Closed 2–5 p.m. & Fri.

Above right: Carved into stone beneath the sands, this multi-layered tomb may have been used for centuries.

Several small villages are scattered throughout the oasis, but the main center is **Bawiti** (population 30,000). With one main street of squat shanty buildings, the place has something of a frontier feel. At first acquaintance, there is no sign of the expected lush oasis greenery, but walk in almost any direction and paved roads give way to sandy trails lined with traditional mud-brick houses and palm groves.

Two thousand years ago, it was a very different story. In the Greco-Roman period Bahariyya prospered as one of the greenest spots in all Egypt, sending its wheat and wine to the Nile Valley. Archaeologists now estimate that the oasis may have had a population of up to half a million. Evidence for this comes from an exciting new archaeological find of a vast and wealthy necropolis, which may contain as many as 10,000 mummies (see box opposite).

Until the necropolis is opened to the public, Bahariyya has little to offer in the way of ancient sites. There are the partial remains of a 26th dynasty temple devoted to Amun-Re, and of another temple raised in honor of Alexander the Great, the only one of its kind in Egypt. There is also a series of ancient burial tunnels, known locally as Qarat al-Firekhi, or Ridge of the Chicken Merchant, because of the thousands of mummified birds discovered there. None of these places are easy to find; ask at the visitor information office for help in locating them.

Just up the main street from the visitor information office is the **Ethnographic Museum,** a grand title for a private house occupied by the owner's naive, life-size sculptures of oasis people.

Otherwise, trips to Bahariyya usually focus on the hot springs. There are many of these, but most are inappropriate for soaking in because they are right beside tracks with a constant stream of local traffic. An exception is **Bir al-Ghaba** (Well of the Forest), about 12 miles (20 km) northeast of Bawiti in a eucalyptus grove. On the way out, the road skirts a flat-topped mountain, known as the Mountain of the Englishman, because during World War I the British manned a lookout post here, on the watch for Italian-sponsored raiding parties. ■

Valley of the Mummies

In March 1999 a team of archaeologists began excavating a suspected desert burial site about 4 miles (6 km) from Bawiti. They dug simultaneously in four spots, and each dig revealed a tomb literally piled with mummified corpses. Stacked in what were probably family vaults, 142 bodies were found, surrounded by scarabs, necklaces, carnelian earrings, and silver bracelets, and accompanied by images of the fertility god Bes.

Further digging in May 2000, some of which took place in front of Fox TV cameras, revealed the tomb of Jed-Khenso-Iufankh. This 26th dynasty ruler of Bahariyya is well known to historians and archaeologists, who had been searching for his whereabouts for decades. At the same time, another seven tombs were opened containing one hundred mummies, some with golden masks. One mummified mother carries an infant mummy on her chest.

The archaeologists estimate that there could be 10,000 more mummies awaiting discovery. While the digging continues, the site is off-limits to the public, but there is talk of turning what has been dubbed the Valley of the Mummies into an open-air museum. ∎

Golden covering of a female mummy found in the valley

The unearthly
beauty of the
White Desert is
spurring an
interest in safaris.

White Desert

A PLACE OF SURREAL ROCK FORMATIONS AND PATCHES OF
blinding white, the White Desert is fast becoming one of the most
popular destinations in the Western Desert. It begins just north of the
oasis of Farafra and continues for about 30 miles (50 km), stretching
for about 12 miles (20 km) on each side of the road. It is best visited
from Farafra Oasis (see p. 210).

White Desert

🗺 199 B3

Part of the 120-mile-long (200 km)
Farafra Depression, the floor of the
White Desert (in Arabic, Sahra al-
Bayda) is a mixture of chalk and
limestone, which gives the appearance of snow. The Bedouin call the
area Wadi Gazar, or Valley of
Carrots, because in some areas the
pinnacle-like rock stacks formed by
wind erosion resemble, well…car-
rots. It is these odd, weathered rock

formations that give the area its distinctive character. You begin to see
them just a few minutes out of
Farafra on the Bahariyya road. Out
of the desert floor rise strangely
rounded shapes that resemble white
sphinxes, weird birds, sunbathers,
stone camels….As the sun shifts,
the white rock takes on pink,
orange, and even blue hues, adding
to the already surreal aspect. Strewn

along the ancient trade route that linked Farafra with the next oasis north of Bahariyya.

Although it is outside the White Desert proper, most excursions to the area include a stop at the **Crystal Mountain,** about 50 miles (80 km) from Farafra. It is less a mountain than a small outcrop of rock right beside the road, but a closer look shows the rock to be quartz crystal. ∎

Huge rock formations sculpted by the wind seem nothing less than a hallucination.

across the ground are iron pyrites in fanciful shapes, and quartz crystals, used by Bedouin to promote salivation and quench thirst in the desert heat.

Another oddity of the White Desert are the springs, of which it has a number, including **Ain al-Sarru, Bir Makfi,** and **Ain al-Wadi.** They are marked by hillocks rather than depressions, formed when sand catches on the vegetation that flourishes around the water. The plants are forced to grow ever higher to avoid being smothered, and eventually a hill is formed.

In **Wadi Hennes,** at the northern end of the White Desert, there are some unexcavated Greco-Roman ruins, including a structure that is thought to be a watchtower, as well as some tombs. They lie

Exploring the desert

Would-be explorers should not be lulled into a false sense of security just because the White Desert is relatively close to an asphalt road. As with any desert travel, a guide is essential for safety as well as for discovering the best sites. In Qasr al-Farafra, the three brothers who own Al-Badawiyya Safari and Hotel (see p. 368) have been organizing camel and jeep trips into the White Desert for years. They provide everything necessary for a night out under the stars, including a campfire and Bedouin musicians. Another well-known guide to the area is Amr Shannon, a Cairo-based explorer who has been traveling through Egypt's deserts for more than 20 years. He has camping equipment and will help with jeep rental. He can be contacted via telephone or fax at 02/519 6894, or e-mail ashannon@internetegypt.com. ∎

Farafra Oasis

THE SMALL, ISOLATED OASIS OF FARAFRA IS FAMED FOR ITS picturesque scenery and tranquility. The main population center is Qasr al-Farafra, although it is more a village than a town, with only a few cafés, a small group of municipal buildings, and a couple of hotels. Surrounding it is some of the Western Desert's most beautiful scenery, including the White Desert (see pp. 208–209).

Farafra Oasis
🔺 199 C3

Badr's Museum
🕐 Closed after 5 p.m.

Farafra's history stretches back to pharaonic times, but there are no monuments in the oasis, and what little knowledge we have of the area in that period comes from stelae found in the Nile Valley. The oasis sat on a strategic trade route to Libya and was an important watering point for caravans and armies. But the small number of wells here limited the permanent population and kept it poor until state investment in land reclamation over the last 20 years boosted its economy.

Until a road was built to the oasis just two decades ago, Farafra's isolation helped to preserve its unique character. Most members of the community here belong to a few extended families. Orchards of dates, olives, and apricots are still surrounded by old mud-brick walls. Traditional desert houses sit around the ruined *qasr*, or fort, up the hill, their single-story, windowless facades painted with images of pilgrimages to Mecca and topped with crenellations.

What is there to do in Qasr al-Farafra? You can just wander and relax; and you can visit **Badr's Museum,** a large, fantastical mud-brick house filled with the works of Farafra's most famous son, the artist Badr. Most of his paintings and sculptures portray village life.

As with the other oases, there are several hot springs. The sulfurous waters at **Bir Sitta,** 4 miles (6 km) north of Qasr al-Farafra, are the most famous and are a wonderful place for a soak. ∎

Dakhla Oasis

DAKHLA IS A CLUSTER OF SMALL SETTLEMENTS, STRUNG east-west along the dusty highway. It is perhaps the most attractive of all the Western Desert oases, with stretches of lush orchards partitioned by sweeps of great white dunes.

The "capital" of the oasis is **Mut**, a sparse, small, low-rise town. While not particularly picturesque, it is friendly and has decent accommodations, a passable restaurant, and the visitor information office. There are hot sulfur pools dotted about, the most accessible being **Mut Talata,** 2 miles (3 km) west of the town center. Of more interest is the medieval town of **Al-Qasr,** some 20 miles (30 km) farther out in the same direction. The town's mud-walled alleys weave a complex pattern linking secluded courtyards and threading through mud tunnels supported by cross beams of roughly cut branches. Parts of it have been dated back to the tenth century, and there is a 12th-century mosque complete with mud minaret. Some doorways have acacia beam lintels carved with the name of the house's owner, a date, and a verse from the Koran. There are 54 such lintels in the village: The earliest dates from A.D. 924.

Another 2 miles (3 km) beyond Al-Qasr, a track leads to the pharaonic era **Al-Muzawaka tombs.** Two main tombs still contain wall paintings, while a third contains four mummies. Farther west still is a turnoff to **Deir al-Haggar,** a recently restored temple dating from the reign of the Roman emperor Nero (A.D. 45–68).

Heading out of Mut toward Kharga, you come to two small settlements, **Balat** and **Bashandi;** both have wonderful old centers, with hardly a right-angle anywhere. Sadly, the lack of modern amenities means that the dwellings have largely been abandoned and are rapidly falling into disrepair. ∎

Bounded by a high escarpment, Dakhla is a collection of green swaths interspersed with sand dunes.

Dakhla Oasis
- 199 C2
Visitor information
- ✉ Al-Thawra al-Khadra St., Mut
- ☎ 092/821 685 or 092/821 686
- ⏱ Closed after 3 p.m.

Al-Muzawaka tombs
- $ $$

Deir al-Haggar
- $ $$

Kharga Oasis

THE LARGEST OF THE WESTERN DESERT OASES, KHARGA
stretches for 120 miles (200 km) along a flat, wide depression. Much
of the depression has been used for land reclamation projects, making Kharga less picturesque than the oases to the north. However,
some of the Western Desert's most impressive archaeological remains
are here, and the surrounding desert with its undulating dunes is
very beautiful.

Christian-era
tombs at Al-
Bagawat are
evidence that the
oases were
staging posts
on an ancient
trading route.

Al-Kharga

🄰 199 D2

Visitor information

✉ Nasser Sq., Al-
Kharga

☎ 092/921 206

🕐 Closed after 2 p.m.
& Fri.

**Archaeological
Museum**

✉ Gamal Abdel Nasser
St., Al-Kharga

🕐 Closed Fri.

💲 $$

Temple of Hibis

💲 $$

**Necropolis of al-
Bagawat**

💲 $$

Qasr al-Ghueita

💲 $$

Qasr al-Zayyan

💲 $$

Qasr al-Dush

💲 $$

The chief town of the oasis is **Al-
Kharga,** capital of the New Valley
governorate. The town center
has little to recommend it apart
from a couple of hotels and the
Archaeological Museum, with
a collection of local artifacts. The
highlight is a small display of pre-
historic tools. At the northern end
of the town is the sixth-century B.C.
Temple of Hibis, dedicated to
the Theban triad of Amun, Mut,
and Khonsu (see p. 246). Almost
opposite the temple are the hilltop
remains of the **Temple/Fortress
of an-Nadura,** built by Roman
emperor Antoninus Pius in A.D 138.
Farther north still is the
fascinating **Necropolis of al-
Bagawat,** containing several hundred Christian-era mud-brick
tombs dating from the fourth to

sixth centuries. Up a track behind
the necropolis stand the dramatic
clifftop ruins of **Deir al-Kashef,**
an early Christian monastery that
overlooked the crossroads of several
trade routes. As you head south
from Al-Kharga, two more ruined
fortresses lie just east of the main
road. **Qasr al-Ghueita** encom-
passes a well-preserved Ptolemaic
temple; Roman **Qasr al-Zayyan**
is close to a modern village.
Most worth seeing of the old
remains is **Qasr al-Dush,** a
Roman temple and fortress near
the town of Baris, some 60 miles
(96 km) south of Al-Kharga.
Emperor Domitian built the well-
preserved Temple of Osiris within
its walls in the first century A.D.
This was the gateway to Egypt for
caravans coming from the south. ∎

A lush belt of greenery filling the Nile Valley, Middle Egypt is the Egyptian heartland. Farming centers cluster around market towns, and everywhere are ancient sites, including the short-lived capital of the "heretic pharaoh" Akhenaten.

Middle Egypt

A girl at Gurna chews on sugarcane.

Middle Egypt

MIDDLE EGYPT IS THAT STRETCH OF THE COUNTRY LYING SOUTH OF CAIRO and north of Luxor, which virtually all visitors skip over by plane or sleep through on an overnight train. However, for anyone who has a hankering to see the "real Egypt," then this is the place to look.

Local village women come down to the banks of the Nile to do their washing.

The term "Middle Egypt" is an invention of 19th-century archaeologists. Egyptians themselves still only speak of Upper and Lower Egypt, terms in use since the time of the first ancient king, Menes (circa 3100 B.C.). But it is a useful handle to describe a region quite different in character from those areas to the north and south. This is very much the heartland of Egypt, largely untouched by either heavy industry or tourism. Not far south of Cairo the cliffs and rocky hills that hem in the Nile withdraw to leave a wide and lushly green plain either side of the river. It is prime agricultural land, cultivated in age-old ways. Farmers still practice flood irrigation, and occasionally you can catch a glimpse of a

waterwheel, or *sakia*, being turned by a blindfolded ox, or a *shadouf*, the ancient implement for lifting water. *Felaheen*, the rural peasantry, work the land by hand, often using tools modeled on designs thousands of years old. Towns are provincial and conservative, to the extent that for all the connection it has with local affairs, Cairo has about as much to do with daily life as New York City.

Unfortunately, this is not quite the rural idyll that it might sound. Year by year, agricultural work fails to provide sufficient employment or income for the area's burgeoning population. The lack of income from industry or tourism results in economic hardship. There is also a historic distrust of the distant authorities in the capital, who are traditionally perceived as being neglectful of the region. These factors, and others, have meant that over the last decade or so Middle Egypt has proved a fertile recruiting ground for extreme Islamic elements. In the early 1990s, when the extremists declared their intention to target Egypt's tourism industry, it was in the areas of Minya and Qena that most attacks on trains and Nile cruisers took place. Leaders of extremist Islamic groups have said that they are no longer threatening foreign visitors, and police have tightened up their protection, but the damage has been done and Middle Egypt remains a no-go zone with tour groups, for whom anxiety overrides curiosity.

Even before the current troubles, however, Middle Egypt has always been a low priority with foreigners. Not only does it lack grand monuments, but there are also few hotels and little public transportation. That may change, as already there are initiatives to make the area more visitor friendly, such as the promotion of a Holy Family pilgrimage route (see p. 222). Though at the moment travel in the region is not recommended, the main sites in Middle Egypt are included in this guide because travel there may soon become safe. The two most appealing sites, the Temple of Seti I at Abydos (see p. 227) and the temple at Dendara (see pp. 229–30), can both be visited from Luxor, a safer and more agreeable base. ∎

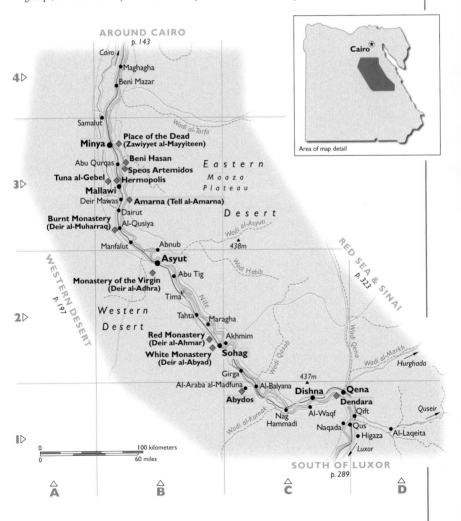

AROUND CAIRO
p. 143

Cairo

Maghagha
Beni Mazar

Samalut

Wadi al-Tarfa

Minya
Place of the Dead
(Zawiyyet al-Mayyiteen)

Abu Qurqas
Beni Hasan
Speos Artemidos
Tuna al-Gebel
Hermopolis
Mallawi
Deir Mawas
Amarna (Tell al-Amarna)
Dairut

Eastern
Maaza
Plateau

Burnt Monastery
(Deir al-Muharraq)
Al-Qusiya

Manfalut
Abnub
438m

Desert

Wadi al-Asyuti

Asyut

Abu Tig
Monastery of the Virgin
(Deir al-Adhra)
Tima

Wadi Habib

Western
Desert

Tahta
Maragha

Red Monastery
(Deir al-Ahmar)
Akhmim

White Monastery
(Deir al-Abyad)
Sohag

Girga

Al-Araba al-Madfuna
Abydos
Al-Balyana
Dishna
Qena
Dendara

Nag
Hammadi
Al-Waqf
Qift
Qus
Al-Laqeita

Naqada
Higaza

Wadi al-Kornak

Luxor

437m

Wadi Qasab

Wadi Qena

Wadi al-Markh

Hurghada

RED SEA & SINAI
p. 323

Quseir

WESTERN DESERT
p. 197

0   100 kilometers
0   60 miles

SOUTH OF LUXOR
p. 289

A   B   C   D

Cairo

Area of map detail

Minya & around

A PROVINCIAL CAPITAL 150 MILES (240 KM) SOUTH OF Cairo, Minya has a relaxed atmosphere that belies its reputation as a center for extremist opposition to the government. The high-profile police presence aside, it is a pleasant Nile-side town with some fine, if badly neglected, architecture testifying to its former prosperity as a center of the cotton industry. It makes a good base from which to explore several important archaeological sites in the area.

A group of schoolchildren head out into the fields around Minya.

Minya
🅰 215 B3
Visitor information
✉ Corniche al-Nil
☎ 086/343 500
🕐 Closed Fri.

Beni Hasan
✉ Abu Qirkus
💲 $$

Minya's small-town life centers on **Tahrir Square,** which is fringed by old colonial town houses built by Italian architects for local cotton magnates in the early years of the 20th century. Though shabby, the buildings retain a great deal of charm. The sidewalks out front are filled with coffeeshop tables and chairs, occupied by patrons puffing on waterpipes and playing games of dominoes and backgammon, games made surprisingly noisy by the Egyptian habit of slamming pieces down on the table. Closer toward the river, one block in from the attractive tree-lined Corniche, is a lively *souq* (street market), which, in season, is dominated by large, pyramidal mounds of watermelons.

If there is little to see in Minya, there is plenty in the neighboring area. As public transportation to the ancient sites is limited and time consuming, it is advisable to rent a taxi for the day. The local tourist office can help with arranging this.

About 3 miles (5 km) south of town, on the other side of the river, is an immense cemetery known locally as Zawiyyet al-Mayyiteen, or **Place of the Dead.** Believed to be one of the largest burial grounds in the world, it contains thousands of mausoleums. Mud-brick domes mark the Muslim tombs, and crosses the Christian. Until the 1970s the dead were transported across to the cemetery by felucca, but a new bridge over the Nile has brought to an end that tradition.

A farther 10 miles (16 km) or so south are the rock tombs of **Beni Hasan,** burrowed into cliffs on the east bank of the Nile. Named for an Arab tribe that once inhabited the area, the tombs are pharaonic and date from the Middle Kingdom (2055–1650 B.C.). There are 39 tombs in total, all belonging to various nobles and regional governors, but only four are open to the public. Earlier and far less elaborate than the famed tombs in the Valley

Most impressive of the quartet is the **Tomb of Khnumhotep,** who lived around 1800 B.C. Beside the main entrance, paintings show acrobats dancing, but most of the scenes relate to the rites of officialdom, with peasants weighing grain, scribes recording its storage, and farmers working the fields. Most splendid of all, though, are the

of the Kings (see pp. 276–285) at Luxor, they are nonetheless fascinating for their wall paintings, which vividly illustrate a wide variety of everyday activities of ancient Egyptian life.

Earliest of the four is the **Tomb of Baqet,** famous for its wrestlers, who are depicted in almost 200 different positions. Immediately south is the **Tomb of Kheti,** son of Baqet, with leisurely scenes of dancers, winemaking, and figures playing *senet,* a game similar to checkers. Kheti can be found seated beneath a sunshade attended by his dwarf and fan bearers. The **Tomb of Amenemhet** displays a niche at the rear meant for statues, a later development. It still contains broken effigies of Amenemhet, along with his wife and mother.

scenes on the back wall of hunting, fishing, and netting birds, which include depictions of a vast menagerie of animals such as hippos, crocodiles, and big cats. All must have been quite common in ancient Egypt, but they have long since been hunted to extinction.

From the tombs, the cliffside path goes south for 1.5 miles (2.5 km) to the **Speos Artemidos,** a rock-cut temple built by the queen-pharaoh Hatshepsut (see p. 274). It has the distinctive Hathor-headed columns also found at Hatshepsut's great temple on the West Bank at Luxor (see pp. 274–75), only in this case they are unfinished. Inside the pillared hall, painted scenes depict the queen with various deities.

Minya is also the best base for a visit to Amarna (see pp. 218–221). ■

Looking like eggs in cartons, the domes of Muslim tombs fill Minya's vast Place of the Dead.

Amarna

THE EGYPTIAN EMPIRE WAS STILL IN ITS GOLDEN AGE IN the 14th century B.C. when, barely out of his teens, the pharaoh Amenhotep IV (*R.*1352–1336 B.C.) swept aside the age-old order of gods, temples, and priests of Karnak at Thebes. In their place he elevated the Aten, the sun disk, as the sole deity, renamed himself Akhenaten (He Who Serves the Aten), and founded a wholly new capital Akhetaten (The Horizon of the Aten). Amarna, also known as Tell al-Amarna, is the site of this revolutionary city.

A visit is best made from a base in Minya, which is about 30 miles (50 km) north. Renting a taxi for the day is by far the best way to go, as transportation is also needed to get around the extensive site of Amarna. En route, you will pass through the town of **Mallawi,** where a small museum contains artifacts found in the region. In recent times, however, Mallawi has been a hot spot for unrest, and as a result the local police do not permit visitors to make a stop in town.

The reasons Akhenaten chose this particular site are unclear, but at 240 miles (384 km) down the Nile from Karnak, it could well be that he was looking to put some distance between himself and the enraged establishment. With astonishing speed he erected his new city, complete with palaces, public buildings, and a great temple, on the east bank of the Nile on a crescent-shaped plain bounded by an arc of high cliffs.

However, Amarna served as the capital of Egypt for less than 15 years. It was abandoned shortly after Akhenaten's death, when the priests of Karnak managed to regain religious control. They desecrated the temple and did their best to obliterate all record of the heretic

Amarna

⬛ 215 B3

✉ Tell al-Amarna

💲 $$

The strange face of Akhenaten

One of the most striking aspects of Amarna art is the appearance of the pharaoh himself. In contrast to the sleek, muscled kings of before, Akhenaten is typically portrayed with a bulging cranium and a thin, feline face with protruding lips. His belly is rounded, and his pelvis and buttocks are matronly, almost voluptuous. Scholars speculated for decades that the pharaoh had a deforming disease. But now many believe that the apparent bisexuality of Akhenaten might in fact be rooted in the new religion, because Aten had both male and female aspects. ■

pharaoh and his wayward religion. Akhetaten city not only fell into ruin but was dismantled, and the stones of its palaces and temples reused elsewhere.

Unfortunately, the drama and mystery of the "rebel pharaoh" (and of his almost equally famed wife, Nefertiti) are of far greater interest than the site of his city. What remains today is only the faintest outline, delineated by low mounds of earth and trenches. There are no standing structures, and any finds, such as pottery and statues, have been removed to various museums (a selection was assembled in 2000 and sent on tour to Los Angeles, Boston, and Chicago under the banner "Pharaohs of the Sun: Akhenaten, Nefertiti, Tutankhamun"). Almost all that there is to be seen at

the site of the city are two sets of cliff tombs cut in the rock, one at each end of the former city. These feature colorful wall paintings of life during the Aten revolution.

Of the six northern tombs, the most rewarding are the **Tomb of Huya** (No. 1) and the **Tomb of Mery-Re I** (No. 4). In the latter, on the right-hand wall behind the two pillars, a painting depicts Akhenaten and his temple, which has helped archaeologists visualize what this city might have looked like. Notice also, down in the bottom corner, the relief of blind beggars awaiting alms; a distinctive characteristic of Amarna art was that it focused on nature and human life rather concentrating on the netherworld. The previously formalized and rigid court style is

Akhenaten (far left) ruled from Amarna (above) during Egypt's golden age in the 14th century B.C.

Akhenaten unleashed a creative furor that gave rise to perhaps the finest era of Egyptian art.

Hermopolis
🄰 215 B3
✉ Al-Ashmunein
$ $$

Tuna al-Gebel
🄰 215 B3
✉ Tuna al-Gebel
$ $$

replaced by something approaching naturalism.

There is a second set of tombs far to the south, grouped in two clusters. Of these, the ones to look for are the **Tomb of Mahu** (No. 9), burial place of Akhenaten's chief of police, and the **Tomb of Ay** (No. 25), finest of all the tombs at Amarna. Wall paintings here show palace scenes and the street life of the city, including gossiping neighbors, soldiers, and prostitutes.

All these tombs are of nobles and officials. Where Akhenaten himself was buried remains a great mystery. One possibility is in an unidentified tomb, known as the **Royal Tomb,** hidden in a valley 3 miles (5 km) east of the river. Its wall paintings and texts were virtually obliterated by the priests of Amun, but a few surviving scenes relate to Meketaten, daughter of Akhenaten and Nefertiti. It could be that this was a royal family tomb and the final resting place of the contentious pharaoh himself. Certainly no other tomb bearing his name has ever been found.

WHERE THE WORLD WAS MADE FROM CHAOS

Visitors with their own transportation can include two other sites in a trip to Amarna, both with strong mythical associations. Five miles (8 km) northwest of Mallawi are the remains of the famed city of **Hermopolis.**

According to one ancient Egyptian tradition, it is here that Creation began, with a primordial mound from which the eight creator gods first emerged to fashion the world out of chaos. From early dynastic times, the site became a center for the cult of Thoth, the ibis-headed god of wisdom, healing, and writing. He also assumed the form of a baboon, often endowed with an enormous erect penis. A pair of giant sandstone baboons now mark the entry to the site, but they are minus their phalluses, which were probably hacked off by early Christians. The Ptolemies identified Thoth with the Greek god Hermes, hence the name Hermopolis. Beyond the baboons, the only real monument here is a fifth-century Christian basilica

built with slender granite columns from an earlier Ptolemaic temple.

Rather more remains of the city's necropolis, known as **Tuna al-Gebel,** after the small nearby village. Midway between village and site is the area's oldest monument, one of a series of stelae (inscribed stones) that marked the boundary of the royal city of Akhetaten. It depicts Akhenaten and Nefertiti with their daughters, adoring the sun. Highlight of the necropolis is the catacombs, the galleries of which were once filled with thousands of mummified baboons and ibises—both being sacred to Thoth. Although only a few main corridors are accessible, Egyptologists suspect this subterranean cemetery may extend all the way to Hermopolis, over 4 miles (7 km) distant.

Back above ground is a small "city of the dead" with streets of mausoleums. Grandest of these is the **Tomb of Petosiris,** dedicated to a high priest of Thoth and designed like a temple. Paintings inside show a mixture of two cultures: typical Egyptian scenes, but with all the figures wearing Greek dress. A small hall behind the tomb displays a well-preserved "mummy" of a young woman who drowned in the Nile in about 120 B.C. In fact, there are no indications of any embalming—it is the dry desert air that has preserved the corpse. ■

The stubs of slender columns mark the site where, according to ancient Egyptian tradition, Creation began.

Leading to God?

American Egyptologist James H. Breasted called Akhenaten "the world's first idealist…the earliest monotheist, and the first prophet of internationalism." His elevation of the Aten—previously just one aspect of the sun god Re—to supreme status, subsuming all attributes of other gods, foreshadows the one God of Jews, Christians, and Muslims. However, although Akhenaten insisted on one supreme god, he perceived himself and Nefertiti as extensions of that god, and therefore also deserving of worship. ■

The Holy Family in Egypt

According to biblical tradition, the Holy Family of Joseph, Mary, and the newly born infant Jesus came from Bethlehem to Egypt to escape Herod's "massacre of the firstborn." They remained for roughly four years. What they did and where they went during that time, the Bible does not say, but Coptic traditions link a surprising number of sites with the visit.

The genesis of many of these links lies with Theophilus, patriarch of the Coptic Church some time about A.D. 500. Theophilus had a dream in which the places where the Holy Family stayed in Egypt were revealed to him. Historical common sense supports at least the first of these sites, Farma in North Sinai (see p. 336), formerly Pelusium, a Roman seaport, which was the gateway to Egypt on a well-trodden caravan route from Judea (now Israel). From here the holy itinerants are said to have journeyed across the Delta region. A popular local tradition connects them with numerous places including Sakha near the town of Kafr al-Sheikh, where a church has a stone reputed to bear the footprint of Jesus, and the Virgin Mary Church in Mostorod, near the town of Bilbeis. Thousands of pilgrims come to this church every August because they believe the Holy Family stayed there.

At Matariyya, a northeastern suburb of Cairo, is the Virgin's Tree. A gnarled sycamore, this is supposedly descended from a tree that shaded Mary during a rest stop. It has been attracting pilgrims for centuries, who have been in the habit of hacking off pieces, leaving the poor plant in a fairly terrible state.

According to tradition, the Holy Family then passed through the settlement of Babylon, now known as Coptic Cairo (see pp. 118–121), sheltering in a cave that is now a part of the Church of St. Sergius. Another

Coptic iconography adorns the Church of Shenouda in the White Monastery at Sohag.

Cairo church, in the southern suburb of Maadi and easily accessible by subway, hosts the next link in the journey south. This fourth-century church claims to occupy the site of a Jewish synagogue on the banks of the Nile from where the family took a boat for Upper Egypt. Copts believe that the stairway from the courtyard of the Church of the Blessed Virgin down to the river is the original, which the Holy Family descended.

The southernmost point associated with the holy route is the town of Asyut (see p. 224), 230 miles (370 km) south of Cairo. Between Maadi and Asyut, countless more villages and churches lay claim to being host to the travelers, boasting ancient churches, holy wells and trees, and myriad tales of miracles. What is undeniable is that Middle Egypt has a great density of ancient churches and monasteries, evidence of a long-standing Christian tradition.

Since 2000 the Egyptian tourism ministry has been working hard to package and market this "holy route," angling to attract some of the pilgrimage trade down from Jerusalem. June 1 has been unofficially designated Holy Family Day, this being the date that Theophilus dreamed that Joseph, Mary, and Jesus made their entry into Egypt. Hopes are that modern-day pilgrims from around the world can be persuaded to do likewise, joining a proposed annual anniversary procession beginning in Farma and moving on to explore some of the other associated sites, many renovated in anticipation of the hoped-for influx of visitors. It is a scheme that offers the chance for little-known places, which have lain well off most visitors' maps, to forge a valuable relationship with the lucrative tourist industry. ∎

Dating from 500 A.D., the White Monastery represents Christianity's long-standing tradition in Egypt.

Asyut

EVEN BEFORE THE TROUBLES BEGAN IN MIDDLE EGYPT,
Asyut was never a major tourist stop. It is the largest and least
pleasant town in the region and has few sights. However, believed to
be the southernmost point reached by the Holy Family, and reputedly the place in which they stayed the longest, Asyut is now being pro-
moted by Egypt's tourist authorities as a venue for Christian pilgrims.

Asyut
🅰 215 B2

Access to the monasteries is
only possible by taxi or
private vehicle, as there is
no public transportation.
Asyut can be reached by
daily flights from Cairo or
by bus. There are
accommodations, although
quality is poor.

The town has a history stretching
back as far as the pharaonic era.
Evidence of this remains at **Al-
Qusiya,** the present name for the
ancient settlement of Meir, where
17 tombs of ancient Egyptian
princes and rulers of the region are
open to the public. Wall reliefs
include delightful scenes of daily
life, sports, papyrus manufacture,
viticulture, and hunting. Finds
from the site are displayed at a
museum on Gomhuriyya Street
in central Asyut. In the 19th century, the town was famous for its slave
market, the biggest in Egypt, with
"merchandise" brought up from
Nubia and Sudan. Goods at the
souq are more conventional these
days, but there are a few old *khans*
(merchants' hostels) to look at.

The two monasteries associated
with the Holy Family are a short
way out of town. The **Monastery
of the Virgin** (Deir al-Adhra), 6
miles (10 km) to the north, is built
around the caves of Dirunka, where
the family is reputed to have shel-
tered. It resembles a great fortified
campus, large enough to accommodate up to 50,000 pilgrims who
attend the Feast of the Virgin
(Moulid al-Adhra) in August each
year. The **Burnt Monastery**
(Deir al-Muharraq) is a farther 20
miles (32 km) north, near the
desert's edge. It, too, is built around
a cave sanctuary that is supposed to
have been home to the Holy Family
and is now the core of a church.
This monastery also has an annual
feast, in the last week of June. ∎

Sohag

SOHAG, 80 MILES (130 KM) SOUTH OF ASYUT, IS AN attractive rural town, with a large Christian community, that is doing its best to woo visitors. Claims to fame include two of Egypt's most celebrated monasteries and a weaving center that produces Egypt's finest textiles, a craft that goes back to the pharaonic era.

Sohag's monasteries, which lie about 6 miles (10 km) south of town, are far smaller and more modest than those at Asyut, but also far more evocative. From a distance, the **White Monastery** (Deir al-Abyad), with its limestone walls, resembles an Egyptian temple with sloping walls like a pylon. Parts of the building are actually purloined from older structures, and some of the stone blocks on the wall of the monastery's church bear pharaonic hieroglyphs. In its heyday around 2,000 monks lived here, but today there are only a handful. Each year during the week of July 14, thousands of pilgrims come for the Feast of Shenouda, honoring the monastery's fifth-century founding saint. The nearby **Red Monastery** (Deir al-Ahmar),

built of red brick, was founded by St. Bishoi, a reformed robber and follower of St. Shenouda.

Just across the Nile from Sohag is the small town of **Akhmim,** center of an ancient weaving tradition. Legend has it that pharaohs were buried in shrouds of Akhmim silk. The lustrous vestments of early Coptic Christians (seen in the Coptic Museum in Cairo; see pp. 118–19) also came from here. Still produced, Akhmim cloth remains highly prized and extremely expensive when it can be found. It is best to get it directly from the weavers' workshops. It makes for one of the most splendid buys in Egypt. Akhmim also has a small **open-air museum** with a 34-foot-high (10 m) standing statue of Merit-Amun, daughter of Ramses II. ∎

Local children receive a Christian education at the ancient Coptic **White Monastery.**

Sohag
🅼 215 B2

Abydos

AS MODERN MUSLIMS ALL ASPIRE TO VISIT MECCA AT LEAST once in their lifetime, so ancient Egyptians tried to make a pilgrimage to Abydos, cult center of the god Osiris. Those who couldn't make it while living were often brought here posthumously for burial, because the Egyptians believed that the entrance to the underworld lay in the desert hills just west of this site.

Abydos

🗺 215 C1

✉ Al-Araba al-Madfuna

💲 $$

Because of its associations with the afterlife, many Egyptian pharaohs constructed cenotaphs at Abydos. It once covered a huge area, with various temple complexes, necropolises, and a town centered upon the great Temple of Osiris, built by Seti I. Though it is seldom visited since the troubles began in the early 1990s, Abydos can easily be seen in a day trip from Luxor, perhaps with a visit to Dendara temple (see pp. 229–230) on the way. A taxi for the whole day should cost no more than about $30 to $40, and the tourist office in Luxor can help with the arrangements.

The site of Abydos is 6 miles (10 km) west of the village of Al-Balyana, which lies on the main Nile-side highway. From here a well-surfaced road leads through

Above: Carved deities decorate the entrances to the seven shrines in the Temple of Seti I.

Above right: Seti I is depicted on a wall relief in his temple with the god Horus.

fields of sugarcane to another small hamlet, Al-Araba al-Madfuna, on the edge of the ruins.

Although there are the remains of several complexes, the most complete, and the one that everyone has been coming to see since its discovery about 1830, is the **Temple of Seti I.** The second pharaoh of the 19th dynasty, Seti I (*R.*1294–1279 B.C.) came to power about 30 years after the collapse of Akhenaten's Amarna regime (see pp. 218–221). Seti was eager to erase all trace of this heretical interlude, and his reign was characterized by a return to Old Kingdom styles of art, while politically he strove to restore stability and recover lost territories. In all this, he was largely successful, laying the foundations for a new pharaonic golden age presided over by his son and successor, Ramses II. In fact, it was Ramses who largely completed the Abydos temple.

As it survives today, the entrance pylon and first and second forecourts are almost entirely gone, and the temple is entered via a portico leading straight into the hypostyle hall. The first part of this hall was completed following Seti's death, as most of the reliefs depict Ramses II in the presence of various gods and goddesses. As you penetrate deeper within the inner hypostyle hall, the sunken reliefs are noticeably finer—in fact, they are regarded as some of the most remarkable to be found in Egypt. These were executed during the reign of Seti and, again, depict the pharaoh in the presence of deities, notably Osiris, lord of the underworld, and Horus.

Beyond the column-filled halls are seven shrines devoted, from left to right, to Seti himself, Ptah, Re-Harakhte, Amun-Re, Osiris, Isis, and Horus. It is unusual to have so many gods and goddesses honored in one temple, but it is thought that

the aim was to reconfirm faith in the pre-Amarna gods. More fine reliefs cover the walls of the shrines, many retaining much of their original coloring. False doors are painted on the back wall of each shrine, apart from that of Osiris, which has a real door leading through to a suite of inner sanctuaries.

From the inner hypostyle hall a corridor goes to a southern wing. On one side of this corridor the walls have a particularly fine relief of Seti and his son—Ramses II—lassoing a bull, while opposite is what is known as the "kings' list." Beginning with Menes, the traditional founder of Egypt, reliefs list 34 pharaohs in roughly chronological order, ending with Seti. Editing deleted undesirables such as Hatshepsut (see p. 274) and the Ak-henaten and his heirs (see p. 218–221).

Behind the temple proper is an unusual structure known as the Osireion, a cenotaph constructed by Seti I. Unfortunately, it is half buried and mostly inaccessible as it is surrounded by stagnant water, but the sloping entrance tunnel has a splendid, spooky atmosphere. ∎

Dendara

ALTHOUGH IT BELONGS TO A TIME LONG AFTER THE ERA of the great pharaohs had passed, the Greco-Roman Temple of Hathor at Dendara offers a fantastic ancient Egyptian experience. It is one of the very few temples that remains almost completely intact, with a massive stone roof, dark chambers, underground passages, and towering columns topped by Hathor-headed capitals.

Dendara

◮ 215 C1

✉ 3 miles (5 km) W of Qena

💲 $$

The temple stands just outside the town of Qena, a small agricultural center with the dubious distinction of possessing an air base that acted as a staging post for the abortive mission to rescue the U.S. hostages from Iran in 1980. The easiest way to visit is on a day excursion from Luxor, just over 35 miles (56 km) to the south. If you get an early start, it is also possible to squeeze in a few hours at Abydos (see pp. 226–27).

Hathor was the goddess of pleasure and love. She is usually represented as a cow, or a woman with a cow's head or ears, or a woman whose headdress is a sun disk fixed between the horns of a cow. According to mythology, she first suckled Horus, then later became his wife, and their union produced the minor god Ihy. She was identified by the Greeks with Aphrodite.

Left: The columns at Dendara were badly damaged by early Christians who attempted to obliterate the faces of the goddess Hathor.

There were shrines to Hathor on this site as early as Old Kingdom times (2686-2181 B.C.), but the existing temple is Greco-Roman dating from between 125 B.C. and A.D. 60. As foreign rulers, the Greco-Romans were eager to emphasize dedication to Egypt's gods and hence a legitimacy to the throne, so the design of this place emulates exactly that of temples gone before.

As at Abydos, the temple lacks its entry pylons, and instead entry is directly into the **hypostyle hall.** Dating from the first century A.D. and raised by the Roman

Right: A local woman clad in a voluminous black *abbeyya* sits on a street-side *mastaba,* or bench.

emperor Tiberius, the hall has 24 columns, each with a four-sided capital carved with the face of the cow-eared goddess. The ceiling of the hall has kept much of its original coloring and represents a chart of the heavens, including the signs of the zodiac (which were

Despite lacking a main entrance pylon, the facade of the Temple of Hathor at Dendara is still impressive.

introduced by the Romans) and the sky-goddess Nut and other deities sailing their solar boats across the cosmos. Reliefs on the walls show Roman emperors making offerings to Egyptian gods.

This great hall leads through to the smaller, and earlier, **Hall of Appearances,** so called because it is here that the statue of the goddess "appeared" for religious ceremonies and processions. Beyond is the **Hall of Offerings,** with a list of offerings depicted on one of the walls. Straight ahead is the enclosed area of the **Sanctuary,** the most sacred part of the temple, into which only the pharaoh and high priests could enter. It housed Hathor's statue and ceremonial bark (boat). Once a year these were carried in procession to the river, placed on a boat, and sailed up to the temple at Edfu (see pp. 293–94) for a conjugal reunion with Horus. Ancient Egyptians celebrated in a two-week festival by imitating the gods and getting drunk.

Around the sanctuary is a series of dimly lit **side chapels** (it is a good idea to bring a flashlight),

some of which are home to colonies of bats. After exploring the ground level of the temple, go up to the roof—stairways ascend on either side of the Hall of Offerings. Reliefs on the stairs illustrate the New Year procession, when Hathor's statue was carried up to the roof at dawn. On the north are twin chapels, one of which contains a plaster cast of the famous Dendara ceiling; the original was removed by Napoleon's expedition in the early 19th century and now graces the Louvre in Paris. Views of the surrounding countryside from the roof are magnificent.

It is also worth walking around the outside of the temple. On the rear wall, two defaced reliefs of Cleopatra and her son, Caesarion (the outermost figures), feature in a procession of deities. There are also several buildings, now largely ruined. Closest to the main gate is a Roman birth house, or *mammisi,* dedicated to the god Horus. It has beautiful carvings on the wall facing the temple, with tiny figures of Bes, the dwarf god of fertility, on the capitals of the columns. ■

S leepy Nile-side Luxor boasts the greatest concentration of pharaonic monuments anywhere in Egypt, including the great temple complex at Karnak, one of the most awe-inspiring pieces of architecture ever built.

Luxor

The face of Queen Nefertari

Luxor

THE MODERN TOWN EXISTS AS LITTLE MORE THAN A LIFE-SUPPORT SYSTEM for the millions of visitors who descend each year, drawn by the fabulous array of antiquities. Tourism accounts for around 85 percent of the local economy, so present-day inhabitants of Luxor are just as much in thrall to the temples and tombs as their ancient ancestors were.

Boats once carried the gods across the sky, and their worshipers between the lands of the living and the dead.

At the height of its power, Thebes had a population of nearly one million. Vast manpower, combined with the immense wealth brought in by foreign conquests, allowed the Thebans to build the most elaborate places of worship for their local god Amun, whom they united with the sun god Re to worship as Amun-Re. Built on the east bank of the Nile, these temples greeted the rising sun each morning. Over on the west bank was the land of the dead, where the sun went down each day. There the pharaohs, deified by their subjects as living gods, built their own funerary monuments.

Thebes was preeminent for 500 glorious years until the end of the New Kingdom and the last of the Ramses (1069 B.C.), after which power returned to Memphis in the north. The city persisted during Greco-Roman times, but

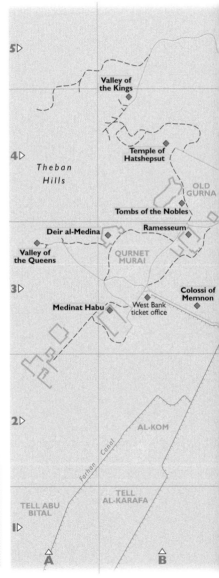

by the time the Arabs conquered Egypt in the seventh century, it was forgotten. Not until Napoleon's 18th-century expedition to Egypt were the temples rediscovered and identified as the ancient city of Thebes, known through classical accounts. To the Arab villagers, who had lived among the sand-covered ruins, this was Al-Uqsor, the Palaces, a name corrupted by Europeans to Luxor.

By the mid-19th century, the first cruisers were already on the Nile, as Luxor became a must for adventurous travelers. "[Luxor] is a place where one could stay a very long time and in a perpetual state of astonishment," wrote Gustave Flaubert, French author, in 1850 in a letter home. Published accounts spread the word, and from the 1860s onward Luxor has welcomed eager tourists. ■

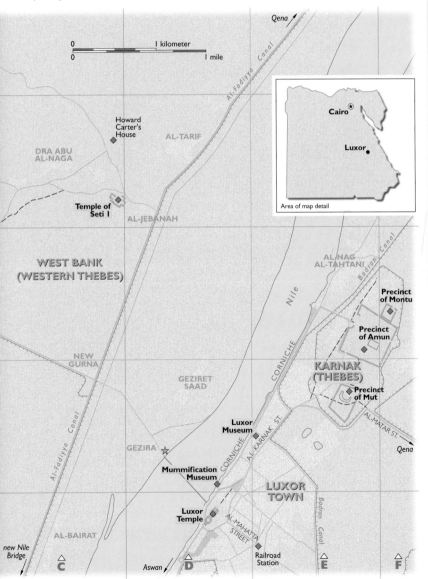

0   1 kilometer
0   1 mile

Qena

Al-Fadiyya Canal

Cairo ✳

Luxor ●

Area of map detail

Howard Carter's House

AL-TARIF

DRA ABU AL-NAGA

Temple of Seti I

AL-JEBANAH

WEST BANK (WESTERN THEBES)

AL-NAG AL-TAHTANI

Badran Canal

Nile

Precinct of Montu

Precinct of Amun

NEW GURNA

GEZIRET SAAD

CORNICHE

KARNAK (THEBES)

Precinct of Mut

AL-MATAR ST.

Qena

Al-Fadiyya Canal

Luxor Museum

GEZIRA

AL-KARNAK ST.

Mummification Museum

CORNICHE

LUXOR TOWN

Badran Canal

Luxor Temple

AL-MAHATTA STREET

new Nile Bridge

AL-BAIRAT

C

Aswan

D

Railroad Station

E

F

With tourism
their lifeblood,
vendors at a
Luxor store
offer travelers
both modern
amenities and
souvenirs of
the ancient.

Luxor town

ONCE THE TERRIFIC HEAT OF THE DAY HAS PASSED,
Luxor's Nile-side boulevard, the Corniche, is the perfect place for an
evening stroll. Horse-drawn carriages canter by on one side, river-
boats churn the water on the other, and as the sun drops spectacularly behind the Theban Hills to the west, lights sparkle in the trees.

It all has a very Victorian air, one
that is majestically reinforced by
the **Winter Palace Hotel** (see
p. 370). Built in the 1880s, when
long-distance travel was the
preserve of the wealthy, this
appropriately named establishment
provided a palatial retreat for
aristocrats and royalty seeing out
harsh northern European winters
in the balmy climes of southern
Egypt. In 1922 the hotel's guests
were the first to learn of Howard

Carter's discovery of the tomb of
Tutankhamun via a posting on
the bulletin board. If you want to
read up on Carter's find, then
Aboudi's Bookshop in the
Tourist Bazaar, a two minutes' walk
north of the Winter Palace, has an
unsurpassed selection of titles on
all things Egypt-related. Luxor's
tourist office is housed in the same
complex.

Continue up the Corniche and
you reach **Luxor Temple** (see

Luxor
🅰 215 C1
Visitor information
✉ Tourist Bazaar,
Al-Karnak St.
☎ 095/372 215
🕐 Closed Fri p.m.

pp. 237–41). Across the road from the temple ticket office is the wharf for the local ferry over to the West Bank. Curving inland of the temple is Al-Karnak Street, the town's main thoroughfare. At its southern end is the **Luxor Wena Hotel,** another of the town's grand old places (in fact, Luxor's oldest hotel), but now sadly run down and dilapidated.

The intersection of Al-Karnak Street and Al-Mahatta Street (Station Street, because of the railroad station at its eastern end) marks the center of town. Most of the stores are devoted to souvenirs, but there is nothing here that can't be found cheaper in Cairo. The same goes for the disappointing *souq,* or bazaar, just north of the mosque on Karnak Street. There is another mosque just a short walk

farther north, beside a small green triangle of parkland, and standing next to it you can look right along the length of the **Avenue of Sphinxes** to the main pylon of Luxor Temple.

Immediately to the west is a narrow sidestreet with a curbside canopy offering shelter from the sun for the horses that draw the tourist carriages. The canopy has been erected by the Brooke Animal Hospital *(Tel 02/364 9312),* an offshoot of a clinic begun by an English woman, Dorothy Brooke, in Cairo in 1934 called the Hospital for Old Warhorses. There are now several of these Brooke hospitals throughout Egypt providing free veterinary treatment for the country's much abused horses and donkeys.

At the point where this sidestreet joins the Corniche is the **Mummification Museum** (see p. 242). You can continue north up the Corniche past a series of modern hotels, which are low rise enough not to cause offense. One or two have gardens out front where it is possible for

A horse-drawn carriage, or calèche, is the favored way for visitors to get around town.

Mummification Museum

🅰 233 D2

✉ The Corniche, opposite Mina Palace Hotel

☎ 095/381 502

🕐 Closed 1–4 p.m.

💲 $$

nonresidents to sit and have a cold drink. Farther along is the **Luxor Museum** (see pp. 244–45), and on beyond that **Chicago House** *(Tel 095/372 525),* the Egyptian base of the highly respected Oriental Institute of the University of Chicago, which has been working on the pharaonic sites here since 1924.

From Chicago House, it is only a walk of perhaps five minutes or so more, north along the Corniche alongside the Nile, to reach the entrance to the vast temple complex of **Karnak** (see pp. 246–253), the greatest of all the pharaonic temples.

An attractive alternative to walking around town is to ride in a horse-drawn carriage (known locally as a calèche), dozens of which cruise the main streets of town through until the early hours of morning. Make sure you agree a price with the driver before you start the ride. ■

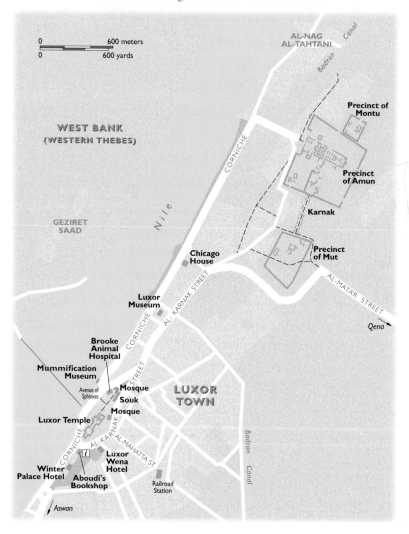

Luxor Temple

SET BESIDE THE NILE AND SURROUNDED BY THE MODERN town, Luxor Temple is one of the most beguiling of all Egypt's pharaonic monuments. Compact and simple in plan, it can be visited in an hour, but the wealth of reliefs and serenity of the site make it worth spending far longer. To catch it at its most atmospheric, visit at night when dramatic lighting brings the place to life.

Just as the temple today lies at the center of the modern town of Luxor, in pharaonic times it sat at the heart of the capital of Thebes. Built on the site of earlier places of worship, it was raised by Amenhotep III (*R*.1390–1352 B.C.), the 18th dynasty "sun king," whose lengthy reign represented the zenith of ancient Egypt's power and prestige. Later he would build an even greater temple on the West Bank, possibly the greatest ever built in Egypt, but that has vanished apart from two lone guardians (see p. 255).

Luxor Temple owes its excellent state of preservation to two factors: It was covered by sand, and the village of Luxor was built on top of it. Vacationing French writer Gustave

Flaubert, visiting in 1850, described houses built among the capitals (the columns buried below) and chickens and pigeons nesting in the great stone lotus leaves. Excavation work, begun in 1885 and still on-going, removed the sand and the village and revealed the temple.

It is approached by an **Avenue of Sphinxes,** which originally went all the way to Karnak, 2 miles (3 km) to the north. Traveling around Luxor today, you keep finding the groove of this avenue between modern buildings, along with bits of half-forgotten, stray statuary. In the temple, the sphinxes come to a halt before the enormous **first pylon.** This is the work of Ramses II, ancient Egypt's other great builder-pharaoh.

A guardian leans against a sphinx, part of the avenue leading to the temple.

Luxor Temple

🔺 233 D1

✉ The Corniche

💲 $$ by day, $ by night

Temples were constantly built and rebuilt (Karnak being the prime example), and a hundred years after the death of Amenhotep III, his monument was expanded—and virtually usurped in the process—by his distant successor. It is Ramses II who is depicted on the pylon's reliefs, slaying Hittite foes at the Battle of Kaddesh. The pylon was originally fronted by six colossal statues of Ramses II, two seated and four standing, and two obelisks. Two statues and one obelisk were carried off to Paris, where the latter now stands in the Place de la Concorde. "How bored it must be….How it must miss its Nile," commented Flaubert.

Beyond the pylon is another addition, the **Great Court of Ramses II,** surrounded by two rows of papyrus-bud columns. Perched high in one corner, on top of the bricked-up colonnade, is the 13th-century A.D. **Mosque of Abu al-Haggag,** which the people of Luxor demanded be left

intact when archaeologists cleared their village from the temple precincts. Dedicated to a local holy man, the mosque still plays an important role in local life, maintaining an unbroken tradition of worship on this site stretching back over 3,000 years.

If you happen to be in Egypt at the right time, it is well worth aiming to be in Luxor for the *moulid* (festival) of Abu al-Haggag, one of the biggest local events of the year. During the raucous festivities, giant floats move through the densely packed streets, while the crowds are entertained by musicians, dancers, and horse racing. A giant boat is also paraded around town in a curious echo across the ages of the pharaonic Opet Festival (see box p. 240). The exact date of the moulid, which lasts two days, varies, but is usually around two weeks before the beginning of Ramadan.

In the western corner of the court is a small bark shrine with triple chapels dedicated to Amun, Khonsu, and Mut, for use in the Opet Festival celebrations. Also look for the diminutive statue of a shapely woman in a diaphanous gown at the foot of one of the colossal statues of Ramses; this is his wife, Nefertari, whose exquisitely decorated tomb is one of the highlights of a visit to the West Bank (see pp. 264–66).

The temple as built by Amenhotep III begins with his **grand processional colonnade.** Its 14 columns are almost 65 feet (20 m) high and probably inspired the even more imposing Great Hypostyle Hall at Karnak (see p. 250). Unfinished at the time of the pharaoh's death, the hall was completed by his grandson Tutankhamun, who added the outer walls, with their scenes of the Opet Festival. On the right-hand side is the floating procession from

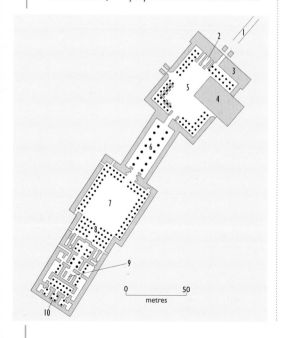

0   50
metres

Tooth brushes are the restoration tools for the Preservation of the Temple,

Karnak to Luxor (look for the fattened sacrificial bulls being led by shaven-headed priests), while on the left-hand side is the better-preserved return.

Highlight of the temple is the paved open-air **Sun Court of Amenhotep III,** enclosed on

A stonemason renovates the chest and head of a statue at the Temple of Luxor.

three sides by colonnades of perfectly proportioned lotus columns. The Corniche passes close by at this point, and the traffic is visible through the columns as flashes of color, with an added soundtrack of horn beeps and engine noise. It has the effect of making the court seem part of the modern town, like some small Italian piazza.

Evenings are an especially beautiful time to be here, when the columns may be lit orange against deep turquoise skies, and bats flit past overhead.

The fantastic cache of statuary, now displayed at the Luxor

Opet Festival

Amun, one of the gods of creation, was the most important deity of Thebes. Once each year, the priests of his great temple at Karnak carried the images of Amun and the other two gods in the local triad—Amun's wife, the war goddess Mut, and their son, the moon god Khonsu—

in the gods' portable barks to Luxor Temple for the Opet Festival, a celebration marking the annual flooding of the Nile. On arrival, the gods were placed in their special shrine and the celebrations would begin. Later, they would travel back on the river, escorted by the barge of the pharaoh himself. ■

Museum (see pp. 244–45), was discovered in 1989 in a pit under the court. On the south side of the court is the **hypostyle hall,** with four rows of eight columns, leading through to an antechamber and the temple's roofed inner sanctuaries. Roman legionaries sealed the entrance to the inner temple and enclosed the whole complex in a fortified encampment sometime between the fourth and sixth centuries A.D. It is the remains of this fortress—in the form of furrows and the foundations of walls—that you see scarring the grassy area around the perimeter of the temple. The Romans also transformed the entrance to the inner temple into a niche, flanked by Corinthian columns, that served as a shrine to the imperial cult. Here, local Christians were offered a choice between obeisance or martyrdom. Worn paintings of Roman emperors are still visible near the top of the wall.

The niche-shrine is now punctured by an off-center doorway giving access to a small, square, second antechamber. This leads through to the **Bark Shrine,** rebuilt by Alexander the Great, who is depicted on the walls (he is the one shown with the bare chest and angular skirt) before the god Amun (with raised flail and towering crown).

The final chamber is the "holy of holies," the oldest part of the temple, the **central sanctuary** where the image of Amun was kept—but the statue is gone and only the base remains. ∎

The Mosque of Abu al-Haggag sits between the main entrance pylon and the hypostyle hall.

Making mummies

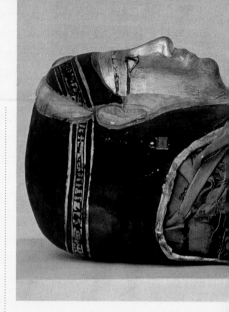

Originally the ancient Egyptians buried their dead directly into the sand, where the hot, dry conditions allowed the fluids responsible for decomposition to drain away, at the same time preserving the soft tissue of skin, hair, and nails. As burial practices became more elaborate for the wealthy, the simple hollow in the sand was replaced with a bench-shaped superstructure, a *mastaba*, over a brick-lined burial chamber. Here the body lay in a wooden coffin, so the natural preservation once achieved by the dry sand had to be replaced with artificial techniques.

Mummification practices became increasingly sophisticated through time, with recent excavations indicating that certain techniques were in use as early as 3400 B.C. These gradually developed during the Old Kingdom period (2686–2181 B.C.), and although initially restricted to royalty, mummification was gradually extended through all ranks of nobles.

Mummification developed into a major industry, employing embalmers, funerary priests, and those who provided the necessary materials. Once the body had been handed over by the family, it would be washed and placed on a large embalming table. The embalmers would loosen the brain with a fine metal probe inserted through the back of the nose. Then they made an incision on the lower left side of the body with an obsidian blade

Mummification Museum

This recent addition to Luxor's sight-list is devoted to Egyptian burial practices, although the emphasis is not on the actual bodies. Below street level in the Corniche embankment, the museum is a little difficult to spot; it is opposite the Mina Palace Hotel *(Tel 095/381 502, closed 1–4 p.m.)*. Inside the dimly lit hall, a series of explanatory wallcharts lead into the exhibits. While nicely designed, they are pretty skimpy on information, leaving out all the gruesome bits that everybody really wants to know about.

There is one mummy on display, that of Masaharti, a high priest of Amun-Re of the 21st dynasty (tenth century B.C.). Perhaps chosen because of his remarkable state of preservation, Masaharti has hair and a beard, and peacefully composed features that give the impression of sleep. There is also a cache of mummified animals (including a ram, cat, fish, and baboon), but otherwise the exhibits concentrate on the implements and materials used in the mummification process. No pictures are needed to cause unease at the sight of the instruments used to scrape the brain out of the skull and for the disemboweling of the body. Another cabinet contains many of the materials necessary for mummification, such as natron salts, bitumen, sawdust, and linen. There are also canopic jars, some beautiful painted coffin lids, and a statue of the jackal-headed god, Anubis, who was patron of embalmers and the guardian of cemeteries.

It is a small collection, and probably takes no more than half an hour to visit. Afterward, visit the museum café with an open-air Nileside terrace offering uninterrupted views across to the West Bank. ■

Above: As well as royalty, nobles and their children were mummified. Right: A mummy in the Egyptian Museum at Cairo

and all internal organs (except the heart as the seat of wisdom and the kidneys as too difficult to get to) were removed and treated separately prior to burial inside the four canopic jars.

The eviscerated body was then covered with a great pile of dry natron salt for 40 days in order to dry it out. It was then washed and the skin anointed with a range of oils, spices, and resins. The embalmers wrapped the mummified body in layers of linen, and priests recited the incantations needed to activate the amulets placed within the wrappings.

The standard mummification process took 70 days; the linen-wrapped mummy placed inside its wooden coffin was then ready for the funeral. Priests, ceremonial dancers, mourners, and servants carrying the funerary equipment went in procession to the tomb. Setting the coffin upright by the tomb, the priest performed the "Opening of the Mouth" ceremony in order to reawaken the soul and restore the senses, which were then sated with offerings of incense, flowers, choice cuts of meat, and wine. The mummy was finally laid to rest in its tomb surrounded by items ranging from those used in daily life to those made specifically for burial.

Mummification ended with the spread of Christianity in the fourth century A.D., although some mummies have been found clutching crosses. Most of the mummies in museums today originated in the Luxor area and the royal necropolises centered on the Valley of the Kings (see p. 276). The other major burial ground was Saqqara (see pp. 148–151), where burials are still being discovered. ■

Something of a rarity in Egypt, the exhibits at Luxor Museum are beautifully lit and displayed, and well labeled.

Luxor Museum

THIS IS ARGUABLY THE BEST MUSEUM IN EGYPT, WITH ITS collection of ancient Egyptian funerary items and statues found in and around Luxor. It contains just a fraction of the antiquities displayed at Cairo's Egyptian Museum (see pp. 70–79), but that is to its advantage. The treasures here are thoughtfully displayed in an attractively lit and air-conditioned environment, and—for a change—everything on display is well labeled.

Luxor Museum
- 🅰 233 E2
- ✉ The Corniche
- ☎ 095/380 269
- 🕐 Closed p.m.
- 💲 $$. Camera $, video camera $$$

The layout is simple: It is one large hall with two levels, connected by a ramp. There is just a single side gallery, immediately off to the right on entering. In it are 16 of the 24 mostly life-size statues discovered by chance while archaeologists were collecting earth samples at Luxor Temple in 1989. Each stands on its own, and visitors can walk around and examine the pieces from all sides. Pride of the find, standing at the head of the hall, is an 8-foot-tall (2.5 m) red quartzite statue of the temple's builder, **Amenhotep III**, which, according to eminent Egyptologist George Hart of the British Museum, "for its serene beauty is unrivaled among the thousands of sculptures surviving from ancient Egypt."

Amenhotep III presided over

what is considered to be a golden age of Egyptian art, and much evidence for that is contained in this museum. Displayed in the entrance hall is an impressively massive **head of the pharaoh,** part of a colossus that belonged to his lost funerary temple on the West Bank (see p. 255).

Around the corner in the main hall is a touching life-size calcite dyad of the crocodile god **Sobek,** with his arm resting paternally around a young Amenhotep III's shoulders. Two fat crocodiles contentedly basking on the block behind are pure Disney. Anyone who has previously found ancient Egyptian sculpture rigid and obsessed with death has some pleasant reevaluating to do.

There are plenty of fine pieces from other periods in this main hall too, particularly exhibit No. 61, a statuette of a youthful **Tuthmose III** *(R.1479–1425 B.C.)* that is so flawlessly smooth it appears to have been cast in pewter.

On the upper floor are the smaller items, much less success-fully displayed in big glass cases. There are a few items from the tomb of Tutankhamun, including sandals, arrows, bronze rosettes that were attached to the pall that covered the sarcophagus, and two model funerary barks, but this is just small fry—all the good stuff from this historic haul is to be found at the Egyptian Museum in Cairo.

Instead, the stand-out items on the upper floor are all related to the rule of **Akhenaten** (here called Amenhotep IV), second son and successor of Amenhotep III, who turned the world of ancient Egypt on its head (see pp. 218–221). His distinctive, almost alien features are immediately identifiable in three sandstone heads hung around the gallery. But most impressive of all is

a reconstructed wall of painted sandstone blocks *(talatat),* which comes from one of the temples erected at Karnak by Akhenaten. These blocks, along with thousands of others, were discovered disman-tled and buried away as infill within one of the great pylons—an attempt by a later pharaoh to oblit-erate evidence of Akhenaten and his heretical ways. Pieced together like some giant jigsaw by archaeolo-gists, the blocks formed a wall, the greater part of which depicts in brightly colored relief incidents of ancient Egyptian daily life. Toward the left are scenes involving the king worshiping the sun god, Aten, standing beneath its rays, each of which ends in a tiny hand holding an ankh (the ancient Egyptian symbol of life). ■

Unmistakably Akhenaten: Feline eyes, elongated face, and sensuous lips

Karnak

Karnak

◭ 233 E2

✉ The Corniche

💲 $$. Open-air
museum $ (ticket
must be bought
outside). Sound-and-
light show $$$

TO THE ANCIENT EGYPTIANS, KARNAK WAS KNOWN AS
Ipet-Isut, The Most Perfect of Places, and you can see why. Despite
being in ruins, it remains spectacular. Possibly the largest temple
complex ever built anywhere, it grew in stages over 1,500 years, added
to by successive generations of pharaohs, and the resulting collection
of sanctuaries, kiosks, pylons, and obelisks acts as a vast open-air
archive of history set in stone.

**Teams of local
artisans are
working toward
the restoration of
the temple
complex at
Karnak.**

During the New Kingdom period
of glory (1550–1069 B.C.), Thebes
was the all-powerful capital of
Egypt, and Karnak was its heart.
More than just a place of worship, it
was the residence of the pharaohs,
the center of administration, a
vastly wealthy treasury, and the keystone of the economy, owning vast
tracts of land and employing tens
of thousands of workers. Ordinary
folk were not allowed in its
precincts, only the priests and royal
retinue entered it.

The Karnak complex had three
compounds. The main precinct,
dedicated to Amun, lay at the center, dominated by the Great Temple
of Amun and containing a large
sacred lake. This was the main place
of worship of the Theban triad of
gods (Amun-Re, Mut, and
Khonsu). Directly to the south was
the precinct of Amun's consort,
Mut, linked to the main temple by
an avenue of ram-headed sphinxes.

To the north was the precinct of the
the old Theban falcon god, Montu.

Although most of this vast
complex was the work of New
Kingdom rulers, including notably
Hatshepsut, Tuthmose III, Seti I,
and Ramses II, the original sanctuary of the Great Temple of Amun
was built during the Middle
Kingdom period (circa 1900 B.C.).
Successive pharaohs expanded out
from this core, with the first
pylon—the present imposing
entrance to the site—dating from
as late as circa 370 B.C. In the postpharaonic age the Ptolemies,
Romans, and early Christians all
also left their mark. When visiting
today, the deeper into the complex
you venture, the farther back in
time you go.

Since Egyptology became a science, Karnak has been subject to
numerous excavations, and various
projects are still ongoing. There
have been major finds here,

Practicalities

The site of Karnak lies about a
mile and a half (2.4 km) south
of the modern center of Luxor. It is
quite possible to walk there down
the Corniche, but as you will be on
your feet exploring over the next
few hours, it may be preferable to
make the trip in a taxi or a calèche.
The site covers 247 acres (100 ha),
so you need at least half a day just
to walk around the many precincts.

Visitors are admitted from 6 a.m.,
and an early start beats the heat;
from about 7 a.m. onward the place
gets very busy with tour groups. It is
much quieter in the afternoon, but
the downside is the intense heat,
and there is little shade. If you have
the time, consider visiting once during the day, and then again in the
evening to experience the sound-
and-light show (see box p. 251). ∎

**Opposite:
Stripped of its
color, Karnak's
Great Hypostyle
Hall still feels a
hall of the gods.**

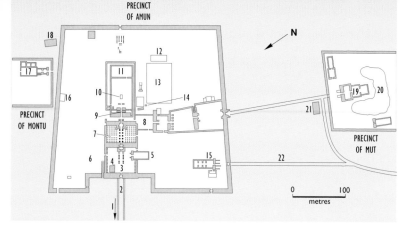

PRECINCT
OF AMUN

N

PRECINCT
OF MONTU

PRECINCT
OF MUT

0   100
metres

including an impressive haul of royal statuary (most now in the Egyptian Museum, Cairo; see pp. 70–79) uncovered in 1903, but today most of the efforts of the archaeologists are concentrated on conserving and systematically restoring the standing monuments.

PRECINCT OF AMUN

For most visitors, the Precinct of Amun *is* Karnak. Even without the neighboring complexes devoted to Mut and Montu, it completely dwarfs anything else in Egypt. The precinct has a complicated plan, combining two axes: north-south and east-west. East-west is the main axis, and the easiest way to explore is to stick to this. If you still feel able to take in more once you have reached the far end, you can walk back via the Sacred Lake and explore north-south.

A canal once connected the Amun precinct with the Nile, to allow for the passage of the sacred barks (see

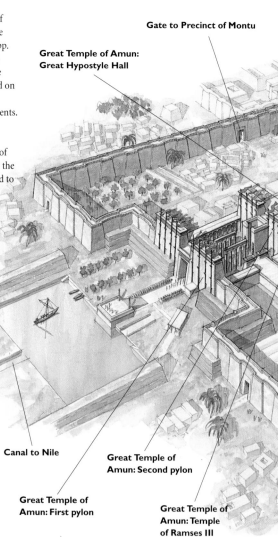

Gate to Precinct of Montu

Great Temple of Amun:
Great Hypostyle Hall

The Precinct of Amun at Karnak at the height of its New Kingdom period of glory

Canal to Nile

Great Temple of Amun: First pylon

Great Temple of Amun: Second pylon

Great Temple of Amun: Temple of Ramses III

p. 240). Ramses II built a quay beside the canal, and it is this quay—flanked by a short processional avenue of ram-headed sphinxes, each with a statue of the king between its paws—that forms the impressive approach to the **first pylon** and entrance. Massive as it is, the pylon is unfinished, as you can see by the unequal heights of the two sides. If you stand close to the gate, you can make out an inscription left by Napoleon's

expedition (see pp. 39–40) high up on the right-hand jamb of the gate.

Beyond is the **Great Court** (everything at Karnak is "great") of the Amun Temple, which contains a real grab-bag of ancient remains. To the left is the **Shrine of Seti II,** composed of a trio of small chapels for the sacred barks of Amun, Mut, and Khonsu. If you have already visited Luxor Temple, you will have seen similar chapels in the great court there. Opposite

KEY TO SITE PLAN

Karnak

1 To ticket office
2 Avenue of Sphinxes
3 Great Court
4 Shrine of Seti II
5 Temple of Ramses III
6 Open-air museum
7 Great Hypostyle Hall
8 Cachette Court
9 Obelisks of Hatshepsut
10 Sacred Bark Shrine
11 Festival Temple of Tuthmose III
12 Sound-and-light grandstand
13 Sacred Lake
14 Café
15 Temple of Khonsu
16 Temple of Ptah
17 Temple of Montu

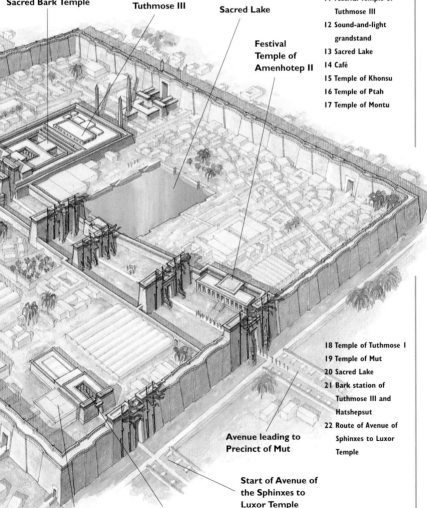

Great Temple of Amun: Sacred Bark Temple

Great Temple of Amun: Festival Temple of Tuthmose III

Sacred Lake

Festival Temple of Amenhotep II

18 Temple of Tuthmose I
19 Temple of Mut
20 Sacred Lake
21 Bark station of Tuthmose III and Hatshepsut
22 Route of Avenue of Sphinxes to Luxor Temple

Avenue leading to Precinct of Mut

Start of Avenue of the Sphinxes to Luxor Temple

Temple of Opet   Temple of Khonsu

the shrine is a sphinx with the features of Tutankhamun. To the right is a small **Temple of Ramses III,** a miniature version of his temple at Medinat Habu (see pp. 258–59), and older than the court, which explains the odd way it crashes through the wall. One

are they usually so hypnotically regimented. It is hard to think of a space in any other building, ancient or modern, that so imbues the viewer with a sense of his or her mortality.

To state the facts: The hall is filled with 134 columns, which are

Displaced sphinxes that once lined a processional route cluster in the Great Court

lone papyrid column stands near the center of the court, all that is left of a kiosk built by Taharqa, a 25th dynasty Nubian pharaoh. He ruled more than 600 years after Ramses II, whose pink-granite colossi stand just behind, fronting the **second pylon.**

Ramses II himself did not actually build the pylon (credit for that goes to Horemheb), but he was in the habit of adding his cartouche and likeness to the monuments of his predecessors. Pause for breath here, because after passing through the second pylon you are greeted by one of the most magnificent of spectacles, the dizzying **Great Hypostyle Hall.** To describe it, as many guidebooks do, as a forest of columns is to undersell it. Tree trunks are rarely this massive, nor

roughly 50 feet (15 m) high, except for the center 12, which are 69 feet (21 m) tall. It takes six adults to stretch their arms around a column's girth, and it has been calculated that a crowd of 50 people could comfortably stand on one of the splayed column tops. Originally they supported a roof, so that the whole hall would have been enclosed and only dimly illuminated by sparse shafts of light admitted through small clerestory windows. Between the columns would have stood statues of the pharaohs. The whole effect would have been terrifying, and any visitors must have felt that they were trespassing in the hall of the gods themselves.

You leave through the **third pylon,** raised by Amenhotep III

(*R*.1390–1352 B.C.), the pharaoh responsible for Luxor Temple. Beyond is a narrow court that also lies on the temple's secondary axis. Four obelisks once marked this juncture, erected by Tuthmose I and III, but only one remains standing. Sections of the other three lie in ruins.

Continuing to the east on the main axis, the **fourth pylon,** built by Tuthmose I (*R*.1504–1492 B.C.), serves as the entrance to the earliest part of the temple. Immediately beyond, a small hypostyle hall contains later additions in the form of the **Obelisks of Hatshepsut.** Only one still stands (a second lies beside the nearby Sacred Lake). It is the tallest obelisk in Egypt at almost 100 feet (30 m) high, and although shaped from a single piece of granite, it appears to be of two stones of different colors. The story behind this is that when Tuthmose III finally came to power (see p. 274), he had a wall built around the obelisks to hide the hieroglyphs that glorified his hated stepmother Hatshepsut. He could not cover the top portion, as it carried dedications to Amun, so for centuries that part was more exposed to the elements and has taken a lighter tone through the effects of weathering.

From this point on, the temple is in a much more ruined state and it becomes increasingly hard to understand what all the elements are. Little remains of the fifth and sixth pylons, which stand close together, but just beyond them is a small court with two granite pillars carved with giant floral emblems representing Upper Egypt (the lily) and Lower Egypt (the papyrus). The boxlike structure ahead is the **Sacred Bark Shrine,** which still contains the plinth on which would have rested the bark of Amun. These barks were scale-model boats representing the vessels on which

A 3,200-year-old sentinel: One of two colossi of Ramses II fronting the temple's second pylon

Sound-and-light show

Three times every evening Karnak puts on a 90-minute, Hollywood-style sound-and-light show. The action starts at the avenue of ram-headed sphinxes, and then the audience follows as the narrative moves through the Great Court and Great Hypostyle Hall to a finale at the Sacred Lake. The commentary is pure bathos, but it is worth enduring for the opportunity of a starlit walk through the temple. Obtain your ticket from the temple ticket office; times are posted there. ∎

the gods traveled the heavens. Priests would have carried them aloft on poles during festivals and processions, including the local Opet Festival. The inner walls of the shrine are decorated with depictions of offering rites, while the outer walls show festival scenes,

temple is a small roofless vestibule famed as the Botanical Room because of the fine painted reliefs of plants and animals.

From here you can walk back around the south side of the temple beside the **Sacred Lake,** which once supplied the temple with

Filled by groundwater, the Sacred Lake provided water for the priests' ablutions.

Opposite: Wall reliefs are like a massive picturebook detailing the triumphs and activities of the pharaohs.

parts of which still have their original coloring.

The very earliest temples at this site stood where the central court now is. Across the open area, you reach the **Festival Temple of Tuthmose III,** built by the pharaoh as a memorial to himself. Curiously, the columns around the perimeter are square in section, while those in the center are round and larger at the top than at the base. Egyptologists speculate that they may represent tent poles, symbolic of the kind of military pavilion that might have been familiar to this pharaoh, who led his army on numerous campaigns. In the early Christian era this hall was used as a church, and you can still make out haloed saints painted on the columns. On the east side of the

water. There is a café beside the lake, and beyond is the first court of the precinct's north-south axis.

PRECINCTS OF MUT & MONTU

This subsidiary axis is basically a processional way between the various precincts of Karnak. The first court, by the café, is known as the **Cachette Court** because a haul of some 900 stone statues and statuettes was unearthed here in a deep pit in the early 20th century. It is thought that these were surplus statues. The priests of Karnak no longer had room for them, but at the same time could not discard them because of their hallowed nature. So they buried them. That way they stayed within the temple precincts, but out of the way. A similar cache was found buried beneath a court at Luxor Temple. Several of Karnak's statues now stand in front of the pylon to the south, the first of a series of four that ends with an avenue of sphinxes leading to the largely destroyed **Precinct of Mut.** The centerpiece is the ruined Temple of Mut, built by Amenhotep III, partly surrounded by another sacred lake. Throughout the precinct are granite statues of the lion goddess Sekhmet, the "Spreader of Terror."

As you return to the main Amun precinct, on your left is a monumental gateway covered with reliefs and with a winged sun-disk beneath a curving cornice. This belongs to the **Temple of Khonsu** and marks the original start of the Avenue of Sphinxes that joined Karnak to Luxor Temple a mile and a half (2.5 km) to the south.

Backtracking across the Amun temple, go out on the north side and to the left is an open-air museum with a collection of statuary found throughout the temple complexes. A separate ticket is required; buy it before entering Karnak.

Against the northern enclosure wall of the Amun precinct, just inside the gate leading to the Montu precinct, is the small **Temple of Ptah.** Ptah is the creator god who thought the world into being, and whose cult center was the ancient capital of Memphis. The temple was begun during the reign of Tuthmose III and expanded under the Ptolemies.

The nearby gate leads into the **Precinct of Montu,** smallest of Karnak's three walled compounds. Montu was the falcon-headed warrior god, the original deity of Thebes, and the enclosure contains his ruined temple as well as a sacred lake. The area is very dilapidated and is often closed to the public. ■

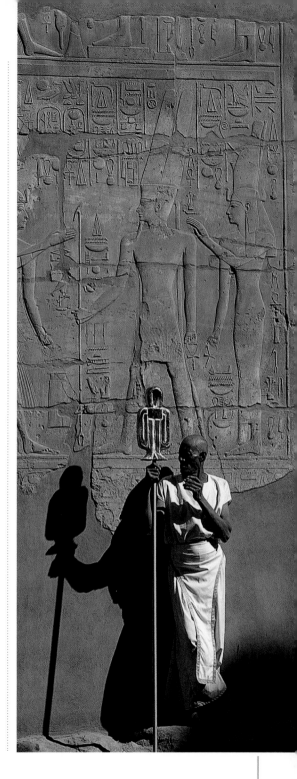

A group of early morning visitors step ashore on the West Bank.

Exploring the West Bank

Across the Nile from Luxor town lie the temples and tombs of the West Bank. Whether you explore them by air-conditioned tour bus, rented taxi, or by bicycle (see pp. 256–57), there are a few basic ground rules to bear in mind.

The first and most crucial rule is to set off early. By noon the sun is ferocious. It saps away the energy, and all appreciation of the monuments is then reduced to how much shade they offer. Secondly, do not attempt too much. Ancient Egypt overload sets in quickly in the heat, and about two or three sights is the limit before most visitors' eyes begin to glaze over. Don't feel guilty about retreating to the hotel during the afternoon for a siesta or relaxation beside the pool. About the time you have recovered, the temperature will have dropped slightly, and you can then visit the museums in town, Luxor Temple by night, or Karnak for the sound-and-light show.

Unfortunately, everybody else is likely to have had similar advice, so the West Bank is at its busiest in the early morning. The Valley of the Kings and the Temple of Hatshepsut are perpetually crowded, but some sights—including Deir al-Medina, Medinat Habu, and the Tombs of the Nobles, which are no less interesting—are only visited by the tour groups if they have time after they have worked through the A-list. Heading to these places first means a good chance of having them to yourself.

Individual tickets are required for each temple, tomb, or group of tombs. These have to be bought at the West Bank ticket office (*Tel 095/311 662;* see maps pp. 232 & 257). As tickets are valid only for the day of purchase, you have to decide your day's itinerary in advance. A large board lists all the sights and admission fees, which average at about $3.50 per sight. If you want to see everything here, you would end up spending just short of $100 on entrance alone (but you'd probably need to allow at least a week). The office opens at 6 a.m. If you are hoping to secure a ticket for the Tomb of Nefertari (see p. 264), you need to be in the line by at least 5:30 a.m., as the number of people allowed into the tomb each day is restricted to the first 150 visitors. ■

Colossi of Memnon

Twin figures of
Amenhotep III
greet the dawn.

BESIDE THE ROAD TO THE WEST BANK MONUMENTS, IN A
dusty clearing among the sugarcane fields, these celebrated statues
are virtually all that remain of one of Egypt's greatest temples.

Each carved from a single piece of
stone, the colossi are 59 feet (18 m)
high and were famous in antiquity
for a bell-like tone emitted each sunrise by the more northerly of the
two. This mysterious sound led the
Greeks to believe the statues were of
the immortal Memnon, who each
morning was greeting his mother,
the dawn goddess Eos. Archaeologists
think the noise could have resulted
from the passage of air through the
pores of the stone, caused by the
warming of the sun's first rays. The
noise ceased following a restoration
of the statue by Roman emperor
Septimius Severus in A.D. 170.

We now know that the giant
seated figures are the New Kingdom
pharaoh Amenhotep III. The smaller carved figures at his feet are his
wife, Tiye, and mother, Mutemuia.
They stood here before the entrance
pylon of the king's mortuary tem-

ple, just as Ramses II stands before
the first pylon at Luxor Temple.
However, it is believed that this
temple was much larger. Archaeologists have calculated that it surpassed even Karnak in size, but it
has almost completely vanished.
Repeated plundering and ancient
earthquake damage reduced it to
rubble, which was then eroded
away to nothing by the annual
flooding of the Nile. This temple
was unique in that it stood on the
low-lying plain. Each year the rising
waters must have flooded the outer
halls and courts, leaving only the
raised inner sanctuary dry.

Aside from the colossi, all that
remains of the temple are a carved
reerected stela and some column
bases. Luxor Museum (see pp.
244-45) and Cairo's Egyptian
Museum (see pp. 70–79) display
pieces of statuary from the site. ■

Colossi of
Memnon
▲ 232 B3

CYCLING THE WEST BANK

Cycling the West Bank

The numerous temples and dozens of tombs of the West Bank spread over several miles, making it impractical to explore on foot. Tour buses and rented taxis are the usual options, but if you are in reasonably good shape, then there is no better way to get around than by bicycle.

Bicycles are ideal for stop-start sight-seeing, but be prepared for long inclines and the heat.

Bicycles can be rented by the day for just a few dollars at several places along Al-Mahatta Street in Luxor town (see p. 235). You can transport them across to the West Bank on the local ferry, which departs every ten minutes from a dock in front of Luxor Temple. Alternatively, you can rent a bicycle on the West Bank from the village shops just up the hill from the ferry landing. Try the bike out first to make sure that it is roadworthy. Remember to take some bottled water—it is essential to drink plenty to avoid dehydration.

The road to the monuments runs almost perfectly straight through fields watered by a network of small irrigation canals. After crossing a combination of a particularly large canal and a major road intersection, you'll see off to the right the domed mud-brick structures of **New Gurna** ❶, a model village designed in 1946 by Egypt's "architect of the people," Hassan Fathy (1900-1989). Made with traditional materials, it was constructed to rehouse the inhabitants of Old Gurna, but in the end they refused to move (see p. 270).

A mile farther on, you spot the first of the West Bank monuments, the **Colossi of Memnon** ❷, a lone pair of statues standing sentinel in the fields (see p. 255). Just a few hundred yards beyond, a small, single-story

building off to the left houses the **West Bank ticket office** ❸ (Tel 095/311 662), the only place you can purchase tickets for the sights (see p. 254). Past the ticket office the cultivation ends abruptly as the land begins to climb up to the Theban Hills. Take a right at the big junction and cycle parallel to the edge of the fields, soon passing the **Ramesseum** ❹ (see pp. 267–69) on your right. Huddled on the slopes to the left are the brightly colored houses of **Old Gurna** ❺, many painted with pharaonic motifs and the aircraft, ships, and black-cubed Qaaba that indicates the occupant has made a pilgrimage to Mecca. In such villages you may see children leading goats, women making bread by a traditional method, and farmers with water buffalo—day-to-day sights familiar from the scenes painted on the walls of the ancient tombs.

About a mile farther on you come to a T-junction; turn left. As you begin to cycle up a gradual rise, off to the right is **Howard Carter's House** ❻, recognizable by its dome. This is where the dogged Egyptologist lived during his search for an unrobbed tomb, which ended in success at the tomb of Tutankhamun. For years there has been talk of turning the place into a museum, but with nothing to show yet. Go straight on for another mile and a half

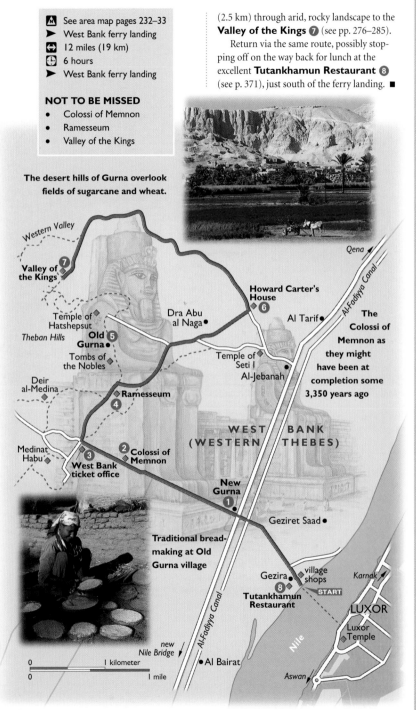

- ▲ See area map pages 232–33
- ► West Bank ferry landing
- ↔ 12 miles (19 km)
- ⊕ 6 hours
- ► West Bank ferry landing

NOT TO BE MISSED
- Colossi of Memnon
- Ramesseum
- Valley of the Kings

(2.5 km) through arid, rocky landscape to the **Valley of the Kings** ❼ (see pp. 276–285).

Return via the same route, possibly stopping off on the way back for lunch at the excellent **Tutankhamun Restaurant** ❽ (see p. 371), just south of the ferry landing. ∎

The desert hills of Gurna overlook fields of sugarcane and wheat.

Western Valley

Qena

Al-Fadiyya Canal

Valley of the Kings ❼

Howard Carter's House ❻

Al Tarif

The Colossi of Memnon as they might have been at completion some 3,350 years ago

Dra Abu al Naga

Temple of Hatshepsut

Theban Hills

Old Gurna ❺

Tombs of the Nobles

Temple of Seti I
Al-Jebanah

Deir al-Medina

Ramesseum ❹

WEST BANK (WESTERN THEBES)

Medinat Habu

West Bank ticket office ❸

Colossi of Memnon ❷

New Gurna ❶

Geziret Saad

Traditional bread-making at Old Gurna village

Gezira

village shops

Karnak

START

Tutankhamun Restaurant ❽

LUXOR

Luxor Temple

new Nile Bridge

Al Bairat

Nile

Aswan

Al-Fadiyya Canal

0   1 kilometer
0   1 mile

Ramses III is depicted on the massive entrance pylon with raised flail and gripping the hair of his vanquished foes.

Medinat Habu

OFTEN BYPASSED BY TOURISTS HEADING STRAIGHT FOR the more famous Valley of the Kings and Ramesseum, this magnificent complex, dominated by the Temple of Ramses III, is the best preserved monument on the West Bank. It contains more than 2,700 square miles (7,000 sq km) of decorated surfaces, and to explore the place properly can take up to half a day.

Medinat Habu
- 232 B3
- $$. Tickets from West Bank ticket office only (see p. 254)

No one is quite sure where the name (City of Habu) comes from, although there was a temple to a Hapu, son of Amenhotep, just to the north of here. Built as a power base for Ramses III (*R.*1184–1153 B.C.), the last of the great pharaohs of Egypt, at its height Medinat Habu certainly resembled a walled city, with temples, palaces, chapels, and accommodations for the priests and officials.

It was the administrative center for the region, and its great fortified walls offered refuge to the area's inhabitants in times of trouble. Later, during the Christian era, a Coptic town of churches and dwellings was built on and around the site, only to be abandoned in the ninth century A.D. after an outbreak of plague. As you approach today, you can still make out the ancient mud-brick houses built on top of the even more ancient enclosure walls.

Entrance is via the **High Gate,** a very unpharaonic, three-story structure designed along the lines of a Syrian fortress and commissioned to commemorate a Middle Eastern victory. Upstairs were the king's private apartments, decorated with reliefs of him being entertained by lithe dancers. Unfortunately, the staircase is in such a dilapidated condition that it is no longer possible to go up.

Through the gate is the great court and the approach to the massive main temple. Before that, off to the left, are the **Chapels of the Divine Adoratrices,** a series of small 25th-dynasty mortuary chapels contained in one well-preserved block dedicated to the priestesses of Amun. To the right is the **Small Temple,** begun in the 18th dynasty under Hatshepsut and constantly expanded until Roman times. It is hard to pay too much attention, though, when you are being visually mugged by the fantastic spectacle of the **Temple of Ramses III.**

Looking like an extension of the mountains behind, the **entrance pylon** is immense. Hyperbolic scenes of the king defeating the Libyans and Sea Peoples, both of whom attacked Egypt during Ramses III's reign, decorate the pylon. Similar scenes are depicted in the **first court,** including scribes counting piles of severed hands and tongues and, over on the wall to the left, Ramses standing on the carved heads of captives, which protrude from the walls like medieval gargoyles. Elsewhere, figures and hieroglyphs are incised so deeply into the stone that they provide nesting places for birds.

What is especially fine about this temple is that parts of the wall reliefs, ceilings, and columns remain in their original painted state, colored with vivid primary blues, yellows, and reds, giving some idea of how riotously bright these places must once have been. This is particularly so in the **second court,** which is in an excellent state of preservation, apart from the damage done by early Christians, who hacked away the giant figures of Ramses when they converted the court into a church; look for crosses carved into pillars. The **hypostyle hall** is in a worse condition, with only stubs of columns to indicate the presence of the courts, but there are a number of **side chapels,** with walls covered with reliefs depicting feasting and worship.

West of the temple are the remains of the **Royal Palace,** although these are no more than traces and outlines, while in the right-hand corner nearest the road is the fetid black **Sacred Lake.** Once the site of Osiris worship, the lake is still reputed by local villagers to have magical properties able to bring fertility to the barren. ■

KEY TO SITE PLAN

Medinat Habu
1 Ticket office
2 Entrance
3 Ptolemaic pylon
4 High Gate
5 Sacred Lake
6 Small Temple
7 Chapels of the Divine Adoratrices
8 Entrance pylon
9 First court
10 Royal Palace
11 Second court
12 Hypostyle hall
13 Side chapels

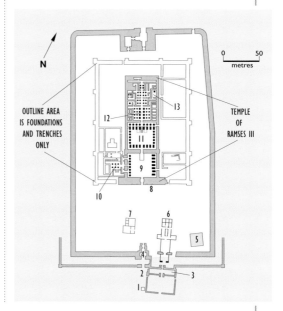

Deir al-Medina

ALL THOSE MAGNIFICENT TEMPLES AND TOMBS ON THE
West Bank dedicated to the glory of ancient Egypt's kings, royals,
and nobles—somebody had to build them. Traces of these largely
unsung artisans and craftsmen are usually few, but Deir al-Medina
provides a fascinating exception, because it was here that the workers
engaged in the building and decoration of the monuments lived
and were buried.

Excavations at this site have
revealed a **Workers' Village** of
about 70 dwellings enclosed within
a protective wall. The ruins, while
only a few bricks high, clearly show
the layout of the houses, each with
an entrance opening off the narrow
streets, leading to three or four
rooms, with stairs down to cellar
spaces and up to what must have
been roof terraces. In places the
stone floors still bear the marks
made by opening and closing
doors. Remnants of foodstuffs discovered here by archaeologists
show that the workers existed on a
diet of fish and cereals, supplemented by fruit, honey, and occasionally meat. They brewed and
drank beer.

Much of our knowledge of
these people comes from limestone
fragments called *ostraca* inscribed
with accounts, records, and personal reminders. Archaeologists have
found thousands of these ancient
Post-It notes amid the houses. They
tell us who lived here and where
exactly, their names, what their
work was, even how much they
earned (payment being in grain
and food). More than any other site
in Egypt, here you feel the presence
of the ancient Egyptians.

Nestled right beside the village is
its small **necropolis.** Tombs here
took the form of a walled courtyard
with a chapel, beneath which was
the burial chamber. Often the
chapel was surmounted by a brick
pyramidion (mini-pyramid), and
some of these have been restored to
their original state. Farther west,
climbing up the valley side, you'll
find a few more simple tombs,
hewn out of the rock. Three of
these are open to visitors and are
well worth a look inside for the
beautiful wall paintings, rendered
predominantly in warm tones of
yellows, ochers, and golds.

Closest to the parking lot is
the **Tomb of Inherkhau,** a
foreman who lived during the
reigns of both Ramses III and
Ramses IV. Inherkhau is depicted
frequently, in some instances bald-
headed and in other places with
black curly locks. However, the
scene in this tomb everybody
remembers is that of a stylized
long-eared cat killing the serpent
Apophis under a holy tree.

**Left: Inherkhau
dressed as a
priest with the
distinctive shaven
head and the
leopard skin.**

Deir al-Medina
- 232 B3
- $$. Tickets from
  West Bank ticket
  office only (see
  p. 254)

Next along is the **Tomb of Sennedjem,** described in hieroglyphs as a "servant in the Place of Truth," which is the ancients' name for the Valley of Kings, where most of the inhabitants of Deir al-Medina were employed. Although today it is a distance of several miles by road to get between the two sites, they are actually almost adjacent, lying either side of a rocky hill. It is possible to walk from one to the other in half an hour. When Sennedjem's tomb was first opened in 1886, it contained a rich cache of funerary equipment, now exhibited at the Egyptian Museum in Cairo (see pp. 70–79). The tomb is still worth visiting for the beautiful paintings found there.

A little further up the slope is the **Tomb of Peshedu,** another servant in the Place of Truth. To enter his tomb you pass between two symmetrical representations of Anubis, the jackal-headed god, but the most famous scene is immediately to the right in the burial chamber; it shows Peshedu crouching by a stream under a palm tree.

Up the valley from the Workers' Village and necropolis, along a rough path, is a small **Ptolemaic temple** dedicated to Hathor and built in the third century B.C. It is a very modest affair—a mud-brick wall around a compound—but painted bas-reliefs inside have kept some of their color. In the early Christian period it was taken over for use by the Copts, which is where the name of this whole site comes from: Deir al-Medina, Monastery of the City. ■

Simple stone walls mark out dwellings and streets where laborers and craftsmen lived.

Valley of the Queens

Valley of the Queens
A   232 A3
$ $$. Tickets from the West Bank ticket office only (see p. 254)

A WIDE WADI IN THE SOUTHERNMOST PART OF THE Theban necropolis, the Valley of the Queens is where royal brides, princes, princesses, and members of the royal court were buried. At least 75 tombs are burrowed into the rock, of which only a handful are ever open to the public—but that includes what for many is the highlight of the West Bank, the beautiful Tomb of Nefertari.

The bunker-like entrances to tombs dot the rocky hillside.

Opposite: Nefertari, "the most beautiful," wears a white linen gown painted to give an impression of transparency.

If you have already visited the Valley of the Kings, then you know what to expect here: a craggy, sun-blasted landscape pocked with the small black openings of tunnel-like entrances. Of the tombs that can be visited, three are of sons of Ramses III, builder of the great temple at Medinat Habu (see pp. 258–59). These are all fairly modest endeavors, tunneled straight and level into the rock face with few steps or slopes and consisting of a single, fairly short corridor with one or two small side rooms. When discovered by an Italian expedition early in the 20th century, all had been completely looted in antiquity, but the wall decoration was remarkably well preserved and constitutes a great treasure in itself. Colored reliefs cover every surface

of the tombs. These depict a ritual journey of the souls of the princes, beginning in the company of their father, who introduces them to various deities in the afterlife. Deeper into the tomb the princes are left alone in front of the gods.

The **Tomb of Khaemwaset** belongs to the eldest son. He is easy to pick out in the reliefs because of his distinctive hairstyle, collected in a tress and falling sideways over his ear—look for him in the second chamber, on the right, following behind his father, shown wearing the classic blue-and-gold pharaoh's headdress. In the final chamber is the prince alone making offerings to a seated Osiris, lord of the afterlife, whose face is painted green, the color of regeneration.

The **Tomb of Amunher-khepshep** is that of the designated heir to throne, who died at about age 15 (of what we don't know). As in his brother's tomb, the scenes on the walls show his father, Ramses III, introducing him to the gods and guardians of the afterlife. In the farthest chamber a glass cabinet contains the skeleton of a fetus wrapped in bandages. Guides will tell you how Amunher-khepshep's mother was pregnant at the time of his death, and in her grief she aborted the child and entombed it with her dead son. In reality, the fetus was discovered elsewhere in the valley and has no proven connection with this tomb.

On the way to the tomb of Amunherkhepshep you can usually

also enter the **Tomb of Titi,** wife of a pharaoh from the 20th dynasty. The tomb is simple, but lavishly decorated. There are scenes depicting guardians of the underworld, and Hathor is shown pouring Nile water to rejuvenate the queen.

All the above, while certainly worth visiting, pale before the **Tomb of Nefertari,** which is by far the most stunning tomb in all

Egypt. So fabulous is it that it even justifies the extraordinary entrance fee of LE100 ($30). As breathing increases humidity which in turn causes the salt crystalization so damaging to plaster, visitors to the tomb are limited to 150 per day, with a maximum of ten in the tomb at any one time. Each visitor is also limited to only ten minutes in the tomb. Despite the cost, demand for

tickets is high. In order to have any chance of getting one, you need to be at the West Bank ticket office well before it opens (see p. 254).

Nefertari (whose name means "the most beautiful") was the favorite wife of Ramses II, the New Kingdom pharaoh known for his monuments of self-celebration, such as the Ramesseum and Abu Simbel (see pp. 267–69). But it is a

mark of the pharaoh's respect for his wife that at Abu Simbel he dedicated a temple to her, where the queen is represented in large statues equal in size to those of the king—most queens in pharaonic art only come up to their husband's knees. Similarly, Nefertari's tomb appears as an exquisite labor of love.

Entered via a steep stairway, the tomb consists of an antechamber

The goddess Isis presents Nefertari to the scarab-headed god Khepri.

A tomb guardian ensures no touching and no lingering, with ten minutes only allowed per visit.

with annex, and then a second stairway leading down to the burial chamber. Every surface is adorned with scenes of the queen, usually wearing a flowing, partially transparent white gown and a vulture headdress, in the company of the gods. Four years of restoration, financed by the Getty Research Institute and completed in 1992, have resulted in a blaze of color that is, quite literally, breathtaking.

In the antechamber, to the left of the entrance stair, Nefertari plays *sennet,* a checkers-like game, while to the right the role call of gods starts with a seated Osiris holding a flail, followed by jackal-headed Anubis. On the inside of the arch is the goddess Neith, and then Harsiesis leads Nefertari before seated figures of Re-Harakhty and

Hathor. Some of the best scenes in the tomb are through in the annex, including the queen facing the ibis-headed god of wisdom, Thoth, and consecrating tables of offerings in front of Osiris (left) and Re (right).

Scenes down the second staircase show (on the left) Nefertari making offerings to the goddesses Isis and Nephthys, while opposite she does likewise with Hathor and Selkis. As in the upper chambers, the burial chamber has an astronomical ceiling of gold stars on blue. The queen's pink granite sarcophagus was originally located at the center of the hall, between the four pillars, but only a few fragments were found when the tomb was rediscovered by archaeologists in 1904, plunderers having got there first, way back in antiquity. ∎

Ramesseum

Two young girls
face the mighty
Ramses II—3,000
years their senior.

AS IT EXISTS TODAY, THE RAMESSEUM IS NO MORE THAN three small tableaus of ruins, with a field of ridges, holes, and bases to indicate where the rest of the complex once stood. But its reputation far outstrips its physical presence. Famed Egyptologist Jean-François Champollion called it the "most noble and pure in Thebes as far as great monuments are concerned," while the English poet Percy Bysshe Shelley immortalized it in verse (see p. 269).

Its reputation rests with its creator, pharaoh Ramses II (*R.*1279–1213 B.C.) of the 19th dynasty, mightiest ruler of all, who wore the double crown of Egypt for 67 years. Construction of the Ramesseum began soon after Ramses II took the throne, and it was probably only finished around the 22nd year of his reign. Intended as his grand

and immortalizing mortuary complex, in its completed state the Ramesseum had a central main temple flanked by small temples to his mother, Tuya, and favored wife, Nefertari, palaces, administrative buildings, and vast areas of store-houses. No effort was spared to make this the greatest of all monuments, but later dynasties

Ramesseum
△ 232 B3
$ $$. Tickets from the West Bank ticket office only (see p. 254)

Columns portray
the pharaoh in
the guise of
Osiris, Lord of
the Underworld.

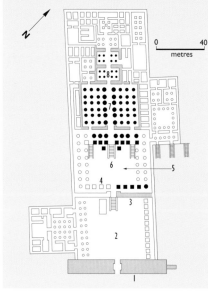

0 ___ 40
metres

KEY TO SITE PLAN

Ramesseum
1 First pylon
2 First court
3 Second pylon
4 Fallen colossus of
  Ramses II
5 Entrance
6 Second court
7 Hypostyle hall
8 Astronomical Room

dismantled the Ramesseum to use the stone in building their own temples. Early Christians took over what was left and converted the remains to a church, further damaging the pagan statues and reliefs.

What remains today are parts of Ramses II's main temple. Its layout inspired Medinat Habu (see pp. 258–59), which was built by Ramses III, and it may be a good idea to visit there first to help understand what you are looking at here.

Whereas at Medinat Habu visitors experience the building as intended—approaching the first pylon, passing through into the first court, the second, and then the hypostyle hall—at the Ramesseum the visitors' entrance is from the side, directly into the **second court.** This was originally enclosed by a double row of columns, of which just the bases remain.

On the left is a part of the **second pylon,** with four colossi of Ramses II in the form of a mummy,

his arms crossed holding a flail and a scepter in the manner of the god Osiris. Beside them are the head and shoulders of a freestanding **colossus of Ramses II,** now toppled and smashed. The king's cartouche is plainly visible on his right shoulder. Estimated to have stood over six stories high, this is not only the largest freestanding statue ever made in Egypt, but also possibly one of the most titanic works of sculpture achieved in human history. What makes the task even more astounding is that the stone block for the statue came from the quarries at Aswan and had to be shipped some 150 miles (240 km) to the north. The feet of the colossus are planted in the first court of the temple, where the statue originally sat.

Across the second court are four more Osiride pillars, and before them a black granite head of the pharaoh that belonged to one of two statues that stood here. Its twin was removed by Giovanni Belzoni (see pp. 80–81) in 1816 and is now displayed at the British Museum in London, although the lower half remains here in place, to the left of what was the main stairway up to the **hypostyle hall.**

Only 29 of the original 48 papyrus columns of the hall are still standing, but they all have beautifully decorated and colored capitals. The surrounding walls show scenes of Ramses II's military victories, while on the far wall, on the right-hand side of the doorway, is a bit of historical graffiti—the inscribed and dated name BELZONI.

On the far side of the hall is the **Astronomical Room,** so called because of its ceiling, which depicts a celestial calendar of the constellations. This ceiling probably had a practical use in helping to determine the timing of religious ceremonies. ∎

Ozymandias

I met a traveller from an antique land
Who said: Two vast and trunkless legs of stone
Stand in the desert....Near them, on the sand,
Half sunk, a shattered visage lies, whose frown,
And wrinkled lip, and sneer of cold command,
Tell that its sculptor well those passions read
Which yet survive, stamped on these lifeless things,
The hand that mocked them, and the heart that fed:
And on the pedestal these words appear:
"My name is Ozymandias, king of kings:
Look on my works, ye Mighty, and despair!"
Nothing beside remains. Round the decay
Of that colossal wreck, boundless and bare
The lone and level sands stretch far away.

English poet Shelley (1792–1822) never visited Egypt. His verse is fantasy, inspired by a visit to London's British Museum, where he may have seen the head of Ramses II, known to the Greeks as Ozymandias. ∎

Guardians & thieves

The mud-brick houses of Gurna have lined the mountainside above the magnificent temple remains of Thebes for generations. Prior to that, if 18th-century travelers' accounts are to be believed, the Gurnawis, as they are known, lived in the tombs themselves, many of which are little more than caves.

A child in the village of Gurna wears a shawl that typifies the bright colors seen around here.

On any given day, groups of tourists can be seen talking to the villagers and taking pictures of the brightly colored houses. The fact that people still live in and among the ancient monuments provides a continuity between ancient and modern that visitors find as fascinating as the pharaonic tombs and temples they have come to see. Many sit and have tea in the villagers' homes, often the only chance they have to interact with ordinary Egyptians during their stay in the country. Some of the villagers earn a living making small reproductions of pharaonic statues or little dolls that they sell to tourists. A few have set up small kiosks selling soft drinks or have opened "alabaster factories" making carved reproductions of pieces of famous pharaonic statuary. However, a century ago it was a very different kind of cottage industry that made the Gurnawis infamous.

About 1875, valuable antiquities began showing up in the marketplace, prompting the Egyptian authorities to suspect someone had found, and was plundering, an unknown tomb. Inquiries led to the village of Gurna, specifically to the Abdel Rassoul brothers. Initially they protested their innocence until, in the spring of 1881, a disagreement caused a disgruntled family member to blow the whistle and lead government officials to the stash. A crevice high up on a cliff face near the Temple of Hatshepsut was revealed as the opening of a massive shaft leading down into the mountainside. By the faint light of candles, officials were able to make out piles of sarcophagi inscribed with the names of some of the most famous pharaohs of the New Kingdom, including Tuthmose III, Seti I, and Ramses II. In all, the mummies of 40 pharaohs, queens, and nobles were found there.

It seems that the New Kingdom priests realized that the bodies of their kings would never be safe from violation in their own tombs, no matter what precautions were taken against grave robbers, so they moved them to this communal grave. When the cache was found by the authorities, the mummies were immediately removed to Cairo, where many of them are now on display at the Egyptian Museum (see pp. 70–79).

Ever since, the Egyptian government has been eager to get rid of the village of Gurna. In the 1940s it sponsored architect Hassan Fathy to create a new village, known as New Gurna (see p. 256), on agricultural land nearer to the river, but the Gurnawis refused to be tempted down from their traditional hillside homes. The Gurnawis insist that whatever tomb-robbing did exist in the past is now over.

However, the authorities also contend that the houses of Gurna prevent the excavation of other, as-yet-undiscovered tombs in the hillside. Moreover, they say, the presence of the village destroys the "panorama" of the area. Most visitors would disagree and contend that the colorful village is a spectacle in itself. Nonetheless, plans are again afoot to move the entire village to a specially built desert settlement some miles distant. ∎

Right: Brightly decorated Gurnawi houses add a welcome splash of color in the otherwise dusty, barren landscape.

Tombs of the Nobles

Tombs of the Nobles

🅰 232 B4

💲 $$. Tickets from the West Bank ticket office only (see p. 254)

ANCIENT EGYPT OVERLOAD MEANS THAT AFTER DOING all the must-sees, most visitors are too weary for yet more tombs. But the burial chambers that riddle the hillside between the Ramesseum and Hatshepsut's temple are very different. Belonging to nonroyals, like governors, mayors, and scribes, these modest little burial complexes offer a glimpse of a more human side of ancient Egypt.

The frizzy locks of a guest at Ramose's banquet are sculpted into limestone with supreme skill.

Set among the painted houses and yards of the hillside village of Gurna, the tombs are not always easy to find. Signs are few and you have to watch carefully for the modern, bunker-like entrances. Some 14 are open to visitors; divided into five groups, each requires its own ticket (bought in advance from the West Bank ticket office; see p. 254). All of the tombs are heavily decorated, but unlike those of the kings and queens, where the images are of a divine nature related to the afterlife, scenes in the Tombs of the Nobles depict the living, with the day-to-day activities of life as it was 4,500 years ago.

TOMBS OF RAMOSE (NO. 55), USERHET (NO. 56), & KHAEMHET (NO. 57)

Lying immediately north of the Ramesseum, behind an alabaster factory, this trio is just off the main road. Ramose was a governor of Thebes during the reigns of Amenhotep III and Akhenaten. His tomb is larger than most, with a hypostyle hall supported by a forest of columns. Only one wall is painted; it depicts the deceased's funeral, with a procession carrying the funerary furniture and a crowd of wailing women. Other surfaces are decorated with sculpted reliefs that are masterful in their definition and texture and ability to convey life. Khaemhet's tomb, which would have been crafted at the same time (he was Amenhotep III's court scribe and overseer of granaries),

shares the same high quality of workmanship. On the left-hand wall of the first vestibule is a particularly fine depiction of Khaemhet making food offerings in the form of bread and geese.

TOMBS OF KHONSU (NO. 31), USERHAT (NO. 51), & BENIA (NO. 343)

This cluster of tombs lies 100 yards (90 m) east of the previous group. Khonsu was an adviser to Tuthmose III, and unlike the ones described above, his tomb is covered with colorful reliefs, although many are badly damaged. On the right-hand wall of the first vestibule, down near the bottom, is a funeral procession beside a pyramidal tomb, very much like those at nearby Deir al-Medina. The tombs of Userhat (not to be confused with Userhat, No. 56) and Benia are also highly decorated. The last one has three painted limestone statues in a niche, representing Benia sitting between his mother and father.

TOMBS OF NAKHT (NO. 52) & MENNA (NO. 69)

Egyptologists speculate that these two tombs, dating from the reign of Amenhotep III, were the work of the same artist. Both are covered in images of rural life, depicting the sowing, plowing, and harvesting of crops; hunting and fishing; and, in the tomb of Nakht, winemaking—figures pick the grapes off vines, while others trample the fruit. In the same tomb is one of the most famous pieces of pharaonic art, reproduced on posters and tourist bazaar papyri—three female musicians, one playing the lute, one a harp, and one a wind instrument.

TOMBS OF NEFER-RONPET (NO. 178), DHUTMOSI (NO. 295), & NEFER-SEKHERU (NO. 296)

About 100 yards (90 m) west of the tomb of Menna, this grouping of three is probably the least essential of all the Tombs of the Nobles, although two of them have ceilings with attractive geometric designs.

TOMBS OF SENNEFER (NO. 96) & REKHMIRE (NO. 100)

These two tombs are the highlights of the area. Sennefer was a senior official at the time of Amenhotep II, and a man obviously very much in love with his wife. On the four pillars that support the deeply subterranean burial chamber, the couple are shown no less than 14 times, always touching and holding. The ceiling is wonderfully informal—the artist exploited the unevenness of the rock to give an almost three-dimensional quality to a spread of vines snaking across the chamber and hung with bunches of grapes.

Although roughly of the same age, the Tomb of Rekhmire is completely different in character. Where that of Sennefer suggested intimacy, this one is almost bureaucratic in its fastidiousness. It is also quite wonderful. Rekhmire was a governor under Tuthmose III and Amenhotep II, a time when the Egyptian empire was expanding, so one wall (left on entering the vestibule) shows tributes extracted from foreign countries, including baboons, monkeys, and a giraffe from Nubia, weapons, carts, horses, and a bear from Syria, and pots

from what might be Crete. In the narrow chapel, in which the height of the ceiling climbs sharply from the entrance, the walls serve as huge storyboards. One side depicts the funerary banquet, while the other has scenes of temple-building, with laborers making mud bricks, sculptors working on two colossi, and the setting up of an obelisk. ∎

The depiction of the three musicians is one of the most famous of ancient Egyptian wall paintings.

Temple of Hatshepsut

A FIRM FAVORITE WITH THE TOUR BUSES, HATSHEPSUT'S temple is a showpiece of the West Bank. Its setting is superb—the temple rises in a series of broad terraces that at the topmost level join with a great bay of limestone cliffs. Close up, though, there is far less to be seen than at many other sites, and what there is, is often obscured by the crowds.

The Tomboy Queen

Identifiable by her cow ears, the image of Hathor adorns capitals at her chapel.

Temple of Hatshepsut

🅜 232 B4

💲 $$. Tickets from the West Bank ticket office only (see p. 254)

Much of the mystique of the temple has to do with the personality of Hatshepsut herself, ancient Egypt's only woman pharaoh. As a daughter of Tuthmose I she had been married off to her half-brother and heir to the throne. He duly succeeded to the throne as Tuthmose II, but died in his early thirties, leaving one young son whom he named as his successor, Tuthmose III. At first, stepmother Hatshepsut acted as regent for the young king, but later usurped him altogether and declared herself pharaoh. To legitimize her position she was portrayed in statues and reliefs with all the regalia of kingship, including the royal false beard. She held the throne until her death—though there is some speculation that Tuthmose III might have had a hand in this, after being kept so long in waiting.

The site of her temple is often refered to as Deir al-Bahri, after a Coptic monastery *(deir)* that once stood here. The original ancient Egyptian name was the far more evocative Djeser-djeseru, Sacred of Sacreds. Three temples stood side by side, but the two neighbors have not survived. Hatshepsut's temple very nearly didn't make it either. Her successor, Tuthmose III, vandalized the place out of spite at being kept off the throne. When discovered in the mid-19th century the temple was in ruins, and its present appearance is largely due to massive reconstruction by a Polish-Egyptian team that has been

working on site since 1961. It is debatable how successful this rebuild is—one travel magazine described the place as resembling a Romanian bus depot. Exaggerated the comment may be, but the temple definitely has a clean-lined, almost brutal modernist feel to it.

Only the core of the temple has been re-created; missing is the sphinx-lined causeway and the monumental entrance pylon that it would have led up to. Beyond the pylon would have been the first court, now a dusty flat area where the lower ramp begins. Most people pass straight on up, but first take time to look around the **lower colonnade,** which depicts scenes of fishing and birds being caught in nets (right-hand side), and the transportation of the queen's great obelisks from the Aswan quarries to Karnak (left-hand side).

For years now, the second court has served as an open-air workshop for masons chipping away at new blocks for the temple. The finished stone goes up the second ramp to the upper terrace, which is closed to visitors and likely to remain that way for years to come. Instead, you can view the carved reliefs around the **second-level colonnade,** which on the right-hand side show the queen's divine "birth" (more propaganda to emphasize her right to reign as pharaoh), and on the left-hand side tell the story of an expedition to the land of Punt. Nobody is quite sure where this Punt was, but the best guess is that

it equates to what is now Ethiopia or northern Somalia. There is a detailed scene of ships being loaded up with sacks and animals, and myrrh trees being carried in baskets. Look, too, for the reception of the Egyptian embassy by the king of Punt and his queen, who is almost elephantine in appearance.

Beyond the Punt scenes is the small **Chapel of Hathor,** which was originally approached by its own separate ramp up from the first court. It is crowded with columns, with capitals in the form of the features of the cow goddess. At the back of the chapel, just to the left of the entrance (usually barred) to the sanctuary, there is a carved relief of Hathor in the form of a cow licking the hand of Queen Hatshepsut. ■

A hot-air balloon drifts over Hatshepsut's terraces, offering its passengers a bird's-eye view.

Valley of the Kings

ON FIRST APPEARANCES IT IS JUST A SUN-SCORCHED, ARID valley between steep-sided rocky hills. But this is the one of the richest archaeological sites on Earth. During the greatest period in ancient Egyptian history, practically every pharaoh was buried here, in deeply sunk tombs of extraordinary beauty, decorated from floor to ceiling with mysterious images of the afterlife. These subterranean chambers were filled to overflowing with vast treasures, and although almost everything was looted in antiquity, it is impossible not to entertain the thought that maybe, even today, some magnificent cache secreted away still remains, waiting to be discovered.

Mortuary temples, lined up along the edge of the floodplain, where the cultivation ended and the dry slopes of the Theban Hills began, kept alive the memory of the dead pharaohs. But the actual bodies were hidden away in this secluded valley, with only one easily guarded entrance. The secretive tombs were intended to preserve the pharaoh's mummies for eternity. It is sad that they should have so completely failed, but ancient tomb robbers got there long before archaeologists did.

Each tomb was designed to resemble the underworld, with a long, inclined corridor descending into either an antechamber or a series of pillared halls, and ending in a burial chamber. No two tombs are exactly the same, although they all share common features. Early tombs have a right-angled plan, later tombs have one straight axis. In the earliest tombs only the burial chamber received decoration, but beginning with the 19th dynasty (Ramses I in 1295 B.C.) the wall

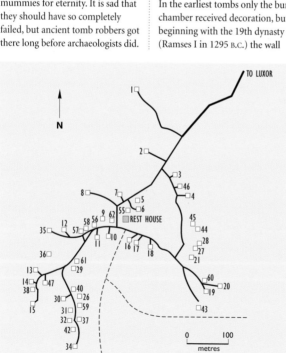

KEY TO SITE PLAN

Valley of the Kings. The numbers below are the KV tomb numbers and are only those referred to in the text.

2 Ramses IV
5 "The lost tomb"
6 Ramses IX
8 Merenptah
9 Ramses VI
10 Ameemesses
11 Ramses III
17 Seti I
34 Tuthmose III
35 Amenhotep II
43 Tuthmose IV
57 Horemheb
62 Tutankhamun

paintings were carried through into all parts. These scenes were copied from the books of the afterlife such as the Amduat, Litany of Re, and Book of the Dead, and act as a guide to the afterlife. They depict the protocol the king must carry out, presenting himself to the various gods and goddesses. So that the deceased could live as they had on Earth, the tombs were provided with furniture, papyrus scrolls, amulets, jewelry, ritual objects, statues of gods, and *ushabti*, miniature effigies of the king that would carry out any tasks or labors on his behalf in the afterlife.

Despite the ancient architects' best efforts, they were repeatedly thwarted by robbers who despoiled most of the royal mummies and carted away the treasures buried with them. Before the era of the pharaohs was over, most of the tombs had been emptied. A further two-and-a-half millennia of looting and scavenging meant that by the time the archaeologists began excavating here in the early 19th century, anything that could possibly be carried away had been. Almost. Howard Carter's find (see pp. 278–79) proved that the robbers had not got everything.

Tutankhamun, though, is regarded as a unique stroke of good fortune, unlikely to be repeated. Few serious archaeologists believe that there are more royal tombs to be found, and rather than treasure-hunting, the priority in the Valley of the Kings is now to study and better understand the finds already at hand.

So many tombs riddle the Valley of the Kings that Egyptologists have been kept busy here for nearly two centuries.

Valley of the Kings

🅜 232 B4

💲 $$. Tickets from the West Bank ticket office only (see p. 254)

VISITING THE VALLEY

Tickets for the Valley of the Kings cannot be bought at the site. They can only be had from the West Bank ticket office (see p. 254), located near the Colossi of Memnon. One ticket is good for any three tombs, excluding Tutankhamun's, which has its own separate ticket. If you want to visit more than three tombs, then you need more than one ticket. There is a rest house at the entrance to the valley where you can buy over-priced bottled water and soft drinks, and beyond that a *tuf-tuf*— a noisy tractor inappropriately dressed up to look like a train— ferries visitors up to the first tombs.

To date, 62 tombs have been discovered here, although not all belong to pharaohs. Each one is assigned a KV, or Kings' Valley, number, usually in the sequence in which it was found. Not all the tombs are accessible to the public, and some of those that are open at the time of writing may well be closed when you visit, as part of an ongoing program of renovation. At the most popular tombs (which include those of Tutankhamun and Ramses VI) be prepared to line up. Be prepared also to sweat: Most tombs involve the descent of two long, steep staircases with the air getting steadily hotter and clammier the deeper you get.

TUTANKHAMUN

The tomb that everyone rushes to is Tutankhamun's. It is not really deserving of the clamor; it is small and for the most part undecorated, and all the treasures have been removed to the Egyptian Museum in Cairo (see pp. 70–79). All that remains is the large granite sarcophagus. The story of his discovery is far more interesting than the now empty chambers.

Born in 1892, Howard Carter came to Egypt from Britain as a

teenager and began as a humble junior draftsman responsible for copying wall paintings. He joined the Egyptian Antiquities Service in 1899 and was appointed inspector for Upper Egypt. Intrigued by the Valley of the Kings and convinced that a number of royal tombs lay undiscovered there, he teamed up with a wealthy English aristocrat, Lord Carnarvon, and began patient excavations.

Together the two explored the valley for ten years without success. Finally losing heart, Carnarvon announced he was not prepared to finance any more exploration when, on November 4, 1922, work-men discovered a flight of steps. Uncovered, they led down to a walled-up entrance whose plaster face bore the seals of a little-known pharaoh, Tutankhamun. Carter resealed the tomb and telegraphed Carnarvon, who arrived on the 23rd. It took a another few days to reclear the door and the sloping corridor beyond it. On November 26 they stood before a second intact door, from which Carter removed a few stones and looked in. Asked by Carnarvon if he could see anything, Carter replied, "Yes, wonderful things." What he might more accurately have said was, "The most magnificent and unimaginable cache of glittering art and treasures ever discovered."

So much was stashed in three small chambers that, looking at photographs of the find, you would think the two men had discovered a badly kept junk store. It was to take Carter ten solid years to record, remove, and catalog all the items.

In the meantime, the discovery of these "wonderful things," which had lain undisturbed and unseen for thousands of years, took not just archaeology but the whole world by storm. As Carter labored to conserve the treasures, at the

The steep staircases at the narrow entrance to the tomb of Tuthmose III

same time he was obliged to satisfy an endless stream of VIP visitors and the world's press. Tutmania became the craze of the 1920s. The Folies Bergère in Paris added "Tutankhamun's Follies" to its showgirl review, London seriously considered calling the latest

OTHER TOMBS

There are too many tombs to see to describe them all, but the following are some of the more interesting. They are listed in chronological sequence, which is the ideal way to visit to witness the evolution of tomb design and wall paintings.

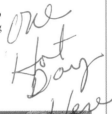

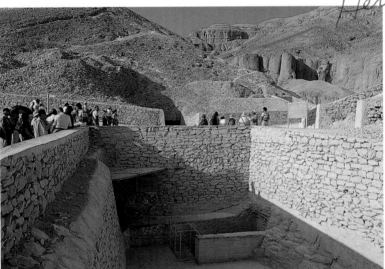

extension to its subway system Tutancamden (it passed through Tooting and Camden Town), while in Russia Tutankhamun's chambers inspired the mausoleum in Red Square, and its occupant, the corpse of Lenin, was said to be embalmed with a fluid based on one used by the ancient Egyptians. So immense was the impact of Tutankhamun on all aspects of life that Pope Pius XI was led to comment of the find, "It's not an exhumation, it is a resurrection."

For all that, Carnarvon and Carter's prize was the burial of a very minor king, and it can only be wondered what the intact tomb of a Ramses II or Amenhotep III might have held. We can be sure that it would have put Tutankhamun's haul to shame.

TOMB OF TUTHMOSE III (KV 34)

Kept off the throne by Hatshepsut (see p. 274), when he eventually did attain power Tuthmose III (1479–1425 B.C.) established himself as one of Egypt's greatest pharaohs. It was during his reign that the Valley of the Kings assumed the character of a royal necropolis, and he was one of the first to be buried in it. His tomb is one of the most difficult to reach, at the far end of the valley, with the entrance in a narrow defile some 100 feet (30 m) above ground. It is necessary to ascend a steep wooden staircase to the entrance, then to make an equally steep descent down the rock-hewn corridor. Just before the bottom is a shaft, now traversed by a narrow gangway;

A tour group braves the heat to listen to their guide before descending into the tomb of Tutankhamun.

Building a royal tomb

No sooner did Seti I ascend the throne of Egypt in 1294 B.C. than he began planning and building his royal tomb. First, stonecutters quarried away at the valley's limestone and shale, carving out hallways and chambers (above left). Other craftsmen followed, transforming this crude cave into an intricately ornamented grave.

The insets depict the stages in crafting an ageless portrait, as the stonecutters first chisel out a chamber, leaving behind raw rock walls (1). A coat of plaster then creates a smooth surface (2) on which an artist renders his subject in rough outline (3). A master painter makes corrections and adds details (4) to guide the bas-relief sculptor who follows (5).

Finally, another artisan gives the portrait its royal finish (6).

The size of the workforce varied from a few laborers to more than a hundred. Breathing must have become difficult as workers inhaled air laden with plaster and stone dust. To deal with the darkness deep in the tomb, burrowing away hundreds of feet into the hillside, they burned pottery lamps fitted with linen wicks and fueled with oil or fat mixed with a bit of salt to inhibit smoke.

Lavishly decorated, the tomb of Seti I is the longest and deepest of all those discovered in the Valley of the Kings.

When their work was nearly complete, laborers hauled a stone sarcophagus (top right) down to the burial chamber.

Seti I died in 1279 B.C., and the grave builders had just 70 days—while the priests mummified his body—to ready the tomb to receive the pharaoh's remains. ■

Decorations like these in the tomb of Seti I were a guidebook to help the dead pharaoh from this world to the next.

similar shafts appear in other tombs and they are the source of much debate. One theory has it they were to protect the burial hall from flooding by torrential rains, another that they were traps for unwary thieves. Alternatively they may have some yet unrevealed ritual meaning. The burial chamber, which is oval-shaped like a cartouche, has peculiar stick figures rather than the fuller characters of later tombs, and script in a style used for writing on a papyrus.

TOMB OF AMENHOTEP II (KV 35)

It is no surprise that the tomb of Amenhotep II (*R.*1427–1400 B.C.) is very similar to that of Tuthmose III, whom he succeeded on the throne. It has much the same plan, only on a considerably larger scale, and the same "prototype-style" wall paintings. When French archaeologists discovered the tomb in 1898, the quartzite sarcophagus still contained the body of the pharaoh, with a garland of mimosas around his neck. The mummy was left in peace until 1928, when it was removed to the Egyptian Museum in Cairo. In one of the small annexes off the burial chamber, walled up in antiquity, the archaeologists also made the surprising find of nine other mummies of royal blood, including Tuthmose IV, Seti II, Amenhotep III, and his wife, Queen Tiye. The bodies of kings and queens were often moved and hidden to foil robbers, who would rip them apart in their search for treasure, but nobody quite knows why

Visit 4

or exactly when they were hidden in this tomb.

TOMB OF TUTHMOSE IV (KV 43)

Tuthmose IV (*R*.1400–1390 B.C.), son of Amenhotep II, enjoyed a peaceful if brief reign. His death would seem to have come prematurely—the artists had no time to finish decorating the tomb before it was required for use. Those figures that do appear, though—in the well shaft and antechamber—now have the fuller-bodied look that most people associate with pharaonic art. The scenes depict various gods, such as Osiris and Hathor, presenting the pharaoh with the key of life, the ankh.

TOMB OF HOREMHEB (KV 57)

Horemheb (*R*.1323–1295 B.C.) had been commander in chief of the Egyptian army before becoming pharaoh. He was a prolific builder who greatly enlarged the temple at Karnak. His tomb displays a change in style from previous ones in that it runs almost straight, with no right-angled bend. It also introduces bas-reliefs, where the figures and symbols are carved out before painting, as opposed to the earlier method of just applying the paint straight to the wall. What is also interesting is that many of the figures are unfinished and left at different stages: Some are just roughly sketched out; some then display corrections by the chief artist; others are partially incised into the rock by a sculptor prior to painting. It gives a fascinating insight into how the tombs were created and gives the enterprise a human slant.

TOMB OF SETI I (KV 17)

This is the longest, deepest, and most lavishly decorated tomb in the Valley of the Kings. It was discovered in 1817 by the famous Belzoni, one of the more colorful characters in the history of Egyptology (see p. 80). The tomb burrows some 390 feet (120 m) down into the hillside in a series of descending corridors and chambers. The upper passages and first four-pillared room all exhibit scenes from the Litany of Re and Amduat. The lower passageway depicts the Opening of the Mouth ceremony in which the king's soul is reawakened and his senses restored. At the bottom is a six-pillared burial chamber with a vaulted heavenly ceiling showing the constellations, and a lineup of deities. In here Belzoni found an empty alabaster sarcophagus of such delicacy it is almost translucent. It now lies at the heart of the eccentric and wonderful Sir John Soane Museum in London.

TOMB OF MERENPTAH (KV 8)

200 steps to the tomb

Merenptah (*R*.1213–1203 B.C.) was one of the many sons of Ramses II. Given the extraordinarily long reign of his father, he was probably already in his fifties when he came to the throne. His tomb sees an increase in the height of the corridors and chambers, and it is the first in which the axis is dead straight, ironing out the sideways jog present in all those that came before. The decoration is very similar to that in the tomb of Seti I: The upper passages contain the Litany of Re, followed by scenes from the Amduat; the lower passages have depictions of the Opening of the Mouth ceremony, although much was destroyed by flooding in antiquity. In the eight-pillared burial chamber is Merenptah's magnificent granite sarcophagus, carved in the shape of a cartouche on which the dead king is depicted with his arms crossed in an Osiride position. Surrounding him is the *uroboros*, the serpent that encircles the world.

TOMB OF RAMSES III (KV 11)

Ramses III (*R*.1184–1153 B.C.), the builder of the glorious temple at Medinat Habu (see pp. 258–59), was the last of the truly great pharaohs. Not all of his tomb is open to the public because excavation work is ongoing in the lowest levels, including the burial chamber, but it is worth visiting for the wall paintings in the upper chambers and passageways. Expert opinion is that technically the reliefs here are poor, but the variety and unusual nature of the subjects portrayed are interesting. In ten small cells off the upper passages are paintings of jugs, pots, and amphorae; of the preparation of food; and of the furniture and weapons of the king. It is the ancient ancestor of *Better Homes & Gardens*. Most famous of all, in the last cell on the left, is a pair of musicians, from which the tomb gets its alternative name, the Tomb of the Harpists. Just beyond this cell is a stubby dead-end and a new parallel corridor starting to the right; this is where the workmen ran into another tomb (KV 10, belonging to Ameemesses) and had to switch direction. Visitors can follow the new corridor down to a pillared hall, which contains paintings of the known human races.

TOMB OF RAMSES IV (KV 2)

A very shallow and bright tomb with no stairs, and with only one wide, reasonably airy, short passage to descend, this tomb has none of the claustrophobic air of its predecessors. It has been open since antiquity and carries the graffiti to prove it. Exposure to centuries of

visitors has led to the deterioration of the wall paintings, but a vibrant depiction of the goddess Nut stretches across the blue ceiling.

TOMB OF RAMSES VI (KV 9)

Strictly speaking, this is the tomb of Ramses V (*R*.1147–1143 B.C.) *and* Ramses VI (*R*.1143–1136 B.C.). The earlier Ramses began the tomb and was first interred here, but then it was later extended by his brother and successor. Egyptologists still puzzle why Ramses VI did not build his own tomb, as was customary, and the best guess is that it was down to simple economics; at this period in history, ancient Egypt was in a weakened and bankrupt state. Little is known about Ramses VI, but his tomb, though very simple in plan, has perhaps the most sophisticated decoration of any. Its walls contain a vast encyclopedia of texts and images detailing the nightly journey of the sun-god Re through the underworld, and his victorious emergence each morning. This rebirth occurs at the center of the east wall of the burial chamber, with the sun disk being raised by the elongated arms of Nut, the "Lady of the Sky and Stars, Mother of the Sun." The same goddess also stretches along the ceiling, swallowing the sun, which travels through her elongated form to be reborn.

TOMB OF RAMSES IX (KV 6)

The closest open tomb to the site entrance, this is also one of the last to be dug in the valley (just as the tomb of Tuthmose III, one of the earliest, is right at the far end). Again, characteristic of these later Ramessid tombs, it has a simple plan of one relatively short, wide sloping corridor with few steps. The decoration is very similar to that in the tomb of Ramses VI. ∎

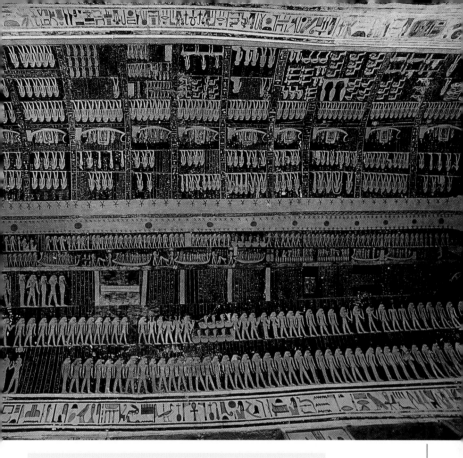

The lost tomb

In 1995 archaeologist Kent Weeks was directing a mapping project in the Valley of the Kings and wanted to relocate KV 5, an ancient tomb entered in 1825, dismissed as unimportant, and subsequently forgotten. The roadway at the valley's entrance was being widened and he feared it might damage any tombs in its path, and that path, he suspected, lay above KV 5. It took only a week of digging to locate the entrance. The plans for the road were changed, and Weeks and his team got on with clearing debris from the tomb. In doing so, they uncovered an unknown doorway. Beyond it a long corridor stretched out ahead.

What had previously been thought an unimportant small tomb turned out to be a massive complex of 59 chambers. Even more exciting, inscriptions in two of the chambers indicated that this was the burial place of a number of sons of Ramses II, otherwise known as Ramses the Great. KV 5 became the biggest and most newsworthy find since Tutankhamun. Not that there is any treasure involved this time around; ancient grave robbers had taken care of that. However, excavations have since yielded another 44 chambers, bringing the total in the complex so far to 110, making this by far the largest tomb ever discovered in Egypt. ■

Arcing across the ceiling of Ramses VI's tomb, dual images of the sky goddess Nut bracket scenes from sacred texts.

Bringing Egyptology up to date

In the early years of the 20th century, scientific excavation in Egypt began to overtake treasure hunting. Individual enthusiasts backed by wealthy patrons gave way to officially accredited teams of foreign and local archaeologists sifting the sands of Egypt and attempting to make sense of its ancient past.

Howard Carter (kneeling) opens the doors of the inner shrine to discover Tutankhamun's sarcophagus.

The opening of the tomb of Tutankhamun in 1922 is the defining moment in the history of Egyptology. Inevitably the discovery generated something of a political storm, the outcome being that any antiquities found in Egypt—including the entire contents of Tutankhamun's tomb—had to remain there. Archaeology in Egypt became subject to much more stringent rules—but this did not mean a halt to the discoveries.

Less than 20 years after Tutankhamun, in 1939, yet more intact royal tombs were revealed when French archaeologist Pierre Montet made his staggering discoveries at the northern Delta site of Tanis (see p. 169). American discoveries at the pyramid site of Dahshur (see p. 155) uncovered the golden jewels of Queen Weret in 1995, the same year in which fellow American Kent Weeks discovered a whole network of chambers in KV 5, the massive tomb built for Ramses II's children in the Valley of the Kings (see p. 285). It is the largest tomb yet found and it will take many years' work to examine fully, together with several more of the valley's royal tombs, which are currently being studied by international teams of archaeologists.

Barely a year goes by without the report of another significant find. In 2000 it was the discovery of the sunken ancient city of Canopus deep below the waters off the northern coast. This came hot on the heels of the discovery of the so-called palace of Cleopatra (see p. 182), now gradually emerging from beneath the harbor at Alexandria, thanks to the latest developments in underwater excavation.

In 1999 an old-fashioned hunch led to the chance discovery of the Valley of the Mummies (see p. 207), but these days advances in Egyptology are less likely to come from headline-grabbing tomb openings than from meticulous scientific examinations. With new methods of study out in the field there are philologists, epigraphists, engineers, forensic scientists, and geologists analyzing soil, reading striations in stone, and autopsying corpses that are several thousand years old. In the 200 years since the decipherment of hieroglyphics, the techniques available to Egyptologists have developed at an amazing rate: Tiny robot-propelled cameras can investigate deep inside the Great Pyramid, while extraction of DNA samples from mummies lets scientists study them in a virtually nondestructive way.

Egyptologists are now digging for information, not things. Which is not to say there are no more spectacular finds to be made. In the opinion of Dr. Zahi Hawass, Undersecretary of State for the Giza Monuments, and Egypt's leading archaeologist, there are many more finds to be made. "I still say all the time that you never know what the sands of Egypt might hold. And that's why I believe until today we have discovered only 30 percent of our monuments. Still 70 percent is buried underneath the ground." The rediscovery of ancient Egypt is a story still being told. ■

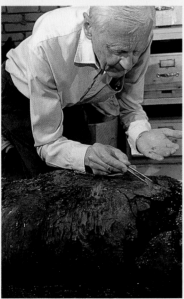

Above: Archaeologist Kent Weeks and his wife, Susan, examine a hallway in KV 5.
Left: Beads are plucked from the mummy of Infaa prior to X-ray examination.
Below: A diver sketches a sphinx in situ.

Temple of Seti I

IN ANCIENT TIMES, THE TEMPLE OF SETI I (ALSO KNOWN AS
Sethos I) was one of the major monuments of Western Thebes. But
lacking the infamy of Hatshepsut or the ego of his son Ramses II,
Seti I's fame has waned, and as a consequence his temple is one of
the less-visited sights hereabouts. It is a case of poor judgment,
though, because it is certainly worth seeing.

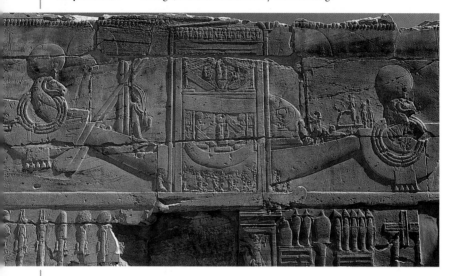

Temple of Seti I
- 233 C4
- $$. Tickets from the West Bank ticket office only (see p. 254)

The reign of Seti I (R.1294–1279 B.C.) was something of a high point. His first success was in restoring order to the country after the instability of the Amarna kings (see pp. 218–19). That accomplished, he expanded the Egyptian empire to include Cyprus and parts of Mesopotamia (modern-day Iraq).

His military achievements were matched by those in the arts. Under Seti's patronage some magnificent buildings were undertaken, including the Great Hypostyle Hall at Karnak (see p. 250), a structure later completed by Ramses II, and the king's temple at Abydos (see p. 227) in Middle Egypt. The tomb created for Seti I is perhaps the most splendid of all those in the Valley of the Kings, and has some of the finest wall paintings.

Unfortunately, the pylons and courts of his mortuary temple here on the West Bank have largely been destroyed, making it seem less significant than it was. Dedicated to Amun, it was originally meant as a place of worship for the king's own cult, and also served as a treasure house for some of the spoils of his military ventures. Only the central part of the building is preserved, including a portico of eight papyriform pillars and, beyond, a hypostyle hall, considerably less grand than at Karnak. However, the bas-reliefs adorning the temple walls are particularly elegant and constitute some of the finest examples of New Kingdom art.

The temple is just off the Valley of the Kings road, but heading in the direction of the river. ■

S outh of Luxor, Egypt looks
less like a mix of Arabia and
Europe and more like the rest of
Africa. Pharaonic monuments,
though few in number, benefit
from magnificent settings beside
the Nile, which here is at its
most majestic.

South of Luxor

The captain of a felucca
maneuvers his craft.

South of Luxor

IF ALEXANDRIA IS EGYPT'S EUROPEAN FACE, AND CAIRO EMBODIES THE
Arab Middle East, then south of Luxor is African Egypt. The banks of the Nile, here broad
and dramatic, are heavy with lush vegetation. Urban centers are few, and even the capital
of the region, Aswan, has a languorous air, stifled into inactivity by the heat.

**Nubian shoeshine boys in colonial livery
await guests at the Old Cataract Hotel
in Aswan.**

Since the time of the pharaohs, this area has
always been the southernmost province of
Egypt, and Aswan (population 150,000) the
southernmost Egyptian town. For centuries,
the cataract at Aswan, where rocks churn up
the river and make it impassable by boat,
marked the dividing line between ancient
Egypt and its equally ancient neighbor to the
south, Nubia. One of history's discarded
empires, Nubia vanished under the onslaught
of the Muslims, but it once encompassed the
lands from beyond Aswan all the way down to
what is now Khartoum in Sudan. In times of
strength, the Egyptians would undertake military expeditions to the south, erecting great
monuments such as the imposing Abu Simbel
to mark out their territorial gains. When
Egypt wavered under weak dynasties, the

Nubians (also known as Kushites) would, in
turn, forge north. In 715 B.C. they succeeded in
taking control of all Egypt and briefly establishing a new ruling dynasty in Memphis.
Later, from their base in Alexandria, the
Greco-Romans managed to maintain a firm
grip on this frontier territory, pursuing a politically sensible policy of assimilation rather
than subjugation. Almost all the surviving
monuments south of Luxor date from this era,
notably the riverside temples at Esna, Edfu,
Kom Ombo, and Philae—the latter two are
striking as much for their location as for their
architecture. The finest way to visit these
sights is in the time-honored way, by boat,
cruising from Luxor upriver to Aswan, or vice
versa (see pp. 306–307).

Viewed from a cruise ship, the banks of
the river are lined with forests of palm trees,
banana plantations, and rows of crops. Signs
of life are few, largely because villages have
traditionally been built back from the water's
edge to avoid being inundated during the
annual floods. Villagers usually appear at sunset, coming down to the Nile to wash their
dishes, water the animals, and socialize. The
women are often carrying pots or water jugs
balanced amazingly on their heads.

The influence of Nubia is still felt greatly.
Even though no country or political entity
called Nubia exists, there is still a Nubian people. Until the 20th century, many of them lived
along the Nile south of Aswan, their ancient
homeland. But following the completion of
the first Aswan Dam in 1902, villages had to be
abandoned in the face of rising waters. When
the High Dam was built in the 1960s, the
whole region was inundated. Many moved
north, and now a large proportion of the
inhabitants of Aswan and surrounding villages
are Nubians, distinguished from the rest of the
Egyptians by being taller and darker. They
speak their own language and also have their
own traditional culture (see p. 296). ■

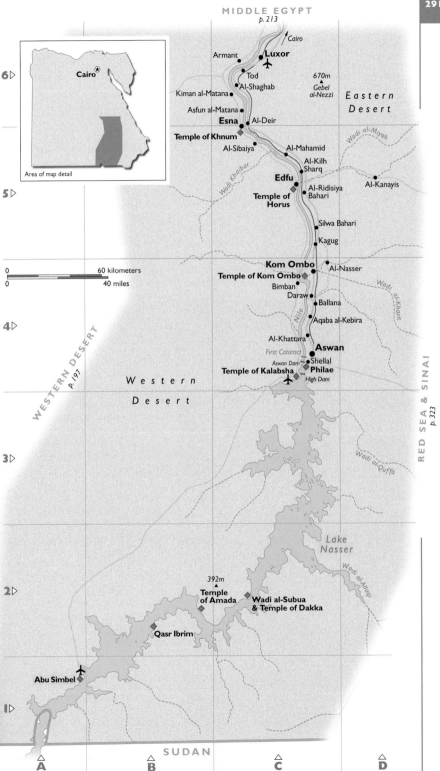

MIDDLE EGYPT
p. 213

Cairo

Armant
Luxor
Tod
Al-Shaghab
Kiman al-Matana
Asfun al-Matana
Esna
Al-Deir
Temple of Khnum
Al-Sibaiya
Al-Mahamid
Edfu
Al-Kilh Sharq
Al-Kanayis
Temple of Horus
Al-Ridisiya Bahari
Silwa Bahari
Kagug
Kom Ombo
Al-Nasser
Temple of Kom Ombo
Bimban
Daraw
Ballana
Aqaba al-Kebira
Al-Khattara
First Cataract
Aswan
Shellal
Aswan Dam
Philae
Temple of Kalabsha
High Dam

670m
Gebel al-Nezzi

Eastern Desert

Wadi al-Miyah
Wadi Khaibar
Nile
Wadi al-Kharit

WESTERN DESERT
p. 197

Western Desert

RED SEA & SINAI
p. 323

Wadi al-Quffa

Lake Nasser

Wadi al-Allaqi

392m
Temple of Amada
Wadi al-Subua & Temple of Dakka

Qasr Ibrim

Abu Simbel

SUDAN

Cairo
Area of map detail

0   60 kilometers
0   40 miles

6 ▷
5 ▷
4 ▷
3 ▷
2 ▷
1 ▷

A   B   C   D

Esna

Temple of Khnum
- 291 C5
- Tourist bazaar
- $$

EASILY VISITED AS A DAY TRIP FROM LUXOR, ESNA (ISNA), 30 miles (48 km) to the south, is a busy little agricultural center on the west bank of the Nile. Its prime attraction, and the reason that many cruise ships stop here, is the Temple of Khnum.

Although only the hypostyle hall is left of Esna's temple, it is in good shape.

The temple is buried in the middle of the modern town, sunk in a pit almost 30 feet (9 m) below the level of the surrounding buildings. Constructed in Ptolemaic and Roman times, it was dedicated to Khnum, the ram-headed god who created humankind on his potter's wheel using clay from the Nile.

It was one of the last great temples to be built in Egypt. Even so, it has not lasted as well as some of the monuments built centuries earlier, and all that remains today is the columned **hypostyle hall.** This is the work of the Roman emperor Claudius and dates from the third century A.D. Twenty-four columns with lotus-flower capitals support the roof of the hall. An astronomical theme decorates the ceiling, showcasing a large zodiac, and the wall reliefs include a scene depicting a king netting wildfowl. Some walls have hymns to Khnum, one written almost entirely with hieroglyphs of rams, another written with crocodiles.

Originally, a ceremonial way linked the temple to the Nile, which is just a short distance to the east. Remains of the **ancient quay,** with cartouches of Roman emperor Marcus Aurelius, lie just south of the place where the modern cruise ships dock.

Nowadays a covered tourist bazaar connects the temple and river, and visitors are required to run a gauntlet of pushy salesmen offering thin cotton scarves, *galabiyyas* (the long robe commonly worn by rural Egyptians), and the handwoven baskets for which the area is known. Bargain hard if you are going to buy. Each Saturday morning the town also hosts a busy **camel market.**

Just to the north of Esna, two barrages, one with a hydroelectric generator, also act as bridges over the Nile. Both have locks that the cruise ships have to pass through as they travel from Luxor to Aswan and back. ∎

visit 930 5/2/07

Edfu

EASILY THE MOST SPLENDID OF THE SERIES OF NILE-SIDE
monuments between Luxor and Aswan, Edfu's Temple of Horus is
the most complete of its kind. It was built by the Greco-Romans long
after the true era of the pharaohs had passed, but it conforms exactly to the principles of ancient Egyptian architecture. Visit Edfu (Idfu)
to see what virtually every other temple in Egypt would have looked
like in its original form.

Temple of Horus
- 291 C5
- Tourist bazaar
- $$

A small, dusty regional center for
the sugarcane trade, the town of
Edfu lies about halfway between
Luxor and Aswan, roughly 70 miles
(112 km) from each. It's an easy day
trip by bus from either, and all
cruise ships stop off here. The
Temple of Edfu is some distance
inland from the river moorings,
and there is a thriving local trade in
horsedrawn calèches ferrying visi-
tors from one to the other. The ride
costs no more than a couple of
dollars. The approach to the temple
is via the obligatory tourist bazaar,
with streetside stalls peddling goods
that are easily resisted.

Until the mid-19th century, as a
commonly reproduced drawing by
Scottish artist David Roberts
(1796–1864) shows, the temple was
almost completely buried, with
sand filling the interior practically
to the ceiling. A part of the village
of Edfu stood on its roof. Auguste
Mariette, the founder of Cairo's
Egyptian Museum (see p. 80),
began excavation in the 1860s.
Today the whole of the temple has
been revealed, and the village is
pushed back so that the mud-brick
houses line the top of the com-
pound walls overlooking the
cleared forecourt below.

Unfortunately for visitors, the
impact of the temple is lessened
somewhat by having to approach
from the rear and walk along the
length of the side wall to view the
splendor of the main **entrance
pylon.** This massive structure

was erected by Ptolemy XII
(*R.*80–51 B.C.), father of Cleopatra,
and is decorated with twin scenes
of the pharaoh grasping the hair of
his enemies, with a staff raised
about to smite them. The deities
Horus and Hathor look on.
Ptolemy XII was in fact the ninth

**Temple guardians
past and present:
Horus, in the form
of a hawk, and a
local villager**

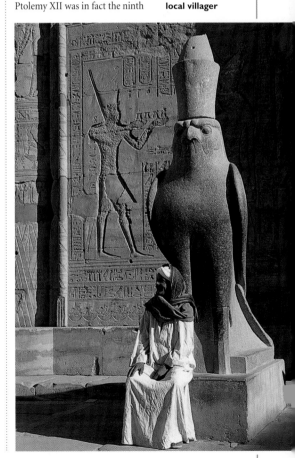

Unusually, the two towers of Edfu's great entrance pylon are perfect mirror images of each other.

of his dynasty to add to this temple, which Ptolemy III began 180 years earlier, in 237 B.C.

Flanking the entrance gate are two **statues of Horus** as a falcon. According to Egyptian mythology, Horus was the child of Isis and Osiris, the fertility god who was killed by his brother Seth, the god of chaos (see box p. 309). Ancient Egyptians believed that Horus avenged his father's death at Edfu by fighting and killing Seth. Many of the wall reliefs inside the temple deal with this cataclysmic battle, with Seth represented as a diminutive hippopotamus.

Immediately beyond the pylon is the immense, paved **peristyle court** surrounded by colonnades composed of columns with capitals sculpted in various forms. Also in the court, standing before the entrance to the first hypostyle hall, is a colossal black granite statue of Horus as a falcon wearing the double crown of Egyptian kingship.

There are two **hypostyle halls,** each with 12 great columns supporting the roof, and beyond them an empty antechamber, off

which is a doorway leading to a staircase. Long, straight, and narrow, this gives access to the roof with fine views over the town to the Nile and green fields beyond. It is usually necessary to pay one of the guardians some *baksheesh* (a tip) to get access.

Back downstairs, directly ahead from the antechamber, is the innermost core of the temple, the **sanctuary of Horus.** The shrine, carved from a single block of gray granite, stands 13 feet (4 m) high. As you face the sanctuary a doorway on the right leads out into a small unroofed court where a flight of steps leads up to what is known as the **New Year Chapel,** worth a look for the blue-colored sky goddess Nut stretched across the ceiling.

To the outer side of the temple, a flight of steps leads down to a small **Nilometer.**

Also, don't miss the colonnaded **birth house,** across the forecourt from the temple's great pylon, which is a focus for an annual festival reenacting the divine birth of Horus and the reigning pharaoh. ∎

Kom Ombo

niset 5/2/07

JUST 30 MILES (48 KM) NORTH OF ASWAN, KOM OMBO occupies the Nile-side site of the ancient city of Pa-Sebek, the Domain of Sobek, a center for worship of the crocodile god of that name. All traces of the city are long gone—and the crocodiles that used to bask on nearby sandbanks have been hunted to extinction —but the remains of a fine waterfront temple are well worth a visit.

Cruise ships provide the best means of transportation to the ruins of Kom Ombo.

The best way to approach Kom Ombo is by river. If you are lucky enough to approach from the south by cruise ship, as your boat rounds the headland the ruins come spectacularly into view. Otherwise, reach the town by car, bus, or train from Aswan.

Like those at Esna and Edfu, the temple is postpharaonic, begun by Ptolemy VI (*R*.180–145 B.C.) and completed during Roman times, probably replacing an earlier structure here. Unusually, it is dedicated to two gods, Sobek and Horus the Elder, the falcon-headed sky god. Symmetrical along its main axis, the temple has two of everything; each half is devoted to one god.

You approach not from the front but from the side, via a small **Ptolemaic pylon** that formerly acted as a gate into the temple compound. This is at a right angle to what would have been the main pylon, now completely vanished, eroded by the river. Instead, the main remaining structure is, as at Esna, a **hypostyle hall** with eight great lotus-capital columns. It is fronted by a paved forecourt ringed with the stubs of columns bearing some well-preserved reliefs, complete with ancient coloring.

Off to the right is a small **Chapel of Hathor,** dedicated to the wife of Horus. It is now used to display a collection of mummified crocodiles. On the far side of the temple are a deep well and a small pond where crocodiles, sacred to Sobek, may have been raised. ■

Temple of Kom Ombo

◭ 291 C4

✉ Corniche al-Nil

$ $$

Nubian culture

Nubian lands may have gone, drowned 200 feet (60 m) below the surface of Lake Nasser, but the culture of the Nubians remains very much alive and vibrant.

When they were forced to abandon their villages in the 1960s and '70s and move, the Nubians re-created their traditional dwellings anew elsewhere. Made of mud-brick, their houses typically have domed or vaulted ceilings and are plastered or whitewashed. Each is decorated individually with claustrawork—moldings and tracery in mud. The highly distinctive decoration also often includes ceramic plates set into the plaster of the external walls around the doorway. Such houses can be seen in the Nubian villages around Aswan and in Ballana near Kom Ombo. There is nothing else like it in Egypt.

Just as unique is Nubian music, the fame of which has spread far beyond the Nile. Played on traditional instruments such as the oud (a pear-shaped guitar) and *douff* (a shallow drum), the music is characterized by a softly rolling, undulating rhythm, with a kind of swaying lilt. Melodies are simple and voices dry, twangy, and soulful. It's like an Egyptian form of the blues. One of the biggest names is Ali Hassan Kuban, a septuagenarian former tillerman from a small village near Aswan. He grew up playing at weddings and parties, but he is now a regular fixture on the international world music scene and has toured all over Europe, Canada, and the United States. Almost as well-known is Hamza al-Din, a Nubian composer born in Wadi Halfa, the Sudanese town at the southernmost end of Lake Nasser. He is widely respected in the West for his semiclassical compositions written for the oud.

Visitors to Aswan are usually able to experience Nubian music as part of a floor show at a local restaurant or hotel, performed by troupes wearing gleaming white *galabiyyas* (gowns) and embroidered waistcoats. It is also not uncommon to see a wedding, particularly on a Thursday, which is the big wedding night

throughout Egypt. Nubian wedding festivities last three days. On the first night, the bride and groom celebrate separately with their respective friends and families. On the second night, the bride takes her party to the groom's home and both groups dance to traditional music until the small hours. Then the bride returns home and her hands and feet are painted in beautiful designs with henna. The groom will also have his hands and feet covered in henna, but without any design. On the third day, the groom and his party walk slowly to the bride's house in a procession, singing and dancing the whole way.

Women visitors who want to get a taste of Nubian culture can have their hands "tattooed" with henna at some of the villages around Aswan—it looks great and you are able to spend time with Nubian women. Ask at the tourist office, which may be able to help. Expect to pay between $5 and $10 depending on the size of the design. ■

Above: Nubians boast a rich musical culture; these women wearing embroidered gowns stage regular shows in Aswan as well as take part in wedding festivities.
Below: Women in front of the distinctively decorated wall of a Nubian mud-brick dwelling

*Al Reuephe
Places!*

Aswan

TO MOST VISITORS ASWAN IS A ONE-NIGHT STOPOVER EN
route to Abu Simbel. However, with a vibrant street market, a
fascinating museum, idyllic midstream islands, and a couple of
intriguing pharaonic sites in the vicinity, it is definitely worth a longer
visit. If you can, take two or three days to enjoy what is one of the
most peaceful and relaxing spots in Egypt.

Historically, Aswan has always been
Egypt's southern frontier town, the
"gateway to Africa." It lies at the
First Cataract, one of six sets of
rapids in the Nile (the other five are
all in Sudan) between here and
Khartoum that made the river
impassable for boats. Hence water-
borne traffic has always had to stop
here, and the town has thrived over
the centuries as a trading post. In
ancient times the area was known
as Sunt, but later the Copts called
the place Souan, meaning "trade,"
from which comes the Arabic
"Aswan."

Elephant caravans from the
south once brought gold, perfumes,
the skins of lions, leopards, and
cheetahs, ostrich feathers and ivory
tusks, and slaves, first for the
pharaohs, then later for the harems
of Islamic Cairo. Aswan was also an
important military garrison, a base
for expeditions into Nubia and
Sudan. This garrison role continued
right into the latter part of the 19th
century, when the town was a mar-
shaling point for Anglo-Egyptian
forces sent down to Khartoum to
quell the Mahdist Uprising (1881–
1898) against the government.

About this time the town began
to gain popularity among wealthy
Europeans as a winter resort. The
dry heat was deemed to be good for
all kinds of ailments. Archaeologist
Gaston Maspero (director of excavations in Egypt 1899–1914)
deplored the influx of foreigners,
complaining that what had been an

unspoiled village was rapidly being
turned into a copy of the French
Riviera.

The main legacy of the early
"excursionists" is the development
of the Nile-side **Corniche,** created
to provide moorings for the
steamers. It is the most attractive
waterfront boulevard in Egypt,
looking over a beautiful stretch of
the Nile, dotted with palm-crowded
islands and with a backdrop of pure
white sand hills rising from the
water's edge on the far side.

One block inland from the
Corniche is the *souq* (market),
which, although no longer carrying
the kind of unusual wares that once
came in on the African caravans, is
still a riot of bright colors and exotic fragrances. Things to look for
include spices, patterned textiles,
and local jewelry made to traditional Nubian designs.

At the southern end of the
Corniche, at the point at which it
curves sharply inland, are the
Ferial Gardens, a peaceful little
public park on a gentle rise of land.
Beyond the gardens are the rather
more private grounds of the **Old
Cataract Hotel** (*Abtal al-Tahrir
St., tel 097/316 006*), another wonderful leftover from the early age
of tourism. Opened in 1899, it is a
great pink mansion of a place with
Moorish interiors, vast high, wide
corridors, and the most magnificent of dining halls, which could
double as a stage set for *The Thief
of Baghdad.* Most splendid of all,

Aswan

🔼 291 C4

Visitor information

✉ Railroad Station Sq.

☎ 097/312 811

🕐 Open 9 a.m.–3
p.m. & 6–8 p.m.

though, is the setting, on a rocky outcrop high above the river. A big old wooden terrace makes the finest spot in Egypt to take an early-evening apéritif. French president François Mittérand was a frequent visitor, and other distinguished guests have included Winston Churchill, Jimmy Carter, Prince Charles and Princess Diana, and, perhaps most famously of all, Agatha Christie, who wrote part of *Death on the Nile* (1937) while staying here. The hotel appears prominently in both the book and the movie of the book, made in 1978 and starring Peter Ustinov and Bette Davis. Unfortunately, in recent years the hotel has instituted a residents-only policy, and non-guests are allowed no farther than the main gate. It may, however, be possible to make a reservation for dinner (see p. 372).

SOUTH OF THE CENTER
Beyond the grounds of the Old Cataract Hotel stands a large, modern, light sandstone building, the **Nubian Museum.** A recent addition to the Aswan cultural scene, the museum opened in 1997. It is a rather belated attempt to preserve and honor the culture of the region's indigenous people, a culture that was dealt a near fatal blow with the creation of the High Dam in the 1960s (see p. 312). The lake that formed behind the dam completely submerged the Nubian heartland causing countless villages to be abandoned, forcing their inhabitants to migrate. The museum houses a collection of artifacts

Seen from the south, Aswan town is to the right, beyond the Old Cataract Hotel, while Elephantine Island is on the left against the sand hills of the west bank.

Nubian Museum
- Map p. 300
- Corniche al-Nil
- 097/319 111 or 097/319 222
- Open daily 9 a.m.–1 p.m. & 6–9 p.m.
- $$

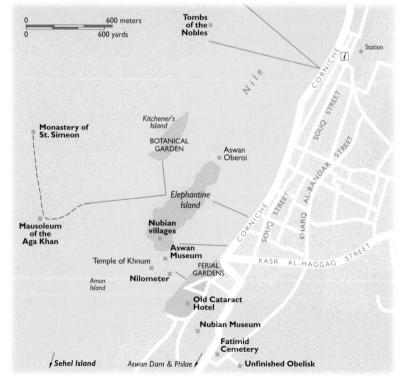

0	600 meters
0	600 yards

Tombs of the Nobles

Station

CORNICHE

Nile

SOUQ STREET

Monastery of St. Simeon

Kitchener's Island

BOTANICAL GARDEN

Aswan Oberoi

KHARQ AL-BANDAR STREET

SOUQ STREET

Elephantine Island

CORNICHE

Mausoleum of the Aga Khan

Nubian villages

Aswan Museum

KASR AL-HAGGAG STREET

Temple of Khnum

FERIAL GARDENS

Amun Island

Nilometer

Old Cataract Hotel

Nubian Museum

Fatimid Cemetery

↙ Sehel Island

Aswan Dam & Philae ↙

Unfinished Obelisk

from the region, which are logically organized to tell the story of the development of this part of the Nile Valley from prehistory, through the pharaonic age, the coming of Christianity and Islam, right up to the building of the dam—although with no mention of the consequences. Exhibits are well displayed, and labeling is in several languages, English included. There are good, large-scale models of Philae and of Abu Simbel, which are well worth seeing before you visit the temples.

Most striking of all is a series of beautifully decorated facades, reconstructions of typical Nubian dwellings. In the museum's large, terraced garden there is a reconstructed Nubian house and a cave containing rock art rescued from areas now inundated with water.

High on top of the hill to the south of the museum is **Nubian House** (*Nubian Museum Rd., tel 097/326 226*), a modest café with a terrace offering superb views over the Nile and First Cataract. It is a wonderful place for sunset drinks. To get there, turn left out of the museum and head straight on up the hill; it is a walk of about 20 minutes, or just a brief taxi ride. Have the taxi wait to avoid walking back along empty, unlit roads.

Below the museum is the vast **Fatimid Cemetery,** a burial ground with many small, domed mausoleums dating back to the ninth century. Some of these tombs belong to local saints—these are usually strewn with flags and often visited by locals seeking blessings. Walk through the cemetery and out of a gate on the far side to reach what is known as the **Unfinished Obelisk.** One of Aswan's most curious sights, this is a huge obelisk perfectly shaped on three sides but still attached to the bedrock on the fourth. It was abandoned after a flaw was discovered in the stone. Nearly 140 feet (42 m) in length, had it been completed it would have been the largest, heaviest

Life along the Nile flows past the guests on the terrace at the Old Cataract Hotel.

Guess who's stayed here... Condo Rice (yesterday) Churchill along time ago

5★ hotel so faded

The wait staff wear that turkish fez. nice touch

This house is decorated in traditional Nubian style, more African than Middle Eastern.

Unfinished Obelisk
✉ Off Airport Rd.
💲 $$

obelisk ever attempted. Archaeologists speculate that it was intended for Karnak (see p. 246), a twin for the obelisk of Tuthmose III, which has since been removed and now stands on the Piazza San Giovanni in Rome. If you do not feel like walking (the quarry containing the obelisk is just over a mile/2 km from the center of town), tours to Philae temple usually stop here on the way back. Alternatively, a taxi should cost no more than a couple of dollars.

THE NILE & ITS ISLANDS

Shopping in the souq is fun, and the museum and obelisk are interesting, but the real attraction in Aswan is the river—broad and blue, and a conduit for cooling breezes that bring relief from the

Obelisks

Archaeologists believe that the obelisk originated as just an irregularly shaped, upright stone, which gradually developed into the familiar elongated, tapering, four-sided shaft with a point on top. Especially common in New Kingdom times, obelisks were often erected in pairs before temple entrances. They are always inscribed, commemorating victories, jubilees, or other notable events. Monolithic and regal, Egypt's obelisks have also always been

Aswan's Unfinished Obelisk

regarded as something of collectors' items by powers abroad. The Assyrians removed two to Nineveh (in modern-day Iraq), the Romans carried off no less than three to Rome, and the Byzantines pilfered another to adorn the Hippodrome at Constantinople (now Istanbul).

The mighty industrial powers of the modern age also felt compelled to embellish their capitals with Egyptian megaliths, and in the 19th century yet more obelisks were removed from Alexandria and Karnak in Luxor and reerected in New York, London, and Paris. ■

relentless heat. The best thing to do is get out on the water. One option is to rent a felucca, the traditional lateen-sailed boats that gracefully skim the Nile (see box p. 304). Another alternative is to visit some of the many islands.

Preeminent among the islands is **Elephantine Island,** so called for the giant gray granite boulders off the southern end of the island, which resemble a herd of bathing elephants. A local ferry service shuttles across every 15 minutes or so between about 6 a.m. and 10 p.m., departing from the Corniche in front of Thomas Cook's office.

Long before the existence of Aswan, the pharaonic-era town of Sunt was on the southern end of the island, protected from attack by the turbulent waters. It was known as the Gate of the South and was also the center of the cult of the ram-headed Khnum, creator of humankind. Partly excavated ruins cover this part of the island and include a late-dynasty temple devoted to Khnum, with the remains of pillars painted by the Romans.

Overlooking the ruins is the modest **Aswan Museum,** which has lost its best artifacts to the Nubian Museum (see pp. 299–300). However, the museum building was formerly the residence of Sir William Willcocks, the English architect of the Aswan Dam (see p. 311), and it still has a fragrant flower-and-herb garden. From the museum a path goes southward to a sycamore tree, marking the location of an ancient **nilometer.** Steps incised in the rock lead down to a square chamber at water level. The walls are marked off in Arabic, Roman, and faint pharaonic numerals. You can also view the nilometer from the river, the only vantage point from which it is also possible to see inscriptions carved into the surrounding rock with cartouches bearing the names of Tuthmose III and Amenhotep III.

The central part of Elephantine Island is thick with palms, cut through by looping pathways. Among the groves are two **Nubian villages,** with houses painted in oranges, yellows, and blues, the tightly grouped buildings separated

Visitors crowd the entrance to the Aga Khan's desert mausoleum.

Aswan Museum & nilometer
✉ Elephantine Island
💲 $$

Aswan is all about the river, and the best way to appreciate the place is to get on a boat.

by narrow baked-earth alleys. The banks of the east side of the island make a fine place to sit with nothing but the river, a blue sky, and the palms of the next island as a view. This is **Kitchener's Island,** named after Lord Horatio Kitchener (1850–1916), now chiefly remembered for Britain's famous "Your Country Needs You" World

War I recruitment poster. He was given the island in the 1890s when, as consul general, he effectively ruled Egypt on behalf of the British. Although a military man, Kitchener also had a passion for horticulture, which he indulged here by turning the entire island into a botanical garden, importing plants from other parts of Africa,

Renting a felucca

Felucca captains hustle for business along the Corniche. Prices are almost wholly dependent on your bargaining skills, although the official government price for a boat capable of seating up to eight people is roughly $5 per hour. A three- or four-hour trip, for

instance, to Sehel Island and back with an hour's wait included, costs about $12 to $15. By far the nicest time to be out on the water is at sunset. Pack a picnic and a few bottles of beer and feast while drifting, watching a blood red sun drop below the horizon. ∎

from India, and from as far afield as Southeast Asia. With plenty of shade from the broad leaves overhead, it is a beautiful place to while away an afternoon. Get here by felucca from the Corniche or from the east side of Elephantine Island.

Also worth visiting is **Sehel Island,** a little less than 3 miles (4 km) upriver from central Aswan. It is a beautiful run of about an hour in a felucca. The island has two summits, both of which provide superb views of the foaming waters around the First Cataract. There are pharaonic-era ruins and a picturesque Nubian village full of clamorous children eager to offer themselves as guides. All invitations should be firmly declined, as there is nothing to be guided around.

ACROSS THE RIVER

Completely uninhabited, the West Bank of the Nile is pure desert. Other than to tramp the dunes, there are three main reasons to cross (most easily achieved by local ferry from the railroad station end of the Corniche). The first reason is to visit the **Mausoleum of the Aga Khan,** which is the small, white, domed building high up on the sandy slopes opposite the Old Cataract Hotel. It holds the body of Muhammad Shah Aga Khan III (1877–1957), the Pakistani-born 48th Imam, or spiritual leader, of the Ismaili sect of Islam. Once regarded as the richest man in the world and offered his weight in diamonds on his diamond jubilee in 1945, the Aga Khan liked to winter in Aswan. When he died, his wife, the Begum Aga Khan, a former French beauty queen, oversaw the construction of this fine monument, which in form is inspired by the Fatimid tombs in the cemetery over the river. Until her own death in July 2000, the Begum (or in her absence, the gardener) placed a red rose on his sarcophagus every day. She now lies entombed beside him.

About a mile into the desert from the ferry landing is the **Monastery of St. Simeon** (Deir Amba Samaan), founded in the seventh century, rebuilt in the tenth, and inexplicably abandoned some time in the 13th never to be occupied again. Considering how long the monastery has lain abandoned, it remains in surprisingly good shape. Located at the head of a desert valley, it is an impressive sight, looking far more like a fortress in a movie set than a religious institution. Its outer walls are 30 feet (9 m) high in parts, with the lower courses composed of rock and the upper parts made of mudbrick. Inside are the remains of a church, with a painting of Christ in the domed apse, a central keep, a vaulted refectory, stables, and a rock chapel painted with saints. A fun way of getting to the monastery is to rent a camel from the pack down at the ferry landing. The round-trip including waiting time should cost about $10. Otherwise, it is a hard, extremely tiring trudge through soft sand.

The third of the West Bank sights is the **Tombs of the Nobles,** a series of rock-cut tombs in the high cliffs to the north of Kitchener's Island. These are the burial places of the dignitaries of ancient Sunt. They date from the Old and Middle Kingdoms, with some much later Roman tombs lower down the cliff face. There's a ticket office at the site, and one ticket is good for all the tombs. The best preserved of them all is the **Tomb of Prince Sirenput II** (No. 31), dating from 12th dynasty (1985–1795 B.C.), which contains six small Osiride statues of the tomb's occupant, as well as some fine wall paintings depicting Sirenput with his family. ∎

Monastery of St. Simeon
✉ West Bank
$ $$

Cruising the Nile

Running the length of the country, the Nile was ancient Egypt's highway. The pharaohs traversed their realm by river, it was the route for traders and invaders alike, and in death, the ancients even took boats to the underworld. Only over the last century, with first railroads, then air travel, has the river been surpassed as a mode of transportation. And still, for anyone with time, a cruise on the Nile remains by far the best way to experience Egypt.

Travelers have gazed out over the country from the deck of a boat since as far back as the fifth century B.C., when the Greek chronicler Herodotus took passage through Egypt. But it was a combination of Napoleon's expedition (1798–1801) and the firm, stabilizing rule of Muhammad Ali (*R*.1805–1847) that opened up the Nile to the curious. At this time, the Holy Land and Egypt came to supplant the Grand Tour of Europe as a part of any wealthy young gentleman's education. Each fall, when the temperatures cooled and the winds got up, intrepid tourists would arrive in Alexandria by liner, from where they would travel down to Cairo, hire a dragoman (guide), select a suitable *dahabiyya* (large sailboat), scuttle it to get rid of the rats and vermin, gather provisions in the *souq*, retrieve the boat, and then set off. The pace was languid, taking anything from 6 to 12 weeks to cover the 530 miles (850 km) between Cairo and Aswan. Besides visiting the sights, these early tourists enjoyed such activities en route as picnicking in tombs and digging for antiquities.

From the 1870s sailboats were replaced by steamers, all of which were owned by Thomas Cook, the Henry Ford of sight-seeing, who introduced the world to package tourism. Known as "excursionists," Cook's customers were looked down upon by more independent travelers, most notably by Mark Twain, writing in 1870: "In the morning the lost tribes of America came ashore and infested the hotels and took possession of all the donkeys: They went in picturesque procession; tried to break

Above and right: The ancient Egyptians didn't have the benefit of lounge decks or onboard swimming pools, but a boat on the Nile has always been the way to travel.

a fragment off the upright [Cleopatra's] Needle; made noise for five hundred, collided with camels, dervishes, effendis, asses, beggars and everything else; shoved the donkeys off their corns and looked at the charming scenery of the Nile."

Since Cook made Nile cruising affordable, it has been the staple of any visit to Egypt. Unfortunately, the threat of terrorist attacks in Middle Egypt has meant that since the early 1990s cruise ships are no longer permitted to sail south of Cairo or north of Luxor. These days, those wishing to journey by river have to be content with sailing between Luxor and Aswan, a voyage of three or four days. Nights are spent on the boat at dock, days are filled with excursions, typically including all the sights of Luxor, Esna, Edfu, and Kom Ombo,

NILE RITZ

then Aswan. The temples of Philae and Abu Simbel are usually optional extras.

Levels of luxury are as high as you are prepared to pay for. Top-of-the-range boats come with plush carpets, icy air-conditioning, and swimming pools. At the other end of the scale, there are boats on which conditions leave a lot to be desired. It is very much a case of getting what you pay for. The most reputable boats are managed by international hotel chains, for example Mövenpick or Sheraton. Cairo-based travel agencies such as Abercrombie and Kent *(Tel 02/393 6255)* and, the people who started the whole business, Thomas Cook *(Tel 02/574 3955)*, also have their own boats with excellent reputations. ■

Philae

A TEMPLE COMPLEX ON AN ISLAND IN THE NILE DEVOTED to the goddess Isis, Philae is arguably the most romantic of Egypt's monuments, harmonizing perfectly with its watery setting. Getting there is only possible by small motor launch, which is a wonderful experience in itself.

Philae

⬛ 291 C4

✉ Aglika Island

💲 $$. Sound-and-light show $$$

"There are four great recollections of a traveler, which might tempt him to live forever: the sea view of Constantinople, the sight of the Coliseum by moonlight, the prospect from the summit of Vesuvius at dawn, and the first glimpse of Philae at sunset."
—Dr. R.R. Madden, 1827

First, there is a taxi ride to the boat landing at Shellal, just south of the old Aswan Dam (see p. 311), about 5 miles (8 km) south of Aswan town center. After purchasing temple tickets, would-be visitors walk out to the jetty, off which is moored a flotilla of small boats with Nubian captains. These water taxis hover, waiting for a full complement of eight passengers before they cast off and ride low in the water, headed for Aglika Island and its splendid ruins.

But as recently as 30 years ago the launches would have been heading for Philae Island, which is where the temple complex was originally constructed back in the Ptolemaic era. After the building of the Aswan Dam at the end of the 19th century, the level of the Nile

rose, completely submerging the temple for six months of the year. Visitors would row out to peer down through the translucent green waters to the courts and columns below. In the 1960s, when the new High Dam threatened to put the island underwater forever, the temples were dismantled and removed stone by stone and then reconstructed on the nearby higher terrain of Aglika Island, which was even landscaped to resemble the original Philae.

Philae rose to importance during the time of the Ptolemies and was the main cult center of Isis (see box opposite), drawing pilgrims from all over the Mediterranean basin. So popular was worship of Isis that the site survived well into the Christian era as

one of the last outposts of paganism. It was not officially closed until A.D. 550. Early Christians then transformed the main temple's hypostyle hall into a chapel and added churches to the island, but none of these have survived.

The motor launches dock at the ancient quay on Aglika Island. The first structure visitors pass, just off to the left, is a "kiosk," a small open temple, erected by Nectanebo I (R.380–362 B.C.). Although now little more than a paved area with a row of columns at the rear, it is the oldest monument on the island. Beyond is a large court enclosed by two long colonnades; that to the west has windows overlooking the river, while the one to the east is interrupted by a series of ruined structures. The most notable of

There is no setting to equal Philae, viewed here at night.

Isis & Osiris

Together Osiris and his consort/sister Isis ruled the country. However, the evil Seth, brother of Osiris and Isis, began to plot against them. He tricked Osiris into climbing into a chest, which he then sealed and flung into the Nile. The chest washed up on the shores of Lebanon (Byblos), where it was eventually found by Isis and returned to Egypt. Seth, however, intercepted the chest, hacked Osiris' body into 14 parts, and scattered them throughout the Nile Valley. Isis sought out each part and briefly revived Osiris to conceive a child, Horus, who using the magic of his mother then defeated Seth and restored divine order. As pharaohs identified themselves with Horus, so Isis was their divine mother. She became identified as the goddess of women, sex, and purity, and Isis worship spread throughout the Roman empire, with cult temples as far afield as what is now Hungary. For the first two centuries of Christianity's history, she was its chief rival. Some scholars believe that the Virgin Mary cult was Christianity's attempt to win over the Isis worshipers. ■

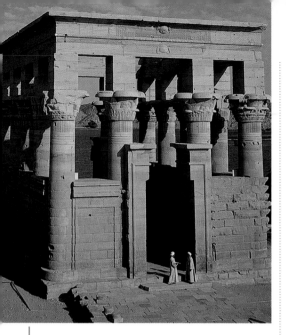

similarly grand gateway at Edfu (see p. 293). It is decorated with scenes of the ruler dispatching enemies, also familiar from Edfu. On the walls of the passage leading between the two towers of the pylon are inscriptions left by Napoleon's troops. They commemorate a French victory over the Mamluks at the Battle of the Pyramids (see p. 40).

Beyond the pylon is a forecourt with elegantly carved columns; in fact, everything about this temple is extremely refined and delicate, making it a favorite with Egyptologists as well as casual visitors. Off to the left is what's known as the **birth house** (or *mammisi*), which is where the pharaohs reinstated their legitimacy as mortal descendants of Horus by taking part in rituals celebrating the god's birth. At the bottom of the rear wall is a scene of Isis giving birth to Horus in the marshes, while on the left-hand wall she is shown suckling the infant. Unfortunately the goddess has suffered defacement at the hands of Christian iconoclasts.

Back in the forecourt, a second pylon gives access to the inner temple, where, beyond a small hypostyle hall, a series of vestibules get lower and darker, culminating in the innermost holy sanctuary. Dimly lit by two apertures in the ceiling, the **sanctuary** contains a stone pedestal dedicated by Ptolemy III (*R*.246–221 B.C.) and his wife Berenice (portrayed in several beautiful mosaics at the Greco-Roman Museum in Alexandria; see pp. 180–81).

If the caretaker can be persuaded to open the gate, a staircase on the west side of the temple gives access to upper rooms decorated with reliefs dwelling on the resurrection of Osiris after his dismemberment by Seth (see box p. 309). You can see Isis gathering

The Kiosk of Trajan has come to symbolize Philae, but it is not part of the temple proper.

these is the **Temple of Arensnuphis,** dedicated to a very obscure Nubian god.

At the head of the court is the first pylon of the **Temple of Isis,** the centerpiece of the island. The pylon was raised by Ptolemy XII, the pharaoh responsible for the

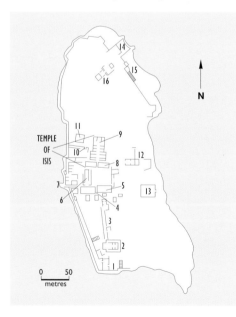

It is hard to believe that the whole complex has been transported stone by stone from another island, now sunken.

up her brother's limbs. It is also possible to get up onto the roof.

OTHER MONUMENTS

Beside the main Temple of Isis, east of the second pylon, is the small **Temple of Hathor.** It is in a fairly ruinous state, but you can still make out two Hathor-headed columns, distinguished by their flared wigs. It also possesses a particularly fine relief of musicians with the ugly dwarf-god Bes playing harp.

Just to the south is the most famous of Philae's monuments, the very distinctive **Kiosk of Trajan,** nicknamed the Pharaoh's Bedstead, for obvious reasons. Built under the Roman emperor of that name (circa A.D. 100), it served as a royal landing for the temple. The kiosk is a curious thing in that it combines a typically classical structure of columns and lintels with pharaonic trimmings, such as the floral column capitals. In its original form it would have had a wooden roof. Reliefs on the screen walls feature Emperor Trajan making offerings to Isis, Osiris, and Horus.

Like all Egypt's major monu-

ments, Philae hosts a bombastic **sound-and-light show,** but it is certainly the best of its kind. It consists of an hour-long tour through the floodlit ruins. The cost is $10, including the boat ride, but it is worth it for the magical ambience of being on the island after dark. There are three shows a night, but performance times vary seasonally, so check details with your hotel receptionist or at the Aswan tourist information office.

ASWAN DAM

Just upriver from the First Cataract, the Aswan Dam was constructed by the British between 1898 and 1902. At the time it was the largest of its kind in the world. It released Egypt from being at the mercy of unpredictable fluctuations in the level of the Nile. It also opened up vast new areas to cultivation and provided the country with most of its hydroelectric power. Now surpassed both in function and as a tourist attraction by the High Dam (see pp. 312–13), it is still worth a brief visit for the views of the river below—access is by road atop the dam. ∎

High Dam

EGYPT HAS A LONG HISTORY OF DAM BUILDING. THE earliest recorded dam is believed to have been on the Nile near Cairo, where a 49-foot-high (15 m) structure was built about 2900 B.C. to supply water to the capital at Memphis. A project to rival anything built by the pharaohs, the High Dam (Sadd al-Ali) contains almost 20 times the amount of building material used in the Great Pyramid.

High Dam

🗺 291 C4

Visiting the dam
The easiest way to visit the dam and temples is to rent a taxi from Aswan. It is about a 15-minute ride. A round-trip with an hour's wait should cost about $8.

As early as the 1950s it was evident that the Aswan Dam (see p. 311) was not big enough to counter the annual flooding of the Nile. Nor could it any longer satisfy Egypt's needs for power. President Gamal Abdel Nasser had the answer in a new, bigger dam. After the World Bank reneged on a promised loan under pressure from the United States, Nasser nationalized the Suez

Canal to generate revenue for the project, precipitating the Suez Crisis in which France, the U.K., and Israel invaded the canal zone (see pp. 42–43). In the end, the Soviet Union offered funding and expertise. Work began on the High Dam in 1960 and was completed in 1971, outlasting Nasser by a year.

The resulting structure is 12,562 feet (3,830 m) across the top, 3,214

feet (980 m) wide at its base, and 364 feet (111m) at its highest point. Over 35,000 people helped build it, and 451 of them died during the construction. It is by no means the largest dam in the world (America's Hoover Dam is over twice as high), but it is impressive nonetheless. The benefits of the dam also have been huge. Egypt's area of cultivable land has increased by more than 30 percent, while evaporation from Lake Nasser, the reservoir that backs up behind the dam, has brought rainfall to previously arid areas. The High Dam's hydroelectric station has doubled the country's power supply.

Since a dam burst would wash most of Egypt into the Mediterranean, security is paramount. The hills around bristle with aerials, radar, and missiles. Visitors are allowed though. There is a visitors' pavilion at the eastern end of the dam with models and photographs, and at the western end a giant lotuslike tower stands as a monument to Soviet-Egyptian friendship.

Visible from the dam, on the west side of Lake Nasser, is the **Temple of Kalabsha.** Like Philae, this temple was originally sited elsewhere (in this case, 30 miles to the south) but had to be moved to avoid being submerged by Lake Nasser. The German government financed the rescue project and was presented in return with the temple's gateway, which is now in the Berlin Museum. Kalabsha was built during the reign of the last of the Ptolemies and completed under the first Roman emperor of Egypt, Augustus, between 30 B.C. and 14 A.D. It was dedicated to the Nubian god Mandulis. Isis and Osiris were also worshiped here. An impressive stone causeway leads up from the lake to the entrance pylon, beyond which are a colonnaded court and

Right: The monument that commemorates Soviet assistance with the dam

Temple of Kalabsha
🅰 291 C4
✉ Lake Nasser
💲 $$

hypostyle hall. Inscriptions on the walls show emperors and pharaohs worshiping with gods and goddesses. Beyond the hall are three chambers, with stairs leading from one up to the roof. The view of Lake Nasser and the High Dam, across the hall and court, is fantastic.

Adjacent to the temple is the **Kiosk of Qertassi,** a smaller, less well-preserved version of Trajan's Kiosk at Philae. Also here is the **Temple of Bayt al-Wali,** carved from rock during the reign of Ramses II. On the walls of the forecourt are several reliefs, detailing the pharaoh's victory over the Nubians (south wall) and his wars against the Libyans and Syrians (north wall). Like Kalabsha, both of the structures were removed here to escape being inundated. ■

Lake Nasser

AS THE WORLD'S LARGEST ARTIFICIAL BODY OF WATER, THE statistics of Lake Nasser are staggering. From the barrier of the High Dam it stretches back over 300 miles (480 km), down into Sudan, and in places spreads to over 22 miles (35 km) in width. It is also the most stunningly beautiful and unspoiled region of Egypt.

Lake Nasser
 291 A1–C4

The massive expanse of Lake Nasser was created as a consequence of the construction of the High Dam.

It is a lake in the desert, with sand-dune shores rolling down to the water's edge. Elsewhere are jagged granite crags topped with white sand, looking for all the world like snowcapped alpine peaks. So far removed from civilization, skies are completely clear, cloudless, and the deepest of blues. At night, stars stretch from one horizon to the other, arrayed like a great open-air planetarium. The lack of human inhabitants has made the reedy lake shores a favorite with migrating birds, as well as with a variety of wildlife including gazelle, foxes, and monitor lizards. The inlets of the lake are the habitat of the only surviving specimens of Nile crocodiles in Egypt, which in recent years have claimed the life of more than one local fisherman. At least 25 species of fish thrive in the lake, including the enormous Nile perch *(Lates niloticus)*. The current record for a catch is 510 pounds (232 kg). The area now draws visitors from Europe and America purely on the strength of the fishing. It is possible to sign up for five-day fishing safaris (see p. 381), or just head out from Aswan for a day.

The only man-made structures anywhere on the lake are a series of ancient Egyptian temples, painstakingly moved out of the path of the rising waters in the 1960s (see pp. 316–17).

Almost the only drawback is how to visit. There are virtually no roads in the area. In fact, the only possible way to explore Lake Nasser is by boat. Currently several outfits operate luxury cruises of three or four days' duration (see p. 353), sailing between the High Dam in the north and Abu Simbel in the south. They stop en route at all the various pharaonic sites.

Most northerly of these sites is **Wadi al-Sebua,** about 85 miles (140 km) south of the High Dam on the west bank of the lake. Built

during the reign of Ramses II, its name means "valley of lions" and refers to the avenue of sphinxes that leads to the temple. Although the temple was only moved from its original site in the '60s, its inaccessibility meant that it was quickly forgotten and allowed to fill with sand. It was only when the first cruise ships started sailing Lake Nasser in the 1990s that it was re-excavated for visitors. Even so, fallen statues of kings still lie half buried in the sand, and the fact that there is nothing but desert around—no ticket office, no souvenir stalls, no guardian—allows the visitor to imagine that they might be the first discoverers of the site.

Dedicated to the gods Amun-Re and Re-Horakhty, the temple is yet another work dating from the reign of the prolific Ramses II. A large statue of the great pharaoh stands to the left of the entrance, and there are ten more representations of him attached to the columns around the first courtyard.

Less than a mile to the north are the remains of the **Temple of**
Dakka, a Ptolemaic structure dating back to the third century B.C., notable for its monumental pylon. You can climb this pylon for amazing views over the surrounding landscape.

Oldest of all the Lake Nasser monuments is the **Temple of Amada,** about 30 miles (48 km) south of Wadi al-Sebua. This dates back to the 18th dynasty, predating Ramses II by a couple of hundred years. It is small with a very simple plan, but contains wall paintings that still have much of their original color.

The only monument to have remained on its original site is **Qasr Ibrim,** which once capped the top of a 235-foot (72 m) cliff. This has been transformed by the rising waters into a rocky island near the center of the lake. The Qasr, or fortress, is a pharaonic and Roman bastion, with a seventh-century sandstone cathedral. Ships generally moor alongside the island to allow passengers to peer over the remains, but because the site is the subject of intense archaeological work, it is off-limits to visitors. ■

The lake water is regulated so that it is 600 feet (183 m) above sea level—204 feet (62 m) higher than the original level of the Nile.

Saving the monuments

The Egyptian government's decision to build a new dam just upstream of Aswan in the 1950s threatened to submerge forever all the ancient sites and monuments along the Nubian stretch of the Nile. Drowning the past to save the future, they termed it. In the end, the monuments were saved by a UNESCO rescue effort that ranks as one of the greatest engineering feats of modern times.

Once the dam got the go-ahead, archaeological missions from many countries, at the request of the Egyptian government, descended on Nubia to explore the threatened area. All portable artifacts were removed to museums, and while some temples were surrendered and allowed to disappear beneath the rising waters of the newly formed Lake Nasser, more than a dozen were salvaged and moved to safety.

Ten of them, including the temple complexes of Philae (see pp. 308–311), Kalabsha (see p. 313), and Abu Simbel (see pp. 319–322), were dismantled stone by stone and rebuilt as close to the original sites as possible, but on higher ground. Several other smaller structures were donated to the countries that contributed to the rescue effort, including the Temple of Dendur, which now forms the centerpiece of the ancient Egypt collection at the Metropolitan Museum of Art in New York.

Undoubtedly the most spectacular part of the whole ambitious project was the preservation of the temples at Abu Simbel. Hewn as they were out of a solid cliff face, there was no question of simply taking the temples to pieces and moving them. Instead various imaginative schemes were proposed. An Italian engineer submitted a plan to lift the temple the height of a 20-story building on hydraulic jacks. The British suggested enclosing the whole site in a vast clear dome under the water.

These ideas proved prohibitively expensive, and in the end UNESCO accepted the plan of Swedish consulting engineers, which called for sawing up the temples and cutting them away from the mountain. In 1964 a cofferdam was built around the site to hold back the already encroaching water of the new lake, while engineers injected a strengthening synthetic resin into the brittle sandstone. The temples were then hand-sawn piece by precisely calculated piece.

At a cost of about 40 million dollars (a third of which was funded by the United States) the temples were cut up into more than

Behind the scenes at Abu Simbel

Beneath a man-made mountain, an immense concrete dome protects the great temple of Ramses II from the tons of rocks piled up in imitation of Abu Simbel's original setting. A concrete dome of this height and span (90 feet by 195 feet) had never previously been attempted at the time, and sceptics doubted that it could be built at all. But in the end, Swedish engineers produced a technical masterpiece almost the equal of the great pharaoh's achievement in building the temple.

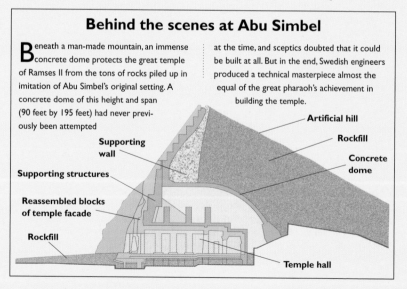

- Artificial hill
- Rockfill
- Concrete dome
- Supporting wall
- Supporting structures
- Reassembled blocks of temple facade
- Rockfill
- Temple hall

The severed face of Ramses II, weighing 19 tons, is carefully lifted before being transported to the new site.

2,000 huge blocks, weighing around 22 tons (20 tonnes) each, and reconstructed like a giant jigsaw puzzle approximately 656 feet (200 m) inland of the water and 212 feet (65 m) higher than the original site. Two great concrete domes covered with rocks and sand were used to reconstruct the shape of the mountain out of which the temples had been cut. Great care was also taken to carefully orient the temples in precisely the correct alignment.

The project took just over four years. The temples of Abu Simbel were officially reopened in 1968, while the sacred site they had occupied for over 3,000 years disappeared beneath Lake Nasser. ■

Abu Simbel

BUILT BY THE MIGHTIEST OF THE PHARAOHS, RAMSES II, with four massive colossi of himself adorning the facade, Abu Simbel is the most famous of the ancient Egyptian monuments after the Pyramids and the Sphinx. It marked the limit of Egypt's domain and was intended to convey the might of the pharaohs to any who approached from the south. More than 3,000 years later, it has lost none of its power to inspire awe.

Twice a year, in spring and fall, the rising sun fully illuminates the gods, positioned deep inside the temple.

Although it has the appearance of being a monument raised to the glory of is builder, Ramses II (1279–1213 B.C.), the temple was dedicated to the gods Re-Harakhty, Amun, and Ptah. Carved from the mountainside on the West Bank of the Nile, it was begun in the pharaoh's fifth regnal year but was not completed until his 35th. With the passing of the great age of the pharaohs, the upkeep of the temple was forgotten, and it gradually became almost completely buried in sand. It disappeared from history completely, mentioned by neither Greeks nor Romans, until its chance rediscovery by the Swiss explorer John Lewis Burkhardt in 1813. As he described the scene, "An entire head and part of the breast and arms of one of the statues emerge still above the surface. Of the adjacent statue, there is almost nothing to be seen, since its head has broken off and its body is covered in sand to above shoulder level. Of the two others, only their headdresses are visible. It is difficult to decide whether these statues are seated or standing."

With such a huge volume of sand piled up against the temple, initial efforts at clearance were limited to finding a doorway to gain entrance to the temple and see what treasures lay within. In 1817 the Italian adventurer in the employ of the British consul, Giovanni Belzoni (see p. 80), succeeded in digging his way inside. He

was to be bitterly disappointed; aside from a few small statues, which he took away, the temple contained none of the hoped-for treasures. Belzoni and crew turned their backs on Abu Simbel after three days and left for good. Over the next decades periodic attempts were made by various parties to clear more of the sand away, but always it blew back. It was not until as recently as 1909 that the temple was finally cleared for good.

VISITING THE TEMPLE
Abu Simbel is usually reached from Aswan. A road connects the two, although most visitors make the trip with EgyptAir, a brief 30-minute flight from Aswan. Flights are timed to give a couple of hours at the temple before returning.

Abu Simbel
- 291 A1
- Lake Nasser
- Open daily 6 a.m.–5 p.m.
- $$$

Opposite: Ankle-high to the pharaoh, children scramble over the colossi of Ramses II at Abu Simbel.

Shuttle buses are provided between the airport and temples. An alternative option is to join a Lake Nasser cruise (see p. 314). These boats moor almost in the shadow of the Ramses colossi, giving passengers the chance to view them both by moonlight and by the first light of dawn.

At 69 feet (21 m) high, the four **enthroned colossi** are the largest surviving sculptures in Egypt. Their hands alone, resting on their knees, are longer than the average person is tall. They sit against a flattened area cut from the mountain to resemble the sloping walls of a temple's pylon. At the feet of the giant statues are bound captives—Africans and Asians—symbolic of the Egyptian kingdom's border foes. Either side of the kings' legs are smaller (though still much larger than life-size) statues of his mother, Tuya, his wife, Nefertari,

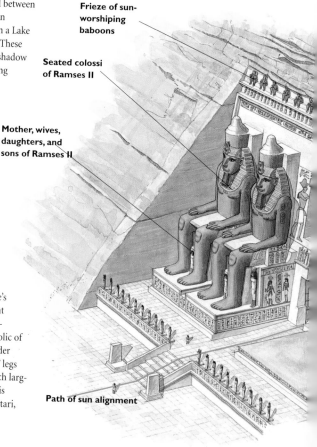

Frieze of sun-worshiping baboons

Seated colossi of Ramses II

Mother, wives, daughters, and sons of Ramses II

Path of sun alignment

Left: The pharaoh, his chief wife, Nefertari, and gods decorate pillars in the small hall.

Below: The temple of Abu Simbel as it might have been at completion some 3,000 years ago

and some of their children. Above the central entrance, between the heads of the colossi, is the figure of the falcon-headed sun god Re.

The interior of Ramses' temple is much less spectacular than its facade. Burrowed 200 feet (60 m) into rock, it has the simplest of plans, with a large pillared hall leading to a small one, also with pillars, and a sanctuary at the rear. Nevertheless, the first pillared hall is still fairly imposing, with eight more statues of Ramses attached to columns supporting a ceiling decorated with Osiride vultures. Reliefs on the walls, some of which still have their original color, depict the pharaoh in battle.

In the small pillared hall,

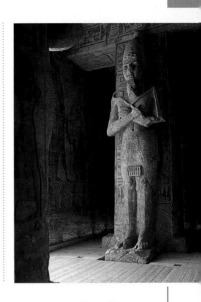

Above: Hewn from rock, 30-foot statues of Ramses II dominate the large pillared hall.

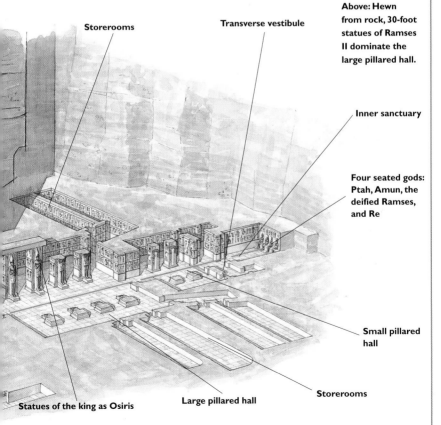

Storerooms

Transverse vestibule

Inner sanctuary

Four seated gods: Ptah, Amun, the deified Ramses, and Re

Small pillared hall

Storerooms

Statues of the king as Osiris

Large pillared hall

Although created in Nefertari's honor, the Temple of Hathor also glorifies her egocentric husband, and twin statues of Ramses II flank each of hers.

Ramses and Nefertari are shown in front of the gods and their sacred barks. The innermost chamber is the **Sacred Sanctuary,** with four small statues of the gods Ptah, Amun-Re, the deified Ramses, and Re-Horakhty.

The temple is aligned in such a way that on February 22 and October 22 every year, the first rays of the rising sun penetrate the temple and illuminate the holy quartet—or at least three of them; Ptah, on the left, remains in shadow. Until the temples were moved up from the lake, this phenomenon happened one day earlier. Some Egyptologists have speculated that these may be the anniversaries of Ramses' coronation and birth.

TEMPLE OF HATHOR

To the north of Ramses' main temple is a far smaller second temple, built in honor of the pharaoh's beloved chief wife, Nefertari. It is dedicated to the goddess Hathor, the deity most closely associated with queenship in ancient Egypt. It, too, is fronted by

a series of colossal figures. Standing about 32 feet (10 m) high, four of these statues are of Ramses and two of his queen. Beside them are the more diminutive figures of the rest of the royal family.

Inside is a single hall with six pillars crowned with Hathor (cow-eared) capitals. The walls are adorned with scenes depicting Nefertari before Hathor and Mut. On the rear wall, the queen is shown as a cow with the king beneath her chin. What is striking is the importance granted to Nefertari, with the queen repeatedly shown on an equal footing with the king. As a pharaonic queen, she is unique in this respect.

A gray door in the mountain-side to the right of the main temple offers quite a bizarre experience. Passing through and ascending a tubular steel staircase, you see the inside of the fake mountain, a vast domed space, filled on one side with cut-stone blocks—the reverse of the monumental facade. The effect is a little like Dorothy pulling aside the curtain to reveal the puny reality of the Wizard of Oz. ■

The desert canyons of the Sinai interior and the underwater world of the Red Sea are natural marvels every bit as wondrous as Egypt's pharaonic heritage.

Red Sea & Sinai

A crimson sea star—part of the famed reef life

Red Sea & Sinai

OVER THE PAST COUPLE OF DECADES EGYPT'S TOURISM INDUSTRY HAS BEEN undergoing a dramatic shift in focus. Where once it was ancient history and the monuments of the pharaohs that proved the big draw, an increasing number of visitors to the country now don't bother with the Pyramids of Giza or temples of Luxor. Instead, they are here for sun, white sands, and turquoise seas, all of which the Red Sea coast and the shores of Sinai have in abundance.

Abdullah, a young Bedouin boy, swims with his companion, Olin the dolphin, at Nuweiba.

Remoteness from the life-sustaining Nile Valley has traditionally kept civilization away from Egypt's extreme eastern edges. Between the Nile and the Red Sea coastline, which extends for 775 miles (1,250 km) from the town of Suez down to the Sudanese border, is the inhospitable expanse of the Eastern Desert. It has proved a daunting barrier. The topography is one of lifeless rocky landscapes, with craggy mountains scored by parched wadis, the local term for a dried-up river bed.

Sinai, the triangular peninsula bounded by the Gulf of Suez and the Suez Canal on the west, and the Gulf of Aqaba and Israel's Negev Desert on the east, is essentially a continuation of the desert. Until now the wild landscapes have been the domain of the Bedouin, roaming with their camels and goats in search of pastures. During the early Christian era, hermits and ascetics valued the remote expanses as somewhere in which they could seek religious enlightenment in solitude. The monasteries they founded still exist.

Sinai remains best known for its religious connections. The word itself probably derives from one of the most ancient of religious cults of the Middle East, that of the moon god Sin. But most people know the name from the Bible; Sinai is the "great and terrible wilderness" negotiated by Moses and his people in their epic 40-year journey from Egypt to the Promised Land—even if the route and the date of their exodus are still matters of debate. It's also here that, as told in the Book of Exodus, God first spoke to Moses, from the burning bush, and on Mount Sinai that Moses is believed to have received the tablets inscribed with the Ten Commandments.

Acting as both bridge and buffer between Egypt and the empires to the north in what we now call the Middle East, Sinai has historically served as a route for trade caravans and armies alike. Most recently that included the Israeli army, which captured the region during the Six Day War of June 1967 and held it until 1982, when Sinai was returned to Egypt under the terms of the Camp David peace treaty.

Since then tourism has boomed and this part of Egypt has gone from wilderness to playground. Resorts in Sinai's Sharm al-Sheikh and Hurghada on the Red Sea have sprung up to offer sunbathing and swimming to northern Europeans looking to escape the cold. The resorts come complete with hotels, casinos, and golf courses, and a complete new set of commandments: from "Do not go topless on the beaches" to "Only drink bottled water."

Thankfully, the wilderness is far from tamed. Inland the desert remains virtually uninhabited, with bare mountains sheltering hidden oases. More dramatic still are the underwater landscapes of the Red Sea, where vast coral reefs provide a home for more than one thousand species of marine life, making for some of the world's richest diving. ■

Mediterranean Sea
GAZA STRIP
Rafah
Pelusium
Al-Arish
Romani
Qantara
ZARANIK PROTECTORATE
Cairo
Suez Canal
DELTA & SUEZ p. 163
Bitter Lakes
S i n a i
ISRAEL
Al-Shatt
Nakhl
Wadi al-Arish
Gebel al-Tih
Taba
JORDAN
AROUND CAIRO p. 143
Ain Sukhna
Zafarana
Serabit al-Khadim
Monastery of St. Anthony
Gebel al-Igma
Monastery of St. Catherine
Nuweiba
SAUDI ARABIA
Monastery of St. Paul
Al-Milga
2285m
2642m ▲ Mt. Sinai (G. Musa)
Mt. St. Catherine (G. Katherina)
Dahab
Gulf of Suez
Gulf of Aqaba
Ras Gharib
ST. CATHERINE PROTECTORATE
Al-Tur
Wadi al-Tarfa
1757m ▲
Gebel Gharib
Ras Zeit
Naama Bay
Sharm al-Sheikh
E a s t e r n   D e s e r t
Gemsa
Al-Gouna
Strait of Gubal
RAS MUHAMMAD NATIONAL PARK
Mons Porphyritis
Hurghada
Giftun Island
MIDDLE EYGPT p. 213
2187m
G. Shayib al-Banat ▲
Mons Claudianus
Wadi Qena
Safaga
Red Sea Mountains
Qena
R E D
Bir Seiyala
Quseir
S E A
Luxor
1477m ▲
Gebel al-Sibai
Ras Abu Aweid
SOUTH OF LUXOR p.289
1160m ▲
Gebel Abu Diyab
Magal Umm Rus
Marsa Alam
Ras Samadai
1505m ▲
Gebel Nugrus
E a s t e r n   D e s e r t
Wadi al-Kharit
1977m ▲
Gebel Hamata
Berenice
Ras Banas
Foul Bay
Aswan
Bir Abu Hashim
1366m ▲
Gebel al-Faraid
Bir Shalatein
1165m ▲
Gebel Natitiai
Bir Abu Safa
Marsa Shaab
Ras Abu Dara
Wadi al-Allaqi
Treaty   Boundary
Halaib
S U D A N

0   200 kilometers
0   100 miles

Cairo ✪
Area of map detail

A   B   C   D

Monasteries of
St. Anthony & St. Paul

In spite of successive restorations, the Monastery of St. Anthony retains its original appearance.

HIDDEN AWAY IN THE BARREN HILLS OF THE EASTERN desert and dramatically set against backdrops of cliffs, are what may be the world's two oldest monasteries. Black-robed monks are welcoming to the few visitors who trouble to make it here to see the splendid ancient wall paintings and murals.

Monasteries of St. Anthony & St. Paul

⚠ 325 B5

🕐 Closed Coptic Christmas (Jan. 6) & Lent

There is no public transportation to the monasteries, and they are best reached on an organized tour from either Cairo or Hurghada, both of which are slightly more than 200 miles (320 km) away. The national tour agency, Misr Travel (*7 Talaat Harb St., Cairo, tel 02/393 0168*),

organizes day trips from Hurghada that include visits to both monasteries.

St. Anthony Abbot (A.D. 251–356) is said to have become a hermit at the age of 18, traveling with a caravan into the Eastern Desert and settling in an isolated mountain cave, where he lived until the age of 105. Since he forbade his many followers to stay near the cave, they camped at the foot of the hill, creating a settlement that formed the basis of the **Monastery of St. Anthony** (Deir Anba Antonius), founded shortly after his death.

Entered through a double-arched gate between twin towers topped by crosses, the monastery compound contains churches, housing quarters, and gardens. It has the pleasing appearance of a small, sandy-colored, walled village. Until quite recently it was largely empty, but since the current Coptic pope, Shenouda III, took office in 1971, all Egypt's monasteries have undergone a renaissance, attracting plenty of new, young would-be monks. From the four monks who maintained St. Anthony's in the early 1970s, numbers are now up to around 80. For the first time in more than a century, the monastery is actually expanding to accommodate the new interest from Coptic Christians in a life of spiritual contemplation.

The oldest structure is the **Church of St. Anthony,** built over the saint's tomb. It contains the largest array of Coptic wall paintings in Egypt, mostly dating from the 13th to 16th centuries, and all beautifully restored during the 1990s.

A path from the west side of the monastery winds steeply up to **St. Anthony's Cave.** The trip to the cave involves climbing some 1,158 wooden steps and the hike takes about an hour. Inside the cave is a small chapel with an altar, but of more interest are the medieval graffiti on the walls. There is also a breathtaking view of the hills and valley below.

The **Monastery of St. Paul** (Deir Anba Bula) is smaller and even more remote than St. Anthony's. It was built in and around the cave where Paul the Hermit lived for nearly 90 years during the third and fourth centuries. Not to be confused with the Apostle Paul, this Paul was born into a wealthy Alexandrian family, but is said to have turned away from society at the age of 16, sickened by Roman inquisitions. Tradition has it that when Paul died, it was St. Anthony who, past the age of 90, made the long trek through the mountains to bury him.

As the crow flies, the two caves and their monasteries are only about 22 miles (35 km) apart, but thanks to the cliffs and rocky hills between, they are around 50 miles (80 km) apart by road. It is possible to emulate St. Anthony's mission and walk between the two monasteries along a mountainous trail. It takes two full days, so camping gear is necessary. A map is available at St. Anthony's Monastery.

St. Paul's cave is contained within **St. Paul's Church,** which is strewn with a number of altars, candelabras, and icons. There is also a sarcophagus which, it is believed, contains the remains of the saint. Note the ostrich eggs, which the monks will tell you are kept as a symbol of Jesus Christ's resurrection. An alternative tale is that they were threaded onto the chains of the oil lamps hanging from the chapel ceilings to prevent rats from climbing down.

In the 17th-century **Church of St. Michael,** also within the monastery, is an icon of the Virgin Mary claimed to have been painted from life by St. Luke in A.D. 40. Outside the monastery there can still be seen an ancient olive press, and the pulley that was used to hoist visitors and provisions over the wall in times of unrest. ∎

Seclusion has a growing appeal, and the number of Coptic monks enrolling at the monasteries is increasing.

Hurghada

Fishing is still an important activity, although the clear waters increasingly act as a bait for tourists to enjoy diving.

HURGHADA (AL-GHARDAKA IN ARABIC), 230 MILES (370 KM) southeast of Cairo on the Red Sea coast, is Egypt's pioneer tourist resort. From its beginnings as a small fishing village, it has developed over the last 20 years into a thriving vacation town filled with beach-front hotels, always full of guests drawn by the promise of year-round sunshine, crystal-clear waters, and good diving.

Hurghada

325 B4

Visitor information

Al-Korah Ave., after EgyptAir Office

065/444 420 or 065/444 421

Open daily 8 a.m.– 8 p.m.

It is a place wholly devoted to tourism. The beaches and sea provide the entertainment during the day, and by night the town lights up with streetside restaurants and bars, and gaudy souvenir shopping malls. Shorts, shades, and T-shirts are the accepted form of dress, and the lambada and other disco themes drown out the call to prayer. Burgers and pizza prevail over felafel and kabobs, with even dishes like borscht and *pelmeni* appearing on menus, catering to the huge flood of Russians who have taken to vacationing here since the collapse of the Soviet Union. There is probably more alcohol consumed in this one town than in the whole of the rest of the country combined. Most visitors fly in directly on charter deals, and their international hotel resorts— Hiltons, Marriotts, Sheratons—

have a full range of amenities, plus their own strip of beach, so that guests need never wander beyond the grounds. The Egypt of ancient monuments doesn't exist here except as icons on T-shirts, and even Arab and Islamic cultures have only the most tenuous of footholds.

One thing that most guests like to do, however, is head out to sea. Nearly all the hotels offer snorkeling safaris out to the reefs that lie off-shore. Many also visit **Giftun Island,** about a 40-minute boat ride from shore. This is a protected area, with a maximum of a hundred people allowed on the island each day. Several tourist camps provide refreshment facilities, dive centers, and rest rooms, but development has been kept to a minimum, and the island remains stunningly beautiful. Fish is usually provided for lunch as part of the package.

It is diving, however, that has really put Hurghada on the map. There are about ten coral islands within day-trip range, all harboring a fantastic array of marine life (see pp. 330–33), including sharks, manta rays, and giant moray eels, as well as myriad shoals of small, brightly colored fish. The numerous local dive centers offer first-timers' courses for novices and a wide array of one-day, overnight, and live-aboard options for the more experienced. Be wary when choosing a dive center, as some outfits are dangerously incompetent. It is generally better to dive with centers attached to the larger hotels and vacation villages, which may be more expensive but keep better maintained equipment and employ professional instructors.

For the less adventurous, there are glass-bottom boats, which allow views of the coral marine life below while sitting comfortably in an air-conditioned cabin. Alternatively, there is the Sindbad Submarine,

which goes down to depths of below 66 feet (20 m) to drift among the fishes. It can be found moored offshore from the Sindbad Beach Resort. For a closer look at sea creatures if you don't want to dive, Hurghada also has the **Red Sea Aquarium,** with tanks containing a large number of species that are found swimming freely around the nearby reefs.

Red Sea Aquarium
- The Corniche, Al-Dahar
- 065/548 557
- Open daily 9 a.m.–10 p.m.
- $

Two children make themselves secure on a camel in anticipation of a ride along a Hurghada beach.

An alternative to the unregulated development of Hurghada exists 12 miles (20 km) north at the brand-new resort center of **Al-Gouna.** Founded by one of Egypt's biggest tycoons, it includes a number of international hotels, several clusters of villas, upscale shopping centers, and a brewery and winery producing Sakkara beer and Obelisk wine. It is an exclusive setup, and a big hit with the Egyptian jet set. Pick of the accommodations is the Sheraton Miramar (see p. 373), built on nine islands connected by bridges and designed by Indianapolis-born architect Michael Graves. It is a pastel-colored, postmodern desert fantasy to turn the Disney Corporation—one of Graves's previous clients—green with envy. ■

Reef life

The coral reefs of the Red Sea are Egypt's crowning natural glory—every bit as spectacular, in their own way, as pharaonic wonders like the Pyramids that usually head the itineraries of most visitors. No adjectives or glossy underwater photographs can adequately prepare you for that magical moment when you don a mask and poke your face into the warm waters of this seductive dreamscape.

A golden butterflyfish, one of the myriad marine species

Egypt has over 500 miles (800 km) of reef-lined Red Sea coastline, stretching from the border with Israel in the north down to the border with Sudan in the south.

The Red Sea is essentially a water-flooded rip in the earth's crust, torn between the African and Asian landmasses. Along either side run chains of desert mountains. Narrow and constricted, the Red Sea is well over a mile (1.6 km) deep in places. Its reefs are mostly steep walls that plunge dizzyingly, rising at some spots to form offshore shoals and coral islands before plunging again. Because of the great depth, sediment never manages to drift upward, and as a result the waters are extremely clear. Between these subterranean cliffs and the shore are shallow fringe reefs, beginning where the water is no more than chest height on an average adult, and ideal for snorkeling.

Marine life

Coral is what makes a reef. Thought for many centuries to be some form of flowering plant, it is in fact an animal. Corals are minute polyps, anemonelike creatures that have a calcareous or horny outer skeleton and feed off other small organisms that live in the sea. They group together in colonies and accumulate into beautiful formations of many shapes. When corals die, the next generation grows up on top of them. Over a long period of time, they build up into reefs. These coral reefs form a mini-ecosystem supporting more than a thousand species of marine life.

At its southern end, the Red Sea runs through narrow straits and shelves to a shallow sea, a geographical bottleneck that has effectively prevented much migration. As a result, the Red Sea is home to a huge number of endemic species (ones that are not found elsewhere).

Many of the fish are brilliantly colored and swim in huge shoals that swathe the reefs with blues, golds, and yellows, or glitter and shimmer like jewels against the background of ultramarine water. The blue-green parrotfish, the numerous kinds of wrasses, beautiful yellow butterfly fish, and silvery damselfish graze the reef, gnawing away at the algae-clad surface. These are preyed on by predators such as groupers, scorpionfish, snappers, and morays. In turn, this group of fish form the menu for higher predators, including dolphins, barracuda, and sharks.

The most commonly encountered types of shark are white or black-tipped reef sharks. Hammerheads, tiger sharks, and the huge, plankton-eating whale sharks are generally found in deeper waters only. Turtles are common, especially the green turtle.

Such a high density of underwater life makes for a competitive environment. All species have necessarily evolved methods to prevent themselves ending up as dinner for some other, bigger fish. A large number carry some kind of spine or poisonous toxin to deter would-be predators. Few species are actually aggressive, but many can inflict painful, occasionally fatal injuries in self-defense. The stingray, for example, has sharp feather-shaped quills in its tail, which is whipped forward at any who get too close. The spiny lionfish, and the stonefish and scorpionfish, which are both well camouflaged to

Right: A diver explores a coral-encrusted wreck, one of several sunken vessels resting on the bed of the Red Sea.

resemble seabed rocks, all have stout dorsal fins, which are erected when the fish is threatened and are strong and sharp enough to puncture skin. Even coral can be well armed. Fire coral can inflict irritating burns if it comes into contact with exposed flesh. The simple rule of thumb for divers and snorkelers is do not touch and you won't get hurt.

EXPLORING THE REEF

Sinai and the Red Sea coast are perhaps second only to Australia's Great Barrier Reef when it comes to diving. If you want to learn to dive, plenty of courses are available along the coast, particularly in the tourist hubs such as Hurghada and Sharm al-Sheikh (see p. 381 for some recommendations). They vary greatly in professionalism and price, so shop around. Instructors should belong to an internationally recognized body, the largest of which is the Professional Association of Diving Instructors (PADI).

Most of Egypt's best diving is on the offshore reefs and islands: Some of the most famous names include a site known simply as **The Islands,** off the Sinai coast at Dahab; **Ras Muhammad,** just south of Sharm al-Sheikh; and, farther to the south off the mainland coast, **The Brothers, Daedelus Reef.** Serious divers will want to head down south of Quseir, where a series of dedicated dive camps are being established to take advantage of virgin reefs, until recently off-limits because of their proximity to the Sudanese border.

Dive resorts such as Kahramana around the small, dusty crossroads settlement of **Marsa Alam** give access to the **Abu Dabbab reef,** where a trail through a large underwater cavern leads to three huge coral towers rising up from the seabed.

If you don't dive, or don't want to, snorkeling can also reveal spectacular underwater sights. Most of the best displays of fish are in shallow water anyway, and if you simply paddle along the surface, face down, you'll be treated to vivid displays of tropical color and an eerie, dreamlike sensation of flying. You don't even have to get wet: Operators at resorts like Hurghada and Sharm al-Sheikh have glass-bottom boats, and even submarines, from which you can view the reef. ■

Humbug dascyllus

Yellowtail barracuda

male

female

Red Sea steephead parrotfish

Oceanic white shark

Lionfish

Elkhorn

Red Sea coral-grouper

Giant moray

Fire coral

Common stonefish

Whale shark

Hammerhead shark

Dolphin

Sergeant-major

One spot snapper

Chocolate-tip chromis

Racoon butterflyfish

Jewel fairy basslet

Acropora valenciennesi coral

Montipora tuberosa coral

Arabian smoke angelfish

Masked butterflyfish

Red Sea fairy basslet

Citron gobi

Blue triggerfish

Coneshell

Bearded scorpion fish

Acropora hemiprichii

Abudjubbe's wrasse

Bluespotted ribbontail ray

South of Hurghada

ALTHOUGH AT PRESENT, SOUTH OF HURGHADA IS OFF THE tourist map of Egypt, that is all about to change, as much of the Red Sea coastline has already been sold off to developers, modern-day alchemists aiming to transform white sands and turquoise seas into gold—or piles of the folding green stuff, at least.

Some of Egypt's most attractive new hotels enjoy prime beachfront locations along the Red Sea coast.

Safaga
325 C4

The hottest concepts in coastal development are the so-called tourist centers, planned on an ambitious scale to incorporate not just hotels, restaurants, and entertainment facilities, but also schools, hospitals, and housing for service workers and their families. Several of these are in advanced stages of completion along the coast between Hurghada and the next town to the south, the port of **Safaga,** 32 miles (52 km) to the south. Of little interest to visitors, Safaga is a center for the export of phosphates from local mines, which comes to life once a year when it becomes a busy embarkation point for Muslims traveling to Mecca during the annual *hajj* (pilgrimage).

The mineral-rich Red Sea Mountains, which erupt south of Hurghada, were being quarried for their gold, copper, and other precious metals and stones as far back as pharaonic times. There are no monuments to the ancient Egyptians in the area, but at **Mons Claudianus,** 30 miles (48 km) inland of Safaga, are Roman-era quarries. Here black-flecked granite was hacked out, transported to the Nile, and shipped to Rome, where it was used in the construction of the Pantheon and Trajan's Forum. It was impossibly remote; for the prisoners sent to work here—and their soldier guards—the experience was the ancient Near East equivalent of being banished to Siberia. You can still see the tiny cells that these unfortunates inhabited. There is also an immense cracked pillar, left where it fell 2,000 years ago, a small temple, and numerous partly formed columns and capitals. Some of the hotels along the coast organize trips to the site and also to **Mons Porphyritis,** north of Hurghada, where the Romans quarried porphyry, the precious white-and-purple crystalline stone frequently used for sarcophagi.

By and large, the developers' bulldozers have yet to travel south beyond Safaga, and the scenery down here has a raw, untouched beauty. There are few visitors to appreciate it other than dedicated divers, whose interest lies more with the underwater landscapes, which are said to be at their best toward the Sudanese border, where military permits are required to take a boat out. A few selected

companies take divers out; try Red Sea Diving Safaris *(Tel 02/337 9942, www.egypt.com/redsea)* or Wadi Gimal Divers *(Tel 02/417 0046)*.

The largest town of note down this way is **Quseir,** 53 miles (85 km) south of Safaga. In pharaonic times, it was from here that boats sailed for the Land of Punt, as depicted in reliefs at the Temple of Hatshepsut (see pp. 274–75). Under the Romans, the Islamic leaders, and the Ottoman Turks, it remained a bustling port where Eastern spices were offloaded onto caravans to continue west, and pilgrims rested en route to Mecca. Quseir ceded its status as a major port and shipbuilding center when the opening of the Suez Canal rendered it redundant. The town experienced a brief flourish of prosperity from phosphate processing early in the 20th century, but that has all but died. Today, it has an end-of-the-world feel. Dominated by a 16th-century Ottoman fortress, the town center is sparse and low lying, with old coral-block buildings with wooden balconies lining the waterfront. Color is added by a scattering of domed tombs belonging to pious pilgrims who died en route to or from Mecca. A few miles to the north of town, occupying the site of the old pharaonic-era harbor, is one of the most paradisical hotels in the country, the Mövenpick Quseir (see p. 374). Designed to resemble a small stone village, it overlooks a sandy cove with gloriously clear waters, in which swim shoals of exotically patterned fish. ∎

A boatbuilder at work in Quseir, although most of the industry has moved north to Suez

Quseir
◮ 325 C3

Northern Sinai

SINAI'S NORTHERN AND SOUTHERN REGIONS CONTRAST greatly in character. Whereas the south is mountainous and fringed with beaches, the north is a great plateau that slopes downward toward the Mediterranean shore, where pale dunes rise from coastal salt marshes. There are few settlements, although Al-Arish is a popular resort with Egyptians and has ambitions to attract some of the foreign vacation trade.

Almost the only foreign traffic across northern Sinai is carried on the nearly daily bus service running between Cairo and Tel Aviv, which crosses the border at the divided town of Rafah. The bus follows the ancient route for trade and invasions since pharaonic times. Highlight of the journey is crossing the Suez Canal at **Qantara.** Traffic is driven onto a busy roll-on/roll-off ferry for the brief 10-minute sail. Other than the passenger ferries at Port Said, this is about the only opportunity there is to get on the canal. Even this may disappear following the construction of a new suspension bridge.

About 18 miles (30 km) east, just before the small settlement of Farma, is a signposted turning for **Pelusium.** This was the fortress town that guarded Egypt's eastern

frontier for centuries. It has a colorful history. The Persian army of Cambyses is said to have captured the garrison here without a fight by driving cats (the sacred animal of the goddess Bastet; see p. 168) before them. It is also here that Ptolemy XIII captured the Roman general Pompey, had him murdered, and presented the head to Julius Caesar (see p. 34). The town was abandoned in the Islamic era and unfortunately has weathered to nothing. Ongoing archaeological excavations have found little beyond a Roman amphitheater.

Continuing east, the coastal road passes ramshackle villages inhabited by Bedouin, their nomadic ways now abandoned. Much of the coast is dominated by the swampy lagoon of **Lake Bardawil,** separated from the Mediterranean by a limestone ridge. It acts as a great fish farm; two gates close the lake off from the sea between April and October, when the fish breed. The rest of the year, it provides an income for around 3,000 local fishermen.

Stretching from the eastern edge of the lake is the **Zaranik Protectorate,** an 85-square-mile (220 sq km) area of lagoons and marshes that provides a resting point for numerous species of migrating birds (see p. 158) on their journey between Europe and Africa. Visiting is encouraged.

Al-Arish, about 22 miles

Left: A Bedouin woman in traditional dress sells her wares at the market in Al-Arish.

Zaranik Protectorate
🗺 325 B6
Visitor information
✉ Just off main highway
🕐 Open sunrise to sunset

Al-Arish
🗺 325 B6
Visitor information
☎ 068/363 743
🕐 Closed after 2 p.m. & Fri.

(35 km) beyond Lake Bardawil, is the peaceful, small-town capital of the North Sinai region. Its origins are as a Roman garrison town called Rhinocolorum (Noses Cut Off), after the fate of dissidents exiled there. However, its misfortune has been to lie in the path of every invading army, with the result that it has been razed and then rebuilt on countless occasions over the centuries. Most recently, the town was largely abandoned in 1967 when the Israelis captured Sinai, and only reinhabited after 1982. Hence, Al-Arish has little to show for its history, and few tangible tourist attractions. The place does come to life, though, every Thursday morning for the weekly market, filling with noise and color as Bedouin from numerous tribes descend to buy and sell. There are fruit, vegetables, clothes, plastic items, hens, and even the odd camel. Most interesting of all are the traditional Bedouin handicrafts: embroidered dresses, beadwork, rugs, silver, and jewelry—although much of the best work is transported directly to Cairo for sale. The market is also a traditional place for Bedouin men to meet to resolve their differences and for women to advertise their availability for marriage.

The other main attraction is the beach, lined with endless groves of bowed palms. Although the water is significantly cooler than the Red Sea and there are no reefs, Al-Arish has the advantage of being undeveloped and quiet. However, because Al-Arish is not used to foreigners, women should not wear bikinis. Local girls swim clothed. ■

Local Bedouin tribesmen limber up for camel races held regularly in northern Sinai.

Southern Sinai

SOUTHERN SINAI IS A GREAT, JAGGED, RUST-COLORED expanse of mountains, with drifting sands carpeting its valleys and plains. Almost completely uninhabited and bisected by a single surfaced road, this region is difficult to explore but extremely rewarding.

St. Catherine
🔼 325 B5

Sinai's booming tourist industry is based on its beaches and reefs (see p. 330), but a trip into the interior can be every bit as spectacular and memorable. Many of the larger resort hotels organize inland safaris, ranging from half-day excursions by jeep to week-long treks on camels.

An alternative is to go trekking on foot. This is certainly the most rewarding way to experience the terrain. The base for a number of good hikes is the village of **St.**

Catherine, near the monastery (see p. 340) of the same name. The village lies right at the heart of the mountainous region of the peninsula, but is readily accessible by bus. It is also at the center of the **St. Catherine Protectorate,** a 1,680-square-mile (4,350 sq km) mountain park created by prime ministerial decree in 1996. It contains a unique high-altitude desert ecosystem, as well as some stunning scenery and a number of historical sites. The protectorate has set up

three half-day walking trails, which start and finish in the village. Each has its own trail guide describing the flora and fauna. The trail up to **Wadi Arbaeen** takes in the Rock of Moses, with 12 fissures said to have gushed water when struck by the prophet, and passes the house of a Bedouin named Ramadan. Some years ago Ramadan rescued four hyrax, an indigenous but very elusive rabbitlike creature that is actually a distant relative of the elephant. He now has a colony of some 40 of these animals. Trail booklets, available from the visitor center at the monastery, can direct you to Ramadan.

Ambitious treks requiring the services of Bedouin guides and camels can be organized at the village of **Al-Milga,** near St. Catherine, through Sheikh Musa, a local tribal leader *(ask at the monastery visitor center)*. One worthwhile excursion that can be arranged through the sheikh is to **Blue Valley,** a round-trip of about 8 miles (13 km). It owes its name to Belgian "landscape artist" Jean Verame, who in 1980–81 painted all the large rocks in the valley a deep blue to symbolize peace. It makes a very surreal sight.

Roughly 40 miles (64 km) west of St. Catherine is **Wadi Feiran,** a twisting, high-walled valley full of palms. The Cairo–St. Catherine bus passes through, but if you have your own transportation you can stop and explore. This was the earliest Christian stronghold in Sinai, and a convent is set high up (*no visitors*).

Continuing west toward the coast, motorists can detour north to the remains of a pharaonic temple at **Serabit al-Khadim.** It dates back to the 12th dynasty and is dedicated to the goddess Hathor. Next to it is a New Kingdom shrine to Sopdu, god of the Eastern

Right: Rocks in the Blue Valley, painted that color by a Belgian artist in 1980–81

Desert. Throughout the temple's many courts, inscriptions list the temple's benefactors, who included Hatshepsut and Tuthmose III. The temple also marks the site of old turquoise mines. Despite its remote location, turquoise was mined here as far back as the Old Kingdom. In

the nearby **Wadi Mukattab** (Valley of Inscriptions), more stelae and rock inscriptions, some dating back to the 3rd dynasty, give further evidence of the turquoise mining that was carried out here. ■

Early alphabet

In the turquoise mines of Serabit al-Kadim, archaeologists found crude carvings of a fish, an ox-head, and a square. These signs are quite different from Egyptian hieroglyphics. The Semitic people who carved them were perhaps writing in the earliest known phonetic alphabet—one where each character represents a sound, not an object. ■

St. Catherine's & Mount Sinai

MOUNT SINAI IS REVERED BY JEWS, CHRISTIANS, AND
Muslims alike as the place where Moses received the Ten
Commandments. And, according to belief, it was in the valley below
that God spoke to him from a burning bush.

Nestled in the shadow of the sacred
mountain is the **Monastery of St.
Catherine** (Deir Sant Katreen),
where communities of monks have
lived almost uninterruptedly since
its founding in the sixth century.
Before the monastery, there was a
chapel on this site, established in
the fourth century A.D. by the

Empress Helena at the place where
tradition says that Moses saw the
burning bush. This soon became a
place of pilgrimage, and in the sixth
century a fortified monastery was
added by the Emperor Justinian to
protect the monks and pilgrims
from raiders. It was not until much
later that the establishment was

**A Greek
Orthodox monk,
whose ancestral
brethren have
looked after St.
Catherine's for
over 1,660 years**

Chapel

Dispensary

Library and icon
collection

Walls of Justinian

Chapel of the
Burning Bush

Round tower

**Monastery of
St. Catherine**

⛰ 325 B5

✉ St. Catherine, South
Sinai

☎ 069/470 341 or
069/470 343

🕐 Closed after noon &
Fri. and Sun.

$ Donation

dedicated to St. Catherine. She was an early Christian saint who was martyred in Alexandria in the fourth century. After being tortured on a spiked wheel (hence the catherine wheel firework), she was beheaded. According to legend her body was carried away by angels, to be found, uncorrupted, six centuries later by monks on Mount St. Catherine (Gebel Katarina), a neighbor of Mount Sinai and at 8,665 feet (2,642 m) the highest mountain in Egypt.

Once entailing a difficult and dangerous journey for would-be visitors, the monastery is now served by a good road connecting it to the Red Sea resorts. Many people visit on a half-day trip arranged by their hotel and, as a consequence, the small village of St. Catherine close by the monastery is often choked with tour buses and people,

A mosaic of the Transfiguration adorns the apse of the monastery's basilica.

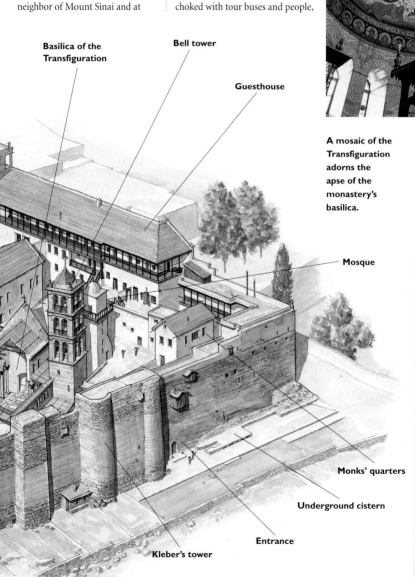

Basilica of the Transfiguration

Bell tower

Guesthouse

Mosque

Monks' quarters

Underground cistern

Entrance

Kleber's tower

icons held by the monastery, including some of the oldest in existence, dating back to the fifth century. St. Catherine's library also has the most important collection of religious manuscripts after the Vatican. The monks' reluctance to allow access to these valuable documents is understandable; in the 19th century a German scholar borrowed one of their rarest, the fourth-century *Codex Sinaiticus,* and never returned it. It is now held by the British Library. However, scholars worldwide will soon have access to at least a part of the monastery's collection via the Internet, as the computer-savvy monks are adding them to St. Catherine's website.

Behind the basilica, the **Well of Moses** marks the place where the patriarch is believed to have met his future wife, Zipporah. Close by is a large bush protected by a wooden lattice; this is a transplant of what was claimed to be the original **burning bush.** Uniquely for a Christian monastery, St. Catherine's contains a **mosque** within its walls, opposite the entrance to the basilica. It was built for a Bedouin who worked for the monks. It has probably also helped avoid attacks by Muslims over the centuries.

Outside the high walls are the monastery gardens, with an orchard of olive and apricot trees shading a cemetery, from which the monks' bones are periodically exhumed and transferred to the nearby **Charnel House.** This rather macabre display of skulls and assorted bones is usually open to visitors. The robed skeleton is that of Stephanos, a sixth-century guardian of the Mount Sinai path.

Tourists and pilgrims witness dawn from the summit of Mount Sinai.

especially in the mornings. One way to avoid the crowds is to make your own way to St. Catherine's by regular public transportation and find accommodations in the village; there is plenty of choice.

Entry to the monastery is through a small postern in the imposing curtain wall, which in places is up to almost 9 feet (3 m) thick. Because of its working nature, most of the monastery is off-limits to the public. The only building open is the **Basilica of the Transfiguration** (also known as the Church of St. Catherine), added by Justinian in the sixth century. Even much of this is roped off, but it is worth visiting for the splendid display of priceless icons in the antichamber. These are just a small sample of some 2,000

Monastery of St. Catherine

Remember that St. Catherine's is still a functioning monastery, not a museum piece. It is home to about 20 monks. They are Greek Orthodox and not Coptic, and most are from the monasteries of Mount Athos in Greece.

MOUNT SINAI

At a height of 7,500 feet (2,285 m), Mount Sinai (in Arabic, Gebel Musa, the Mountain of Moses) towers over St. Catherine's Monastery. It is identified with the biblical Mount Horeb, where Moses spent 40 days and received the tablets bearing God's command-ments. Some archaeologists and historians dispute this claim and place Mount Horeb variously in Saudi Arabia and Jordan, but that hardly seems to deter the hordes of pilgrims who turn up here each day. Visitors here are not just the religious; coming after a visit to the monastery to watch the sunrise from the top of Mount Sinai is de rigueur for almost all travelers coming to Sinai. Consequently the predawn hours on the mountain can be a distinctly unsacred mix of tour groups tripping over sleeping backpackers and church groups singing rival hymns. The views, however, are spectacular and are worth the climb.

There are two ways up the mountain. For the fit, there are the 3,750 **Steps of Repentance,** supposedly hewn by a pentitent monk; this is the most direct route. There are several votive sites en route, including the **Gate of Confession,** where a monk once heard pilgrims' confessions. More meandering but slightly easier on the leg muscles is the **camel path,** which begins behind the monas-tery. On average, depending on your fitness, it takes about two to three hours to climb to the summit. Bedouin with camels place them-selves strategically along the route to offer their services to anyone with faltering legs.

The camel path joins up with the last 750 Steps of Repentance at **Elijah's Basin.** This mountainside hollow is dominated by a 500-year-old cypress tree marking the spot where the Bible recounts that God spoke to Elijah as he hid from Jezebel. If you spend the night, this is where you are asked to sleep.

There are self-composting toilets and stands selling tea and snacks. Even in summer it gets cold and windy in the early hours of morn-ing, so warm clothes and a sleeping bag are a must. There is no space to pitch a tent. From here it is a short climb to the summit to watch the sunrise.

On the summit itself is the Greek Orthodox **Chapel of the Holy Trinity,** built in 1934 on the ruins of a fourth-century church. It contains beautiful paint-ings and ornaments, and a small mosque. However, these were so desecrated by tourists in the 1980s that the chapel is usually kept locked. The summit also offers a breathtaking panorama of the whole southern Sinai right across to the Gulf of Aqaba. ■

Part of the flight of the 3,750 Steps of Repentance

The Bedouin

Although increasingly they are a settled people and have largely traded their camels for pickup trucks, the original inhabitants of Sinai, the Bedouin, still maintain many of their nomadic traditions.

Modesty is paramount for Bedouin women and heads are always swathed in heavy scarves.

There are 14 Bedouin tribes on the peninsula. Most claim ancestry from the horsemen of Arabia (now Saudi Arabia), and they refer to themselves as Arabs rather than Egyptians. One tribe, however, is a significant exception: the Jabaliya are said to be descended from 200 soldiers brought from Romania in the sixth century to defend the monks of St. Catherine's Monastery.

Traditionally, Bedouin lifestyle has involved a constant search for pasture for their livestock, moving on as each area of vegetation was exhausted, to return the next year. This was supplemented by a little cultivation, fishing, and some trading. Each tribe roamed its own territory and had exclusive use of particular oases. At every new grazing spot, the tribe pitched its black, goat-hair tents, known as *bayt shaar,* or hair houses.

Not having permanent settlements, strong emphasis was—and, indeed, still is—placed on family and tribal structures. A nomadic existence also meant owning no more than a person was able to carry. Wealth was accrued in terms of goats or camels, or in the weight of a wife's jewelry. For this reason, the jewelry is large and chunky, valued by mass rather workmanship.

Equally distinctive is Bedouin clothing. Girls under the age of 12 wear bright peacock dresses, but from puberty they must cover up in black cloaks. The colorful stitched embroidery on these robes and their hoods also has a meaning; red means the wearer is married, blue means she is not. Some tribal women still sport the distinctive leather face masks, hung with coins, and have their faces tattooed and eyes ringed with kohl like raccoons. Even the most urbanized of men still prefer the practical flowing white robes to trousers and shirts. Though Muslims, the Bedouin also have their own pagan superstitions and practices and their own common law (*urf*), according to which they administer their own justice.

Since the 1960s, there have been continued attempts to change all this and bring the Bedouin under central government. Schools, clinics, and housing settlements have been provided. Although this outside interference has been resisted, and some tribes do still roam the desert with their flocks, particularly in northern Sinai, most have now forsaken their nomadic ways. Stone houses with tin roofs and TV antennae have replaced the tents. Beginning in the 1980s, tourism has also had a profound effect. Exposure to massive numbers of not just Westerners, but also urban Egyptians, has, unsurprisingly, led to many Bedouin giving up age-old means of income for jobs in construction, taxi driving, or the service industries. Resort towns such as Dahab are full of "Bedouin" hotels and restaurants.

Fortunately, many Bedouin have been able to parley traditional skills—such as finding water, navigating by the stars, tracking, and an extensive knowledge of Sinai's plant and animal life—into a living as tourist guides. A number are also employed as rangers looking after the environment of St. Catherine Protectorate. Future development in Sinai, it is to be hoped, can continue to utilize the unique abilities of the former nomads, rather than teaching them to sell refreshment and wait on tables. ■

Above: Bedouin men in typical attire of white head scarves gather for a feast.
Below: Women prepare to weave the highly distinctive cloth of the Sinai Bedouin, used for rugs, bed coverings, and saddlebags.

Once the domain
only of Bedouin,
coastal **Sinai** is
rapidly developing
as a sun and sand
tourist hotspot.

Sinai Coast

THE SOUTHEAST COAST OF SINAI, FROM THE BORDER WITH
Israel at Taba down to Ras Muhammad at the tip of the peninsula,
features some of the world's most incredible underwater scenery. It
is a snorkeling and scuba-diving paradise that has spawned an ever
increasing number of specially built small resorts, all whitewashed
and pristine because the builders have only just moved out.

Sharm al-Sheikh
🅰 325 C4

Visitor information
There are no visitor centers
in Sinai. Hotel receptionists
will be able to offer advice
and assistance in planning
and booking trips.

Thirty years ago there was nothing
here. The most venerable resort is
Sharm al-Sheikh, which is little
more than 20 years old. Neighboring **Naama Bay** is half that age.
The two occupy bays either side of
a rocky headland. Both are Las
Vegas-style strips, a single highway
lined with hotels and shopping centers. On one side is the sea, on the
other the jagged, purplish mountains, and, beyond those, the desert.

A palm-fringed boardwalk skirts
the beach, lined with cafés and bars.
Sunshine is guaranteed, although
given that temperatures frequently
top 105°F (40°C), this is not a summer place. Peak seasons are fall,
winter, and early spring, before the
heat builds up.

Most visitors are European
(predominantly French, German,
and Italian) twenty- and thirty-
somethings, here for the diving and

snorkeling. Despite the ever growing number of visitors, the offshore reefs remain teeming with fish. Every hotel has its own boats, dive centers, and instructors. And there are many independent outfits as well. You don't have to be an expert to dive: You can be taught on the spot. Popular local dive spots include the stunning **Near** and **Middle Gardens,** and the even more incredible **Far Garden,** all reached by boat.

Serious divers sign up for a day trip to **Ras Muhammad,** Egypt's first national marine park, which lies 18 miles (30 km) southwest of Sharm al-Sheikh at the very southernmost point of Sinai. It is a protected area of 320 square miles (829 sq km) of land and sea, including Tiran Island, of which only a small part is accessible to visitors. All of the thousand-plus species of marine life found in the Red Sea are represented here, including sharks, barracuda, and giant rays, making a trip here an experience not to be missed. Both snorkeling and diving are possible, but the number of boats allowed each day is limited, so you may need to make reservations in advance with one of the many dive operators in Sharm al-Sheikh or Naama Bay (see p. 380).

Back in Sharm, there are all sorts of other water-based activities offered including sailing lessons, windsurfing, parasailing, and glass-bottom-boat trips. Most hotels also offer a wide variety of excursions into the Sinai interior to places such as the Monastery of St. Catherine (see p. 340) and Mount Sinai (see p. 342), and farther afield to Wadi Feiran (see p. 339) and Serabit al-Khadim (see p. 339).

Vacationers who have jetted directly into Sharm even head off on day trips to Cairo for a quick peek at the Pyramids, involving a

grueling 14 hours' travel time there and back. Evenings are more than adequately filled dining at a plethora of open-air restaurants, which take valiant stabs at cuisines from Japanese to Mexican. After dessert there are numerous discos, bars, and clubs to sample.

Sharm al-Sheikh and Naama Bay are the most complete of Sinai's resorts, but there are plenty of others coming. About 50 miles (80 km) to the north, **Dahab** has long been a favorite with budget travelers and the backpacker crowd, who pay just a few dollars a night for a bamboo hut on the beach. The place exists in a late-1960s time warp, where the spirit of Woodstock lives on. Most visitors are content to do little more than sprawl on throw cushions beneath

Holidaymakers live it up at a Sharm al-Sheikh nightspot.

the palms, dozing, reading, and letter-writing to a sound track of Jimi Hendrix, Bob Marley, and Pink Floyd, occasionally raising themselves for a brown-rice stir-fry or pizza at one of the many small beachfront cafés.

But there is more to it than that; there is also a modern resort area, known as **Dahab City,** with tranquil beachside hotels and chic restaurants, and not a hint of a hippy influence. Dahab also has the requisite fine diving, with the most famous—and most dangerous—of sites being the **Blue Hole,** a 215-foot-deep (66 m) shaft that has been known to claim several lives in a year.

Farther north again along the coast is **Nuweiba,** which is several small settlements strung together with a backdrop of beautiful mountain scenery. It started life during the Israeli occupation as a farming cooperative *(moshav)* and has since become a full-fledged small town with a commercial center, Nuweiba City. It has also spawned a neighboring Bedouin village, Tarabeen, and a port area to the south, from where there are twice-daily sailings to Aqaba in Jordan.

Far less polished than Sharm al-Sheikh and Naama Bay, Nuweiba tends to cater more to moderately affluent Egyptians. Part of the reason for this is also that the diving, which is the big attraction for most Europeans, is considerably less good here than it is down to the south. One unique plus, however, is Nuweiba's dolphin, a female named Olin. In the early 1990s the dolphin was befriended by a young Bedouin villager, Abdullah, and the two would regularly swim together. She's stuck around ever since and is now a major draw for tourists, who turn up by busload each day for a chance to swim with her. Abdullah and the village entrepreneurs take visitors out in a boat and rent snorkels for a small fee.

Taba, the northernmost of the Sinai resorts, is right up on the border with Israel—the Israeli resort of Eilat is just a few miles beyond the checkpoints. Until very recently, besides the border guards, there was nothing but a bus station and a Hilton Hotel. However, a new resort development called Taba Heights is under construction, which its planners hope will very soon rival Sharm al-Sheikh in popularity. Several hotels are already operating, with casinos, shops, restaurants, dive centers, and an airport to come. ■

A stretch of unspoiled Sinai coastline at Sharm al-Sheikh

Travelwise

Spices piled in the shape of pyramids on a stall in Luxor

TRAVELWISE INFORMATION

PLANNING YOUR TRIP

WHEN TO GO

Climate

Egypt is good for vacations year-round. However, summer temperatures can be extreme, especially in the south of the country, where the majority of the pharaonic sites are concentrated. If at all possible, avoid June, July, and August, when daytime temperatures in this area can regularly top 100°F. If you do visit at this time, be prepared for early rising, as dawn is the best time for exploring the sites.

Luxor and Aswan make for ideal winter destinations, as even in January skies are clear and temperatures balmy. Unfortunately, the north of the country does experience the cold; winter days in Cairo can be overcast and evenings chilly, while it rains frequently in Alexandria. The best times to visit the country as a whole are spring and fall, which manage to avoid both clouds in the north and extreme heat in the south.

Ramadan

Try not to visit during the holy month of Ramadan, in which all observant Muslims fast during daylight hours. Many restaurants and cafés are closed, stores and offices keep erratic hours, and all schedules are disrupted.

The exact dates of Ramadan change every year as Islam follows a lunar calendar, but in 2002 it falls around November.

CALENDAR OF EVENTS

See also National and Religious Holidays (on p. 355). For more information consult the Egyptian Tourist Authority (see p. 356).

January

Book Fair A three-week festival of literary culture with displays by local and foreign publishers

held at the Cairo Exhibition Grounds

Wust al-Balad Art Festival
A two-week-long program of exhibitions, theater, poetry, and music at galleries, cafés, and other venues in downtown Cairo

February

International Fishing Tournament
Held at Hurghada on the Red Sea and attended by anglers from all over the world

Ascension of Ramses II
On February 22 each year the sun penetrates into the inner sanctuary of the temple at Abu Simbel, illuminating the statues of the gods within.

July

International Festival of Oriental Dance
Belly dancing festival throughout Cairo in which famous Egyptian practitioners give showcase performances and lessons to international attendees

August

Tourism and Shopping Festival
Countrywide promotion of Egyptian products, with participating stores offering discounted prices

September

Alexandria Film Festival
Small-scale international film festival

Experimental Theater Festival
Ten days of international fringe theater performed at a variety of venues throughout Cairo

October

Alexandrias of the World Festival
Four-day celebration attended by delegations from all the cities bearing the name Alexandria (there are over 40 in the world)

Pharaohs' Rally
An 11-day, 2,900-mile (4,700 km) motor vehicle race through the desert, beginning and ending at the Pyramids and attracting competitors from all over the world

Birth of Ramses II
On October 22 the sun's rays penetrate the temple at Abu Simbel.

Commemoration of the Battle of Al Alamein
Services are conducted at this pivotal World War II battle site attended by former combatants of Allied and Axis countries.

November

Arabic Music Festival
A ten-day festival of traditional Arabic music held at venues throughout Cairo

December

Cairo International Film Festival
A 14-day festival with screenings of recent films from all over the world plus celebrity guests

WHAT TO TAKE

Pack clothing that covers your legs and—especially if you are female—as much skin as possible. Not only will this help protect against sunburn, but it will also provide an appropriate degree of modesty in an Islamic country whose citizens cover up and appreciate their visitors doing the same. Of course, if you are hitting the beaches of Sinai or the Red Sea coast, then pack a bikini or swimming shorts. Women need head scarves inside mosques, and it is wise to get into the habit of carrying one at all times.

Leave the portable drugstore at home—pharmacies are easy to find in Egypt and are very well stocked. Most pharmacists speak English and are competent to make basic diagnoses. Stomach ailments are the biggest concern, so you might want to take a suitable drug for immediate use. Consult your doctor before leaving home.

Other handy items include a small flashlight for poorly lit tombs and museums, earplugs for noisy hotels, an alarm clock (wake-up calls rarely happen), and possibly an instant Polaroid camera—locals love keepsake photographs.

TRAVEL INSURANCE

Always take out adequate insurance when you travel, especially for medical needs. Costs for emergency surgery or medical repatriation home can be exhorbitant. Make sure that the policy covers all the activities that you are likely to undertake, for example diving.

ENTRY FORMALITIES

Visas
You need a valid passport and a visa obtainable in advance from an Egyptian embassy or consulate in your country. Apply at least one month in advance. Alternatively, you can acquire a visa on the spot on arrival at Cairo or Luxor airport for $15. The visa is good for a stay of up to three months.

CUSTOMS

Travelers over the age of 18 may bring one liter of alcohol, one liter of perfume, 200 cigarettes, and 25 cigars into the country.

Travelers may be asked to declare video cameras, boom boxes, and laptop computers if customs officials require it, and they may be subject to an import tax. Alternatively, the items may be written into the traveler's passport to ensure that they leave the country again and are not sold in Egypt.

Currency restrictions
There are no restrictions on the import of foreign currencies; you are supposed to declare all you have when you enter, but in practice this is never required.

Drugs & narcotics
Medicines for personal use

should be clearly labeled. Obtain a statement from your doctor if you are importing a large number of pharmaceuticals, or if they are of a restricted type.

EMBASSIES

For details and information on visas, customs controls, and restrictions, contact the relevant Egyptian embassy or consulate.

United States
3521 International Court NW, Washington D.C. 20008
Tel 202/895-5400
Fax 202/244-4319
Consulates in Chicago, Houston, New York, and San Francisco

Canada
454 Laurier Ave. East, Ottawa, Ontario, K1N 6R3
Tel 613/234-4931
Fax 613/234-9347
Also in Quebec

United Kingdom
2 Lowndes St., London SW1
Tel 020-7235 9777

Australia
1 Darwin Ave., Yarralumla, Canberra, ACT 2600
Tel 02/6273 4437
Fax 02/6273 4279
Consulates in Melbourne and Sydney

HOW TO GET TO EGYPT

CHOOSING A TICKET

Egypt is a relatively cheap destination, and you can also save money by shopping around for the airline ticket, going out of season, and planning ahead. At the minimum you should investigate the savings available through advance purchase ticketing, such as Apex. Some of the major airlines flying to Egypt are:
EgyptAir
United States:
720 5th Ave.
New York, NY 10019

Tel 212/247-4880
Fax 212/664-1075

Canada:
151 Bloor St., Toronto, Ontario M5S 1S4
Tel 613/960-3203
Fax 613/960-1436

United Kingdom:
29/31 Piccadilly, London W1V 0PT
Tel 020-7734 2343
Fax 020-7287 1728

American Airlines
United States or Canada:
Tel 800/222-2377

United Kingdom: Tel 0845-601 0619

British Airways
United States: Tel 800/247-9292
United Kingdom: Tel 0345-222 111

United Airlines
United States: Tel 800/538-2929

PACKAGE TOURS

It can be invaluable to have a local agent. Confirming flights, negotiating for better hotel rooms, arranging for drivers and guides, securing hard-to-get tickets, all waste untold hours that could be more usefully spent seeing the sights. There are two main ways of achieving this. The first is to fly independently and then spend your time with a tour company. Among the best companies are:

Abercrombie & Kent
U.S.: 1520 Kensington Rd., Suite 212, Oak Brook, IL 60523-2141
Tel 800/323-7308
Fax 630/954-3324
www.abercrombiekent.com
Cairo: Tel 02/393 6255

American Express
Cairo: 15 Qasr al-Nil
Tel 02/574 7991
e-mail tours@amexegypt.com

Misr Travel
Cairo: 7 Talaat Harb St.

Tel 02/393 0168
e-mail misrtrav@aol.com

National Geographic Expeditions
P.O. Box 65265
Washington, D.C., 20035-5265
Tel 888/966-8687
www.nationalgeographic.com
e-mail ngexpeditions@
nationalgeographic.com

Thomas Cook
U.S.: 1881 Broadway at 62nd St.,
New York, NY 10023
Tel 212/586-1166
www.thomascook.com
Cairo: 17 Mahmoud Bassiouni,
Downtown
Tel 02/574 3955

Expect to pay between $180 and $250 per person per day, all inclusive, for a customized itinerary.

Your second option is to buy a vacation package that includes flights, hotels, and sight-seeing from one of the many companies that advertise their packages in travel magazines.

ARRIVING BY AIR

Most visitors arrive in Cairo, though international flights also arrive at Alexandria, Luxor, Hurghada, and Sharm al-Sheikh airports. Cairo International Airport is 15 miles (25 km) northeast of the city center. Most hotels arrange pick-ups for guests. Although a regular bus service to central Cairo exists, it departs from the domestic terminal some distance away. There is no effective link between the international and domestic terminals. If you need to make your own way to the city center, the best option is a taxi. Official "limousines" make the trip for $10. The journey can take anything between 30 minutes and an hour, depending on the traffic.
Note: A departure tax exists, but this is usually prepaid as part of your air ticket.

English language information:
02/291 4255 and 02/291 2266

GETTING AROUND

BY AIR

The national carrier EgyptAir, along with its subsidiary Air Sinai, has a comprehensive network of domestic services linking the major cities and tourist areas. At present Alexandria, Asyut, Aswan, Abu Simbel, Al-Arish, Hurghada, Kharga Oasis, St. Catherine's, and Sharm al-Sheikh all have domestic airports. Bahariyya and Siwa Oases, Marsa Alam, on the Red Sea coast, and Taba in Sinai are all due to gain airports in the near future.

Round-trip ticket prices are roughly double the one-way fare, and there are no special deals or passes. In Cairo, all domestic flights depart from terminal one. If possible, arrange with your tour company for pick-ups and drop-offs, as public transportation to and from regional airports is often nonexistent. Confirm each flight locally, as overbooking is common. Signs at airports are poor and often wrong, so don't rely on them. To be safe, when a flight boards, show your boarding pass to the gate attendant, who will either nod yes or turn you away.

EgyptAir has offices at:
Cairo: Nile Hilton Hotel, tel 02/578 0444
Alexandria: 19 Midan Zaghloul, tel 03/492 0778
Luxor: Winter Palace Arcade, tel 095/380 580
Aswan: Corniche, tel 097/315 000
Sharm al-Sheikh: Naama Bay Road, tel 069/661 056
For EgyptAir overseas offices see page 351.

BY TRAIN

Egypt's rail network is, to all practical effect, limited to a

single extended line shadowing the Nile from Alexandria on the northern coast all the way down to Aswan in the south.

Services between Cairo and Alexandria are excellent. There are three types of train: *turbini*, *fransawi*, and local. The first two are express, and there are several of each every day, while the local makes numerous stops at small Delta towns. The faster services make just one or two stops, completing the journey in around two and a half hours. Passenger coaches are air-conditioned and seating is comfortable. Beware when traveling to Alexandria because there are two stations; the first is Sidi Gaber, in the eastern suburbs of the city, and then the train continues on to terminate at Cairo Station (Mahattat Masr), in the center of town.

Heading south from Cairo, three tourist trains depart daily for Luxor (a ten-hour journey) and Aswan (13 to 16 hours depending on the service), the best of which is the luxurious Wagon Lits sleeper ($92 one way, including dinner and breakfast). One-way fares on the other two less comfortable trains (one a morning departure, the other overnight, but with no sleeping berths) are $15 to Luxor and $18.50 to Aswan. Tickets for all three services must be bought at least two or three days in advance. In the case of the Wagon Lits, reservations are made at a small office just south of the main Cairo train station building. Seats for the other two services are bought from the ticket office beside platform 11.

Cairo's metro (subway) system makes for a good way of getting around the city (see map on page 388). It is efficient, clean, and rarely crowded. Unfortunately for visitors, it has been designed with the commuter in mind and the lines primarily service the suburbs,

GETTING AROUND/PRACTICAL ADVICE

stopping at few places of interest (although there are convenient stations for Coptic Cairo, the Opera House, and Ramses train station). A third line, currently under construction, will be of greater value to the visitor because it will connect downtown with Islamic Cairo and Zamalek. Stations are easily identified by signs with a big red M in a blue star. Tickets are bought down in the underground concourses and cost 50pt (15 cents) for a ride of up to nine stops. Signing is in Arabic and English and the system is extremely easy to use. The service starts at about 5 a.m. and closes around 11:30 p.m. The first carriage is reserved for women only. Women who want to ride in this carriage should make sure they're standing at the right place on the platform as the trains don't stop for long.

BY BUS

When it comes to getting around, if you aren't flying, then the way to go is trains for any travel north-south, but buses when it comes to going east and west. So from Cairo, if you want to head out to the Western Desert and its oases, or over to the Red Sea coast and Sinai, the best way is by bus. The country is covered by several companies, each of which has its own territory. In Cairo they all operate out of one giant bus station, called Turgoman Garage, which is in the district of Bulaq, between the city center and the Nile. To call it a bus station is a bit of an exaggeration because it's nothing more than a huge parking lot with a few wooden cabins where tickets are sold. It is an exceptionally confusing place, and it is essential to be accompanied by a guide, or even better have a tour company arrange the ticketing for you. Buses are modern and air-conditioned, and departures to most destinations are frequent.

NILE CRUISES

Experiencing Egypt without a Nile cruise is like going to Las Vegas and not gambling. The traditional cruise has always been from Cairo down to Luxor (see p. 306), but since the early 1990s fears for tourists' safety have meant that boats are no longer allowed to sail through Middle Egypt. Instead, cruisers sail for three or four nights between Luxor and Aswan, typically stopping off at Esna, Edfu, and Kom Ombo en route. Every big hotel company or tour operator has a boat on the Nile. In particular, Abercrombie & Kent's 40-passenger *Sun Boat III* and 84 passenger *Sun Boat IV* are notably luxurious and serve excellent food.

LAKE NASSER CRUISES

Even better than a Nile cruise is to sail the length of Lake Nasser from the High Dam at Aswan down to the magnificent temple of Abu Simbel. There are five boats currently sailing the lake and, of these, two stand out far above the rest. The M.S. *Eugénie* and M.S. *Qasr Ibrim* are supremely luxurious, designed to look like late 19th-century floating palaces. Both have pools, Jacuzzis, and fantastic French cuisine. Passengers are pampered with such treats as cocktails served in the desert and their own private sound-and-light performance in front of Abu Simbel Temple. The boats are run by Belle Epoque Tours of Cairo (Tel 02/516 9653 or 02/516 9654 or 02/516 9656 fax 02/516 9646, e-mail eugenie@soficom.com.eg).

BY CAR

There are very few places in Egypt where you would want to rent a car and drive yourself. Traffic in and around Cairo and Alexandria is nightmarish. Observance of traffic rules is negligible, and almost every

vehicle carries the bumps and dents to prove it.

Driving in the south of the country is less harrowing, but the continued threat of terrorism means that private cars must travel in police-escorted convoys that travel at set times. Opportunities for sight-seeing are therefore limited, as the traditional freedoms of having your own transportation are severely curtailed.

Perhaps the only parts of the country in which driving is an attractive option are Sinai and the Red Sea coast. Many of the major hotels in resorts such as Hurghada, Sharm al-Sheikh, and Naama Bay have international car rental desks. Rates are not particularly cheap, typically $50 to $60 a day, depending on the model. If you think you may want to rent a car, remember to take your driver's license with you.

PRACTICAL ADVICE

BUSINESS HOURS

Banks, government offices, and most businesses are open 8:30 a.m. to 2 p.m. Sunday through Thursday. They close on public and religious holidays. It is usually possible to find a hotel bank that is open 24 hours.

Stores normally do not open until at least 10 a.m. but remain open until 10 p.m. or later, especially during summer. Many close on Friday, the Islamic holy day, or at the very least for Friday prayers, which occupy an hour around noon. Many stores and private businesses also close on Saturdays, including foreign embassies and consulates. Christian businesses close on Sunday.

COMMUNICATIONS

MAIL
Stamps may be purchased at post offices and hotel bookstalls.

Postcards and letters up to half an ounce (15g) cost the equivalent of 25 cents to most countries and take around a week to ten days to reach the United States, and four or five days to Europe. Sending mail from the mailboxes at major hotels instead of from those on the street helps ensure a quicker service.

If possible, avoid sending packages home. These can only be mailed from a city's central post office (which in Cairo is close to Ramses train station) and it involves a long and tortuous process of form filling and customs inspection. When you are buying in the bazaar, some shopkeepers will offer to handle mailing as part of the deal.

General delivery
Larger offices have a free general delivery (*poste restante*) service. The letter needs to have the recipient's name and be addressed "Poste Restante, Central Post Office" and the name of the town. Take proof of identity, preferably a passport, when collecting. American Express has a client mail service at its main offices.

TELEPHONES
The best that can be said is that Egypt's telephone system is improving. The easiest way of making a call is to use the card phones that are found on most street corners. There are two kinds, of which the distinctive yellow-and-green booths of Menatel are by far the most common. Cards are sold at various shops and kiosks, flagged with a little sticker in the window, and come in units of 10, 20, and 30 Egyptian pounds. Rates for calling Europe and the U.S. via Menatel are 5.6 Egyptian pounds (roughly $1.50) for the first minute and then 4.5 Egyptian pounds for each additional minute. Calls made from your hotel carry a heavy surcharge.

The international dialing code for Egypt is 20.
To call from Egypt to the U.S. or Canada, the code is 00 1.
To call from Egypt to the U.K., the code is 00 44.

FAX
Fax machines are available at main post offices and at most three- to five-star hotels. From a telephone office, a one-page fax to the U.S. or U.K. costs about $3.50. Hotel rates are a lot more.

E-MAIL & ONLINE SERVICES
Cairo, Alexandria, Sharm al-Sheikh, Dahab, Hurghada, Luxor, and Aswan all offer online services via privately owned internet cafés. These allow you to use the internet and send e-mail at a quarter-hour, half-hour, or hourly rate (typically one hour costs the equivalent of $3). Connections can be infuriatingly slow, a result of too much demand on insufficient international bandwidth. If you are traveling with a laptop and want to connect, you may have problems because of the variety of phone sockets in use in Egypt. In older hotels, phone cables are usually wired right into the wall.

CONVERSIONS
Egypt uses the metric system.
Useful conversions are:
1 mile = 1.6 kilometers
1 kilometer = 0.62 mile
1 quart = 0.95 liter
1 liter = 1.06 quart
1 U.S. gallon = 3.79 liters
1 pound = 0.37 kilograms
1 kilo = 2.2 pounds
1 ounce = 28 grams
1 foot = 0.3 meter
1 meter = 39.37 inches

ELECTRICITY
Egyptian electrical appliances have plugs with two round pins. Electrical voltage is 220 volts AC, 50 Hz. American and British appliances will need adaptors.

ETIQUETTE
Though Egypt is an Islamic country, few special rules apply to the visitor. The main concern is to dress modestly. For women this means avoiding shorts and sleeveless tops and wearing pants or skirts that come below the knee. In more conservative areas, such as Islamic Cairo, and when visiting mosques or churches, shoulders must be covered. Because Western women are perceived to be more lax in their modesty, they are frequently hit upon by Egyptian men. It is usually harmless, but can nevertheless be annoying. It is also generally easy to shrug off: Avoid eye contact; do not beam wide smiles; do not respond to invitations, come-ons, or obnoxious comments.

One advantage for women is that they often have their own lines, at train station ticket offices, for example, and these are always much shorter than the corresponding men's lines. Not that Egyptians are very good at standing in line anyway—it does not pay to be too polite or you will never get to the front.

In central Cairo and Luxor, in particular, beware of touts who stop you on the street to ask where you are from; invariably, stopping to chat ends up with a time-consuming visit to a perfume or papyrus shop. Beware also of shopowners who tell you that the museum or temple to which you are obviously heading is closed, and why not spend time and have tea at my shop? Of course, the museum or temple is not closed, but you would be amazed how many people fall for this ploy. Not all Egyptians are looking to part visitors from their cash, but a healthy dose of skepticism is useful.

LIQUOR LAWS
Few Egyptians consume alcohol because the Koran warns

against substances that cloud the mind. At the same time, they are tolerant of others who wish to do so, particularly foreign visitors. Locally produced beer and wine and imported hard liquor are readily available in hotel bars and in many restaurants, especially those in more touristed areas. The farther you get from the big cities and resorts, however, the harder it is to find alcohol. Until recently it could not be found at Siwa Oasis at all. Discretion should still be shown anywhere in Egypt, and alcohol should not be consumed on the streets.

MEDIA

NEWSPAPERS
The English-language daily (not Sunday) *Egyptian Gazette* is available throughout the country, as is the *Al-Ahram Weekly*, both government-owned newspapers. The weekly *Cairo Times* is less well distributed, but makes for a better read. *Egypt Today*, a monthly glossy magazine, is worth picking up for its what's-on listings. The same publishers also put out useful pocket-size quarterlies: *Alex Today*, *Red Sea Today*, and *Sinai Today*.

TV CHANNELS
Cairo-based Nile TV broadcasts news and current affairs exclusively in English and French from early each morning until past midnight. In addition, most hotels offer satellite TV with CNN, BBC World, and MTV at the very least.

RADIO
FM95 broadcasts news in English on 557 kHz at 7:30 a.m. and 2:30 and 8 p.m. daily. BBC and Voice of America (VOA) broadcasts can be picked up on medium wave at various times of the morning and evening. The BBC can be heard on both 639 kHz and 1320 kHz, and VOA on 1290 kHz.

MONEY

The unit of currency is the Egyptian pound (LE), which is

divided into 100 piastres (pt). Bills come in denominations of 25 pt, 50 pt, and 1, 5, 10, 20, 50, and 100 pounds. Different colors and sizes make them easy to identify. There are also 5, 10 and 25 pt coins, but these are of practically no value at all and are rarely encountered by most visitors. Carry lots of small-denomination notes (50 pt and LE1) for taxis and tipping.

Major international credit cards are widely accepted in most hotels, restaurants, and tourist establishments. ATMs are common in all larger centers and tourist resorts, and allow cash withdrawals on American Express, Visa, and MasterCard. Other than in regions such as the Western Desert, it is becoming increasingly easy to travel in Egypt on just plastic.

NATIONAL & RELIGIOUS HOLIDAYS

National holidays
January 1 (New Year's Day)
April 25 (Sinai Liberation Day)
May 1 (May Day)
July 23 (Revolution Day)
October 6 (National Day)

Religious holidays
Egypt's major holidays are all religious. Because the Islamic calendar is 11 days shorter than the Gregorian (Western) calendar, its holidays fall 11 days earlier each year. Dates of Islamic holidays are also approximate because they depend on the sighting of the moon. The following are public holidays in Egypt:

Eid al-Adha, the Great Feast (March 22–25 in 2002)

Moulid an-Nabi, Prophet's Birthday (May 24 in 2002)

Ramadan (November 5 to December 4 in 2002)

Eid al-Fitr, the Small Feast (December 5–7 in 2002).

PHOTOGRAPHY & VIDEO

Although quality film and processing are available throughout Egypt, some stores do not always take good care of their stock. Film is often stored in direct sunlight and high temperatures, which adversely affects the quality, so be careful where you buy from. When you're shooting, the intense glare from the sun and its reflection on the water may bleach your photographs of color. To minimize this, make use of the best times to shoot in the early morning and late afternoon.

Note that most sights in Egypt charge an additional photography fee of two to three dollars. If you do not wish to pay, you may be forced to surrender your camera at the ticket office during your visit. For video cameras the fee rises up to $20 to $30 per sight, so think twice about taking the camera with you at these sights.
    In this guide, information about these fees where applicable is given in the sidebar for each sight.

Be cautious when pointing cameras at anything other than tourist sights. It is forbidden to photograph bridges, railroad stations, anything military, airports, and many other seemingly innocuous public structures, including factories. Anybody who does so risks having their film confiscated. Egyptians are also sensitive about what may be perceived as backward aspects of the country, such as donkey carts or dilapidated buildings. Always ask before photographing people, especially women.

REST ROOMS

Toilets in most hotels and restaurants are the Western sit-down variety and are generally clean and well maintained, but public rest rooms elsewhere can be fairly awful. Some toilets are of the squat kind and are very uncomfortable if you have never used this kind of facility before. Only in better hotels will toilet paper be provided; most toilets simply come equipped with a water squirter for washing yourself when you are finished. For this reason, it is a good idea to always carry packets of disposable tissues with you (these are available cheaply all over Egypt).

TIME DIFFERENCES

Egyptian time is seven hours ahead of Eastern Standard Time, and two hours ahead of British Summer Time.

TIPPING

For most services, *baksheesh,* (tipping) is expected. Ten percent is customary in restaurants. Tip 50 pt to LE1 for small services, such as a porter carrying your bags or when a guard shows you something off the beaten track at an ancient monument. Do not be intimidated into tipping when you do not believe that it is warranted.

TOURIST OFFICES

The Egyptian Tourist Authority runs tourist offices in most countries.

United States
630 5th Ave., Suite 1706,
New York, NY 10111
Tel 212/332-2570
Fax 212/956-6439
Also in Los Angeles & Chicago.

Canada
1253 McGill College Ave.,
Suite 250,
Montreal, Quebec H3B 2Y5
Tel 514/851-4606
Fax 514/861-8071

United Kingdom
Egyptian House, 170 Piccadilly,
3rd Floor West, London

WIV 9DD
Tel 020-7493 5283
Fax 020-7408 0295

Australia
1 Darwin Ave., Yarralumla,
Canberra, ACT 2600
Tel 02/6273 4260
Fax 02/6273 4629

INTERNET INFORMATION

The Egyptian Ministry of Tourism has a good website with travel information and reservation advice at:
www.touregypt.com.

TRAVELERS WITH DISABILITIES

Although some of the larger hotels are wheelchair accessible, generally speaking Egypt is a difficult place for anyone with a mobility problem. Sidewalks are high with a plethora of steps, and many of them are badly maintained. Ramps are few, public facilities don't necessarily have lifts, and gaining entrance to many of the ancient sites is all but impossible owing to their narrow entrances and steep stairs. Public transportation is also basically inaccessible. Anybody with mobility problems wishing to visit Egypt should make special arrangements with their tour operator.

EMERGENCIES

EMERGENCY TELEPHONE NUMBERS

For the tourist police call 126.

For an ambulance call 123.

For the fire service call 125.

EMBASSIES & CONSULATES

Most countries have an embassy in Cairo, and several (including the United States and United Kingdom) also maintain a consulate in Alexandria.

United States
5 Latin America St.,
Garden City, Cairo
Tel 02/795 7371
Fax 02/797 3200

Canada
5 Al-Saraya al-Kubra St.,
Garden City, Cairo
Tel 02/794 3110
Fax 02/796 3548

United Kingdom
7 Ahmed Ragheb St.,
Garden City, Cairo
Tel 02/794 0850
Fax 02/794 0959

Australia
World Trade Centre, 11th floor,
1191 Corniche al-Nil, Cairo
Tel 02/575 0444
Fax 02/578 1638

HEALTH

Medical care in Egypt is not good. If you become ill, the best advice is to fly home. If you are in immediate need of medical attention, your embassy will have a list of recommended doctors.

Inoculations
None are essential. It is sensible to be vaccinated against tetanus and hepatitis (A and B), but that is true whether you are traveling or not. Egypt is not in a malarial zone, but there is a risk of malaria in the Fayoum area from June through October. If you intend to travel to this region, you should consider taking antimalarials. Other insect-borne diseases, such as dengue fever, typhus, filariasis, and West Nile fever, do occur along the Nile but the risk to travelers is minimal. It is wise, however, to take steps to avoid insect bites by using an effective repellent.

If you require a particular medication, take an adequate supply, as it may not be available locally. For peace of mind, take part of the packaging showing the generic name rather than the brand, which will make getting replacements easier.

Food & water
Doctors recommend sticking to mineral water. There are several good local brands widely available such as Baraka or Siwa. Fruit and vegetables should always be washed before eating. For this reason, avoid salads in restaurants where it is impossible to tell how clean the ingredients are.

Sunburn & heat sickness
Do not underestimate the power of the sun. Try to stay out of the sun between 11 a.m. and 3 p.m. At the very least, always wear properly applied, high SPF suntan lotion and a hat. Keep neck and arms well covered, and protect your eyes with good-quality sunglasses. Drink plenty of fluids to prevent dehydration. Long, continuous periods of exposure to high temperatures and insufficient fluids can leave you vulnerable to heatstroke, a serious, occasionally fatal, condition.

LOST PROPERTY

To report a crime or loss of belongings, report to the tourist police rather than the local police. Tourist police generally speak English. Even so, filling out the necessary forms is a long and arduous process and can take up half a day.

FURTHER READING

There is a vast and ever growing array of publications on all aspects of Egypt and Egyptology. Many of these titles are available in bookshops in Egypt, often at prices cheaper than those you will find at home.

FICTION & LITERATURE

Cavafy, Constantine
Collected Poems (1935)
The Alexandrian Greek poet who inspired Durrell

Christie, Agatha *Death on the Nile* (1937)
Detective Hercule Poirot investigates the murder of an heiress onboard a Nile steamer. Christie herself cruised the Nile.

Durrell, Lawrence
Alexandria Quartet (1960)
Made up of *Justine, Balthazar, Mount Olive,* and *Clea,* these four books tell the tale of bohemian expat life in 1930s Egypt.

Gedge, Pauline *Lords of the Two Lands* (2001)
Ancient Egyptian trilogy bringing to life the little documented 17th dynasty and the struggle of the prince Kamose to expel the foreign Hyksos rulers from Egypt

George, Margaret *The Memoirs of Cleopatra* (1997)
Novelization of the life of Egypt's legendary queen, with impressive attention to detail, presenting her as mother and diplomat rather than the scheming seductress as she's so often mistakenly viewed

Jacq, Christian *Ramses Quintet* (1999)
A five-volume populist work by a French Egyptologist that put ancient Egypt's greatest pharaoh at the top of the bestseller lists

Mahfouz, Naguib *Cairo Trilogy*
The judges who awarded Mahfouz the Nobel Prize for Literature considered *Between the Palaces, Sugar Street,* and *Palace of Desire,* the novels that make up the trilogy, to be the laureate's finest work.

Ondaatjie, Michael *The English Patient* (1992)
An award-winning story of love and destiny in World War II, set in Italy and Egypt. The central character, Ladislaw Almasy, was a real person who lived in Cairo.

Soueif, Ahdaf *The Map of Love* (2000) Soueif is an Egyptian, raised in Cairo but educated in English and now very much part of the London literary scene. This massive family saga was shortlisted for Britain's prestigious Booker Prize.

NONFICTION

Aciman, Andre *Out of Egypt* (1996)
A memoir of eccentric family life in prerevolutionary cosmopolitan Alexandria by a occasional contributer to *The New Yorker*

Atiya, Nayra (editor) *Khul-Khaal* (1984)
Five women from widely different backgrounds tell their life stories. Published by the AUC Press and widely available in Egypt

Critchfield, Richard *Shahhat An Egyptian*
A classic anthropological study of villagers on Luxor's West Bank. Published in Egypt by the AUC Press

Empreur, Jean-Yves
Alexandria Rediscovered (1998)
Beautifully illustrated exploration of Alexandria's history through its archaeological remains, written by the leader of one of the two teams currently diving the harbor

Fletcher, Joann *Chronicle of a Pharaoh: The Intimate Life of Amenhotep III* (2000)
The builder of Luxor Temple brought to life—right down to the name of his pet cat—in a very readable and captivating way, with plenty of great illustrations

Foreman, Laura *Cleopatra's Palace* (1999)
A profusely illustrated history of the queen and how her legend has grown over the years, brought up to date with the story of the ongoing dives in Alexandria on what is thought may be the ancient royal palace

Ghosh, Amitav *In an Antique Land* (1994) Account of time spent by the author in a small Delta farming village. Affectionate, sympathetic, and extremely illuminating about the life of the Egyptian peasant

Lehner, Mark *The Complete Pyramids* (1997) Everything you ever wanted to know about pyramids, not just those at Giza but the other 80-plus scattered throughout Egypt, written by one of the world's foremost pyramid experts

Quirke, Stephen and Spencer, Jeffrey (editors) *The British Museum Book of Ancient Egypt* (1995) The authoritive who's who and what's what of ancient Egypt in encyclopedic form

Reeves, Nicholas *Ancient Egypt: The Great Discoveries* (2000) Fascinating chronological account of all the major landmarks in the science of Egyptology, from the deciphering of the Rosetta Stone right up to date with robots crawling into the pyramids

Rodenbeck, Max *Cairo: The City Victorious* (1998) Entertaining and highly anecdotal meander through 5,000 years of the city's history, but especially informative on the Cairo of today

Sattin, Anthony *The Pharaoh's Shadow* (2000) Travel literature with a twist as Sattin searches for "survivals" of pharaonic traditions in modern Egypt

Steegmuller, Francis (editor) *Flaubert in Egypt* (1996) Extracts from diaries French novelist Gustave Flaubert kept when he visited the country for a few months in 1849. Bathhouses and bordellos are preferred over ancient monuments.

Tiradritti, Francesco and DeLuca, Araido *Egyptian Treasures From the Egyptian Museum in Cairo* (1999) Hefty and expensive, but the hundreds of magnificent full-color photographs make this just about the most sumptuous book on the artifacts of ancient Egypt. The pictures are backed up by informative essays.

Twain, Mark *The Innocents Abroad* (1869) Twain liked Egypt about the same as he liked most places (very little) and turns his cantankerous wit on Alexandria, the Pyramids, and the Sphinx, all of which are found lacking.

Weeks, Kent *The Lost Tomb* (1998) The story behind the greatest discovery at the Valley of the Kings since Tutankhamun, told by the man who made the find

MOVIES

For such a cinematic country with spectacular monuments, exotic bazaars, and striking desert scenery, Egypt is poorly served on the big screen. The major reason for this is punitive taxes, put in place in the early 1980s, which have kept foreign filmmakers away ever since.

Cairo Road (1950) Anti-drug-smuggling escapade, with Eric Portman and Laurence Harvey, actually shot in Cairo and Port Said

Cleopatra (1963) A four-hour marathon of a film, remembered more for the on-set affair between stars Richard Burton and Elizabeth Taylor

Death on the Nile (1978) Nostalgic period re-creation with Peter Ustinov as Poirot and a cast that included Bette Davis, Mia Farrow, and David Niven, all filmed against fantastic Nile scenery

The English Patient (1996) Winner of seven Oscars, particularly notable for some sensuous desert photography. Alas, although supposedly set in Egypt, the desert was Tunisia, and Venice stood in for Cairo.

Five Graves to Cairo (1943) Wartime espionage thriller directed by Billy Wilder (*Sunset Boulevard, Some Like It Hot*)

Lawrence of Arabia (1962) David Lean's epic biopic of T.E. Lawrence takes place mainly in the deserts of Jordan, but includes episodes crossing Sinai and at military headquarters in Cairo (actually shot in Seville).

The Mummy (1932) The first and best of the mummies, with Boris Karloff in the title role. Some scenes were shot in Cairo's Egyptian Museum.

The Mummy (1959) Produced by Britain's Hammer Studios, this time with Christopher Lee taking the title role, lumbering around London

The Mummy (1999) and *The Mummy Returns* (2001) Comic Saturday matinee-style takes on ancient horror, with the focus on the hero (Brendan Fraser) rather than the monster. The Tunisian desert stands in for Egypt, while Cairo is a mix of studio work and clever montage.

The Prince of Egypt (1998) Animated version of the story of Moses and the Jews' escape from Egypt

Ruby Cairo (1992) Liam Neeson and Andie MacDowall in a thriller about a missing husband, with plenty of travelogue footage of Cairo and Egypt shot on location

The Spy Who Loved Me (1977) Bond goes to Egypt. Roger Moore dispenses with the bad guys at the Pyramids, in Islamic Cairo, and at Karnak, all of which look ravishing.

HOTELS & RESTAURANTS

Egypt offers visitors a broad range of accommodations; construction in the tourism industry is booming and the number of beds is rising rapidly. There is less of a choice when it comes to restaurants. Cairo, Aswan, Luxor, and the established coastal resorts of Hurghada and Sharm al-Sheikh all have a wide choice of hotels from luxury to modest, but it is only in the capital that visitors find anything like an equivalent range of dining options. Elsewhere—in Middle Egypt and the Western Desert, for example—accommodation and dining standards are generally lower.

ACCOMMODATIONS

Hotels

Rooms in international luxury chain hotels may usually be reserved through the hotels' international network, or over the Internet. Reservations at more modest establishments can sometimes be made via the Internet or by e-mail. Try the Egyptian Ministry of Tourism website (see p. 356) for links to useful sites. It is always advisable to make advance reservations, although often far better deals can be arranged once you are in Egypt—perhaps through a local agent—if you are flexible and prepared to shop around.

The big international five-star chains are well represented in Egypt; most have several hotels dotted throughout the country. The Sheraton, Marriott, Hilton, and InterContinental hotels in Egypt have facilities every bit as good as you'll find in any other country in the world. All have air-conditioning, banks, shops, swimming pools, and a full complement of bars and restaurants. Some have fitness centers, others golf courses or diving schools; one even has butlers who wait on guests in its most exclusive rooms. Unfortunately, service is the one area that disappoints. Do not rely on that early morning alarm call from reception, and always double-check all arrangements.

In smaller hotels, service can often be better because of the personal factor. At the same time, facilities are wildly variable. While most mid-range options will have air-conditioning and a restaurant, and perhaps a pool, expect little more. Hot water is not always a given, or might only be available at certain times of the day. It is wise to check before accepting your room.

One of the greatest pleasures of a stay in Egypt can be the historic hotels. Mass tourism came early to Egypt, and as a result the country has some splendid, near-palatial accommodations, built when travel still involved steamer trunks and servants and drinks on the verandah. Alexandria's Cecil (see p. 366), Cairo's Mena House (see p. 361), Luxor's Winter Palace (see p. 370) and Aswan's Old Cataract (see p. 372) are places that, even if you are not staying there, are worth a visit as sights in themselves.

Hotel rates

The range of prices given for hotels is based on the standard full price for a double room. Off season, which in central and southern Egypt covers the summer months, many hotels are prepared to offer guests special rates. It is always worth asking if any such arrangements are available.

Note that quoted prices are usually exclusive of a series of taxes and service charges that can add a further 19 to 23 percent to the final bill.

Alcohol

Many tourist-oriented restaurants and hotel bars serve alcohol (see section on Liquor laws on p. 354), but some smaller restaurants listed here may not.

(see p. 356) · (see p. 366) · (see p. 361) · (see p. 370) · (see p. 372) · (see section on Liquor laws on p. 354)

PRICES	
HOTELS	
An indication of the cost of a double room without breakfast is given by **$** signs.	
$$$$$	Over $200
$$$$	$120–$200
$$$	$60–$120
$$	$30–$60
$	Under $30
RESTAURANTS	
An indication of the cost of a full meal without drinks, tax, and tip is given by **$** signs.	
$$$$	Over $35
$$$	$20–$35
$$	$10–$20
$	Under $10

Hostels

Egypt has 15 hostels recognized by Hosteling International (HI). These are located in Cairo, Alexandria, al-Fayoum, Aswan, Asyut, Hurghada, Ismailia, Luxor, Marsa Matruh, Port Said, and Sharm al-Sheikh. Standards are not very good, but prices are as little as $1 to $5 per night. In a few there are rooms for couples or families, but on the whole the sexes are segregated. Reservations are not usually needed. For further details contact the Egyptian Youth Hostels Association (Tel 02/794 0527, fax 02/795 0329).

Camping

Officially, camping is allowed at only a very few places in Egypt, such as the desert oases and Ras Muhammad National Park in Sinai. Facilities tend to be very rudimentary. There is no Egyptian camping organization.

RESTAURANTS

Only Cairo has anything that could be described as a wide variety of eating places. There it is possible to eat at vegetarian cafés, pizza parlors, Western-style fast-food joints, and ethnic restaurants from a bewilderingly large and varied number of countries. Alexandria is notable for the excellence of its seafood. Outside these main cities, you may find yourself becoming overly reliant on the cafés, bistros, brasseries, and restaurants in your hotel. Reservations at restaurants are rarely necessary, and outside of Cairo they are almost unheard of.

Traditional Egyptian restaurants are fairly rare because, on the whole, Egyptians are not frequent restaurant goers. Instead, what you do find are a great many street food stalls selling *fuul* and felafel (called *taamiyya* in Cairo), the two Egyptian staples, which are eaten for breakfast, lunch, and dinner. You will also see eateries where the windows are filled with great vats of rice, lentils, and macaroni; these three constituents are ladled into a bowl and topped with fried onions and hot tomato sauce to make a dish called *kushari*. It's excellent for a quick fill-up.

On the occasions when Egyptians sit down to dine, it tends to be a very social affair. They begin with many small dishes, known as *meze*, which may include *felafel*, eggplant (*bedingan*), stuffed vine leaves, *hummus*, green salads, and plenty of bread. After that may come soup or a slightly more filling dish such as bread stuffed with ground beef. Only when this has been consumed, is the main course served, typically roast chicken or grilled meats, usually served with both potatoes and rice. In order to digest all that, there follows a lengthy period during which coffee, and maybe sticky, syrupy pastries and fruit, are taken. Some of the company may even smoke a water pipe. The whole procedure can take most of an evening, and as evening meals are eaten late, it's not unusual for Egyptians to still be at the table at midnight. Most local restaurants do not close until the early hours of the morning, and there are some in

Cairo that stay open until dawn. Egypt is not a place for the overly health conscious or for anyone keeping a watch on their figure.

Credit cards

Large hotels and most tourist oriented restaurants accept the major credit cards. Abbreviations used are AE American Express, DC Diners Club, MC Mastercard, V Visa.

In the following selection, hotels are listed under each location by price, then in alphabetical order, followed by restaurants, also by price and alphabetical order.

CAIRO

HOTELS

🏨 FOUR SEASONS
$$$$$
35 GIZA ST.
GIZA
TEL 02/573 1212
FAX 02/568 1616
WEBSITE www.fourseasons.com
Cairo's newest luxury hotel is part of the exclusive First Residence complex, the most expensive real estate in the city, with shops, luxury apartments, and a casino. Levels of service are unmatched, although the location in Giza is not particularly convenient for the major sights except the Pyramids and the Sphinx.
🛏 271 🔄 🅿 🏊 🛗
🅰 All major cards

🏨 CAIRO MARRIOTT
$$$$
SARAY AL-GEZIRA ZAMALEK
TEL 02/735 8888
FAX 02/735 6667
WEBSITE http://marriotthotels
.com/CAIEG
The Egyptian ruler Khedive Ismail built this palace on an island in the Nile to house Empress Eugénie and her suite when she was guest of honor at the grand opening

of the Suez Canal in 1869. The palace (furnished with antiques) and 6 acres of gardens form the core of the hotel, while two modern towers contain the bedrooms, which have all up-to-date facilities. Most have views of the Nile. The garden is a wonderful place to lunch even if you aren't a guest at the hotel.
🛏 1,124 🔄 🅿 🏊 🛗
🅰 All major cards

🏨 CAIRO SHERATON
$$$$
AL-GALAA SQ.
DOKKI
TEL 02/336 9700
FAX 02/336 4601
This sizable 1970s hotel lies on the river, so most rooms have excellent views. Unfortunately it is on the wrong side of the river—the West Bank—which means you have to get taxis everywhere because it's just a bit too far to walk.
🛏 605 🔄 🅿 🏊
🅰 All major cards

🏨 CONRAD INTERNATIONAL
$$$$
1191 CORNICHE AL-NIL
BULAQ
TEL 02/580 8000
FAX 02/580 8080
E-MAIL reservation@conradcairo.
com.eg
This is one of Cairo's new luxury hotels, with a Nile-side location (all rooms overlook the river) just north of the city center—too far to walk to most of the sights but only a couple of minutes in a taxi. The elegant rooms and suites have many amenities, and also have private terraces. Next door is the World Trade Center, containing Cairo's most exclusive shopping mall and top restaurants (see p. 379).
🛏 617 🔄 🏊 🅰 All major cards

⊞ GEZIRA SHERATON
$$$$
3 MAGLIS QUADAT AL-
THAWRA ST.
GEZIRA
TEL 02/736 1333
FAX 02/735 5056
E-MAIL gzher@rite.com

Easy to spot, the Sheraton is in a round tower right on the southern tip of the island of Gezira. All of the luxurious rooms have excellent views of the Nile and the city. Dining options include Spanish, Italian, and Egyptian restaurants. The hotel nightclub hosts some of the biggest names in belly dancing.

🛈 460 🔁 🅢 🅐 🅢 All major cards

SOMETHING SPECIAL

⊞ MENA HOUSE OBEROI

A former royal hunting lodge belonging to Khedive Ismail (*R.* 1863–1879), turned into a hotel in the late 19th century, the Mena House boasts wonderful views courtesy of its location beside the Pyramids; you can float in the garden pool while gazing up at one of the Seven Wonders of the World. The interior is an opulent Orientalist fantasy, enjoyed by a list of past guests that has included Charlie Chaplin, Cecil B. DeMille, and Winston Churchill and President Roosevelt, who met here to finalize plans for the Allied invasion of Europe that would end World War II. If possible, avoid rooms in the modern garden annex, which are quite characterless. Restaurants include The Moghul Room and Khan al-Khalili. The hotel has its own golf course.

$$$$
AL-HARAM ST.
GIZA
TEL 02/383 3222
FAX 02/383 7777
WEBSITE www.oberoihotels
.com/mena.htm

🛈 523 🔁 🅢 🅐 🅢 All major cards

⊞ LE MERIDIEN CAIRO
$$$$
CORNICHE AL-NIL
MANIAL
TEL 02/362 1717
FAX 02/362 1927

By virtue of the hotel's location on the northern tip of the island of Rhoda, all rooms in the Meridien have great Nile views. There are all the usual Meridien facilities and several restaurants, cafés, and bars. A new annex opened in 2001, making the Meridien now one of Cairo's largest hotels.

🛈 1,100 🔁 🅢 🅐
🅢 All major cards

⊞ MÖVENPICK JOLIEVILLE
$$$$
CAIRO-ALEXANDRIA
DESERT HWY.
TEL 02/385 2555
FAX 02/383 5006
E-MAIL movenbyr@eis.egnet.net

If you want to get away from the noise and pollution of the city, this pleasant, modern, low-rise hotel out by the Pyramids is a good bet. The Jolieville makes a convenient base for trips to sights in the environs of Cairo such as Saqqara, Memphis, Abu Sir, and Dahshur.

🛈 240 🔁 🅢 🅐 🅢 All major cards

⊞ NILE HILTON
$$$$
TAHRIR SQ.
DOWNTOWN
TEL 02/578 0666
FAX 02/578 0475
E-MAIL nhilton@internetegypt.com

Egypt's oldest modern, luxury hotel (built in 1958) is aging well; the refurbished rooms are comfortable and spacious, and there is a full range of amenities, including several restaurants, a casino, and a shopping mall. The biggest plus has to be the location, right next door to the Egyptian Museum.

🛈 430 🔁 🅢 🅐 🆆
🅢 All major cards

⊞ RAMSES HILTON
$$$$
1115 CORNICHE AL-NIL
DOWNTOWN
TEL 02/577 7444
FAX 02/575 7152

A towering Nile-side hotel, the Ramses Hilton is behind the Egyptian Museum. It has good facilities (including six restaurants) and the views are terrific—there's a rooftop cocktail bar. But the tangle of four-lane highways surrounding the hotel is discouragingly ugly and makes getting anywhere on foot potentially lethal.

🛈 859 🔁 🅢 🅐 🅢 All major cards

⊞ SEMIRAMIS INTERCONTINENTAL
$$$$
CORNICHE AL-NIL
DOWNTOWN
TEL 02/795 7171
FAX 02/796 3020
E-MAIL cairo@interconti.com

One of Cairo's most attractive modern hotels, the Semiramis has a bright, airy foyer and elegant, generously sized rooms, most with good river views. The hotel has an excellent location, too, beside the Nile and just a few minutes' walk away from the Egyptian Museum.

🛈 730 🔁 🅢 🅐 🅢 All major cards

⊞ BARON
$$$
8 MAAHAD AL-SAHARI
HELIOPOLIS
TEL 02/291 5757
FAX 02/290 7077

Located just off Airport Road in the northern suburb of Heliopolis, this modest three-star overlooks the bizzare hindu architecture of the Baron's Palace (Baron Empain was the founder of the new town of Heliopolis in 1903). The hotel is convenient for the airport or business in the north of the city.

🛈 126 🔁 🅢 🅢 AE, DC, V

🅢 Air-conditioning 🅐 Indoor/🅐 Outdoor swimming pool 🆆 Health club 🅢 Credit cards **KEY**

HOTELS & RESTAURANTS

🏨 FLAMENCO
$$$
2 GEZIRAT AL-WUSTA
ZAMALEK
TEL 02/735 0815
FAX 02/735 0819
This modest but comfortable neighborhood hotel is found among the busy backstreets on the west side of Zamalek. River-facing rooms look down on a sweep of houseboats moored along the Nile.
🛏 157 🔁 🚻 🏧 All major cards

🏨 NOVOTEL CAIRO AIRPORT
$$$
CAIRO AIRPORT
TEL 02/291 8520
FAX 02/291 4794
The airport hotel is the most convenient place to stay for anyone on a short stayover in Cairo or taking an early morning flight. For other visitors to Cairo, however, it is a long way away from the city center and sights.
🛏 207 🔁 🚻 🏊 🏧 All major cards

🏨 ODEON PALACE
$$$
6 ABDEL HAMID SAID ST.
TEL/FAX 02/577 6637
Just off Talaat Harb Street, downtown Cairo's frenetic main thoroughfare, this small, modern hotel is nevertheless a quiet and private place to stay. The top-floor bar, which is open 24 hours, is popular with a local movie business crowd.
🛏 30 🔁 🚻 🏧 AE, MC, V

🏨 COSMOPOLITAN
$$
1 IBN TAHLAB ST.
TEL 02/392 3845
FAX 02/393 3531
A grand 1910 art nouveau building in the heart of downtown Cairo, the Cosmopolitan has been renovated and updated. However, the refit did not extend to all the rooms,

some of which are still very basic, so it is worth asking to view a few before making a choice.
🛏 84 🔁 🚻 🏧 All major cards

🏨 GARDEN CITY HOUSE
$$
23 KAMAL AD-DIN SALAH
DOWNTOWN
TEL 02/794 4969
FAX 02/794 4126
This characterful budget hotel is located just north of Tahrir Square and behind the Semiramis InterContinental. The place has seen better days, but the friendly service compensates for this. Visiting academics and archaeologists affiliated with the nearby American University often stay here.
🛏 38 🔁 🚻 🏧 No credit cards

🏨 HORUS HOUSE
$$
21 ISMAIL MUHAMMAD ST.
TEL 02/735 3634
FAX 02/735 3182
The Horus House is a small, friendly family hotel on the 4th floor of an apartment block in the backstreets of the leafy island neighborhood of Zamalek. It may be some way from the sights, but the area is full of small boutiques, cafés, bars, and some of the city's better restaurants.
🛏 35 🔁 🚻 🏧 AE, MC, V

🏨 HOTEL HUSSEIN
$$
AL-HUSSEIN SQ.
ISLAMIC CAIRO
TEL 02/591 8089
FAX 02/591 8479
This is one of only two hotels in the historic area of Islamic Cairo. The interior is a little institutional, but it has plenty of atmosphere as the rooms overlook bustling Al-Hussein Square and the Khan al-Khalili bazaar, but noise levels are high as a result.
🛏 56 🔁 🚻 🏧 No credit cards

<table>
<tr><th colspan="2">PRICES</th></tr>
<tr><td colspan="2">**HOTELS**
An indication of the cost of a double room without breakfast is given by $ signs.</td></tr>
<tr><td>$$$$$</td><td>Over $200</td></tr>
<tr><td>$$$$</td><td>$120–$200</td></tr>
<tr><td>$$$</td><td>$60–$120</td></tr>
<tr><td>$$</td><td>$30–$60</td></tr>
<tr><td>$</td><td>Under $30</td></tr>
<tr><td colspan="2">**RESTAURANTS**
An indication of the cost of a full meal without drinks, tax, and tip is given by $ signs.</td></tr>
<tr><td>$$$$</td><td>Over $35</td></tr>
<tr><td>$$$</td><td>$20–$35</td></tr>
<tr><td>$$</td><td>$10–$20</td></tr>
<tr><td>$</td><td>Under $10</td></tr>
</table>

🏨 WINDSOR
$$
19 ALFY BEY ST.
TEL 02/591 5277
FAX 02/592 1621
E-MAIL wdoss@link.com.eg
A British officers' club in the early part of the 20th century, the Windsor retains a distinctly colonial air. This is particularly so in the reception area with its creaky old wooden elevator, and the splendid "barrel bar," one of the finest places in Cairo for a post-sight-seeing drink. Old-fashioned rooms are characterful but occasionally verging on shabby, so look at a few before choosing. Advance reservations are advisable.
🛏 50 🔁 🚻 🏧 All major cards

🏨 PENSION ROMA
$
169 MUHAMMAD FARID ST.
DOWNTOWN
TEL 02/391 1088
FAX 02/579 6243
This immaculately run establishment is by far the best of Cairo's budget options. The Roma occupies the uppermost floors of an old apartment building in mid-downtown. Its rooms are high ceilinged with wooden floors

and fans, and there is a lovely breakfast area. As the Roma is always busy, advance reservations are essential.

🛏 32 🔄 🚫 No credit cards

RESTAURANTS

🍴 LE CHAMPOLLION
$$$$
LE MERIDIEN CAIRO (see p. 361)
RHODA
TEL 02/362 1717
Le Champollion's long-standing reputation as one of the city's best restaurants rests on its Mediterranean food. Dining here is an experience enhanced by wonderful Nile views.
🕐 Open 7–11:30 p.m. 🅐
🚫 All major cards

🍴 THE GRILL
$$$$
SEMIRAMIS INTERCONTINENTAL HOTEL
DOWNTOWN
TEL 02/795 7171
Cairo's best restaurant for carnivores, within the Semiramis InterContinental Hotel (see p. 361), also earns top billing for service and has marvelous panoramic views of the river. As if all that wasn't enough, it also has one of the best wine lists in the country.
🕐 Open 7 p.m.–midnight
🅐 🚫 All major cards

🍴 JUSTINE
$$$$
FOUR CORNERS COMPLEX
4 HASSAN SABRY ST.
ZAMALEK
TEL 02/736 2961
A candidate for the title of Egypt's best French restaurant, Justine is a long-established favorite with Cairo's diplomatic community. Reservations are advisable.
🕐 Open 1–3 p.m. & 8–11 p.m 🅐 🚫 All major cards

🍴 VILLA D'ESTE
$$$$
CONRAD INTERNATIONAL

HOTEL
1191 CORNICHE AL-NIL
BULAQ
TEL 02/580 8000
This supremely elegant and highly recommended Italian restaurant sits on the first floor of the Nile-side Conrad International Hotel (see p. 360). The restaurant operates an admirable policy of no mobile phones—a rarity and a blessing in Cairo.
🕐 Open 7:30 p.m.–midnight
🅐 🚫 All major cards

SOMETHING SPECIAL

🍴 ABU AL-SID
One of Cairo's newest and most sumptuous restaurants, Abu al-Sid is decked out in stage-set Orientalia: padded cushions, brass lamps, and spangly bric-a-brac. Lucky diners get to sit cross-legged at low slung *tabliya*. Food is traditional Egyptian. Choose from the likes of *sharkassiyya* (chicken breast with walnut sauce), *sayadiyya* (fish with tomatoes, onions, and red rice), or *molokhiyya*, the green-leaf soup, with rabbit. It's all exceptional. Reservations are necessary.
$$$
57 26TH OF JULY ST.
ZAMALEK
TEL 02/735 9640
🔄 🕐 Open 11 a.m.–2 a.m.
🅐 🚫 All major cards

🍴 ARABESQUE
$$$
6 QASR AL-NIL ST.
DOWNTOWN
TEL 02/574 7898
Entered through a small art gallery, Arabesque exudes intimacy and exclusivity, and is favored by Egyptian movie stars. The menu mixes accomplished Continental cuisine with local specialties, such as kabobs and pigeon.
🕐 Open 12:30 p.m.–3:30 p.m. & 7:30 p.m.–12.30 a.m.
🅐 🚫 AE, MC, V

🍴 FLUX
$$$
2 GAMIAT AL-NESR ST.
MOHANDISEEN
TEL 02/338 6601
This stylish and chic restaurant wouldn't seem out of place on Manhattan's Upper East Side. The food—international fusion in style—is adventurous and accomplished.
🕐 Open 7 p.m.–2 a.m. 🅐
🚫 All major cards

🍴 LA BODEGA
$$$
157 26TH OF JULY ST.
ZAMALEK
TEL 02/735 6761
La Bodega is an elegant and unusual restaurant, bar, and cocktail lounge combination with fabulous decor. The menu ranges wide and includes Middle Eastern and international dishes. The selection of liquor is possibly the best in town, and the lounge even has its own cigar humidor.
🕐 Open noon–5 p.m. & 6 p.m.–1:30 a.m.
🅐 🚫 All major cards

🍴 LA PIAZZA
$$$
FOUR CORNERS COMPLEX
4 HASSAN SABRY ST.
ZAMALEK
TEL 02/736 2961
This airy, conservatory-like Italian restaurant overlooking the Gezira Club serves good soups, salads, and pastas. It is particularly popular for lunch.
🕐 Open 12:30 p.m.– 12:30 a.m. 🅐 🚫 All major cards

🍴 THE MOGHUL ROOM
$$$
MENA HOUSE OBEROI
AL-HARAM ST.
GIZA
TEL 02/383 3444
Some of the best Indian cuisine in the entire Middle East is served here in a sumptuously decorated dining room. French and Italian wines are available, too. Also in the same hotel is the Khan

al-Khalili serving Egyptian cuisine in a dining room with views of the Pyramids.
🕐 Open 12:30–3 p.m. & 7:30 p.m.–12:30 a.m.
🚭 🅰 All major cards

🍴 KHAN AL-KHALILI RESTAURANT/NAGUIB MAHFOUZ COFFEE SHOP
$$$–$
5 SIQQAT AL-BADESTAN
KHAN AL-KHALILI
TEL 02/590 3788
This restaurant/coffee shop complex buried deep in Khan al-Khalili is operated by the Oberoi hotel group. Named for Egypt's Nobel Prize-winning author, the coffee shop does good sandwiches and snacks (and has the only decent toilets in the area). The attached restaurant has attractive Oriental decor and a menu of Eastern and international dishes.
🕐 Open 10 a.m.–2 a.m. 🚭
🅰 All major cards

🍴 S.S. NILE PEKING
$$$
CORNICHE AL-NIL
OPPOSITE THE NILOMETER
OLD CAIRO
TEL 02/531 6388
Part of a chain of popular Chinese restaurants in Cairo, this one has the added attraction of being on a boat. On the lower deck you can choose from a traditional Chinese menu, while the top deck serves a short list of Mongolian specialties from the barbecue.
🕐 Open noon–midnight
🅰 AE, V

🍴 ANDREA
$$
59-60 MARYOUTIA CANAL
GIZA
TEL 02/383 1133
If you fancy eating out in the vicinity of the Pyramids, try this extremely popular garden restaurant. It specializes in grilled chicken and quail, served with a selection of

meze, and accompanied by hot, flat disks of bread that are baked in clay ovens on the premises.
🕐 Open noon–12:30 a.m.
🚭 No credit cards

🍴 L'AUBERGINE
$$
5 SAYYED AL-BAKRY ST.
ZAMALEK
TEL 02/332 0080
L'Aubergine is a backstreet bar/restaurant popular with the local young fashionable set and with expatriates. Unusually for Cairo, the menu recognizes the existence of vegetarians. It changes regularly but is generally an eclectic mix of Lebanese and other international cuisines.
🕐 Open 10 a.m.–2 a.m. 🚭
🅰 AE, DC, V

🍴 CAFÉ RICHE
$$
17 TALAAT HARB ST.
DOWNTOWN
TEL 02/392 9793
A survivor of prerevolution days but extensively renovated in the 1990s, the Café Riche serves traditional Egyptian fare in a room hung with portraits of Egypt's revered cultural pantheon. It's open for breakfast as well and still favored as an intellectuals' drinking den in the evenings.
🕐 Open 8 a.m.–midnight
🚭 🅰 AE, MC, V

🍴 CHANTILLY
$$
11 BAGHDAD ST.
HELIOPOLIS
TEL 02/290 7303
This reliable Swiss Air-owned restaurant has a bakery attached and a pleasant garden out back.
🕐 Open 7 a.m.–midnight
🚭 🅰 All major cards

🍴 CRAZY FISH
$$
2 MARYOUTIA CANAL
GIZA
TEL 02/388 6288

Located opposite the Siag Pyramids Hotel, near the Pyramids, this is a brand new place specializing in seafood, but with meat on the menu in the form of kofta, kabobs, and chicken. Already it's a big favorite with tour groups.
🕐 Open 9 a.m.–1 a.m. 🚭
🅰 AE, MC, V

🍴 SAMAKMAK
$$
92 AHMED ORABI
MOHANDISEEN
TEL 02/347 8232
This excellent fish restaurant is hidden away among the residential blocks in western Cairo. Appetizers include fried calamari and jumbo shrimp, then you choose your own fish from the catch of the day displayed on ice. The house lime juice is refreshing, and beer is available; there are even water pipes for an after-dinner smoke.
🕐 Open 10 a.m.–6 a.m. 🚭
🅰 All major cards

🍴 ABU TAREK
$
40 CHAMPOLLION ST.
DOWNTOWN
This is arguably Cairo's finest *kushari* restaurant—it sells nothing else (see pp. 360 and

p. 385). Take a table and order a bowl; ask for *kebir* (big), *metawasit* (medium), or *sughayyar* (small). Dessert is excellent cold rice pudding (*roz bileban*).
🕐 **Open 24 hours** ❄
❄ **No credit cards**

🍴 ALFY BEY
$
3 ALFY BEY ST.
DOWNTOWN
TEL 02/577 4999
The Alfy Bey is a simple, old-fashioned restaurant, little changed since it opened in the 1930s, which specializes in basic Egyptian fare, particularly grilled meats. Choose from *kofta* (spicy ground meat grilled on a skewer), kabob, lamb chops, and grilled pigeons stuffed with crushed wheat.
🕐 **Open 1 p.m.–1 a.m.**
❄ **No credit cards**

🍴 EGYPTIAN PANCAKE HOUSE
$
AL-HUSSEIN SQ.
The Egyptian take on the pancake is called a *fiteer,* and it's made of layers of flaky pastry. Watching the cook prepare one, as he whirls the dough around his head and pounds it, is quite an experience. You can have a savory *fiteer,* served with cheese, egg, tomato, olives, or ground beef in any combination, or the sweet version, dusted with powdered sugar and coconut.
🕐 **Open 24 hours** ❄ **No credit cards**

SOMETHING SPECIAL

🍴 FELFELA
Its inexpensive local cooking has made Felfela a long-time favorite with tourists and Egyptians alike. Try the *fuul* (mashed beans), served up with garlic, oil, egg, and tomato, or *fuul hosnia,* with cream and eggs

baked in the oven. Order plenty of mezelike *baba ghanoug* (mashed eggplant), *hummus* (chickpea paste), *tahina* (sesame seed paste), and *felafel,* all eaten with bread. Grilled meats include pigeon. The decor is fun (tree trunk tables, aquariums, caged birds), and there is a lively atmosphere. Beer is served.
$
15 HODA SHAARAWI ST.
DOWNTOWN
ALSO 27 CAIRO-ALEXANDRIA HWY.
GIZA
TEL 02/392 2833
🕐 **Open 8 a.m.–midnight**
❄ ❄ **No credit cards**

🍴 MAISON THOMAS
$
157 26TH OF JULY ST.
ZAMALEK
TEL 02/735 7057
You get superb pizzas and generously filled baguettes, as well as breakfasts here, in the closest approximation you'll find in Egypt to a Continental-style delicatessen.
🕐 **Open 24 hours** ❄ **No credit cards**

AROUND CAIRO

🏨 AUBERGE DU LAC
$$$
LAKE QARUN
FAYOUM
TEL 084/572 001
FAX 084/572 002
A beautiful old hunting lodge, with a superb lakeside setting, has been renovated and transformed into a four-star accommodation.
🛏 72 ⤢ ❄ ❄ ❄ DC, MC, V

🏨 SAQQARA COUNTRY CLUB
$$
SAQQARA RD.
BADRASHEIN
TEL 02/381 1282
FAX 02/381 0571
This small, comfortable hotel is set in palm gardens in the

Egyptian countryside. It has a lovely lagoon-style pool. The location is convenient for the sights at Saqqara, Memphis, and Abu Sir, but you will need your own transportation to get around.
🛏 20 ❄ ❄ ❄ **All major cards**

THE DELTA AND SUEZ CANAL

ISMAILIA

🏨 MERCURE FORSAN ISLAND
$$$
GEZIRAT AL-FORSAN
TEL 066/338 040
FAX 066/338 043
WEBSITE www.accoregypt.com
Large and modern in a green setting on the shores of Lake Timsah, this hotel has its own beach and fine views across the water.
🛏 152 ❄ ❄ ❄ AE, MC, V

🍴 GEORGE'S
$$
11 THAWRA ST.
TEL 064/337 327
Opened in 1950 and scarcely changed since then, George's is an atmospheric little fish restaurant and bar on Ismailia's main street.
🕐 **Open noon–11 p.m.** ❄
❄ AE, MC, V

PORT SAID

🏨 HELNAN PORT SAID
$$$$
CORNICHE
TEL 066/320 890
FAX 066/323 762
This large, but somewhat aging, hotel is situated on the beach a few minutes' walk north of the town center, overlooking the point at which the canal joins the Mediterranean. There are several restaurants and a nightclub, as well as many other amenities.
🛏 202 ❄ ❄ ❄ AE, MC, V

HOTELS & RESTAURANTS

🏨 SONESTA PORT SAID
$$$$
SULTAN HUSSEIN ST.
TEL 066/325 511
FAX 066/324 825
Most of the rooms overlook the canal in this fairly modest, business-oriented hotel on one of Port Said's main streets.
🛏 110 🔲 🏖 🦽 All major cards

🏨 HOTEL DE LA POSTE
$
42 GOMHURIYYA ST.
TEL/FAX 066/224 048
The fading old Greek-run establishment in the center of town is a little creaky round the edges, but it's well maintained and has been recently renovated.
🛏 44 🔲 🦽 No credit cards

🍴 AL-BORG
$$
CORNICHE
Some Egyptians will tell you this very modest beachfront restaurant serves the best and freshest fish and seafood in the country. The specialty is a wonderful seafood soup.
🕐 Open noon–midnight 🦽 No credit cards

🍴 NORA FLOATING RESTAURANT
$$
PALESTINE ST.
TEL 066/326 804
About the only way to sail the Suez Canal is to sign up for a 75-minute tour on the Nora. Sailings are for lunch and dinner, and the menu invariably features seafood.
🏖 3 p.m. & 8:30 p.m. 🦽 No credit cards

ALEXANDRIA

🏨 AL-SALAMLEK
$$$$$
MONTAZAH PALACE GARDENS
TEL 03/547 7999
FAX 02/547 3585
E-MAIL salamlek@sangiovanni

.com
The Egyptian president's summer palace is next door to this former royal hunting lodge set in beautiful gardens with fine views over the sea. The rooms are opulently furnished, there is a casino as well as two fine restaurants on site, and you can relax on a nearby beach.
🛏 20 🔲 🔲 🦽 DC, MC, V

SOMETHING SPECIAL

🏨 CECIL HOTEL
The famous Cecil Hotel was built in 1929 in an elegant Moorish style overlooking Alexandria's Eastern Harbor. It featured in Lawrence Durrell's *Alexandria Quartet* as a haunt of the enigmatic Justine, and was used by the British Secret Service as its headquarters during World War II. The signatures of Noel Coward and Somerset Maugham are among those in the guest-book. Now managed by the Sofitel chain, the hotel retains plenty of period charm—notably the grand wrought-iron and wood central elevator—combined with modern five-star facilities. The rooftop Chinese restaurant is very good.
$$$
SAAD ZAGHLOUL SQ.
TEL 03/487 7173
FAX 03/485 5655
🛏 84 🔲 🔲 🦽 All major cards

🏨 HELNAN PALESTINE
$$$$
MONTAZAH PALACE GARDENS
TEL 03/547 4033
FAX 02/547 3378
E-MAIL resh@helnan.com
The uncompromising architecture of this modern hotel on the otherwise sublime Montazah Palace grounds blights the view for everyone else but offers superb Mediterranean vistas

to its guests.
🛏 222 🔲 🔲 🏖 🦽 All major cards

🏨 SHERATON MONTAZAH
$$$$
CORNICHE
MONTAZAH
TEL 03/548 0550
FAX 02/540 1331
The Sheraton is located in the far eastern suburb of Montazah, overlooking the palace grounds and the sea, but quite some distance from the center of town.
🛏 296 🔲 🔲 🏖 🦽 All major cards

🏨 METROPOLE
$$$
25 SAAD ZAGHLOUL ST.
TEL 03/484 0920
FAX 02/486 2040
A fine period hotel (built in 1902), recently renovated and very comfortable, the Metropole has a good, central location and most rooms have a sea view. Beneath the hotel are the Trianon tearooms, a fine place for breakfast.
🛏 66 🔲 🔲 🦽 All major cards

RENAISSANCE ALEXANDRIA
$$$
544 AL-GEISH AVE.
SIDI BISHR
TEL 03/549 0935
FAX 03/549 7690
E-MAIL alexandria@renaissance-htl.com.eg
Most rooms have a sea view in this modestly sized, modern, comfortable hotel in the eastern suburbs not far from the Royal Jewelry and Mahmoud Said Museums.
171 🔲 🔲 🔲 🔲 All major cards

CRILLON HOTEL
$$
5 ADIB ISHAQ ST.
TEL 03/480 0330
The best of Alexandria's budget lodgings is a modest pension occupying several floors of a downtown apartment block. Some of the rooms have French windows opening onto great harbor views, but others are significantly less attractive. Have a look before you accept a room.
36 🔲 🔲 No credit cards

HOTEL UNION
$$
164 26TH OF JULY ST.
TEL 03/480 7350
FAX 03/480 7350
The Union is a good budget option on the Corniche overlooking the harbor. Some rooms have sea views, some have bathrooms, some have both. Ask to view a few before choosing.
37 🔲 🔲 No credit cards

AU PRIVÉ
$$$
14 HOREYYA ST.
TEL 03/484 1881
Tucked down an alley off the main street, this is Alexandria's most fashionable nightspot. Snack at the bar or dine in the restaurant area, where the ambitious French-inclined menu offers dishes of duck, rabbit, seafood, and steaks.
Open 5 p.m.–2:30 a.m.
🔲 🔲 All major cards

SOMETHING SPECIAL

QADOURA
When in Alexandria, the thing to do is to eat seafood at a streetside restaurant. Of the many places where you can do this, Qadoura is one of the best. It is on a backstreet out toward the Fortress of Qaitbey, one block in from the sea. The tram rumbles by the outdoor tables.

As is standard, there is no menu. Instead you pick your fish from the ice-packed selection (which may include sea bass, red and grey mullet, bluefish, sole, squid, and shrimp), and tell the waiter how you want it cooked: baked or grilled. A selection of meze comes with all orders, and there is beer and wine. Take a seat after the sun goes down and make a night of it.
$$$
33 BAIRAM AL-TONSI ST.
ANFUSHI
TEL 03/480 0405
Open 24 hours 🔲 QV

SAMAKMAK
$$$
42 QASR RAS AL-TIN ST.
ANFUSHI
TEL 03/480 9523
The name is a play on the Arabic word for fish, *samak*. It's a toss-up whether this or the Qadoura is the better restaurant, but Samakmak is certainly the better known of the two courtesy of the owner, a famous former belly dancer.
Open 10 a.m.–2 a.m. 🔲 🔲 MC, V

SANTA LUCIA
$$$
40 SAFIYYA ZAGHLOUL ST.
TEL 03/486 4240
Service is black tie at Alexandria's most exclusive restaurant. Even though not quite as glamorous as it once was, the Santa Lucia serves a Mediterranean menu that is still good, and the food is certainly a cut above average.
Open noon–4 p.m. & 7 p.m.–2 a.m. 🔲 🔲 AE, MC, V

BA'ASH
$$
SAFER PASHA ST.
ANFUSHI
TEL 03/480 2815
Safer Pasha is the most wonderful of streets, lined with fish and meat restaurants, all producing great clouds of aromatic smoke from their busy open-air grills. Most places are open around-the-clock and the best time to visit is late. Of the restaurants here **Ba'ash** does great pigeon, while **Abu Ashraf** (tel 03/481 6597) at No. 28 is recommended for fish, and **Muhammad Hosni** at No. 48 for grilled meats.
24 hours 🔲 🔲 V at Abu Ashraf only

ELITE
$$
43 SAFIYYA ZAGHLOUL ST.
TEL 03/486 3592
The Elite used to be a favorite of intellectuals and artists when Alexandria still had an intellectual and artistic scene to speak of before the revolution of 1952. Still run by the redoubtable Madam Christina, it maintains a raffish air and is the only place in Alexandria where you can drink beer and watch the street through large picture windows. The food, though not fine cuisine, is satisfying.
Open 11 a.m.–midnight
🔲 🔲 No credit cards

MALEK AL-SAMAAN
$$
ATTAREEN ST.
ATTAREEN
If you don't read Arabic, look for the street sign showing a tiny bird. The bird is a quail,

HOTELS & RESTAURANTS

which is all that is served at this rough, awning-covered, open-air courtyard restaurant, one of Egypt's most unusual dining venues.
⏱ Open 8 p.m.–late 🚫 No credit cards

🍴 L'OSABUCCO
$$
14 HOREYYA AVE.
TEL 02/487 2506
Run by the same people as Cairo's L'Aubergine (see p. 364), this is a recently opened chic bar-restaurant on two floors, with drinking downstairs and candlelit dining upstairs. The menu changes frequently and is inventive and wide ranging, from salmon felafel to Cajun chicken.
⏱ Open noon–midnight 🅿
🚫 AE, DC, V

🍴 CAP D'OR
$
4 ADIB ST., OFF SAAD ZAGHLOUL ST.
TEL 03/486 5177
Primarily a bar—and an excellent one at that—the Cap d'Or also serves first-rate seafood snacks such as prawns and calamari.
⏱ Open noon–2 a.m.
🚫 No credit cards

🍴 HASSAN BLEIK
$
18 SAAD ZAGHLOUL ST.
The tiny, venerable Lebanese restaurant is through the back of a pastry shop. It may look a little basic, but the food is beautifully prepared. While here, it's worth visiting the wonderful Sofianopoulo Coffee Store next door.
⏱ Open noon–6 p.m.
🚫 No credit cards

🍴 HAVANA
$
CORNER OF HOREYYA ST. & ORABI ST.
TEL 03/487 0661
This is one of Alexandria's wonderful taverna-style bars that whisk up wonders in the

kitchen. In this case the food is anything owner Nagy has found at the market that day, from roast beef to grilled liver or fish. Ask what's on the menu.
⏱ Open noon–2 a.m.
🚫 No credit cards

🍴 MUHAMMAD AHMED
$
17 SHAKOUR PASHA ST.
DOWNTOWN
TEL 03/487 3576
Alexandrians rate this as the city's best restaurant for fuul and felafel. It also offers a range of omelettes and fried cheese, plus all the usual salad and dip accompaniments. You can eat in or take out. Find this place one street west of main Safiyya Zaghloul Street, just north of Saad Zaghloul.
🚫 No credit cards

WESTERN DESERT

BAHARIYYA OASIS

🏨 INTERNATIONAL HEALTH CENTRE
$$$
BAWITI
TEL 018/802 322
Located about 3 miles (5 km) outside the oasis on the road to Cairo, this is a three-star spa built around a sulfur spring, supposed to have therapeutic qualities. There are also a gym, a sauna, and a restaurant.
ℹ 27 🚫 No credit cards

🏨 AL-BESHMO LODGE
$$
BAWITI
TEL/FAX 011/802 177
Basic huts are arranged around a courtyard beside a palm grove watered by Al-Beshmu spring. Some of the huts have air-conditioning and private bathrooms, the rest are equipped with fans and share spotlessly kept facilities.
ℹ 25 🅿 🚫 No credit cards

DAKHLA OASIS

🏨 MUT TALATA
$$$
MUT
TEL 092/821 530
FAX 092/927 983
This small complex consisting of a salmon pink central villa, six chalets, and three canvas tents sits beside a hot spring a couple of miles outside Mut, the main center of the oasis. It is under the same management as the Pioneers Hotel in Kharga.
ℹ 11 🚫 No credit cards

🏨 MEBAREZ HOTEL
$$
MUT
TEL/FAX 092/821 524
This modern concrete hotel on the edge of Mut is reasonable value for money. Some of the rooms are on the shabby side, but they are air-conditioned and have their own fairly clean bathrooms.
ℹ 29 🅿 🚫 No credit cards

🍴 AHMED HAMDY
$
MUT
TEL 092/820 767
Look for this very basic, tiny open-air restaurant on the main road through the oasis, near the Mebarez Hotel. There is no menu; instead there are just two dishes of the day served, with salad and beer, but the food is always fresh and wholesome.
⏱ Open noon–late 🚫 No credit cards

FARAFRA OASIS

🏨 AL-BADAWIYYA SAFARI & HOTEL
$$-$
TEL 02/345 8524
E-MAIL mtt@hotmail.com
This tastefully designed mud-brick hotel is owned by Bedouin brothers and managed by a Swiss woman. There are various styles of room from shared

dormitories to suites with their own living rooms, and the whole package is excellent value. The brothers who own the hotel also organize jeep, camel, and walking safaris into the White Desert. Both the hotel and the safaris are very popular, so it is essential to reserve rooms well in advance.
🛈 30 🚫 No credit cards

KHARGA OASIS

🏨 PIONEERS
$$$
GAMAL ABDEL NASSER ST.
TEL 092/927 982
FAX 092/927 983
The only luxury accommo-dations in all the oases except for the Adrere Amellal in Siwa, the Pioneers is a postmodernist, pink-painted, low-rise hotel. Attractive terraces overlook a central pool area and there are a bar, café, and restaurant. Desert safaris can be arranged.
🛈 102 🄢 🌊 🚫 No credit cards

🏨 KHARGA OASIS HOTEL
$$
KHARGA OASIS
TEL 092/921 500
FAX 092/921 615
This modernist high-rise hotel has a pleasant palm-filled garden and terrace. The rooms are comfortable; most have balconies overlooking the garden and are equipped with air-conditioning and private bathrooms.
🛈 30 🄢 🌊 🚫 No credit cards

MARSA MATRUH

🏨 BEAU SITE
$$$$
CORNICHE
TEL 046/493 2066
FAX 046/493 3319
E-MAIL beausite@hiba.com
Among the many bland concrete blocks that deface this quiet Mediterranean town, the Beau Site stands out

as somewhere individual. Run by the same family since the 1950s, it has a pleasingly personal quality, comfortable rooms, and its own private beach. The restaurant is also very good.
🛈 170 🄢 🌊 🚫 AE, MC, V

SIWA OASIS

🏨 ADRERE AMELLAL
Twelve miles (19 km) outside the center of Siwa, this is possibly the most unique and enchanting accommodations in all Egypt. Lying in the lee of a chalky mountain beside a lake on the edge of the desert, it's a remote eco-lodge built in a traditional Siwan mud-brick and palm-beam fashion. It resembles a small village. Promoting a real back-to-nature ethic, the lodge has no electricity or phone lines; at night the place is lit by candles and flaming torches. A Roman spring in a nearby palm grove serves as a swimming pool. The price includes all meals (gourmet-standard organic food), drinks, and excursions to visit hot springs in the desert.
$$$$$
SIDI JAFAR
TEL 02/735 1924
FAX 02/735 5489
E-MAIL info@eqi.com.eg
🛈 32 🌊 🚫 AE, V

🏨 SHALI LODGE
$$$
SIWA TOWN
TEL 046/460 2299
FAX 046/460 1799
E-MAIL info@eqi.com.eg
In this intimate mud-brick hotel, set in a palm garden just off the main market square in central Siwa, the rooms are arranged around a central pool.
🛈 7 🄢 🌊 🚫 No credit cards

🏨 SIWA SAFARI PARADISE
$$$-$

TEL 046/460 2289
FAX 046/460 2286
This is a three-star complex in a palm garden setting close by the Temple of Amun. It has a variety of accommodation choices: You can enjoy the luxury of a bungalow with air-conditioning, TV, and fridge; pay less for a bungalow without air-conditioning; or go native in a reed hut.
🛈 54 🄢 Some rooms 🚫 AE, V

🏨 AROUS AL-WAHA HOTEL
$$
SIWA TOWN
TEL 046/460 2100
Despite its utilitarian concrete appearance, this is a comfortable place to stay in the center of Siwa. Rooms with private bathrooms are well maintained and have constant hot water; and, although there's no air-conditioning, the rooms do have fans.
🛈 20 🚫 No credit cards

ASYUT

🏨 ASSIUTEL HOTEL
$$
AL-THAWRA ST.
TEL 088/312 121
FAX 088/312 122
The hotel is of middling quality but it's as good as it gets for Asyut. However, it has an excellent riverside position and lovely views from the rooms.
🛈 28 🄢 Some rooms 🚫 No credit cards

MINYA

🏨 MERCURE NEFERTITI & ATON
$$$
CORNICHE AL-NIL
TEL 086/341 515
FAX 086/366 467
The only real contender in town is this four-star hotel with

a good Nile-side location just north of the center. It has a full range of facilities including gym, swimming pool, tennis courts, bar, and restaurants.

🛈 96 ⬚ ⬚ ⬚ AE, MC, V

SOHAG

🏨 MERIT AMOUN HOTEL
$$
EAST BANK
TEL 093/601 985
FAX 093/603 222
The Merit Amoun is a large three-star hotel, which has the advantage of possessing a restaurant (finding somewhere decent to eat can be a problem in Middle Egypt). Also consider the nearby **Cazalovy Hotel,** which is of similar quality to the Merit Amoun but around half the price.
🛈 28 ⬚ Some rooms ⬚ No credit cards

LUXOR

SOMETHING SPECIAL

🏨 AL-MOUDIRA
This is an extraordinary new boutique hotel out in a desert setting on the West Bank, which is built using traditional mud-brick styles but in a grand manner that recalls Italianate villas. Rooms are arranged off a series of courtyards and each has a trompe d'oeil theme. Other beautiful touches include the use of salvaged architectural pieces such as old doors and wrought-iron balconies. By far Luxor's most magical accommodations.
$$$$$
DABAIYYA
WEST BANK
TEL 012/325 1307
🛈 54 ⬚ ⬚ All major cards

🏨 MÖVENPICK JOLIEVILLE CROCODILE ISLAND
$$$$$
CROCODILE ISLAND

TEL 095/374 855
FAX 095/374 936
E-MAIL mpluxor@intouch.com
Occupying its own island in the Nile, 2.5 miles (4 km) south of town, this is Luxor's top hotel in terms of setting, service, and facilities. Accommodations are bungalows set on a lush banana plantation; the well-equipped rooms each have their own terrace. There are several restaurants and the food is excellent. Feluccas (traditional Nile sailing boats) are available for the use of guests; there is even a little zoo and children's playground.
🛈 332 ⬚ ⬚ ⬚ All major cards

SOMETHING SPECIAL

🏨 WINTER PALACE HOTEL
This grand old hotel was built to accommodate the aristocracy of Europe who were flocking to discover ancient Egypt at the turn of the last century. More recently, the hotel has been tastefully refurbished by the Sofitel chain and now has all modern facilities. Half of the rooms overlook the Nile, the rest a splendid garden. There is also a considerably less charming new annex, the New Winter Palace.
$$$$$-$$$$
CORNICHE AL-NIL
TEL 095/380 422
FAX 095/374 087
🛈 356 ⬚ ⬚ ⬚ All major cards

🏨 HILTON LUXOR
$$$$
KARNAK ST.
TEL 095/374 933
FAX 095/382 837
www.hilton.com
Located 2.5 miles (4 km) north of town, the Hilton is convenient for the great temple complex of Karnak, but little else of interest is within walking distance. However, there are shuttle

---

PRICES

HOTELS
An indication of the cost of a double room without breakfast is given by **$** signs.
$$$$$ Over $200
$$$$ $120–$200
$$$ $60–$120
$$ $30–$60
$ Under $30

RESTAURANTS
An indication of the cost of a full meal without drinks, tax, and tip is given by **$** signs.
$$$$ Over $35
$$$ $20–$35
$$ $10–$20
$ Under $10

---

services to the town center, and the hotel has the usual range of luxury features.
🛈 261 ⬚ ⬚ ⬚ All major cards

🏨 HOTEL MERCURE CORALIA
$$$$
CORNICHE AL-NIL
TEL 095/380 944
FAX 095/374 912
This attractive, mid-rise hotel has a superb location on the Nile-front Corniche, midway between Luxor Temple and Luxor Museum. Rooms at the front have a glorious view of the West Bank across the river.
🛈 314 ⬚ ⬚ ⬚ All major cards

🏨 SHERATON LUXOR
$$$$
KHALID IBN AL-WALID ST.
TEL 095/374 544
FAX 095/374 941
WEBSITE www.sheraton.com
The location 2 miles (3 km) south of town, necessitating lots of taxi rides, is a drawback. However, the Sheraton has a pleasant garden setting beside the Nile and good facilities, and offers daily yacht excursions to the temple at Dendara.
🛈 290 ⬚ ⬚ ⬚ All major cards

SONESTA ST. GEORGE
$$$$
KHALID IBN AL-WALID ST.
TEL 095/382 575
FAX 095/382 571
E-MAIL sonesta@iec.egnet.net
This stylish hotel is only a few years old. It has the disadvantage of being some distance south of the center, but is redeemed by its beautiful Nile-side setting. The hotel is known for its excellent Japanese restaurant, which is open to guests and nonguests alike.
🛈 224 🛇 🏊 🖾 All major cards

ISIS HOTEL
$$$
KHALED IBN AL-WALID ST.
TEL 095/373 366
FAX 095/372 923
Owned by a relative of President Hosni Mubarak, this luxury complex stands in beautiful gardens beside the Nile. It's about a mile (1.5 km) south of the center, but it has its own excellent Chinese and Italian restaurants, plus a couple of pools (and a heliport on the roof).
🛈 480 🛇 🏊 🖾 MC, V

HOTEL AL-GEZIRA
$$
BAYARAT AL-GEZIRA
WEST BANK
TEL/FAX 095/310 034
Just up from the West Bank ferry landing is this modest, modern hotel, with rooms overlooking the river. Some rooms have air-conditioning, others just fans. Private bathrooms. Excellent Egyptian food is served in a rooftop restaurant.
🛈 11 🛇 Some rooms 🖾 No credit cards

EMILIO
$$
YOUSEF HASSAN ST.
TEL 095/373 570
FAX 095/370 000
This mid-range hotel in the middle of town is convenient for Luxor Temple and the West Bank ferry. All rooms have private bathrooms and air-conditioning, and there's a pleasant roof terrace.
🛈 48 🛇 🏊 🖾 AE, MC, V

GADDIS HOTEL
$$
KHALED IBN AL-WALID ST.
TEL 095/382 838
FAX 095/382 837
A mile (1.5 km) south of the center of town, the Gaddis offers good value with clean and stylish rooms. There are a smallish pool, three restaurants, and a bar.
🛈 55 🛇 Some rooms 🏊 🖾 MC, V

NUR AL-GURNA
$$
BAYARAT
WEST BANK
TEL 095/311 430
A recent addition to the West Bank, this small hotel is built around a mud-brick courtyard hidden in a palm grove across from the West Bank ticket office. Rooms are decorated with local crafts and fabrics.
🛈 9 🖾 No credit cards

PHARAOH'S HOTEL
$$
BAYARAT
WEST BANK
TEL/FAX 095/310 702
Pharaoh's is the most upscale of the West Bank hotels, located between the West Bank ticket office and the temple of Medinat Habu. Rooms have air-conditioning or a fan, some have private bathrooms, and some have water views of the temple. There is a nice beer garden.
🛈 29 🛇 Some rooms 🖾 No credit cards

AMUN AL-GEZIRA
$
BAYARAT AL-GEZIRA
WEST BANK
TEL 095/310 912
FAX 095/311 205
This modest family-run establishment is in a back alley of a West Bank village just uphill from the ferry landing. The rooms have fans and bathrooms and are kept immaculately clean. There's a lovely roof terrace and small garden. You'll have to compete for rooms with archaeologists who favor the place.
🛈 12 🖾 No credit cards

YMCA CAMPSITE
$
KARNAK ST.
TEL 095/372 425
The site provides tent space and hot showers, and can also offer sites for campers and trailers. The location is midway between the town center and the temples of Karnak.

🍴 MIYAKO
$$$
SONESTA ST. GEORGE HOTEL
KHALED IBN AL-WALID ST.
TEL 095/382 575
This attractive Japanese restaurant is centered on a *teppanyaki* grill at which up to ten people can sit around and watch the chef at work. The decor is stylish, and if the food wouldn't quite pass muster in Tokyo, it makes a welcome change in Egypt.
🕐 Open 7–11 p.m. 🛇 🖾 All major cards

🍴 MÖVENPICK GARDEN TERRACE
$$$–$$
MÖVENPICK JOLIEVILLE
CROCODILE ISLAND
TEL 095/374 855
Nonguests are invited to take the hotel shuttle launch and head to Crocodile Island for the breakfast buffet, lunch, or dinner. All are served on a beautiful terrace overlooking the Nile. Whatever the time of day, it is by far the most pleasurable eating out experience to be found in Luxor.
🖾 All major cards

LA MAMA
$$
SHERATON LUXOR
KHALID IBN AL-WALID ST.
TEL 095/374 544
Pastas, pizzas, and other assorted Italian dishes are served in the hotel garden beside a pool with ducks and pelicans.
🕒 Open noon–11 p.m.
💳 AE, MC, V

PEACE ABOUZEID RESTAURANT
$$
CORNICHE AL-NIL BY KARNAK TEMPLE
The buffet lunch served by this Nile-side terrace restaurant, which is located near the temple, is very popular. For a better experience, however, go in the evening when the à la carte menu includes Egyptian favorites such as stuffed pigeon, and diners can round off the meal with a puff on a sheesha.
💳 No credit cards

TUTANKHAMUN RESTAURANT
$$
BAYARAT AL-GEZIRA
WEST BANK
TEL 095/310 118
Just up from the local ferry landing, this open-air Nile-side restaurant is run by Aam Mahmoud, a former cook at one of the French archaeological missions. There's no menu, just a couple of dishes of the day, often *tagens* (stews cooked in a clay pot). These come with various salads and side orders.
💳 No credit cards

KING'S HEAD PUB
$
KHALED IBN AL-WALID ST.
TEL 095/371 249
The King's Head is an English-style pub, but the king in question is Akhenaten, wearing a Tudor hat. The food ranges from dishes of French fries to a Sunday lunch special of roast beef and Yorkshire pudding. The authentic pub atmosphere extends to traditional games such as darts and billiards.
🕒 Open noon–midnight
💳 No credit cards

RESTAURANT MUHAMMAD
$
NEXT TO THE PHARAOH'S HOTEL
BAYARAT
WEST BANK
TEL 095/311 014
You are basically a guest at Muhammad Abdel Lahi's mud-brick house, where he cooks up good, basic Egyptian food, including chicken, kabob, duck, and *molokhiyya,* the glutinous green-leaf soup that is very much an acquired taste.
🕒 Open noon–10 p.m.
💳 No credit cards

ASWAN

ABU SIMBEL

NEFERTARI HOTEL
$$$
ABU SIMBEL
TEL/FAX 097/400 508
Of only two accommodation options at Abu Simbel, this is slightly the better—and closer to the temples. It has the advantage of a garden with a tree-shaded pool.
🛏 120 💳 🅿 💳 AE, MC, V

NOBALEH RAMSES
$$
ABU SIMBEL
TEL 097/400 294
FAX 097/400 381
The cheaper of the two Abu Simbel hotels, the Nobaleh Ramses lies almost a mile (1.5 km) distant from the temples. Rooms are fairly basic but they are clean and air-conditioned.
🛏 32 💳 💳 No credit cards

ASWAN

ASWAN

🏨 OLD CATARACT
Arguably Egypt's most romantic hotel, the Old Cataract is an oppulent Moorish mansion set on beautiful gardens on a rocky bluff above the Nile. It's a period piece belonging to the days when Aswan was a winter resort for the rich and titled of Europe. Agatha Christie wrote part of *Death on the Nile* here and the hotel features in both the novel and the movie. The large rooms are beautifully furnished and most have balconies with fantastic views of the river. The dining room is of palatial proportions with great horseshoe arches supporting the ceiling. Best of all is the terrace, the perfect place for sunset drinks while watching the sun sink below the desert hills on the far bank.
$$$$$–$$$$
ABTAL AL-TAHRIR ST.
TEL 097/316 006
FAX 097/316 011
E-MAIL hl666@accor-hotels.com
🛏 131 💳 🅿 💳 All major cards

🏨 AMOUN ISLAND CLUB
$$$$
AMOUN ISLAND
TEL 097/313 800
FAX 097/317 190
E-MAIL rashab@starnet.com.eg
This small, island hotel run by Club Med is centered on a former royal hunting lodge. Rooms are modest but all have river views, and the garden setting is stunning. Small motorboats shuttle guests across the river from shore to shore.
🛏 50 💳 🅿 💳 MC, V

🏨 ASWAN OBEROI
$$$$
ELEPHANTINE ISLAND
TEL 097/314 666
FAX 097/313 538

E-MAIL crs@oberoi.com.eg
Its ugly tower dominates the Aswan skyline, but if you stay here you'll enjoy the full complement of five-star facilities in the setting of a luscious Nile island. There's an excellent riverside pool, too.
244 All major cards

NEW CATARACT
$$$$
ABTAL AL-TAHRIR ST.
TEL 097/316 000
FAX 097/316 011
E-MAIL hl666@accor-hotels.com
It may be an ugly, modern high-rise, but guests at the New Cataract get to share the garden, splendid swimming pool, and, above all, the view with those staying at its illustrious neighbor, the Old Cataract.
144 All major cards

BASMA
$$$
ABTAL AL-TAHRIR ST.
TEL 097/310 901
FAX 097/310 907
E-MAIL basma@rocketmail.com
The Basma is a somewhat impersonal hotel south of town beside the Nubian Museum. However, the rooms are comfortable with good views, the staff is friendly, and the rates are highly competitive.
200 AE, MC, V

CLEOPATRA HOTEL
$$$
SOUQ ST.
TEL 097/314 003
FAX 097/314 002
The rooms are clean and comfortable (although occasionally gloomy, so look at a few before choosing) and have air-conditioning and private bathrooms. There's also a rooftop pool. The hotel is located close to the railroad station in the market area.
109 AE, MC, V

HAPPI HOTEL
$$
ABTAL AL-TAHRIR ST.
TEL 097/314 115
FAX 097/307 572
One block back from the Corniche, the Happi is right in the center of town amid the busy market streets. Rooms have private bathrooms and air-conditioning, and guests have use of the rooftop pool at the nearby Cleopatra Hotel for a discounted fee.
64 No credit cards

HOTEL KEYLANY
$$-$
SOUQ ST.
TEL/FAX 097/317 332
E-MAIL mohamed@aswanet.com.eg
This is an excellent budget option. It is located in the thick of the market, and has a variety of rooms ranging from dormitories to new doubles with private bath. There's a small pool on the roof. Internet access is also available to guests.
28 Some rooms No credit cards

RAMSES HOTEL
$$
ABTAL AL-TAHRIR ST.
TEL 097/304 000
FAX 097/315 701
This is good value. The rooms are old, and a little shabby in some cases, but they are air-conditioned and come with private bathrooms, fridge, and Nile views.
112 No credit cards

1902 RESTAURANT
$$$
OLD CATARACT HOTEL
ABTAL AL-TAHRIR ST.
TEL 097/316 000
In a stunning dining room, under a huge domed ceiling, eat a four-course fixed-price menu with French-inspired dishes. The restaurant is sometimes closed to nonresidents, when the hotel is full.
Open 7 p.m.–midnight All major cards

ILE AMOUN
$$
AMOUN ISLAND
TEL 097/313 800
Nonresidents are welcome to dine at the Amoun Island Hotel restaurant, which offers an excellent dinner buffet of meat and fish dishes, plus plenty of meze and salads. Free boats to the island run from in front of the EgyptAir office on the Corniche.
Open 7 p.m.–late All major cards

NUBIAN RESTAURANT
$$
ESSA ISLAND
SOUTH OF ELEPHANTINE
This is a complete Nubian experience. You eat a three-course meal—including meat stews cooked in clay dishes—to the accompaniment of music and dance performed by a Nubian troupe. Free boats shuttle to the island from the Al-Dokka landing stage on the Corniche opposite the telecom building.
Open 7 p.m.–midnight No credit cards

AL-MASRI
$
AL-MATAR ST.
TEL 097/302 576
On a side street off the souq, this place serves kabobs and kofta only. The meat is excellent and comes with bread, salad, and tahina. Very popular with local families, the restaurant is clean, with attractive Arabesque tiled walls.
Open noon–midnight No credit cards

ASWAN MOON
$
CORNICHE AL-NIL
TEL 097/316 108
The Aswan Moon is the best of a string of floating restaurants. The food is basic

HOTELS & RESTAURANTS

(soup, kabobs, chicken, some vegetarian dishes) but good, and the service is friendly. It's also a popular beer-drinking haunt for local felucca captains.
🕐 Open 8 a.m.–midnight
🚫 No credit cards

RED SEA & SINAI

DAHAB

🏨 HILTON RESORT
$$$$
DAHAB BAY
TEL 069/640 310
FAX 069/640 424
WEBSITE www.hilton.com
Far less developed than nearby Sharm al-Sheikh and Naama Bay, Dahab makes for a quieter getaway, and this is the newest and best of the big hotels there. Most rooms are whitewashed and domed and arranged around a central artificial lagoon. There's a fine strip of beach, and water sports and diving facilities are good.
🛏 163 🔶 🏖 🚫 All major cards

🏨 NESIMA HOTEL
$$$
MASHRABA
TEL 069/640 320
FAX 069/640 321
E-MAIL nesima@intouch.com
Accommodations are simple but comfortable domed rooms, some with air-conditioning. It has a great pool with a juice bar overlooking the beach. The hotel's diving center has an excellent reputation; as a consequence, the hotel is often full with dive groups.
🛏 51 🔶 🏖 🚫 MC, V

EL GOUNA

🏨 SHERATON MIRAMAR
$$$$$
AL-GOUNA RESORT
TEL 065/545 606
FAX 065/545 608
WEBSITE www.sheraton.com

Designed by internationally renowned architect Michael Graves, this is one of Egypt's most outstanding modern hotels. A pastel-painted postmodern creation, it looks stunning in its seaside desert setting. Service is exceptional, and in addition to rooms and suites there are 25 "palace" rooms served by butlers.
🛏 338 🔶 🏖 🚫 All major cards

🏨 DAWAR AL-UMDA
$$$$
KAFR AL-GOUNA
TEL 065/545 060
FAX 065/545 601
Part of the exclusive Al-Gouna resort, this is a modestly scaled boutique hotel designed along traditional lines with domes and vaults and adobe walls. At the same time, guests have full use of the resort's facilities, including swimming pools, water sports, and a golf course.
🛏 64 🔶 🏖 🚫 All major cards

HURGHADA

🏨 HURGHADA INTERCONTINENTAL
$$$$$
NEW HURGHADA
TEL 065/446 911
FAX 065/446 910
E-MAIL hurghada@interconti.com
Hurghada's most splendid resort complex has rooms overlooking a garden with several pools. It has a fine private beach, a good diving center, water sports, and numerous bars and restaurants.
🛏 244 🔶 🏖 🚫 All major cards

🏨 JASMINE VILLAGE HOTEL
$$$
NEW HURGHADA
TEL 065/446 442
FAX 065/446 441
E-MAIL info@jasmin-diving.com
At the southernmost end of

Hurghada's sprawling hotel strip, Jasmine is a family resort of bungalow-style accommodations. It has a reputable dive center with its own boats, good water sports facilities, and a playground and zoo for children.
🛏 460 🔶 🏖 🚫 All major cards

🏨 THREE CORNERS EMPIRE HOTEL
$$
MUSTASHFA ST.
AL-DAHAR
TEL 065/549 200
FAX 065/549 212
E-MAIL info@threecorners.com
An unattractive concrete building, the Three Corners Empire nevertheless has an excellent location among the bars and restaurants on the busiest street in central Hurghada (Al-Dahar). Guests have access to a private beach a few minutes' walk away.
🛏 366 🔶 🏖 🚫 All major cards

🍴 BIER KELLER
$$
IBEROTEL ARABELLA, SIGALA
TEL 065/545 086
More a bar than a restaurant, it has a fixed-price menu special every evening. This takes the form of Germanic-type fare such as veal escalope, braised beef, or cabbage roll filled with ground meat. It's raucous and fun.
🕐 Open noon–midnight 🔶 🚫 All major cards

🍴 FELFELA
$$
SHERATON ST.
SIGALA
TEL 065/442 410/1
This branch of the ever popular Egyptian-cuisine Cairo restaurant (see p. 365) overlooks the Red Sea.
🕐 Open 8 a.m.–midnight
🚫 No credit cards

PORTOFINO
$$
GENERAL HOSPITAL ST.
AL-DAHAR
TEL 065/546 250
Right on Hurghada's main street, this is an extremely good Italian and seafood restaurant offering interesting specialties such as fish baked in rock salt.
🕐 Open 12.30 p.m.–12.30 a.m. daily 🆒 🍴 AE, MC, V

ROSSI PIZZA
$$
CORNICHE
SIGALA
TEL 065/446 012
This long-standing divers' favorite serves thin-crust pizzas, seafood, and salads. There's a lively bar attached (see p. 382).
🕐 Open 10 a.m.–2:30 a.m. 🆒 🍴 MC, V

NUWEIBA

SOMETHING SPECIAL

BASATA
Basata means "simplicity," and that's the ethic behind Egypt's oldest eco-resort, founded in the 1980s by engineer and owner Sherif Ghamrway. Some 16 bamboo and mud-brick huts stand on a beautiful, secluded beach 15 miles (24 km) north of Nuweiba. At the resort's heart is a central communal hut with kitchens and lounge area. Guests cook their own food from provisions supplied by Sherif (log what you use and pay later) or eat whatever the designated cook prepares. No alcohol, TV, loud music, or scuba diving are allowed to disturb the New Age atmosphere.
$
RAS AL-BURQA
TEL/FAX 069/500 481
🛏 16 🍴 AE, MC, V

QUSEIR

SOMETHING SPECIAL

MÖVENPICK RESORT QUSEIR
The Quseir Mövenpick is a beautiful, environmentally friendly, resort complex 3 miles (5 km) north of the town center, set around an aquamarine bay. The majority of the accommodations are pretty stone bungalows. There's a gorgeous terraced pool area, from where you can look down into the crystal-clear seawater and watch large, colorful fish dart around. There are lots of activities for children, too.
$$$$
SIRENA BEACH
AL-QADIM BAY
TEL 065/332 100
FAX 065/332 128
WEBSITE www.movenpick-quseir.com
🛏 175 🆒 ⛱ 🍴 All major cards

QUSEIR HOTEL & RESTAURANT
$$
138 PORT SAID ST.
TEL/FAX 065/332 301
Here you can stay in an attractively restored Ottoman house on the waterfront with creaky wooden stairs and clean-lined rooms with decor of exposed stone and blonde pine. Some rooms have air-conditioning, others have fans only. Bathrooms are shared. The ground floor restaurant specializes in seafood.
🛏 6 🆒 🍴 All major cards

SHARM AL-SHEIKH

RITZ CARLTON RESORT
$$$$
RAS UMM SID
TEL 069/661 919
FAX 069/661 920
E-MAIL ritzcarltonssh@sinainet.com.eg
This clifftop hotel has

sumptuous rooms overlooking the sea or mountains (the latter are slightly cheaper). There are also a garden with pools, waterfalls, and fountains, a private beach with its own stretch of reef, and a golf course.
🛏 307 🆒 ⛱ 🍴 All major cards

SOFITEL CORALIA SHARM AL-SHEIKH
$$$$
NAAMA BAY
TEL 069/600 083
FAX 069/600 085
E-MAIL h1970@accor-hotels.com
One of the best hotels in southern Sinai, the Sofitel Coralia is located at the northern edge of the resort cluster, with stunning views across the bay from its Moorish-styled rooms. Complete in itself, the hotel has three pools and a very good array of bars and restaurants.
🛏 302 🆒 ⛱ 🍴 All major cards

SANAFIR
$$$
NAAMA BAY
TEL 069/600 197
FAX 069/600 196
E-MAIL sanafir@access.com.eg
At the heart of Naama Bay, surrounded by shops, cafés, and bars, and just a stone's throw from the beach, the Sanafir is one of the resort's older hotels. However, it is well maintained, and, with several popular nightspots, is a favorite with a younger crowd.
🛏 74 🆒 ⛱ 🍴 All major cards

AMAR SINAI
$$
RAS UMM SID
TEL 069/662 222
FAX 069/662 233
Up on the rocky headland that divides Sharm al-Sheikh Bay and Naama Bay, Amar has been designed by its owner to

HOTELS & RESTAURANTS

look like an Egyptian village. The facilities are good for a budget hotel with a pool, Jacuzzi, and Oriental café. Some of the rooms have excellent views.

🛈 91 🔆 ≈ All major cards

🏨 PIGEON HOUSE
$$–$
NAAMA BAY
TEL 069/600 996
FAX 069/600 995
E-MAIL pigeon@access.com.eg
Inexpensive places to stay are scarce in Sharm al-Sheikh and Naama Bay. This is about the best on offer. Room types range from very basic huts with fans and shared facilities to superior rooms with air-conditioning and private bathrooms. There's a small beach-type bar/café—which is nice, but the sand and water are a good 15 minutes' walk distant.

🛈 68 🔆 Some rooms
🚫 No credit cards

🍴 LA LUNA
$$$$
RITZ CARLTON RESORT
RAS UMM SID
TEL 062/661 919
Reputedly one of the best restaurants in the whole of Egypt, La Luna is supervised by Italian chef Marco Aveta, who gets his ingredients flown in from his home country. He serves a mouth watering mix of pastas, steaks, and seafood.

🕐 Open for dinner only 🔆
All major cards

🍴 BUA KHAO
$$$
SHARM HOTEL
NAAMA BAY
TEL 069/601 391
This is the Sinai branch of an award-winning Cairo restaurant specializing in Thai food, here with a seafood slant. Pleasant decor and friendly service complement authentically spiced dishes.

🕐 Open noon–midnight 🔆
All major cards

🍴 DANANEER
$$
SHAMANDOURA SHOPPING CENTER
NAAMA BAY
TEL 069/600 321
Find this popular place above the Benetton store. It's simple but appealing, with an inviting *mashrabiyya*-style (carved wood window) decor, and a menu that's a mix of traditional Egyptian and seafood.

🕐 Open noon–midnight
All major cards

🍴 AL-FANAR
$$
RAS UMM SID
TEL 069/662 218
The local diving community favor Al-Fanar for its out-of-the-way but on-the-beach location. The restaurant itself is decorated in attractive, Bedouin tent style, but with sunken alcoves offering privacy. The food is, unsurprisingly, fishy, and thoroughly excellent—try the baked snapper, washed down with chilled Stella beer.

🕐 Open 10.30 a.m.–midnight 🚫 MC, V

🍴 SAFSAFA
$$
OLD SHARM MALL
TEL 069/660 474
One of the oldest restaurants in town, the Safsafa is badly located some way inland from the sea and is very small (only eight tables). Despite these disadvantages, it's worth seeking out for the freshest and best seafood in town at great prices.

🚫 No credit cards

🍴 SINAI STAR
$
DOWNTOWN MARINA
This is an unpretentious restaurant run by a local Bedouin sheikh. There are no menus but the likes of shrimp, calamari, red snapper, and lobster, either baked, steamed or fried, are typically available.

All come with bowls of nutty-tasting brown rice and crisp salad. Simple but excellent.

🕐 Open noon–midnight
🚫 No credit cards

SINAI INTERIOR

🏨 ST. CATHERINE'S TOURIST VILLAGE
$$$$–$$$
ST. CATHERINE'S VILLAGE
TEL 069/470 324
FAX 069/470 325
The resort consists of stone bungalows on a rocky hillside about a mile (1.5 km) from St. Catherine's Monastery. All rooms are air-conditioned, but not all have their own bathroom.

🛈 118 🔆 ≈ AE, V

🏨 AUBERGE ST. CATHERINE
$$$
ST. CATHERINE'S MONASTERY
TEL/FAX 069/470 353
This basic hostel is actually part of the monastery complex and was originally intended to provide lodgings for pilgrims. It has recently been overhauled and now offers 150 beds in single, double, and triple rooms on a dinner-bed-and-breakfast basis.

🛈 52 🚫 V

SOMA BAY

🏨 SHERATON SOMA BAY RESORT
$$$$
SOMA BAY
TEL 065/545 845
FAX 065/545 885
E-MAIL salessomabay@sheraton.com
Located 32 miles (52 k.m) south of Hurghada, Soma Bay is a new resort complex dominated by this enormous hotel, built to resemble an ancient Egyptian temple. The Sheraton has every imaginable amenity, including an 18-hole golf course.

🛈 310 🔆 ≈ 🚫 All major cards

SHOPPING IN EGYPT

The best shopping in Egypt is at the bazaar, or *souq*. These places overflow with gold and silver jewelry, hieroglyphic paintings, cotton goods, alabaster figurines, copper- and brassware, musical instruments, and wooden boxes inlaid with mother-of-pearl.

Biggest and most famous of the souqs is Cairo's Khan al-Khalili, a 500-year-old maze of commerce at the heart of the old Islamic city, but there are also good examples in Alexandria, Aswan, and Port Said. These are all places that are interesting to visit even if you don't intend to buy.

When shopping in the souq, remember that the starting price is generally high, and bargaining is expected (except at fixed-price artisans' boutiques). Take your time and enjoy the sport, always remaining cordial. If you can't get a price that you think is fair, just walk away.

Tip: An Arabic phrase to remember is *la shukran* (no, thank you), effective at turning away that street peddler intent on selling you just one more set of postcards.

ANTIQUES & ANTIQUITIES

An antique is defined as an object up to a hundred years old. Antiquities are those over a hundred years old; they cannot be taken out of the country except with a license from the Department of Antiquities.

Do not be fooled into buying "antiquities." To begin with, most antiquities offered to visitors are anything but old. For example, black "basalt" figurines for sale outside many tombs at Luxor are actually painted plaster; drop one and it will disintegrate. "Ancient" scarabs are often in fact newly carved from old bone.

Shopping for antiques is more worthwhile. Hoda Shaarawi Street in downtown Cairo and

26th of July Street in Zamalek both have a number of antiques emporiums that are fun to browse. In Alexandria, the Attarine district is a warren of narrow alleyways all lined with cave-like establishments piled high with furniture and fittings, paintings, and historical bric-a-brac, much of it sold to the dealers by wealthy foreign families fleeing the country in the wake of the 1952 revolution.

ART GALLERIES

Several of Cairo's commercial galleries have selections of work for sale by local painters, photographers, and sculptors. Prices are often very affordable.

Cairo-Berlin Gallery
17 Yousef al-Guindi St., Downtown Cairo
Tel 02/393 1764

Mashrabia Gallery
8 Champollion St., off Tahrir Sq., Cairo
Tel 02/578 4494

Townhouse Gallery
Hussein Pasha St., off Mahmoud Bassiouni St., Downtown Cairo
Tel 02/575 5901

BOOKS

You can find excellent pictorial books of the sights of Egypt and a first-class range of more scholarly works on all things Egyptian from pharaohs to mosques. The American University in Cairo (AUC) Press has a prodigious output of quality titles sold throughout the country, as well as in its campus shops in Cairo. The AUC Press is also the English-language publisher of the works of Naguib Mahfouz (see p. 56).

Most five-star hotels have a small bookshop (where you can also usually get a selection of international press that's just a couple of days old), but other good places include:

Aboudi
Tourist Bazaar, Corniche al-Nil, Luxor
Tel 095/373 390

AUC Bookshop
Hill House, AUC Campus, Tahrir Sq., Cairo
Tel 02/797 5377

Ezbekiyya Book Market
Ezbekiyya Gardens, Midan Ataba, Downtown Cairo
A collection of booksellers housed in small cabins. The stock ranges from antiquarian volumes to textbooks, paperbacks, and magazines; much of it is English language.

Gaddis
Corniche al-Nil, next to Winter Palace Hotel, Luxor
Tel 095/372 142

Lehnert & Landrock
44 Sherif St., Downtown Cairo
Tel 02/393 5324
A small gallery upstairs sells framed prints of early 20th-century black-and-white photographs of Egypt taken by Messrs. Lehnert & Landrock.

L'Orientaliste
15 Kasr al-Nil St., Downtown Cairo
Tel 02/575 3418
Antiquarian bookshop specializing in Egypt and the Middle East. Also carries prints, maps, and old photos

CARPETS & RUGS

Unlike Morocco and Turkey, Egypt is not a big producer of carpets. What you do find, however, are brown-and-beige striped, hardwearing camel-hair rugs of Bedouin origin. These are sold in the narrow covered alleys that run south of the Al-Ghouri Mosque across the road from Khan al-Khalili in Islamic Cairo, and in some of the handicraft shops listed below. Perhaps more distinctive are the carpets belonging to the school of Wissa Wassef, whose art and teaching center lies on the road to Saqqara. Carpets, rugs, and wall hangings produced here depict rural and folkloric scenes in beiges, browns, and greens.

Wissa Wassef Art Centre
Next to the Motel Salma, Saqqara Rd., Harraniyya, 2.5 miles (4 km) south of Al-Ahram Street, Cairo
Tel 02/385 0403

CLOTHES

Cotton is Egypt's biggest cash crop, and although much of it is exported, it is possible to find quality products, including shirts, blouses, and pants, at bargain prices. Look in particular for branches of **Safari,** found in all the big malls and in some hotel shopping complexes. For quality bed linen and such, **Galerie Hathout** in downtown Cairo proudly sells Egyptian goods only, and has beautifully embroidered sheet sets (with a made-in-Egypt tag, of course), tablecloths and matching napkins, down to simple kitchen towels.

Down in Middle Egypt, just across the Nile from the town of Sohag, the village of **Akhmim** is the center of an ancient weaving tradition. Legend has it that pharaohs were buried in shrouds of Akhmim silk. Still in production, the cloth comes in deep, rich colors, with elaborate floral and paisley-style patterns. You can find it at the **Akhmim Gallery** in the arcade of the Old Winter Palace in Luxor.

For something even more exotic, what about the sequinned bras, beaded hip bands, veils, and filmy skirts that make up a belly dancer's outfit? Several specialist emporiums are devoted to dressing dancers.

Most famous is the studio of **Amira al-Kattan,** who makes costumes to order, but there are also a couple of suppliers in Cairo's Khan al-Khalili at the northernmost end of Muski Street. To complete the outfit, pick up a pair of *sagat,* or finger cymbals.

CAIRO
Amira al-Kattan
27 Basra St., Mohandiseen, Cairo
Tel 02/349 0322

Galerie Hathout
Mustafa Kamel Sq., Downtown Cairo

Safari
10 Lotfalla St., Zamalek, Cairo
Tel 02/735 1909

HANDICRAFTS

Khan al-Khalili and the souqs are the place for souvenirs, but for better quality crafts you have to look to specialist shops. Many of these are in Cairo.

CAIRO
Al-Ain Gallery
73 Hussein St., Doqqi
Tel 349 3940
A favorite for intricate metalwork lamps by designer Randa Fahmy, jewelry by Azza Fahmy, clothing and furnishings, fabrics from Akhmim, and rugs from Sinai.

Al-Khatoun
Sheikh Muhammad Abdu St., Islamic Cairo
Tel 02/514 7164
In a restored Ottoman house behind Al-Azhar Mosque, Al-Khatoun sells wrought-iron furniture made in a village just outside Cairo, soft wall hangings, glassware, and locally made leather goods.

Beit Sherif
3 Bahgat Aly St., Zamalek, Cairo
Tel 02/736 5689
This is an interior decorator's dream. It is full of old lamps, tiles, and items of wooden furniture—all the props

necessary to give your house an exotic makeover.

Khan Misr Touloun
17 Ahmed Ibn Tulun St., Islamic Cairo
Tel 02/365 2227
Opposite the Mosque of Ibn Tulun, this is a French-owned gallery selling handicrafts from the villages and oases, including wooden chests, bowls and plates, blown glass, clay figurines, scarves, and woven clothing.

Marketing Link
27 Yehia Ibrahim St., Zamalek, Cairo
Tel 02/736 5123
Here you can buy Bedouin rugs and embroidery from Sinai and the northern Western Desert, handmade paper from Muqattam, and Upper Egyptian shawls.

Nomad
14 Saraya al-Gezira St., Zamalek, Cairo
Tel 02/736 1917
On the first floor of an apartment block overlooking the Nile, Nomad specializes in jewelry and traditional Bedouin craft and costumes.

LUXOR
Egypt Crafts Center
Manshiyya St., Luxor town
This craft center offers products made by village women from all over Egypt, all of whom share in the profits.

SINAI
Aladin
Camel Hotel, Naama Bay
Tel 069/600 700 ext. 355
This shop located in the hotel specializes in Bedouin textiles and lovely Egyptian glass.

Bedouin House
St. Catherine's Village, Sinai
Tel 062/450 155
Owned and run by Bedouin women, this handicraft shop sells embroidery, bead jewelry, and small stone carvings.

JEWELRY

Egypt's gold and silver shops are concentrated in the center of Khan al-Khalili. Jewelry is sold by weight, with a little extra added for workmanship. The day's gold prices are listed in the *Egyptian Gazette*. The most popular souvenirs are gold or silver cartouches with your name engraved in hieroglyphs. Most of the shops in Khan al-Khalili can arrange to have this done.

For something far more original, artist Azza Fahmy produces individual pieces of jewelry inspired by facets of Egyptian history and culture. Her work is sold at the **Al-Ain Gallery** in Cairo (see Handicrafts, above) and at First Residence Mall (tel 02/573 7687). For chunky Bedouin jewelry, visit Nomad (see Handicrafts, above) or visit the Thursday market at Al-Arish in Northern Sinai (see p. 337).

MALLS

In bigger cities like Cairo and Alexandria, malls are becoming ever more popular places to shop. Although they contain little of interest for the visitor, they can be good places to pick up cheap cotton clothing. Being air-conditioned they also offer respite from the heat, and have food courts and cinemas.

Talk of the town is the **First Residence Mall** in the Cairo suburb of Giza, which is part of one of the most expensive bits of real estate in the country, the First Residence Towers. Shop here for Gucci and Louis Vuitton. Also pitched upscale is the **World Trade Center**, full of international brand clothing stores like Benetton and Daniel Hechter, as well as several chic restaurants. The **Ramses Hilton Mall,** beside the Ramses Hilton hotel in the city center, is more family oriented, with lots of cheap clothing and shoes.

First Residence Mall
Giza St., Giza, Cairo

Ramses Hilton Mall
Abdel Moniem Riad Sq., Cairo

World Trade Center
Corniche al-Nil, Boulaq, Cairo

PAPYRUS

Banana-leaf papyrus (see Antiques & Antiquities, above) can be bought everywhere in Egypt, typically painted in sweatshops with crude copies of pharaonic wall paintings. For this kind of quality, pay no more than 50 cents a sheet. For real papyrus, painted with some artistry, visit any of the galleries in the upscale hotels. For a wider choice, and to learn something about the process of making papyrus and its historical usage, visit one of Dr. Ragab's papyrus institutes, which are actually sales centers but with an educational spin—staff takes the trouble to explain what it is that you're buying. A good alternative in Cairo is **Said Delta Papyrus Centre** in Islamic Cairo on Al-Muizz li-Din Allah Street, north of Bab Zuweyla. It's on the third floor above a shoe shop; look for a yellow sign at first floor level.

Dr. Ragab's Papyrus Institute
Nile Corniche, Doqqi, Western Cairo
Tel 02/748 8177

PERFUME

Egypt is a big producer of many of the essences that make up French perfume, and places like Cairo's Khan al-Khalili offer a chance to pick up the scents at source. Pure essences cost anywhere from $3 to $10 per ounce. Beware though of cheaper substances, which are diluted with alcohol or oil. The essences are often sold in small decorated glass vials, which in themselves make a very attractive gift.

SOUVENIRS

Pharaonic knickknacks of all sorts fill Egypt's souqs:

Tutankhamun on a T-shirt, Nefertiti lampshades, pyramid paperweights, Abu Simbel painted on ashtrays. Some of the items are more worthwhile than others; there are attractive castings of artifacts from the Egyptian Museum, cute little scarabs, and interesting jewelry inspired by ancient Egypt. All of this can be found in Cairo's Khan al-Khalili souq in the old Islamic quarter.

The Khan is also a good source of more inventive mementos of Egypt. It's the place to find marquetry backgammon boards for game enthusiasts. Cooks and kitchen genies might appreciate a copper or brass coffeepot and set of cups from the **Coppersmith's Market.** Many visitors choose to lug home *sheeshas,* the cumbersome water pipes (buy from Khan al-Khalili, around the Bayn al-Qasreen area), but remember you'll also need a plentiful supply of tobacco and the little pottery tobacco holders.

Children back home might appreciate a Monopoly board game (in Arabic, of course) or a hieroglyph stamp set, available from the many toy stores that line Muski, the market street running between Khan al-Khalili and downtown Cairo.

SPICES

Khan al-Khalili in Cairo and the souqs in Luxor and Aswan are the places for spices. They come in every conceivable color, and the smell around the stalls is just fantastic. Generally they are fresher and better quality than any of the packaged spices you'll find in the West, and considerably cheaper. Look for black pepper *(filfil),* cumin *(kamoon),* saffron *(zaafaran),* and a purplish dried leaf, which is hibiscus; boiled up, strained, and sugared, this makes *karkadeh,* a delicious sweet crimson drink, served chilled with ice.

ACTIVITIES IN EGYPT

Traditionally, activities in Egypt have focused solely on the sea, in the form of diving and water sports. In recent years, however, tour operators, in conjunction with the Egyptian authorities, have been looking to diversify and to broaden the country's appeal. Desert safaris are one exciting recent development, with several agencies and individuals now making accessible dramatic sandy landscapes previously little seen by visitors.

More unexpected is the rise of golf. This is, after all, a blisteringly hot country with a shortage of fresh water and cultivatable land. Despite these factors, the Egyptian Ministry of Tourism is determinedly grooming the country as a golf holiday destination, with the creation of several courses in recent years and more on the drawing board.

BALLOONING

In Luxor two companies offer early morning balloon flights over the monuments of the West Bank. A champagne breakfast is served as part of the package, and the cost is about $200 per person. Reservations can be made through reception at all the larger hotels, or directly.

Balloons Over Egypt
Tel 095/376 515

Hod Hod Suleiman
Tel 095/370 116

DESERT SAFARIS

Egypt's stunning desert scenery remains one of the country's greatest little-seen treasures. Few visitors get to experience the magnificent sandscapes because of the difficulty of getting out to these remote areas. However, a growing number of local operators are now offering trips into Sinai and the far more impressive Western Desert. Some of these are simply half-day expeditions from popular resorts, others are true safaris of three or four days, undertaken in 4WD vehicles with tents for accommodations.

In Sinai, local Bedouin lead treks into the interior from resorts such as Naama Bay, Dahab, and Nuweiba. Trips usually last half a day and can be arranged at short notice by your hotel. Similarly,

there are some wonderful treks with Bedouin guides to be done from St. Catherine's village (see p. 338). Possibly the best of the Sinai operators is Abanoub Travel, based in Nuweiba. The company runs jeep tours that cost about $35 per person per day, including food. Camel treks are about $10 more.

Abanoub Travel
Tel 062/520 201
Fax 062/520 206

To see the most spectacular desert scenery, it is necessary to head out into the Western Desert, to the oases. Many hotels in Siwa, Farafra, and Dakhla organize one-day and overnight expeditions. Guests staying at the exclusive Adrere Amellal (see p. 369) in Siwa get desert exploration as part of the package. Visitors on a tighter budget could take advantage of the trips offered by the Al-Badawiyya Hotel (see p. 368) in Farafra; the Bedouin brothers who own the hotel arrange highly recommended treks throughout the Western Desert and other areas of Egypt.

Amr Shannon
Tel 02/518 6130

Based in Cairo, Amr Shannon is an artist who has been leading small groups out into the deserts for more than 20 years. You need to provide your own camping equipment and 4WD, but Shannon can help with

rentals. He takes groups of up to 12 people at a flat rate of $300 per person per day. Trips are made several times a year and must be booked well in advance.

Max Adventure Travel
Tel 02/303 5125
Fax 02/303 6123

Max Adventure Travel takes groups out to the Western Desert, and south Sinai, and it is not necessary to have your own transport.

DIVING

Egypt's Red Sea is a diver's paradise of beautiful clear waters filled with teeming marine life. It attracts thousands of visitors each year. Diving is concentrated around the southern tip of the Sinai Peninsula, centered on the resorts of Dahab, Naama Bay and Sharm al-Sheikh, and especially around the fabulous Ras Mohammed National Park. The other big dive center is the Red Sea coast resort of Hurghada. Serious divers head farther south to a few scattered dive centers along the barely developed stretch of coast down toward Marsa Alam, where the best reefs are found around the proliferation of offshore islands and reefs.

A vast number of dive clubs cater for visitors wanting to explore underwater worlds. Almost every large hotel in Sinai and on the Red Sea coast has its own dive center. These places offer introductory dives for first-timers, accredited courses for those who want to get into the sport, as well as more ambitious expeditions for the experienced diver. Some clubs also organize dive safaris to remote sites ranging from one night to two weeks. All equipment is provided. Most clubs are well-equipped and staffed by professionals, but not all, so take care when choosing who to dive with. Prices vary, but not greatly.

Don't choose a dive center purely on the grounds of cost, Most visitors organize diving once they arrive in Egypt, but if you wish to make some inquiries in advance, following are a few recommended outfits. The website www.red-sea.com has an index of dive centers.

African Divers
Sharm al-Sheikh/Naama Bay
Tel /fax 062/660 307

Aquanaut Red Sea
Hurghada
Tel 065/549 891

Camel Dive Club
Sharm al-Sheikh/Naama Bay
Tel 062/600 700

Divers International
Dahab, Hurghada, & Sharm al-Sheikh/Naama Bay
Tel 062/600 865

Oonas Diving Center
Sharm al-Sheikh/Naama Bay
Tel 062/600 581

Red Sea Diving College
Sharm al-Sheikh/Naama Bay
Tel 062/600 313

Red Sea Diving Safari
Southern Red Sea coast
Tel 02/337 9942

FISHING

Surprisingly, the prize place for fishing in Egypt is not the Nile or the Red or Mediterranean Seas, but Lake Nasser. The silt-rich depths of this artificially created lake are home to fish of massive proportions, particularly the Nile perch, examples of which have been caught that weigh up to 220 pounds (100 kg) Because the lake is difficult to get to, and is completely uninhabited, specialist help is required to mount a fishing expedition. There are two companies that offer either boat trips or overland safaris:

The African Angler
Tel 097/316 052 or 02/394 7735

Wild Nuba
Tel /fax 097/309 191

GOLF

The British introduced golf to Egypt back in the 19th century. After the 1952 revolution, when the British were sent packing, there was no one left to play. However, in the last decade there has been a renewed interest in the sport among Egypt's nouveau riche. New suburban desert housing developments on the fringes of Cairo are being built with attached courses, and there are no less than three "golf villages" along the Desert Highway that connects Cairo and Alexandria.

Al-Gouna Golf Course
Al Gouna Resort, Red Sea coast
Tel 065/549 702

Dreamland Golf Resort
6th of October City,
Cairo–Alexandria Desert Hwy.
Tel 011/400 577

Luxor Royal Valley Golf Club
Tel 095/380 522

Mirage City Golf Club
Cairo–Alexandria Desert Hwy.
Tel 02/408 5200

Mövenpick Jolieville Golf Resort
Sharm al-Sheikh
Tel 062/600 635

Pyramids Golf & Country Club
Cairo–Alexandria Desert Hwy.
Tel 02/335 3688

SAILING

A highlight of a trip to Egypt is drifting on the Nile in a felucca, the small, lateen-sailed boats that have been in use since ancient times. They're frequently portrayed in tomb paintings. Boats and their captains are found for rent by the hour all along the Nile, from Corniche-side landings in central Cairo right down to Aswan.

Although taking to the Nile at sunset is a wonderful end to a day's sight-seeing in the capital, the best place to enjoy the languid pleasures of sailing is in Aswan, where the riverside scenery is at its most stunning, and you can employ the boat for an afternoon or evening of island-hopping. Prices should be negotiated for the boat per hour; for an idea of the going rates, check with the local tourist office.

The more adventurous might consider a trip of two or three days on a felucca, sailing from Aswan downriver to Edfu. Days are spent visiting sights en route (including Kom Ombo), often with a stop off for tea at your captain's village somewhere along the way. Food is bought in the market before departure and prepared by the captain. Nights are spent on the boat or camping on an island. It's a very basic existence with no facilities or comforts, but it makes for a memorable experience. Arriving at Edfu, you can catch a bus back to Aswan or onward to Luxor.

Feluccas carry a minimum of six passengers and a maximum of eight, and the cost per person is about $15 to Edfu, although this is negotiable. There is also a small fee for police registration and you must buy your own food. Finding a good captain is essential; it is wise to consult with the local tourist office.

Hermes Travel
Tel 02/303 5105
Fax 02/345 4711
Hermes Travel operates a 50-foot (15 m) yacht on Lake Nasser, with five double cabins. In addition to sailing to all the temples on the lake (see p. 314) on request it can also be captained to the Eastern Desert protectorate of Wadi al-Alagi to link up with 4WDs that can take guests across the desert to the usually off-limits Red Sea port of Berenice. Prices are in the range of $50 per person per day.

ENTERTAINMENT IN EGYPT

Outside of Cairo, visitors will find themselves relying on hotels for their evening entertainments, especially in Luxor and Aswan. Most of the larger hotels put on nightly floor shows of folkloric dancing or belly dancing, or there's always the bar, and sometimes a disco. Cairo, on the other hand, has a vibrant cultural scene with plenty of films, music performances, nightclubs, and bars. For information on what's on, seek out the glossy monthly magazine *Egypt Today*, on sale at most hotel bookstores, which has extensive coverage of events throughout the country.

BARS, CAFÉS, & CLUBS

The majority of Egyptians are Muslims and do not drink. So while alcohol is available, it is generally restricted to places frequented by tourists, such as hotel bars and cafés and upscale restaurants.

CAIRO

Bullseye 32 Geddah St., Mohandiseen, tel 02/361 6888. This is an English pub where you can play darts, as the name hints.

Cairo Jazz Club 197 26th of July St., Mohandiseen, tel 02/345 9939. Jazz and blues are played here nightly.

Crazy House Cairo Land, 1 Salah Salem Rd., Old Cairo, tel 02/366 1082. Stomp through the night at this enormous disco, which opens at midnight.

Deals Sayed al-Bakry St., Zamalek, tel 02/736 0502. For a quieter night out, try this neighborhood bar.

Harry's Bar Marriott Hotel, Saraya al-Gezira, Zamalek, tel 02/735 8888. You can let your hair down at this popular pub with karaoke and DJs.

Jackie's Nile Hilton, Tahrir Sq., Downtown, tel 02/578 0444. Dance venues come and go, but Jackie's has long been the most popular disco in town.

Le Tabasco 8 Amman Sq., Mohandiseen, tel 02/336 5583. For more sedate revelers, this is a fashionable bar/restaurant.

ALEXANDRIA

Cap d'Or 4 Adib St., off Salah Salem St., Downtown, tel 03/487 5177. Bar with seafood snacks

Havana corner of Horeyya and Orabis Sts., Attarine, tel 03/487 0661. The best bar in Egypt

Monty's Bar second floor, Cecil Hotel, Saad Zaghloul Sq., tel 03/480 7224. This classy hotel bar is named for the British general (Montgomery).

Spitfire Bar 7 Bursa al-Qadima St., off Saad Zaghloul St., Downtown, tel 03/480 6503. Seafarers' bar

LUXOR

King Dude Gaddis Hotel, Khaled ibn al-Walid St., tel 095/382 838. There are regular karaoke nights in the bar.

King's Head Pub Khaled ibn al-Walid St., tel 095/371 249. An English-style pub with meals, darts, and billiards

Mars Bar Venus Hotel, Youssef Hassan St., tel 095/372 625. Draft beer, satellite TV, a pool table, and Western music are all to be found here.

Pub 2000 Khaled ibn al-Walid St. This English-style pub pulls in the visitors with its popular happy hour.

ASWAN

Aswan Moon Corniche al-Nil, tel 097/316 108. This restaurant by day becomes boozier as the night wears on.

Isis Hotel Corniche, tel 097/315 200. There's a disco here nightly.

Royal Restaurant, Pub, & Coffeeshop Corniche al-Nil. Beers, snacks, Internet, and satellite TV.

RED SEA & SINAI

Bus Stop Bar & Disco Sanafir Hotel, Naama Bay, Sinai, tel 069/600 197. It's the liveliest place in town.

Café Bedouin Sharm Panorama, Naama Bay, Sinai. No alcohol but romantic and quirky late-night venue for tea and a waterpipe

Hard Rock Café Naama Bay, Sinai, tel 069/602 665. Rock memorabilia and burgers

Papa's Bar Attached to Rossi Pizza, Sigala, Hurghada (see p. 375), tel 0101/154 7851. A place to enjoy live music, DJs, and party spirit

Peanuts Bar Market Place Complex, near Three Corners Hotel, Ad-Dahar, Hurghada. Loud and beery, the bar is open 24 hours.

Pirates Bar Hilton Fayruz, Naama Bay, tel 069/600 136. This terrace bar with mini-lights is a big hit with divers.

BELLY DANCING

The best dancers perform at the nightclubs attached to Cairo's five-star hotels. Venues such as the **Haroun el-Rashid Club** (Semiramis InterContinental Hotel, Garden City, Cairo, tel 02/795 7171) and **La Belle Epoque** (Le Meridien Cairo, Rhoda, Cairo, tel 02/362 1717) attract the biggest names, including Dina, Lucy, and the irrepressible Fifi Abdou. But a night in the presence of the ladies does not come cheap. A seat for such a show costs about $50 a head, with buffet included.

At these belly dancing performances, the main act generally doesn't appear until at least 2 a.m., and the band doesn't call it a night until the sun is creeping up over the Nile. Far less accomplished dancers can be seen at most hotels and tourist restaurants throughout the country, for considerably less cash.

CASINOS

Most of Egypt's international five-star hotels have casinos. These are open to non-Egyptians only, which means that you have to show your passport to gain admission. All games are conducted in U.S. dollars or other major foreign currencies, with a minimum stake of a dollar. Smart casual attire is required.

FOLKLORIC DANCE

Folkloric dance often forms part of dinner entertainment at hotels and tourist restaurants, especially in Upper Egypt.

In Luxor the most elaborate shows are put on at the "Fellah's Tent" in the Mövenpick Jolieville (Crocodile Island, tel 095/374 855, fax 095/374 936 adm. $30) and each Saturday at the Sheraton for the "Nubian Night" (Khaled ibn al-Walid St., tel 095/374 544, adm. $25). Performances at these two places include belly dancing and "stick dancing," performed by men in a highly stylized pantomime of combat involving clashing staves. The price of admission includes a buffet meal; drinks are extra. Stick dancing is also on the agenda at Aswan's Nubian Restaurant (Essa Island) (see p. 373), where there is no admission or cover charge.

There are also a few cultural venues with regular performances, including the municipality-run **Palace of Culture** (17 Corniche al-Nil, tel 097/313 390) in Aswan, and the **Sayyid Darwish Concert**

Hall (Gamal ad-Din al-Afghani St., off Al-Ahram St., Giza, Cairo, tel 02/560 2473) in Cairo. See also the Sufi performances described on page 105.

FOR CHILDREN

Egypt is a very child-friendly place, and the locals really warm to youngsters. Keeping them occupied, though, is another story. In Cairo, kids will enjoy **Dr Ragab's Pharaonic Village** (see p. 131). A trip to **Cairo Zoo** (see p. 131) is less inspiring, although unlike Western zoos, visitors can feed the animals and that can be fun. Donkeys and camels can be ridden at the Pyramids.

MUSIC

Egypt's premier music venue, for classical Western and classical Arabic music, is the Cairo **Opera House** (Tahrir St., Gezira, Cairo, tel 02/737 0601) on the island of Gezira. Its main hall hosts regular performances from a variety of visiting international and local artists. On such occasions a jacket and tie are compulsory for men. The small hall has nightly recitals by ensembles, quartets, and soloists, and is also used by the Cairo Symphony Orchestra, which gives concerts there every Saturday from September to mid-June.

In Islamic Cairo, music evenings, and sometimes theater performances, are occasionally held at the **House of Zeinab Khatoun** (Mohamed Abdu St., Islamic Cairo, tel 02/510 4174) and the **Al-Ghouri Complex** (Al-Azhar St., Islamic Cairo, tel 02/510 0823, see p. 96), especially during Ramadan when there are nightly shows.

In Alexandria, the **Sayyid Darwish Theater** (22 Horeyya St., Alexandria, tel 03/486 5602) hosts occasional classical Western and classical Arabic concerts, often organized by the French, Italian,

or German consulates.

In Aswan, the Palace of Culture (see Folkloric Dance) sometimes hosts performances of Nubian and other local musicians.

SOUND-AND-LIGHT

Many major sights in Egypt present an evening *son et lumiere*, or sound-and-light show, in which the monuments are illuminated by floodlight while a recorded voice narrates history and legends. It is often worth attending for the chance to see these places by moonlight. Sound-and-light shows take place at the Pyramids, the Temple of Karnak in Luxor, Philae at Aswan, and Abu Simbel. Timetables of performances are displayed at the sights or visit www.sound-light.egypt.com.

SPORT

Soccer is the national sport and nothing else comes close in inspiring passions. On big match days, streets empty as fans crowd into coffeehouses to watch the action. The two top clubs both hail from Cairo (Ahly and Zamalek) and meetings of these teams are the high points of the sporting calendar. Major games are played at Cairo Stadium in the northeast of the city, but due to demand tickets can be hard to get hold of. Still, it's fun to join the crowd in the coffeehouse.

Squash also has a sizable following and is the sport of choice of the Egyptian president, Hosni Mubarak. The annual Al-Ahram International Squash Tournament draws competitors from all over the world to compete in glass-enclosed courts set up beside the Pyramids. The Pyramids also feature as the start and finishing point in the annual Pharaoh's Rally. Held every October, this is a desert race for souped up 4WDs and trail bikes.

LANGUAGE GUIDE

The official language in Egypt is Arabic, but English is taught in schools and most people speak a little, especially in Cairo and in the areas with many tourists. However, any attempts on your part to speak only a few words in Arabic will be met with an enthusiastic response.

The following list gives a phonetic transliteration from the Arabic script. Words or letters in parentheses indicate the different form that is required when a woman is speaking or being addressed.

GREETINGS & COMMON WORDS

yes aywa, naam
no la
please min fadlak (fadlik)
thank you shukran
you're welcome afwan
hello salaam aleikum
  response aleikum al-salaam
goodbye maa al-salaama
good morning sabaah al-kheir
  response sabaah al-nur
how are you? izzayak (izzayik)
fine kwayyis(a) al-hamdulillah
God willing inshallah
no problem/don't worry
  maalish
tomorrow bukra
tomorrow morning bukra sobh
after tomorrow bade bukra
today inharda
sorry ana aasif (asfa)

do you speak English?
  bititkallim(i) Ingleezi?
I don't understand Ana mish
  faahem (fahma)
I don't know Arabic Ana mish
  aarif (arfa) arabi
go away imshee
leave me alone bass kifaaya
don't/enough balesh
slowly/bit by bit shawaya
  shawaya

EMERGENCY
help! al-haooni!
thief! haraami!
police bulees
hospital mustashfa

where is the toilet? feyn el-
  twalet?
I'm sick ana ayyaan(a)
we need a doctor ayzeen duktor

SHOPPING
shop dukkan
market/bazaar souk
I would like ana eis(a)

I'm just looking ana batfarrag
  bass
how much? bikam?
may I? mumkin?
that's too much da ketir awi
change fakka
do you have change? maak
  fakka?
no change maafish fakka

good kwayyis
bad mish kwayyis
big kebir
small sughayyar
hot sukn
cold baarid
many kitiir
few olayyel
up foq
down taht
more kamaan
enough kefaya

GETTING ABOUT
street sharia
square midan
stop here hina kwayyis
straight ala tuul
left shimel
right yemeen
next to gamb
behind wara
ticket tazkara
wait istanna
where is the...? fein el...?
how many kilometers? kaam
  kilu?
airport mataar
boat markeb
bridge kubri
bus station mahattat al-autobees
car sayara
church kineesa
embassy sifaara
hotel fonduk
hospital mustashfa
museum mathaf
post office busta
railroad station mahatta

NUMBERS
0 sifr
1 wahid
2 itneyn
3 telaata
4 arbaah
5 khamsa
6 sittah
7 sabbaah
8 tamanya
9 tisah
10 ashara
11 hidaashar
12 itnaashar
13 telataashar
14 arbaatashar
15 khamastaashar
16 sittaashar
17 sabbahtaashar
18 tamantaashar
19 tisahtaashar
20 ashreen
21 wahid waashreen
22 itneyn waashreen
30 telaateen
40 arbaheen
50 khamseen
100 maya
200 mitayn
1,000 alf

EATING OUT
what's that? eh da (di)?
bill al-hisab
the bill please al-hisab lau
  samaht
breakfast iftar
dinner asha

MENU READER

baba ghanoug purée of eggplant, grilled and mashed, seasoned with tahina, olive oil and garlic

felafel (taamiyya in Cairo) mashed broad beans and spices balled up and deep fried

fisiikh salty dried fish

fuul beans mashed into a thick, lumpy paste, usually ladled into a piece of pita-type bread as a sandwich

gebda liver, often chickens' liver (gebda firekh), usually sautéed with lemon or garlic

gibna cheese

    gibna beyda soft, white, like feta

    gibna ruumi hard, yellow, and sharp

hummus paste of ground chickpeas mixed with olive oil

kellawi kidneys

kibbeh minced lamb, burgul wheat, and pine seeds shaped into a patty and deep-fried

kushari rice, macaroni, black lentils, fried onions, and tomato sauce

labneh cheesy, yogurt paste that is often heavily flavored with garlic or mint

mashi stuffed vegetable leaves, typically filled with ground meat, a spicy mix of rice, chopped tomatoes, onion, and spices

shwarma strips of lamb or chicken sliced from a spit, sizzled on a hot plate with chopped tomatoes and garnish, and then stuffed in a pocket of pita-type bread

tahina sesame seed paste

zeitoun olives

MAIN COURSES

bamya tomatoey stew of okra sometimes with lamb

fatteh boiled lamb or chicken served over bread and rice in a garlicky, vinegary sauce

firakh chicken, usually spit roasted

kabob skewered, flame-grilled chunks of meat, usually lamb

kofta ground meat peppered with spices, shaped into small sausages, skewered and grilled

hamam pigeon, usually served stuffed with rice and spices

loubiah French beans cooked in a tomato sauce as a stew with other vegetables and lamb

molokhiyya gluinous soup made from the molokhiyya leaf, often served with rabbit

samak fish

shish tawouk flame-grilled kabob of marinated, spiced chicken, onions, peppers, and tomato

tagen oven-baked dish containing vegetables and/or meat

FISH & SEAFOOD

barbuuni red mullet

buuri grey mullet

gambaari shrimp

istakooza lobster

kaborya crabs

kalamari/subeit squid

muusa sole

salamuun salmon

tuuna tuna

SWEETS & DESSERTS

atayif filled sweet crêpe, deep-fried and dipped in syrup

baklawa layers of wafer-thin phyllo pastry filled with crushed nuts and pistachios and drenched in syrup

konafa vermicelli pastry on a soft cheese or cream base

muhalabiyya milk cream thickened by corn flour or ground rice, often flavored with rose water and served with chopped almonds or coconut sprinkled on

Umm Ali Egyptian version of bread pudding: layers of pastry, with nuts and raisins, soaked in cream and milk, and baked in the oven

FRUIT

ananas pineapple

balah date

batikh watermelon

bortuaan orange

fraula strawberry

gooz al-hind coconut

guafa guava

khookh peach

kummitra pear

limoon lemon

manga mango

mishmish apricot

moez banana

rumaan pomegranate

tufaah apple

tiin fig

DRINKS

ahwa coffee

    ahwa saada with no sugar

    ahwa mazbuut with medium sugar

    ahwa ziyaada very sweet

shai tea

    shai libton teabag tea

mayya water

assir juice

nibiit wine

biira beer

sahlab milky drink thickened with the powdered bulb of a type of orchid, and flavored with chopped nuts and cinnamon

karkade made from boiled hibiscus leaves, served hot or cold

yansoon hot drink made from aniseed

BREAKFAST

ai'ish bread in general

ai'ish baladi wholewheat bread, comes in big round disks

ai'ish shammi white flour bread, like pita

beid egg

ishta cream

laban milk

zabaadi yogurt

zibda butter

GLOSSARY

GLOSSARY

abu saint (literally, father of)
ain well, spring
Aten sun disk, worshiped by
    Akhenaten

bab gate or door
baksheesh tip
baladi adjective meaning
    "country" or "local"
bawab porter or doorman,
    common to all Egyptian
    apartment blocks
bayt house
bir spring, well
birket lake
bismillah in the name of God
Books of the Dead ancient
    theological compositions that
    were the subject of most of
    the colorful paintings and
    reliefs on tomb walls
burg tower

calèche horse-drawn carriage
caliph Islamic ruler
canopic jars pottery jars which
    held the embalmed internal
    organs and viscera of a
    mummified body
caravanserai merchants' inn
cartouche oblong figure
    enclosing the hieroglyphs of
    royal or divine names
corniche seafront or riverfront
    promenade

deir monastery

eid feast
emir Islamic ruler
false door fake, seemingly half-
    open *ka* door in a tomb wall
    which enabled the pharaoh's
    spirit, or life force, to come
    and go at will
fatwa a religious ruling
fellaheen rural workers who
    make up the majority of
    Egypt's population.
felucca sailing boat

galabiyya full-length robe worn
    by men
gebel mountain
gezira island

hajj pilgrimage to Mecca
hamman bathhouse
hantour horse-drawn carriage

haramlik women's quarters
hieroglyphs ancient Egyptian
    form of writing, which used
    pictures and symbols to
    represent objects, words or
    sounds
hypostyle hall hall in which the
    roof is supported by columns

imam prayer leader in a mosque
iwan vaulted hall, opening into a
    central court, in the madrassa
    of a mosque

ka spirit, or "double," of a living
    person
khan another name for a
    caravanserai
khanqah Sufi monastery
khedive Egyptian viceroy under
    Ottoman suzerainty
    (1867–1914)
kom heap of rubble over an
    ancient settlement
Koran Muslim holy book
kuttab Quranic school

madrassa school where Islamic
    law is taught
mammisi ancient Egyptian
    symbolic birth house
mashrabiyya ornate carved
    wooden panel or screen,
    typical of Islamic architecture
Masr Egypt (also means Cairo)
mastaba Arabic word for
    "bench"; a mud-brick
    structure above tombs from
    which the pyramids were
    developed
mihrab niche in the wall of a
    mosque that indicates the
    direction of Mecca
minbar pulpit in a mosque
moulid festival celebrating the
    birthday of a local saint or
    holy person
muezzin mosque official who
    calls the faithful to prayer five
    times a day from the minaret

papyrus paper-like material
    made from the pith of the
    papyrus reed
pasha Ottoman title bestowed
    on politicians and men of rank
pharaoh ancient Egyptian ruler;
    strictly speaking the term
    only came into use in the
    New Kingdom, the rulers
    before that being kings.

pylon monumental gateway at
    the entrance to a temple
pyramid texts paintings and
    reliefs on the walls of the
    internal rooms and burial
    chamber of pyramids

qasr palace

Ramadan holy month during
    which Muslims fast from
    sunrise to sunset

sabil public drinking fountain
Saidi a native of Upper Egypt
sarcophagus large stone coffin
    that typically encases smaller
    wooden coffins
scarab dung beetle regarded as
    sacred in ancient Egypt and
    represented on amulets or in
    hieroglyphs as a symbol of the
    sun-god Re
serdab stone chamber
    containing a life-size, painted
    statue of the dead pharaoh. It
    was provided so that the
    deceased's *ka* could
    communicate with the
    outside world.
sharia street, literally "way." Also
    laws based on Koranic
    precepts.
sharm bay
solar bark wooden boat placed
    in or around the pharaoh's
    tomb; the symbolic vessel of
    transport for his journey into
    the eternal afterlife
stela (pl: stelae) stone slab
    decorated with inscriptions
    or figures
Sufi follower of an Islamic
    mystical order that
    emphasizes dancing, chanting,
    and trances in order to attain
    unity with God
sultan secular title meaning ruler
    or king

tell mound of earth covering an
    ancient site

umm mother of
Upper Egypt general term for
    the country south of Cairo

wadi desert watercourse, dry
    except in the rainy season
wikala another name for a
    caravanserai

WHO'S WHO

(For more pharaohs see Timeline of the Pharaohs pp. 54–55)

Akhenaten (R.1352–1336 B.C.)
Formerly Amenhotep IV, the pharaoh who ushered in a revolutionary period in ancient Egyptian history when he replaced worship of the traditional pantheon of gods with the cult of the sun disk Aten

Al-Ghouri, Sultan Qansuh (died 1516)
Penultimate Mamluk sultan, killed in battle with the Ottoman Turks; left behind a fine architectural legacy.

Ali, Muhammad (1769–1849)
Albanian mercenary who seized power in 1805 in the wake of Napoleon's failed Egyptian expedition, establishing a dynasty that would rule until toppled by the 1952 republican coup

Amenhotep III (R.1390–1382 B.C.)
The Sun King whose 38-year reign represented the zenith of ancient Egypt's power and prestige

Belzoni, Giovanni (1778–1823)
Italian strongman turned ancient Egyptian treasure hunter who supplied the British Museum with key pieces for its ancient Egypt collection

Carnarvon, Lord (1866–1923)
British Egyptologist who was the patron and associate of archaeologist Howard Carter in the discovery of the tomb of Tutankhamun (1922)

Carter, Howard (1873–1939)
British archaeologist who made one of the richest and most celebrated contributions to Egyptology: the discovery of the largely intact tomb of Tutankhamun

Champollion, Jean-François (1790–1832)
French linguist who cracked the code of hieroglyphics when he deciphered the Rosetta Stone

Cleopatra (69–30 B.C.)
To be precise, Cleopatra VII, queen of Egypt and last of the Ptolemaic line. Defeated by the Romans who then absorbed Egypt into their empire

De Lesseps, Ferdinand (1805–1894)
French diplomat famous for building the Suez Canal (1859–1869)

Eugénie, Empress (1826–1920)
Wife of Napoleon III and empress of France (1853–1870) who was guest of honor at the grand celebrations for the inauguration of the Suez Canal

Farouk (1920–1965)
Playboy king of Egypt, reigning from 1936 to 1952 when his administration was brought to an end by a republican coup

Ismail Pasha (1830–1895)
Descendant of Muhammad Ali who ruled Egypt from 1863 to 1879 and presided over the building of modern Cairo and the grand celebrations for the inauguration of the Suez Canal

Mahfouz, Naguib (born 1911)
Egyptian novelist who was awarded the Nobel Prize for Literature in 1988

Mariette, Auguste (1821–1881)
First serving head of the Egyptian Antiquities Service and founder of Cairo's Egyptian Museum

Mubarak, Muhammad Hosni (born 1928)
Current president of the Arab Republic of Egypt

Napoleon Bonaparte (1769–1821)
French general who led an army of soldiers, scientists and artists to Egypt (1798–1803). In military terms the expedition was a failure, but it launched the fledgling science of Egyptology.

Nasser, Gamal Abdel (1918–1970) Charismatic army officer who was one of the ringleaders of the 1952 coup, prime minister (1954–56) and then president (1956–1970) of Egypt

Nefertari (ca 1300–1250 B.C.)
Principal wife of Ramses II, often depicted at his side

Nefertiti (ca 1380–1340 B.C.)
Prinicpal wife of Akhenaten

Ramses II (R.1279–1213 B.C.)
Mightiest of the New Kingdom pharaohs and a supreme egotist responsible for some of ancient Egypt's grandest monuments

Sadat, Anwar (1918–1981)
Succeeded Nasser as Egyptian president and signed the Camp David peace deal with Israel. Assassinated by Islamic extremists

Said Pasha (1822–1863)
Descendant of Muhammad Ali who ruled Egypt from 1854 to 1863 and gave the go-ahead for the construction of the Suez Canal

Tuthmose III (R.1479–1425 B.C.)
The "Napoleon of Ancient Egypt" who led numerous successful military campaigns into Palestine and Syria

Umm Kolthum (1904–1975)
The voice of 20th-century Egypt and the Arab world's greatest ever singer. Known reverentially as Al-Sitt, or The Lady

CAIRO METRO MAP

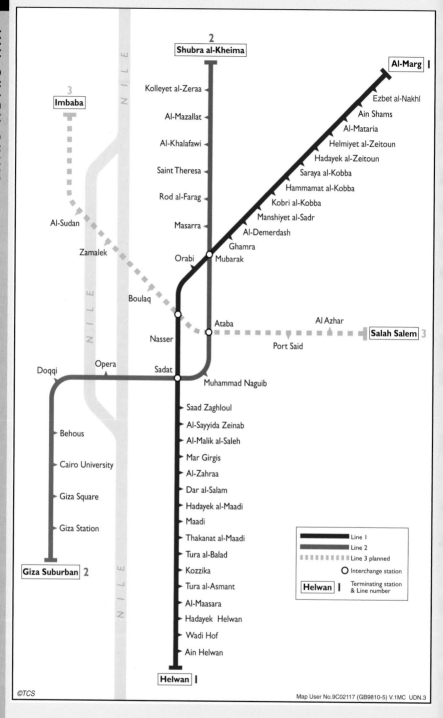

INDEX

Bold page numbers indicate illustrations.

A

Abdelsalam, Shadi 60
Abu al-Abbas al-Mursi Mosque 196
Abu al-Haggag Mosque 238, **240-41**
Abu Mena 201
Abu Qir 196
Abu Simbel 32, 265, 316-17, 318-22, **318, 319, 320-21, 322**
  enthroned colossi 320-21
  relocation 316-17
  Sacred Sanctuary 322
  Temple of Hathor 322
Abu Sir (south of Giza) 144, **146-47**, 146-47
  Pyramid of Neferirkare 147
  Pyramid of Nyuserra 147
  Pyramid of Sahure 146-47
  shaft tombs 147
Abu Sir (Western Desert) 200-201
Abydos 29, 31, 226-27
  Osireion 227
  Temple of Seti I **226-27**, 227
Actium, Battle of 35
Ad-Din, Hamza 296
Aga Khan 305
Aghurmi 204
Agiba Beach 202
Agricultural Museum 141
Ahmose I 31, 54
Ain al-Sarru 209
Ain al-Wadi 209
Air travel 351, 352
Akhenaten (Amenhotep IV) 32, 55, 76, 218, 219, 220, 221, **245**, 245
Akhenaten Center of Arts 128
Akhmim 225
Al-Alamein 201, 201
Al-Ansari, Sherine 56
Al-Aqmar Mosque 101
Al-Arish 336-37
Al-Atrash, Farid 59
Al-Azhar Mosque 90, 96-97, **96-97, 98-99**
Al-Ghouri 96, 104
Al-Ghouriyya 104
Al-Gouna 329
Al-Hady al-Gazzar, Abd 62, 125
Al-Hakim Mosque 90, 100, 101
Al-Hussein Mosque 92
Al-Kamil 115
Al-Kharga 212
  Archaeological Museum 212
  Temple of Hibis 212
  Temple/fortress of an-

Nadura 212
Al-Milga 339
Al-Muayyad Mosque 104
Al-Muzawaka tombs 211
Al-Nasir Muhammad 103
Al-Nasir Muhammad Mosque 113
Al-Qahira see Cairo
Al-Qasr 211
Al-Qusiya 224
Al-Rifai Mosque 109
Al-Sadawi, Nawal 16
Al-Salam Canal 27
Alcohol 66, 354, 359
Alexander the Great 33, 178, 181, 190, 198, 204-205, 241
Alexandria **18-19**, 177-96
  Abu Qir 196
  An-Nabi Daniel Street 190
  Anfushi 196
  Anfushi Necropolis 196
  Attarine Street 190
  Bibliotheca Alexandrina 192, **192**
  Catacombs of Kom al-Shuqafa 184-85, **184**
  Cecil Hotel 188, **188**
  Cinema Metro 190
  Constantine Cavafy Museum 189
  Corniche **191**
  Durrell's House 196
  Eastern Harbor 182-83, **182-83**
  Fortress of Qaitbey 186-87, **186-87**
  Great Synagogue 189
  Greco-Roman Museum 180-81
  history 33-34, 178
  hotels and restaurants 366-68
  Kom al-Dikka **180-81**, 181
  Mahmoud Said Museum 194
  maps 178-79, 189
  Marine Aquarium 186
  Marine Life Museum 186
  Montazah Palace Gardens 195, 195
  Mosque of Abu al-Abbas al-Mursi 196
  Mosque of an-Nabi Daniel 190
  Mustafa Kamel Necropolis 196
  Pastroudi's 190, **190**
  Pharos Lighthouse 178, 181, 182, 186, 187
  Pompey's Pillar 185, **185**
  Ramla Square 188
  Roman theater 181
  Royal Jewelry Museum 193
  Serapeum 185
  Shatby Necropolis 196

Tahrir Square 190
  walk 188-90
Amarna 32, 218-20, **218-19**
  Royal Tomb 220
  Tomb of Ay 220
  Tomb of Huya 219
  Tomb of Mahu 220
  Tomb of Mery-Re 219
Amenemhat III 54, 156
Amenhotep II 55, 282-83
Amenhotep III 31-32, 55, 74, 237, 238, 244-45, 251, 253, 255, 282
Amenhotep IV see Akhenaten
American University in Cairo 83-84
Ammut 46
Amr ibn al-As Mosque 121
Amun 46, 240, 319
Amun-Re 31, 44, **47**, 232, 315
An-Nabi Daniel Mosque 190
Anfushi 196
Anfushi Necropolis 196
Ankh-ma-Hor 151
Antiques and antiquities 377
Anubis 46, **47, 184**, 185, 242, 266
Apis bulls 151, 185
Aquariums
  Alexandria 186
  Hurghada 329
Arab League 123
Arab-Israeli conflict (1948) 42
Archaeological Museum, Kharga 212
Architecture
  contemporary 62-63
  Delta style 170, **171**
  Mamluk 39
  Nubian 296
Arensnuphis 310
Arts 56-63
  architecture 62-63
  art 62
  belly dancing 60, **61**, 62, 382-83
  cinema 60
  literature 56, 58
  music 58-59, 296, 383
  Muslim decorative art 106
  public storytelling 56
Aswan 290, 298-305, **298-99**
  Aswan Dam 290, 311
  Aswan Museum 303
  Corniche 298
  Elephantine Island 303
  Fatimid Cemetery 301
  Ferial Gardens 298
  hotels and restaurants 372-73
  Kitchener's Island 304-305

map 300
  Mausoleum of the Aga Khan **303**, 305
  Monastery of St. Simeon 305
  Nilometer 303
  Nubian House 301
  Nubian Museum 299, 301
  Nubian villages 303-304
  Old Cataract Hotel **290**, 298-99, **300-301**
  Sehel Island 305
  souq 298
  Tombs of the Nobles 305
  Unfinished Obelisk 301-302, **302**
Asyut 222, 224
  Al-Qusiya 224
  Burnt Monastery 224
  Monastery of the Virgin 224
Aten 32, 76, 218, 221
ATMs 355
Atum 44, 46
Auberge du Lac 156, 365
Avedissian, Chant 63
Aye 32, 55

B

Badr's Museum 210
Bahariyya Oasis 206-207
  Bawiti 206
  Bir al-Ghaba 206
  Ethnographic Museum 206
  hot springs 206
  Qarat al-Firekhi burial tunnels 206
  Valley of the Mummies 207
Balat 211
Ballooning 380
Banks 353
Baron's Palace 140
Bars, clubs, and cafés 382
Bartholdi, Frederic Auguste 174
Bashandi 211
Basketry 205, **205**
Bastet 168, **168**
Bawiti 206
Bayt al-Suhaymi 100-101
Bedouin 337, **337**, 344, **345**
Belly dancing 60, **61**, 62, 382-83
Belzoni, Giovanni 80, 269, 283, 319
Ben Ezra Synagogue 120-21, **121**
Beni Hasan 158, 216-17
  Tomb of Amenemhet 217
  Tomb of Baqet 217
  Tomb of Kheti 217
  Tomb of Khnumhotep 217
Bent Pyramid 155, **155**
Berenice II 180, 310
Berenice (port) 25
Bes 44, 46

The world's largest nonprofit scientific and educational organization, the National Geographic Society was founded in 1888 "for the increase and diffusion of geographic knowledge." Since then it has supported scientific exploration and spread information to its more than nine million members worldwide.

The National Geographic Society educates and inspires millions every day through magazines, books, television programs, videos, maps and atlases, research grants, the National Geography Bee, teacher workshops, and innovative classroom materials.

The Society is supported through membership dues, charitable gifts, and income from the sale of its educational products. Members receive NATIONAL GEOGRAPHIC magazine—the Society's official journal—discounts on Society products, and other benefits.

For more information about the National Geographic Society, its educational programs, publications, or how to support its work, call 1-800-NGS-LINE (647-5463), or write to: National Geographic Society, 1145 17th Street, N.W., Washington, D.C. 20036 U.S.A.

Printed in the U.S.A.

ILLUSTRATIONS CREDITS

Abbreviations for term appearing below: (t) top; (b) bottom; (l) left; (r) right.

Front cover: (tl), Pictures Colour Library. (tr), Robert Harding Picture Library. (bl), Gettyone/Stone. (br), Powerstock/Zefa. Spine: Powerstock/Zefa.

1, Eye Ubiquitous. 2/3, Reza/National Geographic Society. 4, Gettyone/Stone. 9, Trip & Art Directors Photo Library. 11, Elk Photo. 12/13, Reza/National Geographic Society. 14/15, Thomas Hartwell. 16/17, Richard Nowitz. 18/19, Reza/National Geographic Society. 20/21, Kenneth Garrett/National Geographic Society. 23, Bradley Ireland Productions. 24/25, Reza/National Geographic Society. 26/7, Patrick Godeau. 28/9, Kenneth Garrett/National Geographic Society. 30, AKG - London. 32/33, Kenneth Garrett/National Geographic Society. 34, Bridgeman Art Library. 35, Patrick Godeau. 36/37, Elk Photo. 38/39, AKG - London. 40, AKG - London. 41, Hulton Getty Picture Collection Ltd. 42, Hulton Getty Picture Collection Ltd. 43l, Hulton Getty Picture Collection Ltd. 43r, David Rubinger/Corbis UK Ltd. 45, Kenneth Garrett/National Geographic Society. 46l, O. Louis Mazzatenta/National Geographic Society. 46r, Kenneth Garrett/National Geographic Society. 47l, The Seeing Eye. 47r, Christine Osborne Pictures/MEP. 50/51, Kenneth Garrett/National Geographic Society. 52/53, Elk Photo. 55, Kenneth Garrett/National Geographic Society. 56, Thomas Hartwell. 57, Peter Sanders Photography. 58/59, Axiom. 59, Hutchison Library. 61, Christine Osborne Pictures/MEP. 62, Patrick Godeau. 63, Bloomsbury Publishing Ltd. 65, Christine Osborne Pictures/MEP. 66, Christine Osborne Pictures/MEP. 67, Elk Photo. 70, Chris Coe/AA Photo Library. 71, Antonio Attini/White Star Publishers. 73, Robert Holmes. 74, Patrick Godeau. 75, Jürgen Liepe. 76, Kenneth Garrett/National Geographic Society. 77, Jürgen Liepe. 78, Bradley Ireland Productions. 79, The Seeing Eye. 80/81, New York Public Library/National Geographic Society. 81, Mary Evans Picture Library. 82/83, The Seeing Eye. 84, Antonio Attini/White Star Publishers. 86, Travel Ink. 88, Christine Osborne Pictures/MEP. 88/89, Elk Photo. 91, Eye Ubiquitous. 92/93, N. Turner/Gettyone/Stone. 94, Christine

Osborne Pictures/MEP. 95, Elk Photo. 96, Christine Osborne Pictures/MEP. 96/97, Elk Photo. 98, Christine Osborne Pictures/MEP. 100, Patrick Godeau. 101, The Seeing Eye. 102, Rick Strange/AA Photo Library. 104, Christine Osborne Pictures/MEP. 105t, J. Morris/Axiom. 105b, D. Winters/Eye Ubiquitous. 106, Antonio Attini/White Star Publishers. 107, Antonio Attini/White Star Publishers. 108/109, Elk Photo. 109, J. Horner/Hutchison Library. 110, Hutchison Library. 111, Hugh Alexander/AA Photo Library. 112/113, H. Sitton/Gettyone/Stone. 114, Bradley Ireland Productions. 114/115, B. McGilloway/Robert Holmes. 116, Elk Photo. 117, Patrick Godeau. 118, Christine Osborne Pictures/MEP. 119, Trip & Art Directors Photo Library. 120, Christine Osborne Pictures/MEP. 121, Trip & Art Directors Photo Library. 122/123, Christine Osborne Pictures/MEP. 124/125, Peter Clayton. 125, Trip & Art Directors Photo Library. 126, Elk Photo. 128, Ancient Egypt Picture Library. 129, Christine Osborne Pictures/MEP. 130, James Davis Worldwide. 131, Gilles Mermet/AKG - London. 133, Robert Harding Picture Library. 134, Elk Photo. 135, Images International Stock Photography. 136, Giulio Veggi/White Star Publishers. 137, Axiom. 138/139, M. Crame/Christine Osborne Pictures/MEP. 140, Christine Osborne Pictures/MEP. 141, Christine Osborne Pictures/MEP. 143, Hugh Alexander/AA Photo Library. 144, Bradley Ireland Productions. 146/147, Kenneth Garrett/National Geographic Society. 147, Kenneth Garrett/National Geographic Society. 148/149, B. McGilloway/Robert Holmes. 150, O. Louis Mazzatenta/National Geographic Society. 151, J. Morris/Axiom. 152, Kenneth Garrett/National Geographic Society. 153t, Peter Clayton. 153b, R Sherridan/Ancient Art & Architecture. 154, O. Louis Mazzatenta/National Geographic Society. 155, Elk Photo. 156, R Strange/AA Photo Library. 156/157, R.Strange/AA Photo Library. 158, M Jelliffe/Hutchison Library. 159t, Richard Brooks/Frank Lane Picture Agency. 159b, Patrick Godeau. 160, Patrick Godeau. 161, J. Morris/Axiom. 162, Eye Ubiquitous. 163, J. Morris/Axiom. 165, Eye Ubiquitous. 166, Reza/National Geographic Society. 167, J. Morris/Axiom. 168, Walter Rawlings/Robert Harding Picture Library. 169, Reza/National Geographic Society. 170, Christine Osborne Pictures/MEP. 171t, Chris Coe/AA Photo Library. 171b, Pictures Colour Library. 172/173, AKG -

London. 173, Hulton Getty Picture Collection Ltd. 175, Christine Osborne Pictures/MEP. 176, Patrick Godeau. 177, J. Morris/Axiom. 179, Reza/National Geographic Society. 180, Reza/National Geographic Society. 181, Images Colour Library. 182/183, S. Compoint/Corbis Sygma. 183, S. Compoint/Corbis Sygma. 184, Stuart Franklin/National Geographic Society. 185, Christine Osborne Pictures/MEP. 186, Elk Photo. 186/187, Elk Photo. 188, H. Gruyaert/Magnum Photos. 190, Christine Osborne Pictures/MEP. 191, Christine Osborne Pictures/MEP. 192, Dermot Tatlow/Panos Pictures. 193, Chris Coe/AA Photo Library. 194, Thomas Hartwell. 195, Christine Osborne Pictures/MEP. 196, Hutchison Library. 197, Elk Photo. 198, Elk Photo. 200, Patrick Godeau. 201, Trip & Art Directors Photo Library. 202, Elk Photo. 203, Elk Photo. 204/205, Elk Photo. 205, R. Strange/AA Photo Library. 206, Kenneth Garrett/National Geographic Society. 207t Kenneth Garrett/National Geographic Society. 207b, Kenneth Garrett/National Geographic Society. 208/209, Elk Photo. 209, M Wilson-Smith/Eye Ubiquitous. 210, Elk Photo. 211, Elk Photo. 212, Elk Photo. 213, Peter Sanders Photography. 214, Christine Osborne Pictures/MEP. 216, Eye Ubiquitous. 217, Christine Osborne Pictures/MEP. 218, Werner Forman Archive. 218/219, AKG - London. 220, François Guenet/AKG - London. 221, Peter Clayton. 222, J. Morris/Axiom. 223, J. Morris/Axiom. 224, Christine Osborne Pictures/MEP. 225, J. Morris/Axiom. 226/227, J. Morris/Axiom. 227, J. Morris/Axiom. 228, J. Morris/Axiom. 229, Robert Holmes. 230, J. Morris/Axiom. 231, Kenneth Garrett. 232, Elk Photo. 234/235, Richard Nowitz/National Geographic Society. 235, Chris Coe/AA Photo Library. 237, Gettyone/Stone. 239, Christine Osborne Pictures/MEP. 240, James Davis Worldwide. 240/241, Trip & Art Directors Photo Library. 242/243, Images Colour Library. 243, Thomas Hartwell. 244, Thomas Hartwell. 245, B. McGilloway/Robert Holmes. 246, Trip & Art Directors Photo Library. 247, J. Morris/Axiom. 250, J. Morris/Axiom. 251, Bradley Ireland Productions. 252, Elk Photo. 253, Elk Photo. 254, Christine Osborne Pictures/MEP. 255, Kenneth Garrett/National Geographic Society. 256, Christine Osborne Pictures/MEP. 257t, Elk Photo. 257b, Peter Sanders Photography. 258, The Seeing Eye. 260, Hutchison Library. 260/261, The Seeing Eye. 262, Robert Harding Picture Library. 263, Kenneth Garrett. 264/265, Kenneth

Garrett. 266, Norbert Schiller/Patrick Godeau. 267, Christine Osborne Pictures/MEP. 268/269, The Seeing Eye. 270, Peter Sanders Photography. 271t, Trip & Art Directors Photo Library. 271b, The Seeing Eye. 272, Trip & Art Directors Photo Library. 273, Elk Photo. 274, The Seeing Eye. 275, John Ross/Robert Harding Picture Library. 276/277, Kenneth Garrett/National Geographic Society. 278, The Seeing Eye. 279, Robert Harding Picture Library. 280/281, National Geographic Society. 282/283, Kenneth Garrett/National Geographic Society. 284/285, Kenneth Garrett/National Geographic Society. 286, Hulton Getty Picture Collection Ltd. 287bl, Kenneth Garrett/National Geographic Society. 287t, Kenneth Garrett/National Geographic Society. 287, S. Compoint/Corbis Sygma. 288, The Seeing Eye. 289, B. McGilloway/Robert Holmes. 290, A. Enock/Travel Ink. 292, B. McGilloway/Robert Holmes. 293, The Seeing Eye. 294, The Seeing Eye. 295, Elk Photo. 296/297, The Seeing Eye. 297, J. Waterlow/Eye Ubiquitous. 298/299, Robert Harding Picture Library. 300/301, Richard Nowitz/National Geographic Society. 302t, Elk Photo. 302b, Bradley Ireland Productions. 303, Trip & Art Directors Photo Library. 304/305, B. McGilloway/Robert Holmes. 306/307, B. McGilloway/Robert Holmes. 307, Elk Photo. 308/309, Patrick Godeau. 310, S. Grandadam/Gettyone/Stone. 311, T. Bognar/Trip & Art Directors Photo Library. 312/313, B. McGilloway/Robert Holmes. 313, B. McGilloway/Robert Holmes. 314, Elk Photo. 315, Eye Ubiquitous. 317, George Geister/National Geographic Society. 318, Richard Nowitz/National Geographic Society. 319, Elk Photo. 320, Bradley Ireland Productions. 321, Elk Photo. 322, Gettyone/Stone. 323, Bradley Ireland Productions. 324, Thomas Hartwell. 326, Patrick Godeau. 327, Patrick Godeau. 328, Axiom. 329, Trip & Art Directors Photo Library. 330, Bradley Ireland Productions. 331, Bradley Ireland Productions. 334, Thomas Hartwell. 335, D. Shaw/Axiom. 336, D. Shaw/Axiom. 336/337, Patrick Godeau. 338/339, Bradley Ireland Productions. 339, D. Saunders/Trip & Art Directors Photo Library. 340, J. Morris/Axiom. 341, Travel Ink. 342, J. Morris/Axiom. 343, Christine Osborne Pictures/MEP. 344, J. Morris/Axiom. 345t, Thomas Hartwell. 345b, Hutchison Library. 346, Thomas Hartwell. 347, Thomas Hartwell. 348, Patrick Godeau. 349, Christine Osborne Pictures/MEP.

Published by the National Geographic Society
John M. Fahey, Jr., *President and Chief Executive Officer*
Gilbert M. Grosvenor, *Chairman of the Board*
Nina D. Hoffman, *Executive Vice President,*
President, Books and School Publishing
Elizabeth L. Newhouse, *Director of Travel Publishing*
Barbara A. Noe, *Senior Editor and Project Manager*
Cinda Rose, *Art Director*
Carl Mehler, *Director of Maps*
Joseph F. Ochlak, *Map Coordinator*
Gary Colbert, *Production Director*
Richard S. Wain, *Production Project Manager*
Michele Callaghan and Lise Sajewski, *Editorial Consultants*
Caroline Hickey, *Senior Researcher*
Lawrence Porges, *Editorial Coordinator*
Verena Phipps, *Contributor*

Edited and designed by AA Publishing (a trading name of Automobile Association Developments Limited, whose registered office is Millstream, Maidenhead Road, Windsor, Berkshire SL4 5GD. Registered number: 1878835).
Virginia Langer, *Project Manager*
David Austin, *Senior Art Editor*
Andrew Renshaw, Marilynne Lanng, *Editors*
Bob Johnson, *Designer*
Cartography by AA Cartographic Production
Richard Firth, *Production Director*
Picture Research by Zooid Pictures Ltd., and Liz Allen, AA Photo Library
Cycle Tour map drawn by Chris Orr Associates, Southampton, England
Cutaway illustrations drawn by Maltings Partnership, Derby, England

ISSN 1536-8602

Printed and bound by R.R. Donnelley & Sons, Willard, Ohio.
Color separations by Leo Reprographic Ltd., Hong Kong
Cover separations by L.C. Repro, Aldermaston, U.K.
Cover printed by Miken Inc., Cheektowage, New York

Visit the society's Web site at http://www.nationalgeographic.com

The information in this book has been carefully checked and to the best of our knowledge is accurate. However, details are subject to change, and the National Geographic Society cannot be responsible for such changes, or for errors or omissions. Assessments of sites, hotels, and restaurants are based on the author's subjective opinions, which do not necessarily reflect the publisher's opinion. The publisher cannot be responsible for any consequences arising from the use of this book.

NATIONAL GEOGRAPHIC
TRAVELER

A Century of Travel Expertise in Every Guide

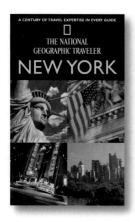

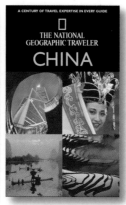

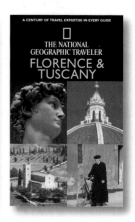

- **Arizona** ISBN: 0-7922-7899-2
- **Australia** ISBN: 0-7922-7431-8
- **Boston & Environs** ISBN: 0-7922-7926-3
- **California** ISBN: 0-7922-7564-0
- **Canada** ISBN: 0-7922-7427-X
- **The Caribbean** ISBN: 0-7922-7434-2
- **China** ISBN: 0-7922-7921-2
- **Costa Rica** ISBN: 0-7922-7946-8
- **Egypt** ISBN: 0-7922-7896-8
- **Florence & Tuscany** ISBN: 0-7922-7924-7
- **Florida** ISBN: 0-7922-7432-6
- **France** ISBN: 0-7922-7426-1
- **Great Britain** ISBN: 0-7922-7425-3
- **Greece** ISBN: 0-7922-7923-9
- **Hawaii** ISBN: 0-7922-7944-1
- **India** ISBN: 0-7922-7898-4

- **Italy** ISBN: 0-7922-7562-4
- **Japan** ISBN: 0-7922-7563-2
- **London** ISBN: 0-7922-7428-8
- **Los Angeles** ISBN: 0-7922-7947-6
- **Mexico** ISBN: 0-7922-7897-6
- **Miami and the Keys** ISBN: 0-7922-7433-4
- **New Orleans** ISBN: 0-7922-7948-4
- **New York** ISBN: 0-7922-7430-X
- **Paris** ISBN: 0-7922-7429-6
- **Rome** ISBN: 0-7922-7566-7
- **San Francisco** ISBN: 0-7922-7565-9
- **Spain** ISBN: 0-7922-7922-0
- **Sydney** ISBN: 0-7922-7435-0
- **Thailand** ISBN: 0-7922-7943-3
- **Venice** ISBN: 0-7922-7917-4